Injury Impoverished

The late nineteenth- and early twentieth-century US economy maimed and killed employees at an astronomically high rate, while the legal system left the injured and their loved ones with little recourse. In the 1910s, US states enacted workers' compensation laws, which required employers to pay a portion of the financial costs of workplace injuries. Nate Holdren uses a range of archival materials, interdisciplinary theoretical perspectives, and compelling narration to criticize the shortcomings of these laws. While compensation laws were a limited improvement for employees in economic terms, Holdren argues that these laws created new forms of inequality, causing people with disabilities to lose their jobs, while also resulting in new forms of inhumanity. Ultimately, this study raises questions about law and class and about when and whether our economy and our legal system produce justice or injustice.

NATE HOLDREN is Assistant Professor in Law, Politics, and Society at Drake University.

Cambridge Historical Studies in American Law and Society

Recognizing legal history's growing importance and influence, the goal of this series is to chart legal history's continuing development by publishing innovative scholarship across the discipline's broadening range of perspectives and subjects. It encourages empirically creative works that take legal history into unexplored subject areas, or that fundamentally revise our thinking about familiar topics; it also encourages methodologically innovative works that bring new disciplinary perspectives and techniques to the historical analysis of legal subjects.

Series Editor

Christopher Tomlins, *University of California, Berkeley*

Previously Published in the Series

Catherine Wells, *Oliver Wendell Holmes: A Willing Servant to an Unknown God*

Michael F. Conlin, *The Constitutional Origins of the American Civil War*

Angela Fernandez, *Pierson v. Post, The Hunt for the Fox: Law and Professionalization in American Legal Culture*

Justin Desautels-Stein, *The Jurisprudence of Style: A Structuralist History of American Pragmatism and Liberal Legal Thought*

William Kuby, *Conjugal Misconduct: Defying Marriage Law in the Twentieth-Century United States*

Rebecca E. Zietlow, *The Forgotten Emancipator: James Mitchell Ashley and the Ideological Origins of Reconstruction*

Robert Daniel Rubin, *Judicial Review and American Conservatism: Christianity, Public Education, and the Federal Courts in the Reagan Era*

Matthew Crow, *Thomas Jefferson, Legal History, and the Art of Recollection*

Oren Bracha, *Owning Ideas: The Intellectual Origins of American Intellectual Property, 1790–1909*

Anne Twitty, *Before Dred Scott: Slavery and Legal Culture in the American Confluence, 1787–1857*

Leia Castañeda Anastacio, *The Foundations of the Modern Philippine State: Imperial Rule and the American Constitutional Tradition in the Philippine Islands, 1898–1935*

Robert Deal, *The Law of the Whale Hunt: Dispute Resolution, Property Law, and American Whalers, 1780–1880*

Sandra F. Vanburkleo, *Gender Remade: Citizenship, Suffrage, and Public Power in the New Northwest, 1879–1912*

Reuel Schiller, *Forging Rivals: Race, Class, Law, and the Collapse of Postwar Liberalism*

Ely Aaronson, *From Slave Abuse to Hate Crime: The Criminalization of Racial Violence in American History*

Stuart Chinn, *Recalibrating Reform: The Limits of Political Change*

Ajay K. Mehrotra, *Making the Modern American Fiscal State*

Yvonne Pitts, *Family, Law, and Inheritance in America: A Social and Legal History of Nineteenth-Century Kentucky*

David M. Rabban, *Law's History*

Kunal M. Parker, *Common Law, History, and Democracy in America, 1790–1900*

Steven Wilf, *Law's Imagined Republic*

James D. Schmidt, *Industrial Violence and the Legal Origins of Child Labor*

Rebecca M. McLennan, *The Crisis of Imprisonment: Protest, Politics, and the Making of the American Penal State, 1776–1941*

Tony A. Freyer, *Antitrust and Global Capitalism, 1930–2004*

Davison Douglas, *Jim Crow Moves North*

Andrew Wender Cohen, *The Racketeer's Progress*

Michael Willrich, *City of Courts, Socializing Justice in Progressive Era Chicago*

Barbara Young Welke, *Recasting American Liberty: Gender, Law and the Railroad Revolution, 1865–1920*

Michael Vorenberg, *Final Freedom: The Civil War, the Abolition of Slavery, and the Thirteenth Amendment*

Robert J. Steinfeld, *Coercion, Contract, and Free Labor in Nineteenth Century America*

David M. Rabban, *Free Speech in Its Forgotten Years*

Jenny Wahl, *The Bondsman's Burden: An Economic Analysis of the Common Law of Southern Slavery*

Michael Grossberg, *A Judgment for Solomon: The d'Hauteville Case and Legal Experience in the Antebellum South*

Injury Impoverished

Workplace Accidents, Capitalism, and Law in the Progressive Era

NATE HOLDREN

Drake University

CAMBRIDGE
UNIVERSITY PRESS

University Printing House, Cambridge CB2 8BS, United Kingdom

One Liberty Plaza, 20th Floor, New York, NY 10006, USA

477 Williamstown Road, Port Melbourne, VIC 3207, Australia

314-321, 3rd Floor, Plot 3, Splendor Forum, Jasola District Centre, New Delhi - 110025, India

103 Penang Road, #05-06/07, Visioncrest Commercial, Singapore 238467

Cambridge University Press is part of the University of Cambridge.

It furthers the University's mission by disseminating knowledge in the pursuit of education, learning and research at the highest international levels of excellence.

www.cambridge.org
Information on this title: www.cambridge.org/9781108448666
DOI: 10.1017/9781108657730

First published 2020
First paperback edition 2021

A catalogue record for this publication is available from the British Library

Library of Congress Cataloging in Publication data
NAMES: Holdren, Nate, 1978– author.
TITLE: Injury impoverished : workplace accidents, capitalism, and law in the progressive era /
Nate Holdren, Drake University, Iowa.
DESCRIPTION: Cambridge, United Kingdom ; New York, NY, USA : Cambridge University Press, 2020. |
SERIES: Cambridge historical studies in American law and society | Based on author's thesis
(doctoral – University of Minnesota, 2014) issued under title: 'The compensation law put
us out of work' : workplace injury law, commodification, and discrimination in the
early 20th century United States. | Includes bibliographical references and index.
IDENTIFIERS: LCCN 2019051255 (print) | LCCN 2019051256 (ebook) | ISBN 9781108488709
(hardback) | ISBN 9781108448666 (paperback) | ISBN 9781108657730 (epub)
SUBJECTS: LCSH: Workers' compensation–Law and legislation–Social aspects–United States–
History–20th century. | Industrial accidents–Law and legislation–Social aspects–
United States–History–20th century.
CLASSIFICATION: LCC KF3615 . H55 2020 (print) | LCC KF3615 (ebook) |
DDC 344.7302/1809041–dc23
LC record available at https://lccn.loc.gov/2019051255
LC ebook record available at https://lccn.loc.gov/2019051256

ISBN 978-1-108-48870-9 Hardback
ISBN 978-1-108-44866-6 Paperback

And even after the new society shall have come into existence, the happiness of its members will not make up for the wretchedness of those who are being destroyed in our contemporary society.
—Max Horkheimer, "Postscript"

If I had a list and if I only knew
I'd write down their names and sing them to you.
And when I got done, I'd sing them again
so you'd all know each one had a name.
—Utah Phillips, "Yuba City"

Yet there is hope. Time and tide flow wide.
—Herman Melville, *Moby Dick*

Contents

List of Tables		*page* xi
Acknowledgments		xiii
	Introduction: Injuries and Abstractions	1

PART I THE ECLIPSE OF RECOGNITION AND THE RISE
OF THE TYRANNY OF THE TABLE

1	Commodification and Recognition within the Tyranny of the Trial	19
2	Injury Impoverished	53
3	Suffering and the Price of Life and Limb	84
	Interlude: Tramped-on and Trampler in the Cherry Mine Fire	119

PART II NEW MACHINERIES OF INJUSTICE

4	The Disabling Power of Law and Market	137
5	Insuring Injustice	175
6	Discrimination Technicians and Human Weeding	218
	Conclusion: Resistance and Aftermath	253
	Coda: Narrative, Machinery, Law	268
Index		279

Tables

5.1 Compensation laws and self-insurance, 1913–1922   *page* 194

6.1 Examinee classifications at Pullman, 1926   235

Acknowledgments

Working on this book touched all of my life, and so I wish a general thank you to everyone who is in my life, for carrying some of the weight and for your patience. I do of course want to name specific friends and colleagues who shaped this project. There are so many that I fear I've left someone out.

I thank first, and most of all, Angelica Mortensen. I am incredibly fortunate to be married to and to be friends with her. She has done more than any other person to make this project possible intellectually, emotionally, and financially. The full list of why I'm grateful for and in debt to her would run as long as this book. I will mention only that she read the entire manuscript closely, providing invaluable line edits and encouragement. Our three children, Kit, Ayla, and Charlotte, have lived with this project for their entire lives. They have asked a few times when it would be done, and have kindly assured me that while grown up books are boring, mine is likely to be less boring than most. I would like it if they read this book someday, but only if they want to. I am very pleased that they are already the kinds of people who have opinions about what they do and do not want to read.

I thank my parents for encouraging me to go to college and later to graduate school. I thank them as well, and my brothers Paul and Trent, for being supportive and proud of me even when I wasn't able to explain what I was doing and why. I also thank my mother-in-law Faith Noe for her enthusiasm and for childcare support at particularly timely moments.

My maternal grandmother, Audrey Miller, passed away while I was writing the dissertation this book is based on. She generously typed many of my papers for me when I was in high school, despite repetitive stress injuries to wrists due to her years employed as a secretary. As usual, I did not understand the significance of this until well after the fact. I have thought of her often as I sat at the keyboard working on this book.

My interest in going to graduate school and many of the intellectual preoccupations that I still have today first arose from my time at Valparaiso University, in the Philosophy Department and in Christ College. Classes with Tom Kennedy, Sandra Visser, Kevin Geiman, and Charles Elder were foundational intellectual experiences for me, as was the mentorship provided by Mark Schwehn. Mark told me to become a historian; as with much of his advice I took a very long time to realize he was right. It was within that context that Angelica and I first became good friends (an early bonding experience we had was reading the philosopher Immanuel Kant and concluding that capitalism was fundamentally immoral; we still talk about that to this day). I also learned a great deal, and deepened my love of intellectual excitement, as a result of conversations with my friends Colin McQuillan and Tzu Chien Tho.

I became a historian largely by accident, by stumbling into courses taught by Barbara Welke and Tracey Deutsch. I have often felt that this was a kind of lottery that it was my great luck to win. Barbara and Tracey became my co-advisors, and soon afterward Susanna Blumenthal became a de facto third advisor. I benefited inestimably from working with the three of them in graduate school and ever since. They have encouraged me to take bigger intellectual risks and to work harder than I otherwise would have. I am a much better historian for it.

Barbara, Tracey, and Susanna served on my dissertation committee, as did Evan Roberts, Jennifer Gunn, and Pat McNamara. I thank all of my committee for their generous support, encouragement, and feedback on my work at multiple stages. They helped me to write and to think better, and to keep writing and thinking. It has been a great pleasure and privilege to work with them.

Christopher Tomlins has been a singular influence on me as a scholar. I have learned so much from what he has written. That has made me all the more grateful for his ongoing and multifaceted engagement with and support for my work.

The quote from Utah Phillips that forms part of this book's epigraph appears with the permission of Joanna Robinson. I thank her for that permission and her enthusiastic response when I described the book. I thank Utah Phillips as well; it was my great pleasure and privilege to have lunch with him before his passing, and to hear so many of his songs and stories. Parts of Chapter 5 of this book previously appeared as

"Incentivizing Safety and Discrimination: Employment Risks under Workmen's Compensation in the Early Twentieth Century United States," *Enterprise & Society* 15, no. 1 (March 2014): 31. I am grateful for Philip Scranton's editorial feedback and the input of the two anonymous reviewers on that article, as they improved the article and helped me to better formulate my larger project in valuable ways. Two other anonymous reviewers at Cambridge University Press gave feedback on my book at an especially key moment, both pressing me on points where I needed to clarify my argument and encouraging me to try to write boldly. I have written a better book for it and I thank them for that.

I have had three academic employers over the course of this project. Given the ongoing crisis of higher education employment as I write this, I wish to state clearly that in my view, employment – and thus the benefits it provides, when it does so – is distributed largely through luck, though that luck is allocated through hierarchical and unequal social structures. As the poet Bertolt Brecht once wrote, "It is true: I work for a living / But, believe me, that is a coincidence. Nothing / That I do gives me the right to eat my fill. / By chance I have been spared. (If my luck does not hold, / I am lost.)"[1] I am grateful for the luck I have had and what I have been provided as a result. I wish that everyone had similar good fortune (*omnia sunt communia*, as it were, everything for everyone) and hold out hope that eventually someday we all will.

The first of my academic employers, the University of Minnesota History Department, was a fantastic place to learn how to be a historian and how to teach, a place of vibrant but never self-important thought. The work-in-progress workshops that the Department hosted are where I learned the most about how to actually do academic writing and where I developed my ongoing love of reading work in progress. The Legal History Workshop and the community that crystallizes around it were especially important to me. It was a joy and a privilege to come back as an alumnus and present a version of Chapter 1 of this book, to an audience even more responsive, energetic, and rigorous than I had remembered.

The Center for Law, Society, and Culture at Indiana University's Mauer School Law hosted me as a Jerome Hall Postdoctoral Fellow. The community of scholars in residence at Indiana and the visiting scholars who came to present work was mind-expanding. Being there

---

[1] Bertolt Brecht, "To Those Who Follow in Our Wake," translated by Scott Horton, *Browsings: The Harper's Blog*, https://harpers.org/blog/2008/01/brecht-to-those-who-follow-in-our-wake/ , accessed June 10, 2016.

encouraged me to make bolder claims about the significance of my work and think more deeply about law. I am especially grateful to Ajay Mehrotra and Ethan Michelson, who directed the Center of Law, Society and Culture, while I was there; Mike Grossberg; Jeannine Bell; Ilana Gershon; Tim Lovelace; Alex Lichtenstein; and my fellow postdoctoral fellow Stacey Vanderhurst.

I have learned a great deal at Drake University's Law, Politics, and Society Department. I am lucky to have Renee Cramer, Matt Canfield, and Will Garriott as engaged, enthusiastic, generous departmental colleagues. Their interest in my work has meant a great deal to me. They are all very busy doing great things but (or maybe because) they are always willing to share their time. I am grateful as well to my students, who are across-the-board fantastic. Their willingness to work hard and to take intellectual risks has helped me maintain some degree of willingness to do so myself. Four students (now former students, as they have all graduated) bear particular mention: Kailey Gray, Phoebe Clark, and my excellent research assistants Natalie Deerr and Collin Vandewalle. In addition to Law, Politics, and Society, I have had two other core intellectual centers of gravity at Drake. One is the Humanities Center. The Center has supported my work financially and, of at least equal importance, provided intellectual community via its Humanities Colloquium events, which I have had the pleasure to both attend and present work at. The other is the faculty writing group it is my pleasure to co-organize and co-facilitate with my friend and colleague En Li, and which is generously supported by Drake's Humanities Center, College of Arts and Sciences, and Office of the Provost. In the writing group I have continued to learn about myself as a writer and have enjoyed hearing about many colleagues' writing projects and processes.

Over the years a great many people contributed to this book in many ways. Friends and colleagues have read and heard parts of this project in the form of written drafts, conference presentations, and informal conversation. Their responses shaped the project intellectually and helped me remember that I was onto something worth pursuing. Many as well offered moral support, advice on how to organize a writing life, and suggestions for how to navigate the institutional worlds I have inhabited. And many have commiserated, encouraged, and sometimes kept me grounded by writing quietly nearby. All of these contributions have mattered so much to this project and to me personally. I thank Megan Brown, Jeff Karnicky, Jen Harvey, Leah Kalmanson, Joseph Schneider, Karen Leroux, En Li, Inbal Mazar, Jeanette Tran, Chris Porter, Laura

Porter, my dean Gesine Gearhard, Lourdes Gutierrez, Godfried Asante, Matt Canfield, Dennis Goldford, Sandi Patton-Imani, Darcie Vandegrift, Kevin Gannon, Heidi Sleister, Mary McCarthy, Art Sanders, Jody Swilky, Cameron Tuai, Sam Becker, Dan Chibnall, Josh Wallace, Ben Gardner, Bill Boal, Lynn McCool, Kevin Carlson, Evelyn Atkinson, Rabia Belt, Heather Berg, Deborah Dinner, Anne Fleming, Alicia Maggard, Dan Platt, Dave Morton, Katie Lambright, Joe Haker, Andy Paul, Brooke Depenbusch, Sam Mitrani, Chad Pearson, Rosemary Feurer, Adam Wolkoff, Kim Reilly, Umut Özsu, Rob Hunter, Chris O'Kane, Kailash Srinivasan, Marianne Le Nabat, Nick Driedger, Matthew Kellard, Eric Tucker, Kim Nielsen, Alice Kessler-Harris, Eileen Boris, David Freund, Pamela Laird, Maggie Levenstein, Ed Balleisen, Chris McKenna, Caitlin Rosenthal, Mitra Shirafi, Fahad Bishara, Dan Bouk, Emily Bruce, Ari Bryen, Carol Chomsky, Kelly Condit-Shrestha, Caley Horan, Danny LaChance, Ryan Johnson, Meg Krausch, Duncan Law, Alison Lefkovitz, Jon Levy, Nicole Pepperell, Jamie Pietruska, Gautham Rao, Raphi Rechitsky, Chantel Rodriguez, Donald Rogers, Sarah Rose, Karen Tani, Evan Taparata, Philip Thai, Felicity Turner, Tiffany Vann Sprecher, Elizabeth Venditto, and Kim Welch. Alex Wisnoski deserves a special mention, for a frequency and quality of support and communication that defies description. Judi Gibbs at Write Guru indexed my book quickly and effectively, and with great patience for my questions as a new author. I am grateful to Stephanie Sakson for her copyediting, which improved the manuscript. I also thank the Cambridge University Press team, Lisa Carter, Debbie Gershenowitz, and Rachel Blaifeder, as well as Baskaran Rajmohan.

I thank as well the institutions that facilitated some of these conversations and these relationships, especially the University of Minnesota's Legal History Workshop and Graduate Workshop in Modern History, the University of Wisconsin-Madison's J. Willard Hurst Summer Institute in Legal History, the American Society for Legal History for supporting the Hurst Institute, the Business History Conference's Oxford Journals Doctoral Colloquium, the Legal Form blog, and Drake University's Humanities Center.

Readers could understandably describe this book as a bit dour. As the long list of people acknowledged here demonstrates, the book has been created in a context of a great deal of intellectual community, which is a genuine gift and joy to be part of. Finally, and in all sincerity, thank you for reading my book.

Introduction

Injuries and Abstractions

This is a book about injuries and abstractions. First, injuries.

Nettie Blom worked in the laundry of a hotel in Yellowstone Park. On June 30, 1900, Blom was operating a machine called a mangle, which used steam-heated and steam-powered metal rollers to iron flat linens. The wet cloth stuck to her hand for a moment too long, and she was pulled into the machine. Blom's hand was crushed and burnt. When a co-worker managed to free her from the machine, Blom's hand looked like "boiled meat." Three of her co-workers fainted at the sight. Blom suffered terrible pain and lost the use of her hand due to her injuries.[1]

We have only partial data on workplace injuries in the twentieth century, but from the data we do have, it is clear that in the United States in this era people suffered injuries at work like Nettie Blom did with appalling frequency. For example, in 1910, US Army Medical Corps physician Major Charles Lynch estimated that the number of deaths due to accidents in mining between 1899 and 1908 totaled 19,775 people. Non-fatal injuries were even more frequent, with more than 5,000 such injuries per year in the years Lynch looked at.[2] And these are only the figures for mining. Employment was incredibly dangerous in this era, with employees harmed regularly. Historian James Schmidt has characterized the pervasive harm to employees in the economy as "industrial violence."[3]

---

[1] *Blom v. Yellowstone Park Association*, 86 Minn. 237 (1902).

[2] Charles Lynch, "Organization of First Aid Instruction," *The Coal Trade Bulletin*, October 1, 1910.

[3] James D. Schmidt, *Industrial Violence and the Legal Origins of Child Labor* (New York: Cambridge University Press, 2010).

The term "violence" is apt because working-class people in this era regularly suffered serious harms to their bodies, their selves, their person, their self-understanding, their lives. Those harms were injustices.

It is hard to specify what exactly an individual loses in an injury. Nettie Blom's loss? One hand. Five fingers. That phrasing separates Blom from her body part, occludes that Blom lost a part of her person. To put it another way, it wasn't just a body part, an object, that became trapped in the Yellowstone Park Association's mangle in 1900. It was Nettie Blom, trapped for minutes that must have felt like an eternity. "I can't describe the pain," Blom said.[4] Trapped in that machine was a human being with a name and a face and a life. The point may feel banal. Of course, every employee injury happens to a human being with a name. Indeed. Every single injury. We often move too quickly away from that fact.

What did Nettie Blom lose? It is hard to say. The body, the person, and the self overlap, and so the body is laden with meaning and feeling. People enduring bodily injury feel corporeal sensation, and they feel emotions that can range across anger, outrage, sadness, shame, humiliation, fear, loss of self-worth – the list goes on. To put it another way, a person who loses a body part in an accident loses whatever that body part and the actions they did with that body part meant to them in the course of their life, and endured whatever their newly injured condition meant to them as well. This kind of loss is as multifaceted as a person is multifaceted. I stress, perhaps belabor, this point about loss's multitude because law's accounting for loss became attenuated in the early twentieth century, at least for employee injuries. I develop this argument over the course of this book.

This book is about injuries and abstractions, so I now turn to abstractions.

Over the years I have worked on this project, I have come to find two quotes especially compelling. The literary critic, essayist, and philosopher Walter Benjamin once evoked an angel flying backward, blown by a storm. The angel watched human history unfold and saw it as an ongoing catastrophe, piling up wreckage into a tower of rubble. As I have spent time with the numbers of injuries that have happened, and still happen – there were 4,836 fatal workplace accidents and 2.9 million non-fatal workplace injuries in 2015 in the United states – I have

---

[4] *Blom v. Yellowstone Park Association*, 86 Minn. 237 (1902).

come to think of much of that rubble as composed of human beings injured and killed.[5]

Benjamin and his angel provide an image for an aerial view. Ta-Nehisi Coates zooms in. In a discussion on slavery in his book *Between the World and Me*, Coates writes:

[R]espect every human being as singular, and you must extend that same respect into the past. Slavery is not an indefinable mass of flesh. It is a particular, enslaved woman, whose mind is as active as your own, whose range of feeling is as vast as your own; who prefers the way the light falls in one particular spot, who enjoys fishing where the water eddies in a nearby steam, who loves her mother in her own complicated way, thinks her sister talks too loud, has a favorite cousin.... You must struggle to truly remember this past in all its nuance, error, and humanity.[6]

We can take Coates's imperative about how to think about slavery as exemplary for how we should think about any large-scale matter of social injustice. In aggregating harms into "indefinable masses" we risk losing some of the truths of those harms. Every harm happens to some specific person who was, in Coates's words, a singular human being. Every person whom Benjamin's angel sees suffering or killed on the earth below is in a certain sense infinite, and so the numbers of the victims are a multitude of infinities. On a large scale, this is a loss so large it defies comprehension. Real human loss defies comprehension at the scale of an individual life as well. Coates's call to keep human singularity in mind while attending to large-scale atrocity is relevant in different ways to different layers of this book, as I hope becomes apparent as the book unfolds. In a sense, this work as a whole is an attempt at a historically

[5] Walter Benjamin, "Theses on the Philosophy of History," in Benjamin, *Illuminations: Essays and Reflections*, ed. Hannah Arendt (New York: Harcourt, 1968), 253–264, 257–258. It is worth noting both that injuries concentrate downward and that accident figures underreport actual accidents. A recent survey of low-waged employees found that 12 percent of people surveyed suffered serious injury on the job in the last three years, but of those injured, only 8 percent filed a workers' compensation claim, and many experienced illegal retaliation for doing so. Annette Bernhardt et al., *Broken Laws, Unprotected Workers: Violations of Employment and Labor Laws in America's Cities* (New York: National Employment Law Project, 2009), 25. It is worth noting as well that injuries are rampant in the global economy. The International Labour Organization estimates that there are two million employment-derived fatalities annually in the global economy. International Labour Organization, *Safety in Numbers: Pointers for a Global Safety Culture at Work* (Geneva: International Labour Organization, 2003), 1. This means 5,000 such fatalities each day. International Labour Organization, "Work-Related Fatalities Reach 2 Million Annually," www.ilo.org/global/about-the-ilo/media-centre/press-releases/WCMS_007789/lang–en/index.htm, accessed April 14, 2014.

[6] Ta-Nehisi Coates, *Between the World and Me* (New York: Spiegel & Grau, 2015), 69.

grounded meditation on that singularity–atrocity relationship and on some of the social conditions that predictably generate certain kinds of atrocity.[7]

As may be apparent, some of my concerns are rather abstract, in the sense that they might be called theoretical, as are some of the perspectives I bring to my subject matter. This is, I would argue, more than a matter of my own proclivities. My object of analysis is in important respects abstract as well, or, rather, my object of analysis is to some extent social, and specifically legal, processes or acts of abstraction.

Nettie Blom went to court. She sued her employer over her injuries. Her employer's attorney argued that the Yellowstone Park Association did not owe her any money because of some technical issues of how the doctrine of liability and negligence worked. These arguments worked. Blom lost her case, receiving no money. The abstractions of legal argument served as a shield held by the Park Association attorney, fending off Blom's claims. Kathryn Carlin suffered a similar injury to Blom, losing a hand in a mangle in a laundry and, like Blom, Carlin sued. She won her case in 1906. The abstractions of legal argument played a role here as well, in this instance facilitating the additional abstractions involved in converting Carlin's injuries into dollar amounts. She was awarded $7,500.[8]

From working on this project I have begun to think about compensation laws as exemplifying a kind of common sense about employee injury. My own personal introduction to this common sense came when a few hundred pounds of lumber fell on me at the factory where I worked during the summer before I moved away to college. An X-ray showed a chip of bone floating in one of my knuckles. Soon after my injury, I made an appointment and met with a lawyer to discuss filing a workers' compensation claim. The lawyer explained to me that my injury was worth a weekly payment for the time it took me to convalesce. The weekly payment was about two-thirds of my pre-injury wage, which meant I would probably get two hundred dollars per week. I felt ambivalent: excited because for me at the time two hundred dollars for a week

---

[7] For other works that I consider a similar historical reflection on singularity and atrocity, see Barbara Young Welke, "The Cowboy Suit Tragedy: Spreading Risk, Owning Hazard in the Modern American Consumer Economy," *Journal of American History* 1, no. 1 (June 2014): 97–121, and Barbara Young Welke, "Owning Hazard: A Tragedy," *UC Irvine Law Review* 1, no. 3 (September 2011): 693–771.

[8] *Carlin v. Kennedy*, 97 Minn. 141 (1906). Adjusted for inflation her award would be about $200,000 today.

sounded like a reasonable amount of money, especially for a week not working. At the same time, I felt offended that the plant managers, with their higher pay rates, would get more for their broken bones if they were to have similar injuries.

I remarked that it felt a little creepy that my hand had a dollar value. The lawyer laughed and agreed that it was creepy. He told me that there were tables that listed the value of all the different body parts, and added with another laugh that one of the highest value body parts was a testicle. Very much a seventeen-year-old boy, I nodded, saying that I supposed I valued my testicles more than my knuckles. Two hundred dollars for one week no longer seemed like a lot of money. I repeated that it was a creepy idea that my body parts in particular had a dollar value, and that in general there were tables written down with the value of body parts calculated in advance. The lawyer replied that a lot of people got hurt at work and that the injuries and the payments for them were all a regular process.[9]

That meeting with the lawyer is where I first encountered what I now think of as the "tyranny of the table," but it is both more and less than tyranny.[10] What I mean by the tyranny of the table is that within compensation laws human lives and human suffering have the fixed monetary values ascribed – no more than that, and not subject to discussion. What doesn't fit into the values of the table? Nearly everything. All of the elements of a human being other than our paychecks.

Experientially my introduction to the tyranny of the table was no big deal. I would occasionally recall this experience in passing in conversation with friends and colleagues ("What's the worst job you ever had before being a teaching assistant?") but I largely forgot about it, shrugged it off. Forgetting the unsettling is for many people a habit both easy and productive of ease. It is easier to go about the world with this habit. It was only after I had written most of the dissertation that was the basis for this book that I really thought about this experience in a serious way. Writing the dissertation retroactively highlighted what I had initially, and

---

[9] In the end I did not file a compensation claim. My mother was concerned it would make it harder for me to get jobs in the future. She had filed a compensation claim for a back injury while working at a shipping company in the 1970s and believed she had been discriminated against in future jobs as a result. Both of my younger brothers would later go on to be injured in different factory jobs. They too did not file compensation claims.

[10] Tyranny is perhaps an unduly polemical term, but my hope is that by the end readers will agree, or at least have seriously entertained the possibility, that law's (in)adequacy to workers' losses is a subject worthy of polemic.

fleetingly, found to be creepy in my personal encounter with employee injury law. One of my goals is for this book to have a similar effect on readers. I hope that when readers finish my book they find our legal handling of employee injury newly unnerving. That is to say, I have attempted in this book to write against the "no big deal" common-sense quality of the tyranny of the table.[11] Thus one major goal of this book is to think outside the tyranny of the table. I hope to make both the table itself and the values and norms behind it more apparent to readers and so perhaps less taken for granted in readers' minds. Ultimately, I question and criticize the tyranny of the table and the system of employee injury law in which it is embedded.

Prior to the tyranny of the table, injured people like Nettie Blom faced what I have come to think of as the tyranny of the trial. Understanding this legal world can shed light on what came afterward. The abstraction-governed legal worlds of the tyrannies of table and trial formed just one domain of the law: employee injury law. That domain existed as one part in a larger machine, an instrument in an ensemble of institutions of domination and control. In the background was the rule of the commodity, creating the problems that fed into both trial and table, composing the concepts and mentalities that animated each and that, in turn, in part, were created by each. Karl Marx called the commodity the cell form of capitalist society, meaning the basic organizational unit or building block.[12] The commodity was a cell in a kind of carceral sense as well, confining people, partially defining the orders given and taken, and the mental universe through which people perceived and understood the society organized by the commodity.

---

[11] I want to stress here that I did not write this book on employee injury and the law thereof because of my personal experience of employee injury. (Like many early-career scholars, I considered other subjects.) Rather, even though I had personal experience of injury, it took writing this book to really reflect on that experience. It was not until several years into this project that I realized I had never really thought about employee injury as part of my family history, and that my family had never really talked about these experiences. Both of my parents, my brothers, my partner, several of my grandparents, and I have all been injured at jobs. It is possible that members of my extended family have as well; I don't know, it's not something we talk about. I suspect that the unremarkable character of injury is both a cause and an effect of the perception that there are relatively few employee injuries.

[12] Karl Marx, *Capital: A Critique of Political Economy*, vol. 1, trans. Ben Fowkes (New York: Penguin Classics, 1990), 90. The rule of the commodity is in important respects, and perhaps entirely, legally constituted. Marx recognized this at least in part. This is apparent in the most historically and empirically grounded parts of *Capital*, the chapters on the working day, machinery, and so-called primitive accumulation.

This is a book, then, about the relationship between injury, abstraction, and law. One of the book's goals is to map the law's imagination, in two facets, the law's social imagination and its moral imagination. By social imagination I mean the ability of the law to adequately represent structural patterns in society such as the power relationships woven into employment, and whether its orientation to those patterns is to obfuscate them, legitimate them, naturalize them, or render them subject to dispute. By moral imagination I mean the ability of the law to perceive individual human beings with a degree of richness appropriate to the expansive humanity – the singularity, as Coates put it – of each individual human being.

This is also a book about capitalism and the social relationships of class that are inextricably woven into capitalist societies.[13] The working class is the group of people who live from wages, that is, from the sale of labor power. Employees are subject to what philosopher Elizabeth Anderson calls private government, meaning coercive power that is not subject to accountability and can be arbitrary.[14] These aspects of

---

[13] In general, in my view, class is not discussed frequently enough. (See Chad Pearson, "From the Labour Question to the Labour History Question," *Labour/Le Travail* 66, no. 1 (2010): 195–230.) This book is animated by what I understand to be a Marxist conception of class, which is not to say the Marxist conception of class. (I am unconvinced that there is a one single Marxist understanding of class or that there is any content to the term "Marxism" that makes it possible to draw clear lines between who is and is not truly a Marxist. That kind of line drawing seems to me a fool's errand.) I conceptualize class in capitalist society as a variety of forms of subjection to commodification. Focusing analytically on class and commodification can help us think about class, commodification, and justice. Commodities and class relationships and the social world they both come from and constitute are often all at once taken as unavoidably given, overlooked, and depoliticized. For a work that connects capitalism and issues of justice admirably, see Nancy Fraser and Rahel Jaeggi, *Capitalism: A Conversation in Critical Theory* (Cambridge: Polity, 2018). There are other valid and useful ways to understand class, such as power and authority (see, for example, the multiple legal historical works of Christopher Tomlins, such as his *Law, Labor, and Ideology in the Early American Republic* [Cambridge: Cambridge University Press, 1993]), class as subjectivity and experience (the most famous version of this approach is E. P. Thompson, *The Making of the English Working Class* [New York: Vintage, 1966]), or class as inequality of wealth (see, for example, David Huyssen, *Progressive Inequality: Rich and Poor in New York, 1890–1920* [Cambridge: Harvard University Press, 2014]). Because capitalism and class are complex and multifaceted, it is good that we have a plurality of analytical approaches available.

[14] Private government is not unique to capitalism, but it is an important characteristic of employment in capitalist societies. See Elizabeth Anderson, *Private Government: How Employers Rule Our Lives (And Why We Don't Talk about It)* (Princeton: Princeton University Press, 2017).

structural constraint that characterize class and employment relationships in capitalism were largely absent from Nettie Blom and Kathryn
Carlin's lawsuits. Capitalism formed the backdrop for, the air in and
around, the courts, and yet that social context was largely abstracted
away in the legal proceedings.[15] This social context lurks in the background of my understanding of all of the events in this book, more
explicitly than it did for the judges in Blom and Carlin's cases, but it is
only occasionally foregrounded.

Like everyone in capitalist society, employers face market imperatives.[16]
These imperatives coerce even well-meaning employers to practice business
in a relatively impersonal manner, relatively indifferent to the well-being of
employees and the working class as a whole. "Nothing personal, just

---

[15] One important part of the social backdrop to these cases was the way in which both paid
and unpaid work are organized in capitalist societies. Blom and Carlyn were injured
while "at work," in a common meaning of the term "work." They were injured while
working for their employers, carrying out their contractually defined roles as sellers of
labor power. They rented their time and energy to their employers, getting (a promise of
later) money and taking commands. For each woman, on the day of their injury, before
they began work they got dressed, probably ate something, and traveled to work. These
actions were not carried out for their employers, but were functional for their employers:
a hungry, sleepless employee is less usable instrumentally. There was, then, work that
occurred off the clock, which was not directly commodified and not under the supervision
of the employer yet still governed by imperatives originating from commodification.
Food, clothing, and shelter had to be paid for, after all, which compelled Blom and Carlin
to have money. For Marxist feminist accounts of the relationship between waged and
unwaged activities in capitalism, see Jeanne Boydston, *Home and Work: Housework,
Wages, and the Ideology of Labor in the Early Republic* (New York: Oxford University
Press, 1990); Mariarosa Dalla Costa and Selma James, *The Power of Women and the
Subversion of the Community* (Bristol: Falling Wall Press, 1972); Silvia Federici, *Caliban
and the Witch: Women, the Body and Primitive Accumulation* (New York: Autonomedia, 2004); Leopoldina Fortunati, *The Arcane of Reproduction* (New York: Autonomedia, 1995); Nancy Fraser, "Behind Marx's Hidden Abode: For an Expanded Conception
of Capitalism," *New Left Review* 86 (March–April 2014): 55–72; Eileen Boris, *Home to
Work: Motherhood and the Politics of Industrial Homework in the United States* (Cambridge: Cambridge University Press, 1994); Alice Kessler-Harris, *A Woman's Wage:
Historical Meanings and Social Consequences* (Lexington: University Press of Kentucky,
1990); Amy Dru Stanley, *From Bondage to Contract; The Straight State: Sexuality and
Citizenship in Twentieth-Century America* (Princeton: Princeton University Press, 2009);
Amy Dru Stanley, "Histories of Capitalism and Sex Difference," *Journal of the Early
Republic* 36, no. 2 (Summer 2016): 343–350; and Christopher Tomlins, "Subordination,
Authority, Law: Subjects in Labor History," *International Labor and Working-Class
History*, no. 47 (Spring 1995): 56–90.

[16] Ellen Meiksins-Wood has made this point in multiple works. For a representative
example, see "Capitalism's Gravediggers," www.jacobinmag.com/2014/12/capitalisms-
gravediggers/, accessed July 13, 2017.

business," is an apt cliché for much of life in capitalist society.[17] This means in part that the ills of capitalism do not primarily result from individual employers' attitudes, beliefs, and moral character but rather from pressures woven into capitalist societies. If anything, employers' moral character is more systemic effect than cause: how one acts becomes who one is.[18]

Law and policy can, with difficulty, intervene to mitigate market imperatives and their effects.[19] Beginning in 1910, state legislatures in the United States began to do exactly this in response to the problem of employee injury, intervening by creating what were called workmen's compensation laws.[20] These laws improved the lives of working-class people in important respects. And yet, in other important respects, compensation laws exemplified the tendency toward treating working-class people impersonally and as objects of instrumental use.

The activist and public intellectual Ella Baker once distinguished between making a living and making a life.[21] While employment is certainly a source of meaning and fulfillment for some people, it is not

---

[17] See H. H. Gerth and C. Wright Mills, eds., *From Max Weber: Essays in Sociology* (Abingdon: Routledge, 1991), 215. That indifference can lead capitalists to undermine elements of society and the natural environment that their industries or that capitalism as a whole requires to function. Nancy Fraser and Rahel Jaeggi discuss that tendency and the conflicts it generates, which they call boundary struggles. See Fraser and Jaeggi, *Capitalism: A Conversation in Critical Theory*.

[18] Jean-Paul Sartre put this as "existence precedes essence." See Jean-Paul Sartre, *Existentialism Is a Humanism* (New Haven: Yale University Press, 2007), 20–23. Martin Glaberman makes a similar point, writing that "consciousness is the result of activity." Glaberman stresses the important point that it is specifically collective activity – social rather than individual existence – that constitutes consciousness. Martin Glaberman, "Work and Working-Class Consciousness," in *Punching Out and Other Writings*, ed. Staughton Lynd (Chicago: Charles H. Kerr, 2002), 121–132, 129.

[19] As I type this, the difficulties of mitigating, let alone averting, catastrophic climate change attest to the power of these imperatives and the difficulty of working against them. See Bill McKibben, "Global Warming's Terrifying New Math," *Rolling Stone*, July 19, 2012.

[20] The laws were called workmen's compensation laws when they were created. For the most part that is what I call them in this book as well. I do so to underline the sexism of the law, but not to express approval of it. That compensation laws were focused on wage-earning men reflected aspects of the social vision behind the laws. That social vision imagined waged work as something only men did and imagined traditionally feminized activities as not work. Alice Kessler-Harris's *In Pursuit of Equity* analyzes how "these gendered habits of mind" shaped social policy in the United States in the twentieth century. Alice Kessler-Harris, *In Pursuit of Equity: Women, Men, and the Quest for Economic Citizenship in 20th-Century America* (Oxford: Oxford University Press, 2001), 18. Jeanne Boydston's *Home and Work* examines how traditionally feminized activities such as housework came to be treated much of the time as not actually work.

[21] Quoted in Barbara Ransby, *Ella Baker and the Black Freedom Movement* (Chapel Hill: University of North Carolina Press, 2003), 261.

equally so for everyone. Furthermore, having money is compulsory, because a living is something one earns rather than being entitled to, which makes employment compulsory for most people as well. This means that, as legal historian Robert Steinfeld has put it, employees "perform often disagreeable tasks for their employers over extended periods of time under the implicit threat that an employer will deny them their principal means of livelihood."[22] And the primary purpose behind the enterprises in which most people work is not to provide either fulfillment (a life) or income (a living), but for the institution to persist and to profit. Employees are those who are used, economic instruments deployed, employed.[23]

The tyranny of the table is of a piece with this social order, a kind of grid that rhetorically and sometimes literally segments persons into parts, and values those parts not in terms of making a life – humanity in its multiplicity and to some extent ineffability – but in terms of making a living: earnings, clear, knowable, simple. Or, rather, simplified, reduced. It is as economic objects, instruments for others' use, that people are valued under compensation laws. This book is intended to dramatize this instrumentalization of working-class people in capitalist society, especially at some of their most vulnerable moments in the aftermath of injuries that resulted from systematically produced industrial violence. This instrumentalization occurs both in the form of relative indifference to their well-being and in the form of efforts to secure that well-being for instrumental reasons rather than because working-class people are human beings who deserve to be treated with respect and dignity.

Some of what I have said is clearly normative in character, as is some of what follows in this book. Historical interpretation cannot avoid normative presuppositions. Interpretations of the American Revolution, for example, as expanding, or failing to expand, human freedom make sense only because the people who make and read those interpretations have in mind some notions of freedom, and a non-normative notion of freedom is impossible. If my book appears normative in some additional way, more than or differently than is common among historians, I would argue that this is not in fact because the book is normative in some qualitatively

[22] Robert Steinfeld, "Coercion/Consent in Labour" (speech at the COMPAS Annual Conference: Theorizing Key Migration Debates, St. Anne's College, University of Oxford, 2008).

[23] See Christopher Tomlins, "'Those Who Are Used': A Commentary on the Employee: A Political History, by Jean-Christian Vinel," UC Berkeley Public Law Research Paper No. 2546331.

different way from other works of history. Rather, this appearance may arise from the fact of this book's explicitness about its normative aspects, and that the views that inform the book perhaps diverge from some relatively widespread normative positions. Ultimately, I leave those assessments up to the reader.

I wish to note as well that much – possibly all – legal history is in some sense meta-normative, in at least two senses. Law is normative. Legal actors make claims based on norms, claims about the meaning, application, enforcement, and stakes of those norms. This means that the object of historical study for legal historians is an important part of the normative life of society. Legal history, by tracing legal continuity and change, traces continuity and change in (at least some of) society's norms. In addition, to the degree that legal historians want readers to draw judgments about those norms, legal historians are in a sense offering normative or prescriptive arguments about how historically existing norms should be understood – legal historians' normative judgments are norms about norms, hence meta-normative. This is often implicit. I have sought to be more explicit about this.

More specifically, I argue in this book that some significant injustices occurred within the history of employee injury law in the early twentieth century. In addition, I argue that historical actors' understandings of justice and injustice within the law changed in the time period I examine. Part of my claim is, therefore, meta-normative, in that I am making a normative argument about different conceptions of justice. Some conceptions of justice can be so attenuated, and some indifferences to injustice can be so egregious, that these conceptions and indifferences themselves are unjust. For an individual to conceive of another person as less than human, even if that conception never eventuates into any other action, is wrong. Similarly, for an individual to be fully indifferent to the well-being of another person is wrong. The wrong is all the greater when the indifference is written into law.

Often legal decisions have consequences in people's lives in the form of greater or lesser access to wealth and power, consequences critics some-times call "material" to provided added rhetorical force. These conse-quences matter a great deal. American society is rife with distributive injustice, historically and still today. At the same time, emphasis on distributive justice should not come at the exclusion of other forms of justice. People ought to have adequate living standards, and people should also be treated with dignity and respect. Feminist political philosopher Nancy Fraser has articulated this in terms of a distinction between justice as redistribution and justice as recognition.[24] Thinking about justice only in distributive terms leaves aside injustices such as disrespect, denial of dignity, and treating people as objects. As the old strike slogan goes, people need both bread and roses.[25] Or, in Baker's words, people need not just a living, but a life. Thus in what follows, I trace changing conceptions of (and indifference to) justice and injustice within employee injury law as well as kinds of injustice perpetrated within or due to employee injury law, some of the time emphasizing issues of distributive justice and some of the time emphasizing justice as recognition.

In addition to its immediate subject matter, this book also offers some general concepts for thinking about law and society. The book is a consciously interdisciplinary attempt to combine historical inquiry with theory, in ways that are appropriate to the book's immediate object and in ways that, I hope, are thought-provoking for readers on issues of law and society more broadly. The book presents concepts like commodification, biopolitics, and disability as a social relationship – which is to say, as political and historical.

The book also presents a kind of meta-concept, a picture of historical change as occurring with minimal contingency. That is to say, this is a

---

[24] Part of the agenda in the background of this book is to show how attention to industrial violence and the law thereof supports Nancy Fraser's insight that class should "be understood as two-dimensional" such that class's "harms include misrecognition as well as maldistribution." Nancy Fraser, "Social Justice in the Age of Identity Politics," in Nancy Fraser and Axel Honneth, *Redistribution or Recognition? A Political-Philosophical Exchange* (London: Verso, 2003), 23. My analysis also disagrees with Fraser in that she argues that the misrecognition harms of class "originated as by-products of economic structure" (p. 23), whereas in my view that misrecognition is not a by-product but inextricably woven into employment relationships in capitalism. To be an employee is in important respects always to be instrumentalized rather than recognized. That condition in turn is constituted by and inextricable from what Ellen Meiksins-Wood has described as the imperative character of markets in capitalist society. Ellen Meiksins-Wood, "The Politics of Capitalism," *Monthly Review* 51, no. 4 (September 1999): 12–26. I see this point as a criticism of what E. P. Thompson called "a political economy which diminished human reciprocities to the wages-nexus." E. P. Thompson, "The Moral Economy of the English Crowed in the Eighteenth Century," in Thompson, *Customs in Common: Studies in Traditional Popular Culture* (London: Merlin Press, 1991), 185–258; 285. As Thompson put it elsewhere, "The injury which advanced industrial capitalism did, and which the market society did, was to define human relations as being primarily economic." Michael Merrill, "An Interview with E. P. Thompson," *Radical History Review* 12 (1976): 4–25. I have found Marcus Rediker's criticisms of what he calls "the violence of abstraction" to be similarly thought provoking. Marcus Rediker, *The Slave Ship: A Human History* (New York: Viking, 2007), 12–13.

[25] Robert Forrant et al., *The Great Lawrence Textile Strike of 1912: New Scholarship on the Bread & Roses Strike* (New York: Routledge, 2014).

story in which there was room for variation in the details, but not in the big picture. I stress that this is not a philosophical position I hold about all historical change as such: there is value in thinking in terms of contingency, and there is also value in thinking otherwise.[26] In modern warfare, when bombs start to fall it is contingent who the exact victims will be, but once the machinery of war is in motion at a sufficient speed, the fact that some people will die is no longer a contingency. A similar point goes for the obfuscated class war that was the early twentieth-century economy. Once the wheels of the process I describe were in motion, it was a given that harms and injustice would happen, even if there were some contingencies about the specifics of what those harms and injustices would be. I do not emphasize the contingencies here, but rather the harms and injustices. I do so above all because I think this offers a useful perspective on my book's subject matter. I also hope that my emphasis on path dependency and necessity in this story can demonstrate the usefulness of those categories for understanding capitalist society.

As I said, this is a book about abstractions. But fundamentally this is a book about people, including Nettie Blom and Kathryn Carlin, who lived in an abstraction-governed society. It is about what we as a society owe one another in terms of just treatment, and about the degree to which our legal and economic system so often falls short of what we owe one another. The story is largely negative, but its telling is motivated by the conviction and hope that we could do better. It is also motivated by the conviction that historical investigation can both enrich and be enriched by engagement with social theory, and that history can enrich collective moral deliberation in the present about who we are and who we could be.

---

[26] John Witt's *The Accidental Republic* illuminates workers' compensation and offers a powerful example of the value of contingency as a concept for historians. John Fabian Witt, *The Accidental Republic: Crippled Workmen, Destitute Widows, and the Remaking of American Law* (Cambridge, MA: Harvard University Press, 2004).

PART I

THE ECLIPSE OF RECOGNITION AND THE RISE
OF THE TYRANNY OF THE TABLE

In the early twentieth-century US economy, working-class people like Nettie Blom and Kathryn Carlyn suffered greatly, regularly enduring incalculable losses. That suffering and loss was not contingent but was a necessary outcome, a path-dependent result of how the economy was organized. Chapter 1 discusses the legal world in which injured people found themselves: a world where the lawsuit predominated as the legal device for dealing with employee injuries. The chapter examines how this legal world often added further suffering to the lives of the injured by abandoning them to post-injury poverty with little real recourse. Individual judges may have felt some remorse at these outcomes, but as institutions that allocated social power the courts were systematically indifferent to the economic well-being of working-class people and to the harms of poverty. The court system, however, was not wholly reducible to its injustices. Alongside massive shortcomings existed practices of recognizing injured people as multifaceted human beings, employee injury as a source of dignitary harms, and injury as (at least some of the time) a kind of injustice.

I focus on these aspects of the court-based system of employee injury law in order ultimately to shed light on the compensation laws that replaced that system. Examining the court system will aid the book's overall goal of making compensation laws appear strange, so that we can think outside the tyranny of the table.[1] Chapter 1 also presents a

---

[1] To some extent, then, this is a genealogical project, in the sense of tracking backward from some current habitual understandings we have of parts of our society. The hope is that by comprehending those understandings historically we might then become somewhat less

theoretical account of commodification, in order to illuminate law's persistent treatment of persons as economic objects, and argues that commodification is, at best, in tension with treating people justly.

In Chapters 2 and 3, the book turns to early twentieth-century reformers' dissatisfaction with the court system's responses to the injury problem. These reformers made arguments about how to change policy to better deal with injuries. In the process, they also offered different implicit definitions of why injuries were a problem. In doing so, they drew on different implied notions of justice. In effect, these actors, despite the important differences among them, defined injury primarily as a problem of loss of income, which meant that the problem law should solve was that of income support. Over time, this approach to the problem of injury tended toward treating injured persons – and working-class people more generally – as economic objects, rather than as political and moral subjects.

Without denying the many shortcomings – indeed, the deep inhumanity – of the court-based system of injury law, there were within the court system some significant ways of dealing with injury law that were lost with the transition to compensation laws. That loss helped give compensation laws their own deep inhumanity. Among the reasons for that loss within the law was a shift toward what theorist Michel Foucault called biopolitics, a new approach to conceptualizing and governing society. Compensation laws introduced new and specifically biopolitical ways to commodify people. Those practices crowded out the momentary, fragmentary forms of recognition of humanity that had existed in courts. As a result, injury as a matter of (in)justice and justice itself as a matter of concern receded within employee injury law. I call this change the moral thinning of injury.

The concerns of the historical actors I examine in these chapters were quite abstract, as is my own theoretical understanding of the social processes in which those actors took part. There is a chance that the arc of this book itself may inadvertently obscure the concrete humanity of injured persons. In an effort to push against that possibility, there follows after Part I an Interlude focusing on a mining disaster in 1909, a disaster that influenced the national turn to compensation laws. This Interlude underlines the human losses involved in employee injury in order to make apparent how little of those losses fit into the abstractions of employee

enrolled in those understandings. See Margot Canaday, *The Straight State: Sexuality and Citizenship in Twentieth-Century America* (Princeton: Princeton University Press, 2009), 11–12.

injury law. Walter Benjamin once wrote that "the tradition of the oppressed teaches us that the 'state of emergency' in which we live is not the exception but the rule. We must attain to a conception of history that accords with this insight." The Interlude attempts to virtuously combine thinking abstractly with attention to concrete lived reality, with two related goals: to make apparent that for every injured individual and their loved ones, each injury was a kind of crisis or multiple crises, and to write history in a way that contributes to the conception of history that Benjamin called for.[2]

---

[2] Walter Benjamin, "On the Concept of History," in Benjamin, *Selected Writings, vol. 4: 1938–1940* (Cambridge: Belknap Press, 2003), 389–400; 392. I attempt, in the words of sociologist Avery Gordon, to "richly conjure, describe, narrate, and explain the liens, the costs, the forfeits, and the losses of modern systems of abusive power in their immediacy and worldly significance." Avery F. Gordon, *Ghostly Matters: Haunting and the Sociological Imagination*, 2nd ed. (Minneapolis: University of Minnesota Press, 2008), xvii. Gordon has criticized the discipline of sociology for having "[b]loodless categories, narrow notions of the visible and the empirical, professional standards of indifference, institutional rules of distance and control," which are inadequate to analysis of violence, injustice, and their effects (p. 21). In addition to avoiding bloodless categories in our investigations of injustice and violence, scholars should investigate the processes by which law and other modalities of rule produce and inflict their own bloodless categories at the same time that they organize the ongoing enactment of violence in society.

Commodification and Recognition within the Tyranny of the Trial

Nettie Blom and people like her found themselves in an abstraction-governed legal world. Much like the market, this legal world was composed of the choices of many individuals yet it added up to something not quite volitional, creating a force to which people had to accommodate themselves.[1] Within this legal (dis)order, the law spoke two dialects, one of commodification and one of morality. To put it another way, within the tyranny of the trial two logics of rule co-existed, one economic and one moral, or perhaps a single logic of rule with both economic and moral facets. This chapter treats these two logics of the court-based system of employee injury law in turn, examining their relationships, their effects on people subject to the law, and the different conceptions of justice implied within them and best suited to evaluating them.

LAW'S SOCIAL IMAGINATION

By the opening of the twentieth century three legal rules had become key within employee injury law: the fellow servant rule, the rule of assumption of risk, and the rule of contributory negligence. The fellow servant rule meant that if an accident was the fault of another employee, the

---

[1] The market itself is legally constituted. See Anne Fleming, "Legal History as Economic History," in *The Oxford Handbook of Legal History*, ed. Markus D. Dubber and Christopher Tomlins (Oxford: Oxford University Press, 2018); Christopher Tomlins, "Organic Poise? Capitalism as Law," *Buffalo Law Review* 64, no. 1 (January 2016): 61; and Nate Holdren, "Some Hasty Musings on Matters Legal and Economic," *Legal Form*, https://legalform.blog/2018/11/18/some-hasty-musings-on-matters-legal-and-economic-nate-holdren/, accessed November 18, 2018.

Military

employer was not liable. Assumption of risk meant that if an employee knowingly worked under risk of injury, then the employee consented to taking that risk; therefore, the employer was not liable should injury result. Contributory negligence meant that if the employee could be shown to have been partially at fault for the accident, then the employer was not liable.[2] Collectively the trio were known as employer's legal defenses. Together these laws meant that injured employees could win lawsuits only by proving that they bore no fault for their injury, did not know they were in danger, and that fault rested solely with their employers. Much of the time employees could not meet this standard. The result was, in the words of treatise writer Charles Labatt, a legal bulwark behind which "'inhumanity,' as several judges have conceded may be predicated of the conduct of employers who are at the same time free from legal liability, has found a secure shelter."[3] Employer security meant inhumane employee insecurity, leaving injured people to bear the personal and financial costs of their injuries based on whatever existing support they happened to have.

Commodification was a core element of employee injury law. This may seem contradictory, given that employee injury law left so many people's injuries uncompensated. A conceptual framework that commodified working-class people, however, was part of how the law reasoned its way toward not compensating injury. In his 1842 opinion in the influential case of *Farwell v. Boston and Worcester R.R. Corp*, Massachusetts Chief Justice Lemuel Shaw ruled that the Boston and Worcester Railroad owed no money to Nicholas Farwell, an injured employee. Shaw argued that an employee "takes upon himself the natural and ordinary risks and perils incident to the performance of such services, and in legal presumption, the

[2] Iowa Employers' Liability Commission, *Report of Employers' Liability Commission* (Des Moines: Emory H. English, State Printer, 1912), 13–18; John Fabian Witt, *The Accidental Republic: Crippled Workmen, Destitute Widows, and the Remaking of American Law* (Cambridge, MA: Harvard University Press, 2004), 22–43; Lawrence M. Friedman, "Civil Wrongs: Personal Injury Law in the Late 19th Century," *American Bar Foundation Research Journal* 12, nos. 2–3 (Spring–Summer, 1987): 351–378. Jonathan Levy's *Freaks of Fortune* interprets the creation of the fellow servant rule in light of the history of insurance in maritime shipping and the broader cultural and intellectual history of risk. Levy argues that the *Farwell* decision, which created the fellow servant rule, treated injured employee plaintiffs in the way that marine insurance law treated ship captains. In doing so the decision brought the maritime rules of risk management into employment relations on land. Jonathan Levy, *Freaks of Fortune: The Emerging World of Capitalism and Risk in America* (Cambridge, MA: Harvard University Press, 2012), 7–21.

[3] Charles Bagot, *Commentaries on the Law of Master and Servant*, vol. 1. (Rochester: Lawyers' Co-operative Publishing Company, 1904), 157.

compensation is adjusted accordingly." Shaw here combined two important notions of commodification that barred compensation. He said that,
legally speaking, employees had by virtue of doing their jobs agreed to
take some degree of chances of harm. This agreement meant that they
could not receive compensation for those "natural and ordinary" harms
because they were presumed to have consented to the chance of injury. In
effect, this framed employees as market actors who had bargained with
employees over the price of labor power and come to agree that as part of
the terms of its sale the employer would pay only for injuries that were
exceptional in character. In a word, the employee was treated, by virtue of
working, as having consented to an agreement that injury would not be
compensated.[4] Hazards of injury is what they had signed on for.

Treatise writer Charles Labatt criticized the social imagination implied
in the argument that employees faced the hazards of work voluntarily,
and so the hazards were rightfully the employee's responsibility. This
perspective, Labatt argued, sidestepped "the ultimate question to be
settled," namely, "whether, as a matter of fact, the servant, confronted
with the alternative of throwing up remunerative work or of encountering
some abnormal peril," actually acted voluntarily.[5] In Labatt's view that
"ultimate question" ought to be answered with a resounding no, because
employment simply was not voluntary. Calling it so "rested upon the
hypothesis that the fear of losing remunerative work does not deprive of
its voluntary quality the action of a servant who enters or continues in an
employment with a knowledge that it involves extraordinary hazards,"
Labatt wrote. "To obtain an adequate support of this hypothesis, it is
necessary to adopt the most extreme doctrines of the laissez faire school of
sociologists."[6] This extreme doctrine wrongly assumed that employers
and employees bargained "on an equal footing" and that the employee
was "a voluntary agent." That view's "essential weakness," Labatt
argued, was that it committed "courts to the anomalous position that
actual constraint is something different from legal constraint. Upon the
average man it is certain that the fear of disagreeable and, it may be,
frightful consequences which almost certainly ensue from the failure to
obtain work from the loss of a position, must always operate as a very

---

[4] *Farwell v. Boston and Worcester R.R.*, quoted in Christopher Tomlins, *Law, Labor, and
Ideology in the Early American Republic* (Cambridge: Cambridge University Press, 1993),
380; pp. 380–384 are illuminating on industrial accidents and law in the nineteenth
century United States; pp. 347–368 deal with the *Farwell* decision in particular.
[5] Bagot, *Commentaries on the Law of Master and Servant*, vol. 1, 166.
[6] Bagot, *Commentaries on the Law of Master and Servant*, vol. 1, 156.

strong coercive influence, indeed. To speak of one whom that fear drives into or detains in a dangerous employment as being a voluntary agent is a mere trifling with words."[7]

This "trifling with words" required mental gymnastics on the part of judges that Labatt had no patience for. "It is simply amazing," he wrote, that "any considerable body of educated men should continue to determine the rights of citizens on the assumption that physical compulsion may be predicated of an act which a servant does because he fears the suffering produced by the stroke of the whip or a bludgeon, and not of an act which a servant does because he fears the suffering" that would result from unemployment.[8]

The idea of ordinary hazard voluntarily assumed by employees represented a certain measure of danger in employment as acceptable. Employers could compel employees to take chances with their well-being, and if employees' well-being suffered as a result, this harm was not the employers' responsibility. Legal decisions, such the influential English case of *Priestley v. Fowler*, often made use of employees' power of exit to justify not holding employers responsible for employees' injuries. That is, courts often held that the fact that employees were legally free to quit meant that they had consented to do the work during which they were injured. This victim-blaming argument failed to account for the ways that employees' ability to quit their jobs was constrained by the consequences of joblessness, and further by the limited set of opportunities that could await the servant after exit. If some measure of danger is ordinary in a job, then that kind of danger is likely present in all jobs of that type; therefore, because having a job is effectively compulsory, there is no exit to a place of safety.[9]

---

[7] Bagot, *Commentaries on the Law of Master and Servant*, vol. 1, 164.

[8] Bagot, *Commentaries on the Law of Master and Servant*, vol. 1, 165. Employment is in important respects compulsory and thus non-consensual, yet it is widely legally considered voluntary. Within labor and employment law, as the legal historian Robert Steinfeld argues, the term "voluntary" does not actually mean free of coercion but rather means coercion of a type that the law finds legitimate and acceptable. Robert Steinfeld, "Coercion/Consent in Labour" (speech at the COMPAS Annual Conference: Theorizing Key Migration Debates, St. Anne's College, University of Oxford, 2008). For extended discussion of the politics of the idea of consent in work, see Tomlins, *Law, Labor and Ideology*, and Christopher Tomlins, *Freedom Bound: Law, Labor, and Civic Identity in Colonizing English America, 1580–1865* (Cambridge: Cambridge University Press, 2010), 338–383.

[9] This paragraph draws on Elizabeth Anderson's discussion of the rhetorical misuse of employees' ability to quit their jobs. See Elizabeth Anderson, *Private Government: How Employers Rule Our Lives (And Why We Don't Talk about It)* (Princeton: Princeton University Press, 2017).

Like Labatt, treatise writer Charles Fall asked some critical questions of legal doctrine's social imagination. The theory written into the law was that employers and employees made contracts with each other, but, Fall wrote, "there can be no contract without a meeting of minds – no contract unless the parties mutually understand the terms, and mutually assent to them." The law often simply assumed such assent was baked into the employment relationship. This meant that the law further implied "that each, at the time [the employment contract] was made, had its terms in his mind." Fall questioned if this actually occurred in the world, and suggested that legislators might consider this matter "as if it were a new question."[10] While the law appealed to social practice to justify itself, and to mask its own intervention into society, the social practice to which law appealed was a fiction that did not accurately represent reality:

If the common experience of ordinary men declares that the danger of injury is seldom thought of at the time of making such contracts, then the fact, which the judges have assumed as the basis of their opinions, does not exist. If, moreover, common experience declares further that workmen are not expected to run their own risks, but to look to their employers for protection, the fact is reversed, the theory falls to the ground together with the hypothesis upon which it rests, and the law should be reversed in favor of the workmen.[11]

Whether or not real people in fact thought like the abstract, artificial person of the law was an empirical question that the legal notion of implied contract did not allow juries to consider. Employees were left bound by a supposed contract they did not in fact partake in creating, a contract that meant they often could not receive compensation for their injuries.

In addition to consent, Shaw's decision in *Farwell* included a second notion of commodification that served to bar compensation: the idea of a wage premium for especially dangerous work. Farwell was relatively well paid by nineteenth-century standards, a point that Shaw used to support the "legal presumption [that] compensation is adjusted" upward for employees who took above-average chances. Farwell's work was, presumptively, better paid because it was more dangerous, and so Farwell had already been paid for his injuries. "The peril of the accident," as historian Jonathan Levy articulates the legal point, "was already

---

[10] Charles G. Fall, *Employers' Liability for Personal Injuries to Their Employees* (Boston: Wright & Potter, 1883), 18.
[11] Fall, *Employers' Liability for Personal Injuries to Their Employees*, 20.

priced into Farwell's wage."[12] Farwell had been paid, in Shaw's words, "a premium for the risk which he thus assumes."[13] Injury was commodified in the employment relationship prior to injury, such that it would be unfair for courts to require employers to make a second payment in the form of a damage award.

Charles Fall argued, based on parliamentary inquiry into the matter, that higher wages in exchange for greater hazard was in fact rare, if the practice existed at all, but courts seem to have been uninterested in that reality.[14] The abstract person discussed in court, the one whose "compensation [was] adjusted," like the person who thought through all the hazards of work and took them on voluntarily, did not have to exist outside "legal presumption" in order to play a role. That fictional person of the law helped Shaw articulate the abstractions to which real persons were subject. Consent and the hazard premium were not treated as empirical matters. Farwell and other employees did not have to consciously agree to risk their bodies and selves in the course of employment. No company official ever had to decide to pay higher wages in order to deliberately pay a risk premium. All of this happened in law, a fiction against which actual persons were measured.[15] When acting within the logic commodification, judges like Shaw depicted employment as a world of voluntary property exchanges. The law and legal actors were thus to an important extent both a cause and an effect of, to borrow a phrase of E. P. Thompson's, "a political economy which diminished human reciprocities to the wages-nexus."[16] They constructed a vision of the world defined by the commodity, decided on the specific meanings thereof, and imposed the consequences on injured people like Nettie Blom.

---

[12] Levy, *Freaks of Fortune*, 8.

[13] *Farwell v. Boston and Worcester R.R.*, quoted in Levy, *Freaks of Fortune*, 8.

[14] Fall, *Employers' Liability for Personal Injuries to Their Employees*, 59–60.

[15] There is a conceptual affinity between this legal person and the average person dealt with in insurance. Both were nonexistent individuals used to govern actual persons. See Dan Bouk, *How Our Days Became Numbered: Risk and the Rise of the Statistical Individual* (Chicago: University of Chicago Press, 2015).

[16] E. P. Thompson, "The Moral Economy of the English Crowd in the Eighteenth Century," in Thompson, *Customs in Common: Studies in Traditional Popular Culture* (London: Merlin Press, 1991), 185–258; 285. For a discussion of the importance of legal assumptions about employment as property exchange within twentieth-century US labor law, see Julius G. Getman, *The Supreme Court on Unions: Why Labor Law Is Failing American Workers* (Ithaca: Cornell University Press, 2016), 16–22.

(NON)COMPENSATION AND DAMAGE

Nettie Blom lost her lawsuit. Many others similarly lost. We lack a comprehensive study of the court-based system of employee injury law, but contemporary empirical investigations repeatedly confirmed high levels of uncompensated injuries, with estimates ranging from 20 to as high as 90 percent of all employee injuries being noncompensable.[17] Whatever the specific numbers, the tyranny of the trial regularly abandoned people like Blom to the vicissitudes of commodity-ruled society. The injured were left to deal with their injuries without financial assistance. The consequences could be quite serious.

The fate of Blom in particular does not seem to have been captured in a historical archive, but other sources help evoke the consequences likely in situations like hers. Upton Sinclair's 1906 social realist novel *The Jungle*, based on Sinclair's research into the lives of Chicago packinghouse workers, dramatized some of the consequences of uncompensated injury. The novel's main character Jurgis Rudkus worked at a slaughterhouse where, in a pivotal scene in the novel, a steer broke loose and charged at Jurgis. He dodged, avoiding severe bodily harm, but in doing so he sprained his ankle. The sprain became progressively more painful, leading Jurgis to miss several weeks of work and to lose his job. In the family's ensuing scramble to pay bills without Jurgis's income, all members of the household feared for their futures, bringing sleepless nights and angry days. Stress-related interpersonal conflict led Jonas, another wage-earning member of the household, to leave, further reducing family income. As a result, several children in the extended family who lived in the same household had to quit school to find waged work. Partly as a result, one of the children, Stanislovas, suffered frostbite that permanently disabled several of his fingers. Later, after Jurgis recovered, Stanislovas tried to

---

[17] Fall, *Employers' Liability for Personal Injuries to Their Employees*, 94. Journalist William Hard estimated that only between 10 and 20 percent of employee injuries were legally compensable under employers' legal defenses. William Hard, *Injured in the Course of Duty* (New York: Ridgway Company, 1910), 54. James Harrington Boyd, an attorney who served on the Ohio Employers Liability Commission, estimated that between 20 and 40 percent of injuries were compensable. James Harrington Boyd, *Workmen's Compensation, or Insurance against Loss of Wages Arising out of Industrial Accidents* (Columbus: F. J. Heer Printing Co., 1911), 77. In 1910 economist E. H. Downey put the figure at around 40 percent. E. H. Downey, *History of Work Accident Indemnity in Iowa* (Iowa City: State Historical Society of Iowa, 1912), 183. Attorney and sociologist Crystal Eastman estimated slightly less than 50 percent. Crystal Eastman, *Work Accidents and the Law* (New York: Russell Sage Foundation, 1910), 121.

avoid going to work on cold days because the chill pained his fingers, prompting Jurgis to beat him to force him to work in order to bring in more money to support the household.[18] In the words of journalist and novelist Jack London, the Rudkus family "dropped down from the proletariat into what sociologists love to call the 'submerged tenth,'" people who were "all wrenched and distorted and twisted out of shape by toil and hardship and accident." These people had been "cast adrift by their masters like so many old horses," abandoned to "the bottom of the Social Pit."[19] The commodity logic of the law of employers' liability imposed poverty on people like Nettie Blom, bringing the market into their lives not as a source of opportunity but as a series of walls standing between them and what they needed.

Like Nettie Blom, Marguerite Murray worked in a laundry and had her fingers stolen by a mangle. After her injury in 1906, Murray sued her employer, the Chicago, Rock Island and Pacific Railway.[20] Unlike Nettie Blom and many other plaintiffs, Marguerite Murray won her trial. She was awarded $15,000. Murray's case was in significant respects a success story, within the limits of the court-based system of employee injury law. As such, her case helps illustrate those limits. Determining the dollar value of injury in the court-based system of employee injury law fell under the law of damages.[21]

[18] Upton Sinclair, *The Jungle* (New York: Doubleday, Page, 1906), 130–159.

[19] Jack London, *War of the Classes* (New York: Macmillan, 1905), 272. Karl Marx referred to what he called "a population which is superfluous to capital's average requirements," or more simply "a surplus population" – surplus, that is, to economic utility. Karl Marx, *Capital: A Critique of Political Economy*, vol. 1 (London: Penguin, 1990), 782. The "lowest sediment" of the surplus population, unable to find employment, lived "in the sphere of pauperism." Many were "the victims of industry, whose number increases with the growth of mines, chemical works, etc., the mutilated, the sickly." Marx, *Capital*, vol. 1, 797. Marx stressed that this poverty was systematically rather than incidentally generated by capitalism, in part because for working-class people access to money was predicated on finding a buyer for one's labor power. For a recent reading of Marx that emphasizes these populations and the social structural forces that generate poverty, see Fredric Jameson, *Representing Capital: A Reading of Volume One* (London: Verso, 2011). In this element, the best part of Jameson's book, Jameson is influenced by the work of the Endnotes collective. Endnotes is among the most intellectually vibrant and ambitious Marxist writing of the twenty-first century. Their writing exists in a series of self-published edited and collaboratively written volumes, available online at https://endnotes.org.uk.

[20] *Murray v. Chicago, R. I. & P. R. Co.*, 152 Iowa 732 (1911). The materials from Marguerite Murray's case are held in the State Law Library of Iowa's bound volumes of the Iowa Supreme Court's Abstracts and Arguments. Pagination reflects the page number in the bound volume.

[21] See George Voorhies, *Treatise on the Law of the Measure of Damages for Personal Injuries* (Norwalk: Laning, 1903).

The law of damages fell into two primary categories, non-pecuniary and pecuniary. The difference instantiated the two logics of commodification within the law, moral and economic. Non-pecuniary damages were for non-financial losses, dealt with later in the chapter. Pecuniary damages were compensation for the financial costs that an injured person suffered over the course of their projected lifespan, such as Murray's lost income and her medical expenses. Pecuniary damages exhibited the commodity logic of employee injury law in a different manner than did the rules of employers' liability.

In his treatise on damages, legal scholar Theodore Sedgwick wrote that damages required "an inquiry into the question of value." That inquiry was not a matter of value in a high-minded sense, but as a matter of price. To put it another way, the inquiry was into the market value of injury, but not into other kinds of values that might inform or define injury and the just handling of injury. Value meant resort to the market. The value of labor was "the market value of [plaintiffs'] labor."[22] "Value in law is generally founded upon the idea of exchange. In the case of the market value of anything, it is the sum of money which the buyers and sellers in the market are willing to give and take for it."[23] "The value of [an employee's] time or service is governed by the current rate of wages."[24]

Lurking in the background here was the rule of the commodity, specifically in its status as what theorist Michel Foucault called "a site of veridiction," a condition in which "the market becomes a site of truth."[25] That is, the market or the commodity determines the truth of value and in doing so occludes other kinds of truths, other kinds of valuation. Under the commodity as veridiction, the answer to the question "what was the value of an injury?" was market price. The answer was simple because the rule of the commodity reduced value to price. Therefore, in considering how to award pecuniary damages, courts used the price of labor power – the wages the injured person had been receiving

---

[22] Theodore Sedgwick, *A Treatise on the Measure of Damages, or, An Inquiry into the Principles Which Govern the Amount of Compensation Recovered in Suits at Law* (New York: John S. Voorhies, 1847), 489.

[23] Sedgwick, *A Treatise on the Measure of Damages*, 490. The language of willing, of consent and voluntary agreement, occluded the compulsory character of employment. See Anderson, *Private Government*, and Steinfeld, "Coercion/Consent in Labour."

[24] Sedgwick, *A Treatise on the Measure of Damages*, 514.

[25] Michel Foucault, *The Birth of Biopolitics: Lectures at the Collège de France, 1978–1979* (New York: Picador, 2008), 32, 31. This notion likewise implies a reduction of persons to labor power, to objects of instrumental, and specifically economic, use.

at the time of their injury and the person's likely earning ability after injury. In Marguerite Murray's case, her attorney set out her pay rate of twenty dollars per month and indicated that she had not been employed since her injury. The accident had left her "unable to earn anything, ... incapacitated for earning by the use of her hands all her life."[26]

The valuing of injury through wage rates meant that pecuniary damages assigned higher and lower values to people's bodies and lives based on their pre-injury income. This generally disadvantaged women, as women were regularly paid lower wages than men in this era.[27] Treatise writer William Osgood noted that this difference in legal valuation was at odds with a common sentiment about people's lives being of equal value: "most people would say that one man's limbs, health, and physical and mental functions were just as valuable as another man's limbs, health, and physical and mental functions. It is indisputable that one man's physical and mental powers are just as valuable to him as another man's physical and mental powers are to him. Yet, when courts and juries are asked to determine the pecuniary value of physical and mental injuries to different individuals the varying business prospects of such individuals

[26] *Murray v. Chicago*, 145 Iowa 212 (1909), 138. Murray and many other women injured on mangles stressed that their injuries meant they would never work again. For example, Kathryn Carlin's lawyer stressed that losing her hand meant Carlin could only "do little things requiring only use of one hand," making it "difficult to imagine an employment open to her in which she can earn any wages" (*Carlin v. Kennedy*, 97 Minn. 141 (1906), 23–24; the materials from Kathryn Carlin's case are held in the University of Minnesota Law Library's bound volumes of the Minnesota Supreme Court's Abstracts and Argument). This worked well in court but wasn't necessarily true: some women went back to work in laundries with one hand. A woman could feed flat linens into a mangle with one hand and a stump. See, for example, Dorothy Richardson, *The Long Day: The Story of a New York Working Girl* (Charlottesville: University Press of Virginia, 1990), 233–234; United States Senate, *Report on Condition of Woman and Child Wage-Earners in the United States, vol. 12: Employment of Women in Laundries* (Washington: Government Printing Office, 1911), 52, 54. This may be counterintuitive, because it is intuitive to assume that to be disabled is to be unable to work. On the history and politics of that sensibility, as part of historicizing the concept of disability, see Sarah F. Rose, *No Right to Be Idle: The Invention of Disability, 1840s–1930s* (Chapel Hill: University of North Carolina Press, 2017), and Sarah F. Rose, "'Crippled' Hands: Disability in Labor and Working-Class History," *Labor: Studies in Working-Class History of the Americas* 2, no. 1 (2005): 27–54.

[27] Women's weekly earnings in manufacturing were about half that of men's in the early twentieth century. Robert A. Margo, "Female-to-Male Earnings Ratios: 1815–1987," table Ba4224–4233 in *Historical Statistics of the United States, Earliest Times to the Present: Millennial Edition*, ed. Susan B. Carter, Scott Sigmund Gartner, Michael R. Haines, Alan L. Olmstead, Richard Sutch, and Gavin Wright (New York: Cambridge University Press, 2006).

influence them in finding varying amounts."[28] In a sense, valuing persons' bodies and lives according to their income was a continuation of a very old practice of social rank. Sedgwick attributed the origins of the law to the medieval Saxon practice of "Weregild, literally a man's money, or the price of man." A person who killed another person could be punished by being ordered to make a payment to the victim's family, a payment called weregild. The amount of this payment was defined by the rank of the victim, so that killing a more high-ranking person would lead to a higher amount paid as weregild.[29] Pecuniary damages worked similarly, except rank was monetary – difference in wages – and the status of higher wages as difference in social rank was often obscured.

Murray and her lawyer argued that her lost earning potential went beyond her pre-injury wage of five dollars per week at the laundry. Murray had been taking piano lessons for several years, with the intent of becoming a piano teacher, a higher paying job than a mangle operator. Murray's music teacher, Estella Belick, testified that Murray "was a very apt pupil ... People heard her play and liked her playing," said Belick, adding: "It would have taken her about from three to four years longer to complete her course, for piano playing so as to be capable to earn money as a teacher." Belick estimated that Murray could reasonably have earned "from twenty to twenty-five dollars a week" teaching or "three dollars a night" if playing piano as a performer.[30] This was a good deal more money than five dollars per week working in a laundry. The defendant objected to the speculation that Murray might earn more wages as a piano teacher but was overruled.[31]

Murray's testimony in court with regard to her piano lessons and career aspirations could be understood cynically – perhaps the lessons were solely for pleasure – but perhaps she really did plan to become a pianist or piano teacher for a living. It is fair to assume that she would have wanted the higher pay that would go with that job. It is also fair to assume she enjoyed other non-financial elements of her musical life. Those other elements did not appear in her case. The loss of her ability to play

[28] William N. Osgood, *Employers' Liability* (Boston: F. H. Hodges, 1891), 25.
[29] Sedgwick, *A Treatise on the Measure of Damages*, 10.
[30] *Murray v. Chicago*, 145 Iowa 212 (1909), 154–154.
[31] *Murray v. Chicago*, 152 Iowa 732 (1911), 81. It is worth noting that the entire enterprise here, including the idea that Murray would have continued to work in a laundry, involved speculation on possible futures. It is also likely that teaching piano was a higher status job than working in a laundry, and that the jury had this in mind in comparing the change in possible futures that came about in Murray's life as a result of her injury.

piano appeared only as a financial loss, a kind of reduction of artistic pursuits to their labor market value. Those pursuits were implicitly made equivalent to any other income-boosting strategy pursued by individuals navigating labor markets.

Lost wages were only one financial cost of Murray's injury. She also needed medical care both in and out of the hospital, and the need of an attendant to help with tasks she was not able to perform one-handed.[32] These needs cost money to meet, or at least had a determinable dollar value. Murray's mother, Florence, had worked as a nurse. After Marguerite's injury, Florence quit her job in order to attend to her daughter. "Her care is constant, because we have her to dress ... and she is not capable of feeding herself in any way, she can't cut her own meat, and she can't peel her own potatoes or anything like that that was necessary to do, break her own eggs or anything.... She is a constant care [sic] all the time, has been ever since she got hurt."[33] Florence Murray speculated about the dollar value of this care:

If I was hired by a stranger, the care I have to give, I would charge at least fifteen dollars a week, because it is day and night work. I have been nursing and have been paid for nursing and know the value of such services.... So far as my daughter is concerned now in her present condition this nursing will certainly have to be continued, and this care and presence of somebody that I have described, because she cannot dress herself, cannot help herself, somebody has got to take care of her.[34]

Under pecuniary damages, losses and the people who bore them were conceptualized according to prices on the labor market. The pecuniary value of a hand or other body part was easily determinable. It was equal to the lost earning potential that the person suffered due to the injury. Pecuniary damages compensated injured plaintiffs for lost income. But how much lost income, for how much working time? To answer this question, courts needed to make a projection of how long the injured person would likely have continued to earn an income had the injury not occurred. To do so, courts often drew on insurance companies' statistical mortality tables and annuity calculations.

---

[32] *Murray v. Chicago*, 145 Iowa 212 (1909), 138–139.

[33] *Murray v. Chicago*, 145 Iowa 212 (1909), 154.

[34] *Murray v. Chicago*, 145 Iowa 212 (1909), 155. Here as elsewhere testimony could play more than one role at the same time. Florence Murray was probably upset while testifying. The spectacle of a mother describing her daughter as unable to dress herself would likely have been moving to the men of the jury. This was both a way to present some of the meaning of Murray's injuries and a way to get higher damages.

In 1873 the Georgia Supreme Court ruled on an appeal in a lawsuit brought by a railroad engineer named Richards. A jury awarded him $3,000 for injuries after he was thrown from the train as a result of problems with the track. His employer, the Central Railroad, appealed. The company contested a statement made by a witness in estimating Richards's life expectancy. The witness was a life insurance agent who said that while he was not an expert on mortality statistics, he was familiar enough with the estimates and averages in tables used by life insurance companies to speak about Richards's likely life expectancy. He included copies of mortality tables with his testimony. The Central Railroad argued in its appeal that since the man was by his own admission not an expert, therefore his testimony on life expectancy should not have been allowed. Georgia Supreme Court Justice Jackson disagreed, writing in his tersely worded decision that "it appears that he was expert enough to have been employed for years about the business of life-insurance and to know what tables were used, and we see nothing wrong in admitting the evidence."[35] While Justice Jackson did not elaborate on his reasons for trusting the man's judgment, it is easy to read this as a kind of faith in the truth and objectivity of statistical tables and professionals in the insurance industry, including insurance sales agents whose statistical expertise was admittedly low.

In 1891 the Pennsylvania Supreme Court heard a case brought by a Mrs. Steinbrunner, after her forty-six-year-old husband was struck and killed by a passenger train. Her lawyer called as a witness a life insurance agent named F. T. Lusk. Lusk's testimony became in part a lesson on the authority and construction of statistical tables. He was asked to name "what authorities are the best" on "the subject of expectation of life," to which he replied that "the actuaries of any of our life insurance companies are authority." In response to questions from both attorneys and the trial judge, Lusk provided an account of the origins and differences between different tables used by the British and American insurance industry. Lusk ultimately said that according to two different tables, the man killed would ordinarily be expected to live an additional 23.8 or 23.81 years longer, depending on the table consulted. In the court's

[35] *Central Railroad v. Richards*, 62 Ga. 306 (1879). On the history of expert testimony, see Jennifer L. Mnookin, "Idealizing Science and Demonizing Experts: An Intellectual History of Expert Evidence," *Villanova Law Review*, 52, no. 4 (2007): 763–802, and Barbara Young Welke, *Recasting American Liberty: Gender, Race, Law, and the Railroad Revolution, 1865–1920* (New York: Cambridge University Press, 2001), 163–166, 237–240.

decision in favor of the injured plaintiff, Pennsylvania's Chief Justice Paxson took to the *Encyclopedia Britannica* to help himself understand and explain the uses and origins of mortality tables. In doing so, he noted what he took to be an important distinction for the use of insurance industry tables for damage awards. Those tables that were derived from the mortality data of the general population were useful for measuring life expectancy, while tables derived solely from insured people, believed to be of above average health, were not. As with *Central Railroad v. Richards*, in *Steinbrunner v. Railway Co.* the insurance agent appeared as the bearer of statistical knowledge, including knowledge of the construction of the tables themselves. That the plaintiffs' attorneys asked these agents to be witnesses attests to the sense of truth and cultural authority that went with insurance tables as well as the expertise and access to privileged information that insurance agents were perceived as having.[36]

In affirming the legal salience of the working knowledge of an insurance agent, Justice Jackson also noted the legal validity of knowledge drawn from and integral to a newly emerging statistical worldview in American culture. In the nineteenth century the life insurance industry used statistics to put itself on a sounder actuarial footing and, of course, to sell insurance. In doing so, the industry not only enrolled people into financial arrangements and communities that shared risk and promoted security, but also enrolled people into a new statistical worldview, within which numerical tables provided greater certainty to projections about the future.[37]

---

[36] *Steinbrunner v. Railway Co.*, 146 Pa. 504 (1892).

[37] While they differ in important ways, historians Barbara Welke and John Witt have both argued that there was a shift toward a statistical mentality in the law and more broadly in society over the course of the nineteenth and early twentieth centuries. This involved a transformation in legal mentality from one of free labor and liberal individualism to one of risk and aggregates, from accidents as inevitable, individualized, and part of the cost of individual freedom to accidents as avoidable, predictable, and statisticalized. Both scholars associate statistical reasoning primarily with the administrative state. Welke, *Recasting American Liberty*, 8–42, 112–118; Witt, *Accidental Republic*, 14–17, 22–42, 138–151, 173–174. Courts' use of mortality tables drew on averages to individualize persons. The difference between this kind of reasoning and that more frequently associated with statistics is the latter is not individualizing but rather aggregating. Foucault called this "massifying" or aggregating power by the term "biopolitics," which he distinguished from discipline, "power over the body in an individualizing mode." Michel Foucault, *"Society Must Be Defended": Lectures at the Collège de France, 1975–1976* (New York: Picador, 2003), 243. To use these terms, biopolitical and disciplinary power could each operate using statistical reasoning. Statistics could be used to aggregate or to individualize. In their use of mortality data for damage determinations, courts did the latter.

COMMODIFICATION

Commodification loomed large within employee injury law, conceptually speaking, in both liability determinations and pecuniary damages. Commodification is an activity people perform, rather than something effortless or automatic. There are structural imperatives that compel commodification. Those pressures help explain the fact that people commodify, but they do not explain how people actually do the activity of commodification.[38]

Commodification is always "a representational act," as historian Stephanie Smallwood has put it. Commodifying involves "particular ways of seeing, evaluating, classifying, and representing."[39] It is, as Karl Marx put it, "an act which takes place entirely in the mind, and involves no physical transaction."[40] Indeed, this mental or representational act has to take place prior to actual acts of commerce. Smallwood has argued for applying "thick description" to practices of commodification: paying close attention to specific social practices at a relatively small scale to show the large-scale context and preconditions for those practices.[41] Doing so can make visible what anthropologist Clifford Geertz has called "the socially established code" and "structures of signification" that form the "social ground" of the activities studied.[42] Acts of commodification draw on specific forms of know-how. Commodification cannot occur without some relatively stable set of institutions and vocabularies through

---

[38] The discussion here is influenced by recent work by historians who have argued that the study of commodification as a social practice is a fruitful line of inquiry within the history of capitalism. See especially Stephanie Smallwood, "Commodified Freedom: Interrogating the Limits of Anti-Slavery Ideology in the Early Republic," *Journal of the Early Republic* 24 (Summer 2004): 289–298; see also Seth Rockman, discussing the "epistemological work" involved in commodification, Seth Rockman, "What Makes the History of Capitalism Newsworthy?," *Journal of the Early Republic* 34, no. 3 (Fall 2014): 451; Edward E. Baptist, "Toxic Debt, Liar Loans, and Collateralized and Securitized Human Beings, and the Panic of 1837," in *Capitalism Takes Command*, ed. Michael Zakim and Gary J. Kornblith (Chicago: University of Chicago Press, 2012), 69–92; Jeffrey Sklansky, "Labor, Money, and the Financial Turn in the History of Capitalism," *Labor: Studies in Working-Class History of the Americas* 11, no. 1 (March 2014): 23–46; and William Cronon, *Changes in the Land: Indians, Colonists, and the Ecology of New England* (New York: Hill & Wang, 1983), 159–170.

[39] Smallwood, "Commodified Freedom," 292.   [40] Marx, *Capital*, vol. 1, 190.

[41] Smallwood, "Commodified Freedom," 294. The term comes from Clifford Geertz, "Thick Description: Toward an Interpretive Theory of Culture," in Geertz, *The Interpretation of Cultures* (New York: Basic Books, 1973), 3–32.

[42] Geertz, "Thick Description," 7, 10.

which people can do the mental work – perform the "representational acts," in Smallwood's words – required for commodification. This book treats employee injury law as regularly carrying out the commodification of working-class people, via conceptual tools present within legal doctrine and via borrowed tools like insurance tables.[43] I call those conceptual tools by the term "commodifying knowledge."[44]

Over different times and places, commodification may be enacted in different ways. At the same time, all acts of commodification involve some common traits. Specifically, commodification involves abstracting away some particulars of what is commodified in order to compare and render similar. In this way, all acts of commodification render their objects comparable with other people or things "as magnitudes of the same denomination, qualitatively equal and quantitatively comparable," in Karl Marx's words.[45] Commodification thus, when applied to people, requires overlooking the individuality, singularity, and, so to speak, infinitude of human persons. Commodified persons are in a sense always nameless and faceless, which is to say, unrecognized.[46]

MONEY AND DIGNITY

To many Americans in the twenty-first century, and to many a century prior, the finding against Nettie Blom would appear unjust. Nettie Blom

---

[43] The whole point of life insurance, and much of accident insurance, was to give dollar amounts for human life, limb, and capacity. See Bouk, *How Our Days Became Numbered*; Levy, *Freaks of Fortune*; Caley Dawn Horan, "Actuarial Age: Insurance and the Emergence of Neoliberalism in the Postwar United States" (PhD diss., University of Minnesota, 2011); Sharon Murphy, *Investing in Life: Insurance in Antebellum America* (Baltimore: Johns Hopkins University Press, 2010).

[44] I use the word "commodifying" here as an adjective. Commodification is an action, and that requires know-how. Commodifying knowledge is my name for that know-how. I suspect that all markets involve some kind of commodifying knowledge. The specific commodifying knowledge used in any given time and place is historical and variable. For example, Walter Johnson has emphasized the role of land surveyors in producing land as a commodity. Surveyors made land visible or legible so it could become present within the commodity world as a system of representations. Walter Johnson, *River of Dark Dreams: Slavery and Empire in the Cotton Kingdom* (Cambridge, MA: Harvard University Press, 2013), 35–38. I use the term "governing knowledge" to refer to knowledge used to have and to exercise power. In social circumstances where people are subjected to commodities, commodifying knowledge is one kind of governing knowledge.

[45] See Marx, *Capital*, vol. 1, 188.

[46] I am indebted here to Susan Schweik's discussion of looking another person in the face, literally and metaphorically. See Susan M. Schweik, *The Ugly Laws: Disability in Public* (New York: New York University, 2009), 286–288, drawing on the work of Emmanuel Levinas and Judith Butler.

was denied money that she deserved; other harms that followed from that denial were likewise unjust. The injustice in denying Blom money was specifically an economic or distributive injustice. The harms that follow from unfair lack of money could perhaps all be called distributive injust-ices as well. As discussed in the next chapter, many people who called for the compensation laws that would soon replace the court-based system of employee injury law based their arguments on notions of distributive justice. While distributive justice certainly matters, it bears mention that Blom suffered other injustices in addition to denial of access to money and the results thereof.

Unlike Blom, Marguerite Murray's legal story had, so to speak, a somewhat happier ending. Murray won her lawsuit, receiving an award for $15,000 in damages. Murray's story would feel more satisfying to many contemporary Americans in part because of issues of distributive justice. Murray got money she needed and avoided the suffering that went with monetary deprivation. I suggest, however, that there is another reason Murray's story feels more satisfying: the court provided some recognition of her situation. In deciding against Blom, the court decided not to give her money specifically because it saw her injury as merely unfortunate rather than unjust. That decision is objectionable not only for reasons of distributive justice, but also of recognition or appropriate meaning. People need goods and services; they also should be treated as people. A term for the human need, right, and moral imperative to be seen as a fellow human being with dignity is "justice as recognition." Imagine if Blom had left the courtroom after her loss and then found a suitcase containing $15,000, which she got to keep. That windfall would make hers a happier story, but it would still remain a story about a person treated unjustly by our legal system, especially in terms of justice as recognition.

Justice as distribution has been a widespread notion in discussion of employee injury law, both by historical actors and by historians. Adding a second concept of justice, justice as recognition, highlights aspects of the court-based system of injury law that we might otherwise miss. Every finding against a plaintiff was not only a distributive injustice but also an unjust denial of recognition. In addition, justice as recognition gives a category to the humiliations that must have been involved in trials, for both losing and winning plaintiffs, who had to sit in court while being blamed for their own injuries by defendants' lawyers, and called useless, disfigured, undesirable, and ugly by their own lawyers. Finally, justice as recognition points out the unjust or at the very least unseemly treatment of injured people under pecuniary damages. It is a violation of human dignity to calculate human worth in dollar amounts. This may well be an indignity that is structurally compelled by the market dependency characteristic of capitalism, but a necessary evil does not become, by its necessity, a good. Thinking about justice as recognition also highlights how, in liability determinations and in the law of damages, the court-based system of injury law did at times carry out some acts of recognition, as part of what I call the moral logic of the law.

MORAL LOGIC

The abstract individual of the law was a market actor, someone who consented to a transaction and was paid. That actor was also a moral actor. Legal historian Susanna Blumenthal argues that the court system was widely understood by nineteenth-century legal elites as pedagogical: part of the function of the law was to cultivate the kind of dutiful, responsible moral subjects needed by a liberal democracy and a free market economy.[47] This same moral-pedagogical vision of law infused employee injury law as well. Negligent injured employees paid the costs of their own injuries, and negligent employers had to pay out. In the process, these negligent actors, or at least other people witnessing the events, learned a lesson about due diligence.[48] That aspect of the moral logic of the law could help create, or at least run ideological cover for, the distributive injustices created by the court-based system of employee injury law. Shaw's arguments in *Farwell* could be understood this way,

---

[47] See Susanna L. Blumenthal, *Law and the Modern Mind: Consciousness and Responsibility in American Legal Culture* (Cambridge, MA: Harvard University Press, 2016) Both Blumenthal and Levy have also shown how nineteenth-century men were often considered morally laudable for taking risks while doing so prudently, and providing security for their dependents, often through the purchase of insurance. See Levy, *Freaks of Fortune.*

[48] Here the idea of two separate logics, one of commodity and one of morality, perhaps breaks down. Some of the time, the commodity logic of the law was itself a moral discourse, and one which could, at least allegedly, be a technique for cultivating responsible moral subjects. Legal theorist Margaret Radin calls the kind of situation where commodification and other standards of value and meaning co-exist by the term "incomplete commodification," and situations where commodity or economic valuation, narrowly understood, is the only form or meaning and value by the term "universal commodification." Margaret Jane Radin, *Contested Commodities: The Trouble with Trade in Sex, Children, Body Parts, and Other Things* (Cambridge, MA: Harvard University Press, 2001).

as the court adding the insult of a lecture on responsibility to the physical and financial injuries Farwell suffered.

There was another aspect to the moral logic of employee injury law. As Charles Fall put it, employers were viewed under the law as "responsible financially, morally, legally for the acts of their agents, whether good or bad, so long as they are done within the general scope of their authority."[49] Understood narrowly this was a statement about the scope of the fellow servant rule. Embedded in this statement, however, was a more expansive sentiment: that employers had moral duties to their employees. This implied that the employment relationship was more than simply an economic transaction. Economic actors owed each other obligations, and were required to be prudent in living up to those obligations. When they failed to do so, the results were moral failings: "negligences," "malfeasances, or misfeasances," "omissions of duty," and "misconduct."[50] As treatise writer Thomas Cooley put it, prudence was a matter of what "circumstances justly demand."[51] Failure to be adequately prudent was thus unjust, as were the injuries that resulted from lack of prudence. As treatise writer Henry Buswell put it, "The law imposes upon every member of the community certain civil obligations and duties in respect of every other member."[52] The law thus reflected and helped create the mutual recognition that people had as members of the same moral and political community. A right to take legal action arose when someone failed to live up to these obligations in a way that resulted in injury.[53]

Damages and liability, then, provided means by which mutual moral obligations in civic life were defined, and through which failings to live up to those obligations could be named and dealt with. People go about their

---

[49] Fall, *Employers' Liability for Personal Injuries to Their Employees*, 7.

[50] Fall, *Employers' Liability for Personal Injuries to Their Employees*, 6.

[51] Quoted in Osgood, *Employers' Liability*, 5.

[52] Henry F. Buswell, *The Civil Liability for Personal Injuries Arising out of Negligence* (Boston: Little, Brown, 1893), 3.

[53] These were different from specifically contractual duties rooted in either explicit or implicit agreements between parties. Over the course of the nineteenth century, employment came to be conceptualized as a contractual rather than a civic matter, as the outcome of protracted struggle between employers, employees, and the state, with the action of judges being especially decisive. Sometimes contractual and civic obligation co-existed, but in general the effects of contract as the concept of employment served to wall off employers from liability and to make injuries not subject to legal action. See Tomlins, *Law, Labor, and Ideology*. To be clear, when employment was civic, the dominant conception at least was always hierarchical and status based, though there were some earlier possibilities for alternative civic statuses of employees. See Tomlins, *Freedom Bound*.

lives and encounter each other (or, in a less atomized formulation, we live together in society) and in the process sometimes people harm each other. Injury law was a way to recognize those harms, to name them, and to make things right or, rather, somewhat more right. Along these lines, treatise writer J. G. Sutherland stressed that the law of damages, like law in general, was about securing rights. Failure to compensate a deserving injured party was a denial of rights and so a "failure of justice."[54] From this perspective, Sutherland criticized judges who seemed to worry about an excess of injury cases "crowd[ing] calendars." These judges missed the forest for the trees: "What are the reasons for establishing and maintaining judicial establishments? Are they not intended to protect the rights of citizens, and to redress their wrongs? And citizens of all classes have the right to resort to them for such purposes."[55] Damages were awarded when there had been an injurious "breach of [the] duties which govern the relations of individuals to each other," as treatise writer Edward Weeks put it.[56] These conceptions of the law's purpose focused on what I have called the moral logic of the law, which differed from the commodity logic of the law.

The economic and moral logics within employee injury law fit with a duality within money as a social institution or social practice. Money facilitates access to means of subsistence, and it also has a symbolic role. It has both power and meaning, often with a moral valence. Philosopher Michael Sandel makes a distinction that can exemplify the difference between money with and without moral meaning, namely, the distinction between fines and fees.[57] A fee is simply a cost of doing business. A fine carries a charge or a tone of disapproval.

Within the court-based system of injury law, the money paid out in damage awards was in part a statement of social meaning. A decision against a defendant signified that the plaintiff had been harmed – and unjustly so. Under the court system, an order to pay damages to an injured worker carried with it the judgment that the injured person had been wronged and that the employer had been unjust. This meant that damage awards were, in Sandel's terms, fines. They bore a mark of

---

[54] J. G. Sutherland, *A Treatise of the Law of Damages*, vol. 1, 3rd ed. (Chicago: Callaghan and Company, 1903), 3.

[55] Sutherland, *A Treatise of the Law of Damages*, 281.

[56] Edward P. Weeks, *The Doctrine of Damnum Absque Injuria: Considered in Its Relation to the Law of Torts* (San Francisco: Sumner Whitney, 1879).

[57] Michael J. Sandel, *What Money Can't Buy: The Moral Limits of Markets* (New York: Farrar, Strauss and Giroux, 2012), 65.

disapproval for the actions of the party ordered to pay. The total fine to be paid was the result of reasoning under two subheadings of the law of damages, pecuniary and non-pecuniary damages. Pecuniary damages were based on financial loss, a kind of thinking which was based on and which enacted commodification. While damages were per se a kind of fine, in their pecuniary variety the fine was calculated like a fee or price, through market values. The two logics of the law, like the economic and symbolic uses of money, overlap with one another. Pecuniary damages were moral money with the amount calculated through economic means; non-pecuniary were moral money with the amount calculated through non-economic means.

MARKETLESS LOSSES

Non-pecuniary damages were non-financial and were a matter of cultural and moral meanings; they were calculated like a fine without discussion of fee or price, without resort to market standards of valuation. Indeed, they put dollar amounts on losses that were priceless. Non-pecuniary damages were a monetization of loss but not a commodification of loss. These damages included all losses that were not immediately financial, such as changes in potential marriageability, both physical and mental pain, and loss of ability to do things like comb one's hair or hold one's child or play piano – anything that could be understood as a harm to a human being.

Sutherland wrote that the law aimed "to afford full redress for personal injuries as well as for all others." This "full redress" was quite expansive, including pain, mental suffering, anxiety, alarm, "wounded sensibility or affection," the "sense of wrong and insult" at having been wrongfully injured, the cost of care, and "mutilation or disfigurement."[58] In short all "detrimental effects" resulting directly from injury were subject to compensation.[59] As treatise writers Joseph and Howard Joyce put it, damages included harms to "all which is a man's own in a strict and proper sense."[60] The entire existence of a person in society, any capacity for one person to harm another person, fell under this capacious definition.

---

[58] Sutherland, *A Treatise of the Law of Damages*, vol. 4, 3594.
[59] Sutherland, *A Treatise of the Law of Damages*, vol. 4, 3595.
[60] Joseph A. Joyce and Howard C. Joyce, *A Treatise on Damages Covering the Entire Law of Damages Both Generally and Specifically* (New York: Banks Law Publishing Co., 1903), 2.

Because only some of a person could fit under pecuniary measures of value, non-pecuniary forms of valuation were required as well.

These kinds of compensation, particularly compensation for pain, were troubling to some judges and legal scholars, who commented that even though the law allowed monetary damage awards for pain and suffering, pain was not actually measurable in dollars. Legal scholar John Bouvier noted that while the feeling of suffering was compensable, this was not intended as "put[ting] up for sale, by agency of a court of justice" the pain and suffering that made the action grounds for a lawsuit.[61] George Voorhies's treatise on damages summarized the law as saying that there was no "fixed rule by which to assess the amount of damages to be awarded for physical pain and suffering caused by an injury. There is no standard amount for the measurement of such damages."[62] Voorhies added:

> No general rule can be given ... for the reason that an injury which would cause little suffering in one person may be a source of great physical pain to another person. It may truly be stated that there is no measure of pecuniary compensation for pain and suffering.... There is no market in which the price of a voluntary submission to pain and suffering can be fixed. There is no market standard of a value to be applied.... The word "compensation" in the phrases "compensation for pain and suffering" is not to be understood as meaning price or value but as describing an allowance looking toward recompense for ... the suffering.[63]

On Voorhies's treatment, at law pain could be translated into a quantity of dollars and yet doing so was not to be understood as attaching a price to pain. This left unanswered the question of how much was enough to constitute recompense for suffering. Similarly, the Georgia Circuit Court judge instructed the jury on how to determine damages in *Vicksburg and Meridian Railroad Company v. Putnam*, saying that "money cannot pay

---

[61] John Bouvier, *A Law Dictionary: Adapted to the Constitution and Laws of the United States of America and of the Several States of the American Union with References to the Civil and Other Systems of Foreign Law*, vol. 1. (Philadelphia: J. B. Lippincott Company, 1892), 804.

[62] Voorhies, *Treatise on the Law of the Measure of Damages for Personal Injuries*, 64–65.

[63] Voorhies, *Treatise on the Law of the Measure of Damages for Personal Injuries*, 66–67. The difference between price and recompense at the turn of the twentieth century is not as clear as Voorhies indicated. In both Bouvier's and Black's respective law dictionaries the term "recompense" is used repeatedly with a sense of equivalence paid through money. If that is not a price, it has in common with price both overtones of exchange and measurement in money. Bouvier, *A Law Dictionary*, and Henry Campbell Black, *A Law Dictionary Containing Definitions of the Terms and Phrases of American and English Jurisprudence, Ancient and Modern* (St. Paul: West Publishing Company, 1910).

for the pain and suffering. It only approaches to it; but he is entitled to some compensation for the pain and suffering. Now, that is left to the enlightened consciences of the jury."[64] In *Goodhart v. Pennsylvania R.R. Co.* the Pennsylvania Supreme Court likewise held that

[p]ain and suffering are not capable of being exactly measured by an equivalent in money, and we have repeatedly said that they have no market price. The question in any given case is not what it would cost to hire someone to undergo the measure of pain alleged to have been suffered by the plaintiff, but what, under all the circumstances, should be allowed to the plaintiff in addition to the other items of damage to which he is entitled, in consideration of suffering necessarily endured. This should not be estimated by a sentimental or fanciful standard, but in a reasonable manner.[65]

The court continued that "some allowance [for pain] has been held to be proper; but, in answer to the question, 'How much?' the only reply yet made is that it should be reasonable in amount. Pain cannot be measured in money."[66] Pain could not be measured in money and yet compensation had to be reasonable. In appeals, courts had to rule whether to uphold damage awards as reasonable or overturn them as unreasonable. It is hard to see anything but a contradiction here. The Pennsylvania court insisted that giving quantities of money in response to pain was not in fact the measurement of pain in money, but what defined a reasonable amount of compensation was whether or not the amount was commensurate with the injury, which meant that courts were in fact measuring pain in money.

Pain and suffering figured especially prominently in accounts of loss in Marguerite Murray's and similar cases. Her lawyer said Murray had suffered "great bodily pain and mental anguish, which latter will endure throughout her entire life."[67] Murray's mother, Florence Murray, corroborated by testifying that Marguerite "suffered constantly day and night" in the hospital immediately after injury and on an ongoing basis after she came home.[68] Florence said that the pain of her injuries disrupted Marguerite's sleep. She slept "when her hands permitted. That would be just a little time and her hands would pain her until she woke up. She could not get her right rest on account of the pain.... Her hands bother her now ... when she gets asleep she groans so we have to wake her up."[69]

---

[64] *Vicksburg and Meridian Railroad Company v. Putnam*, 118 U.S. 545 (1886).
[65] *Goodhart v. Pennsylvania R.R. Co.*, 177 Pa. 1 (1896).
[66] *Goodhart v. Pennsylvania R.R. Co.*
[67] *Murray v. Chicago*, 145 Iowa 212 (1909), 139.
[68] *Murray v. Chicago*, 145 Iowa 212 (1909), 154.
[69] *Murray v. Chicago*, 152 Iowa 732 (1911), 83.

Marguerite Murray herself said "sometimes my hand aches so bad at nights I can't sleep with it."[70]

Accounts of pain blended into depictions of physical harms. Murray said that she was caught in the machine for several minutes. "The drum was hot.... The fingers on my left hand were flattened out like a piece of paper and they were white, all cooked and burned. My right hand they [sic] were mashed."[71] Matt Estis worked in the laundry department under the title of laundry engineer. He freed Murray from the machine by removing the rollers that held her hand. He estimated she was caught in the machine for eight to ten minutes. He said about her injured hand, "I couldn't look at it, it was too bad. It looked like blood all cooked up."[72] A physician who treated Murray the morning after her injury, Dr. J. A. DeArmand, said that in the hospital her "fingers looked like glue, translucent and no evidence of veins or arteries, blood vessels" and "they had the appearance of being parboiled, cooked and bruised."[73] Florence Murray said "The fingers on the left hand seemed to me almost as flat as a board ... just before they were amputated two of her fingers had rotted off."[74]

Accounts of pain and descriptions of physical harm to bodies were common in other suits as well. Nettie Blom said, "I can't describe the pain ... but just to give you an idea, three of the girls fainted" at the sight of her crushed and burnt hand, which looked like "boiled meat."[75] In some suits, the physical appearance of the injured person's body could be used to dramatic effect. For example, Mary McInerny kept her hand covered for much of the trial, which likely built suspense on the part of the jurors and judge. She said she kept her injured hand covered up any time she went out because she didn't want people to see it, further dramatizing herself as vulnerable and as harmed because of her anguish and the changes to her appearance due to her injury. She added, "Very few have seen it with the bandage off until now."[76] McInerny's "until

---

[70] *Murray v. Chicago*, 145 Iowa 212 (1909), 150.

[71] *Murray v. Chicago*, 152 Iowa 732 (1911), 77.

[72] *Murray v. Chicago*, 145 Iowa 212 (1909), 144.

[73] *Murray v. Chicago*, 152 Iowa 732 (1911), 82–83.

[74] *Murray v. Chicago*, 145 Iowa 212 (1909), 154.

[75] *Blom v. Yellowstone Park Association*, 86 Minn. 237 (1902), 49. The materials from Nettie Blom's case are held in the University of Minnesota Law Library's bound volumes of the Minnesota Supreme Court's Abstracts and Argument. Pagination reflects the page number in the bound volume.

[76] *McInerny v. St. Luke's Hospital Association*, 122 Minn. 10 (1913), 119. The materials from Mary McInerny's case are held in the University of Minnesota Law Library's bound volumes of the Minnesota Supreme Court's Abstracts and Argument. Pagination reflects the page number in the bound volume.

now" refers to the moment when she showed her injured hand to the jury. Women like McInerny and their lawyers dramatically uncovered injured hands at critical points in their testimony, displaying them to the jury during the story of the injury and the pain it caused. These descriptions and visual presentations in court helped make the pain and the harms of injury more imaginable and vivid. They also presented the spectacle of an injured woman, which appealed to gendered ideas that men should protect women from harm. This likely had rhetorical effects, in that judges and juries would probably have viewed physical harm to a woman's body with greater horror and sympathy than injury to a man, and may have felt moved to protect these vulnerable women by finding in their favor.[77] Certainly, lawyers for women plaintiffs emphasized the spectacle of harm to women and addressed juries on explicitly gendered grounds.

Courtroom claims to loss included appeals to judges' and juries' sympathies in order to persuade them to compensate injuries, and to do so as generously as possible. Loss could be monetized, and all losses presented in court were appeals for higher awards. At the end of the trial in Murray's suit the trial judge, A. P. Barker, reminded the jury of how expansive the law of damages was. "If entitled to any recovery," Barker said, the jury should award her "such sum as will fully and fairly compensate her for the amount she has paid or incurred for medical services, care and nursing, for loss of earning" and the "pain, suffering and inconvenience caused to her by her injuries" and which she would suffer in the future.[78]

The crushing and burning of parts of one's body obviously causes physical pain. Injuries cause emotional distress as well, beyond physical pain. Mental suffering was compensated because, as treatise writer Archibald Watson put it, "a person's mind ... is no less a part of his person than his body, and the sufferings of the former are often more acute and lasting than those of the latter."[79] This distress too fell under the category of non-pecuniary damages. Florence Murray testified that after her injuries Marguerite "was so nervous and the shock to her system was so severe

---

[77] For an illuminating discussion of gender and injury law based on railway passenger injuries, see Barbara Welke, *Recasting American Liberty: Gender, Race, Law, and the Railroad Revolution, 1865–1920* (Cambridge: Cambridge University Press, 2001), especially 235–246 on legal storytelling.

[78] *Murray v. Chicago*, 145 Iowa 212 (1909), 164.

[79] Archibald Watson, *A Treatise on the Law of Damages for Personal Injuries: Embracing a Consideration of the Principles Regulating the Primary Question of Liability, as Well as the Measure and Elements of Recovery after Liability Established* (Charlottesville: Michie Company, 1901), 485–487.

that we never allowed her alone [*sic*]" because "the minute she was alone she would start worrying about her hands ... the minute she is alone she commences to cry and worry. The doctor told me not to leave her alone at all."[80] Marguerite was "nothing but nerves from one end to the other, she cries and worries if she is left alone at all, and she wishes herself dead."[81] Murray's lawyer said that Murray had been "turned into a nervous wreck" who wished to die as a result of her injuries.[82] Dr. DeArmand described Murray as "nervous, hysterical as the result of the maiming of her hand and pain and being told of the probable hopelessness of the injury, that is the hopelessness of saving much, if any, of the injured hand."[83] When her fingers were amputated, "the hopelessness and the deformity came on her again, and the nervous feeling was again exaggerated. There was a tendency to cry and to blame herself" for her injuries.[84]

In cases of injuries to women, damages took on additional moral overtones, as attorneys for injured women dramatized the gendered effects of injury. Seeking to sway the all-male juries of the day, they invoked the notion that real men protected vulnerable women. During her trial, Marguerite Murray's lawyer argued that the point of law was to protect employees like Murray "from the brutality of men like Schnart, who, absolutely indifferent to the safety of children trying to earn an honest living, order them about like cattle, forcing them into dangerous places, knowing full well what pitfalls are there, and caring little whether or not they fall therein. The rules of law are ... to curb the spirit of selfishness and disregard for human life which occasionally manifests itself in those whom fate has made the masters."[85] Murray's lawyer here invoked the moral pedagogical purpose of the law. Law was to shape the human spirit, or at least its manifestation, in a morally just and socially beneficial direction.

The phrasing here also indicates the gender of this moral pedagogical perspective within employee injury law. The goal of this language was to make jurors want to find in favor of plaintiffs, regardless of whether the plaintiffs were legally entitled to damages. These remarks would have likely resonated with ideas that men ought to protect women and that

---

[80] *Murray v. Chicago*, 145 Iowa 212 (1909), 155.

[81] *Murray v. Chicago*, 152 Iowa 732 (1911), 83.

[82] *Murray v. Chicago*, 152 Iowa 732 (1911), 175.

[83] *Murray v. Chicago*, 152 Iowa 732 (1911), 82. For a discussion of the law of nervous shock, see Welke, *Recasting American Liberty*, 203–234.

[84] *Murray v. Chicago*, 152 Iowa 732 (1911), 83.

[85] *Murray v. Chicago*, 145 Iowa 212 (1909), 190–191.

adults should protect children.[86] This rhetoric, of helpless, dependent "girls" exposed to the brutality of men who treated them like animals had no formal legal standing. There was no rule that said that a despotic employer who acted selfishly and hatefully toward women and girls should be more likely to be liable than a kind employer who acted respectfully, but this probably had moral force with juries because the standards in employee injury law were embedded in larger US culture, which included notions of adult men's responsibility and feminine vulnerability.

Along similar lines, throughout Murray's suit and in those of other women injured in industrial laundries, attorneys referred to the injured plaintiffs as "girls." For example, Martha Ludwig's lawyer, J. W. Pinch, asked the eighteen-year-old Ludwig when she took the stand, "Martha, you are the little girl that was hurt in the laundry?"[87] In his closing argument Pinch referred to Ludwig numerous times as a "little girl" and referred as well to "her little hand."[88] He urged the jury not to let "this little girl ... go out of this court room with nothing and grope her way darkly through to the end of her life with this crippled little hand upon which she has been depending to earn her living."[89]

Pinch evoked the moral-pedagogical purposes of the law, adding that "any man that is prudent, and wants to do what is right with his children or any children, when he puts them up against a dangerous" machine would be sure to look after their safety. The laundry owner did not, Pinch suggested, and so was neither prudent nor concerned "to do what is right with his children or any children."[90] Pinch implored the jury as literal and metaphorical fathers:

---

[86] For a discussion of "judicial paternalism," see Norma Basch, "The Emerging Legal History of Women in the United States: Property, Divorce, and the Constitution," in *Women and the American Legal Order*, ed. Karen J. Maschke (New York: Routledge, 1997), 113–134; 124.

[87] *Ludwig v. Spicer*, 99 Minn. 400 (1906), 116; see also 223, 233, 245, 249. The materials from Martha Ludwig's case are held in the University of Minnesota Law Library's bound volumes of the Minnesota Supreme Court's Abstracts and Argument. Pagination reflects the page number in the bound volume.

[88] *Ludwig v. Spicer*, 99 Minn. 400 (1906), 403–429.

[89] *Ludwig v. Spicer*, 99 Minn. 400 (1906), 404. The defendant's attorney in *Ludwig v. Spicer* pointed out Pinch's rhetoric, noting that Martha Ludwig was "not a little girl, as the plaintiff's counsel says, but a woman." He continued, stressing that she was "a woman 18 years of age, under the statutes of the State of Minnesota, having attained her majority, having the full rights of her status." *Ludwig v. Spicer*, 373–374. This protest proved ineffective, as the jury found in Ludwig's favor.

[90] *Ludwig v. Spicer*, 99 Minn. 400 (1906), 412.

If you want to make people who have charge of your children (if you have any) careful, so that they won't injure them – your little girls and your little boys, perhaps – I don't know as you have any that work in these factories, but there are thousands of them in this city – if you want to make people careful and see to it that they protect these little people or the inexperienced – and I say this little girl ... a pretty little thing, as innocent as a babe unborn, almost; ... if you want to protect the children of this city, the little girls, the young ladies, if you please, anybody that is inexperienced, put to work by masters in places of dangers – concealed dangers – the way you can do it is by the verdict of the jury. When a man understands and when this community is told by the verdict of the jury that they haven't any right to treat a child in the way this child was treated, they will learn better.[91]

As Pinch's remarks show, the moralizing logic of the law could simultaneously engender. He insisted that the men of the jury make an example of an immoral man, by ruling in favor of his client in order to make employers "learn better" to be "prudent," and he framed this in terms of protective fathers and vulnerable, infantilized women. Pinch sought to use the moral logic within the law to help his client win her suit, and in doing so affirmed the cultural construction of men as protectors and women as vulnerable.

At the same time that the law engendered, it also defined ability and disability. Sedgwick noted that the "distress of mind" that resulted from "disfigurement" was also compensable, separately from the physical aspects of the injury, because of the "mortification which [a plaintiff] suffered and will suffer by reason of the mutilation and of the fact that he may become an object of curiosity and ridicule among his fellows" as well as for the "sense of indignity" that a plaintiff (and, Sutherland added, a plaintiff's mother) felt.[92] Ability and gender intersected as well. As Sutherland noted that "mutilation or disfigurement" was "a consideration of especial importance in the case of young women if visible."[93]

At one point in the trial over Marguerite Murray's injuries, Murray's lawyer said "the law would be a farce if it would, under the circumstances in this case, send this crippled, deformed and helpless girl into a life of dependence without some compensation for her wrongs."[94] An important source of mental distress over injuries lay at the intersection of gender

---

[91] *Ludwig v. Spicer*, 99 Minn. 400 (1906), 428.
[92] Sedgwick, *A Treatise on the Measure of Damages*, 76, 79.
[93] Sutherland, *A Treatise of the Law of Damages*, vol. 4, 3594–3595.
[94] *Murray v. Chicago*, 145 Iowa 212 (1909), 191.

and (dis)ability. Disability had different connotations for men than for women. Likewise, gender was performed differently for the able-bodied than for the disabled.[95] Disabling injury suddenly moved a person from one social position to another in ways that could challenge the person's sense of self in gendered and distressing ways.[96]

Murray's lawyer remarked at length on ideas about gender and disability. The loss of her fingers, Murray's lawyer argued, had "impaired her appearance" and as a result "hindered and will hinder her in entering into an advantageous marriage."[97] "Who shall measure," he continued:

the damage to her by reason of the humiliation – the "disgrace" as she felt it? The closing of the doors of society upon her – the lonesomeness of the solitude which must come to her as she sits with her disfigured members wrapped in a shawl or other covering to conceal the deformity. Men may carry disfigurement of the body or the limbs without the burden of distress which it imposes on women; with women such disfigurement sets them apart – leaves them to live in their own world; takes them out of active life and deprives them of every enjoyment.[98]

Florence Murray similarly testified that after her injuries Marguerite "always felt as though it was rather a disgrace to have her fingers so."[99] Mary McInerny's comment in her trial that she generally kept her hand covered in public likely reflects a similar sense of disgrace. Hearing these sentiments said in court must have been painful for the plaintiffs.

---

[95] While I use the term "able-bodied" here and throughout the book I want to stress that it is not the body that determines whether or not someone is able. Disability is socially constructed as marginalization, which mean that the sources of disability lie in institutions and power relationships, rather than being inherent in the bodies of disabled people themselves. Thus to be able-bodied is to be socially constituted as able: in a word, abled.

[96] Paul Longmore's *Telethons* offers a powerful reflection on the relationship between disability, self-identity, and human dignity (and the denial of human dignity), while grounding that reflection in the understanding that disability is a social and political condition with a history. Paul Longmore, *Telethons: Spectacle, Disability, and the Business of Charity*, ed. Catherine Kudlick (New York: Oxford University Press, 2016). See also Rose, "'Crippled' Hands" and *No Right to Be Idle*; Barbara Young Welke, *Law and the Borders of Belonging in the Long Nineteenth Century United States* (Cambridge: Cambridge University Press, 2010); Paul K. Longmore and Lauri Umansky, eds., *The New Disability History: American Perspectives* (New York: New York University Press, 2001); Kim E. Nielsen, *A Disability History of the United States* (Boston: Beacon Press, 2012); and Schweik, *The Ugly Laws*.

[97] *Murray v. Chicago*, 145 Iowa 212 (1909), 138.

[98] *Murray v. Chicago*, 145 Iowa 212 (1909), 186.

[99] *Murray v. Chicago*, 145 Iowa 212 (1909), 155.

Marguerite Murray's lawyer reminded the court that

plaintiff is a woman and there is something about a maimed woman which sort of drives her into seclusion. No one ever saw a woman with a hand off that didn't suggest something uncanny or repulsive. We realize that it ought not to be that way but it is, and this girl in her nervous dread of publicity – in her desire for death to relieve her of what she considers "a disgrace" is simply a human being effected [*sic*] by the ordinary impulse which we cannot control.... The doors of society are closed against her. She is an outcast who must sit alone and contemplate in silence her helpless misery.... [Her injury] not only disables her, but ... from its very nature excludes her from society. There is something uncanny in the absence of hands in the case of a woman which does not appeal to one where the victim is a man. The condition of a man who has lost his hand does not give rise to the feeling of repugnance which we cannot help but feel where the victim of misfortune is a woman.[100]

It is important to stress here the social context that made disability mean exclusion. The loss of a hand or any other change in physical condition does not in and of itself exclude. That loss excludes in an ableist and disabling society; exclusion is not a biological but a social condition.[101] That social condition counted in the courtroom for the sake of defining what the sum total of harms were that Murray had endured and turning that set of harms into a dollar amount.

Murray and her lawyer framed her injuries (and Murray most likely sincerely experienced her injuries) as making it harder for her to pursue the normative activities defining femininity. These included being attractive to men, unencumbered by what she and her lawyer called her disfigurements, and the ability to carry out what at the time were wifely duties of unwaged household labor. Deliberations about damages could thus also draw on the importance of this unwaged labor as part of putting prices on injuries.[102] Murray's lawyer asked her, "What had you done toward learning

---

[100] *Murray v. Chicago*, 152 Iowa 732 (1911), 179.
[101] See Schweik, *The Ugly Laws*, for a discussion of the intersection between disability and notions of public presentability.
[102] We saw this earlier as well in Florence Murray's account of the market value of the care she provided for her daughter. For historical and theoretical accounts of the economic importance of unwaged and usually feminized work, see Jeanne Boydston, *Home and Work: Housework, Wages, and the Ideology of Labor in the Early Republic* (New York: Oxford University Press, 1990); Michael Hardt and Antonio Negri, *Labor of Dionysus: A Critique of the State-Form* (Minneapolis: University of Minnesota Press, 1994), 8; Mariarosa Dalla Costa and Selma James, *The Power of Women and the Subversion of the Community* (Bristol: Falling Wall Press, 1972); Silvia Federici, *Caliban and the Witch: Women, the Body and Primitive Accumulation* (New York: Autonomedia, 2004); and Leopoldina Fortunati, *The Arcane of Reproduction* (New York: Autonomedia, 1995).

cooking and sewing and things of that kind?" She replied, "I could cook, and get meals and I used to do the mending and help mama with the mending.... Since the injury my mother has to help me comb my hair and dress myself and things of that kind."[103] Her lawyer stressed Murray's prior marriageability by noting that she had been "a healthy, able-bodied girl" who "had acquired the art of cooking; ... learned how to sew" and "learned how to play the piano," none of which she could do anymore. Indeed, "she is not able to dress or undress herself or care for herself in any way."[104] She was thus much less desirable as a wife, Murray's lawyer suggested. This loss likely was one source of Murray's feeling that she had been disgraced by her injury. The court-based system of employee injury law moralized and engendered, as part of a single process. In doing so it drew on social conceptions of disability as shame and exclusion, and made that condition compensable.

These remarks indicate an openness within the moral logic of law to understanding people as embedded in social contexts and relationships. Depending on one's social position, one was subject to different kinds of harm. Some of the relationships and social positions recognized in the law were unjust. For example, husbands could receive damages for loss of a wife's "consortium," including services as well as "affection, comfort, and fellowship" and "an undefiled marriage-bed." Fathers could also be compensated for "loss of society of a virtuous daughter" and "destruction of his domestic peace" in cases about the "seduction" of their daughters.[105] These forms of compensation are at best questionable, as they assume hierarchical gendered power relationships. The presence of moral notions in the law is only as good as those notions were. Employee injury law was embedded in and porous to the cultural norms and moral order of its time, and therefore reflected all the limits of its time. This was a facet of the capacity of the law to recognize different kinds of social subjects, and the sorts of harms that were specific to different subject positions – such as the differences between masculine and feminine "disfigurement."

The wide range of non-pecuniary harms strained the meaning of compensation almost to the breaking point, as judges and treatise writers repeatedly noted. Money was all that the law could provide plaintiffs; and yet, how could anyone declare a dollar value for fifteen minutes of agony, inability to marry, and so forth? Within the law, these non-pecuniary

---

[103] *Murray v. Chicago*, 145 Iowa 212 (1909), 150.
[104] *Murray v. Chicago*, 145 Iowa 212 (1909), 138.
[105] Sedgwick, *A Treatise on the Measure of Damages*, 81.

harms were monetizable and that money was determined through non-commodity reasoning. That use of money, to monetize without commodifying, was in important respects arbitrary, in a way that troubled some judges and scholars, because there was no underlying market to serve as the determining measure.[106] Commodification and morality coexisted in the law, but the latter lacked the same stability of veridiction.

In dealing with non-pecuniary damages, courts could not point to markets or other measurements: there was no established going rate for the purchase of an amputated hand or for time spend being burnt and crushed. As such, courts had few pre-existing financial equivalents or conceptual tools to draw on in commodifying plaintiffs' losses. Without a market or other measure to provide epistemic stability, juries were largely left to their own devices to answer seemingly unanswerable questions such as what is the dollar value of fifteen minutes spent conscious while having one's fingers crushed and burnt? What is the price of feeling disgraced? The lack of a market as measurement meant that in the law of non-pecuniary damages the other logic within employee injury law came to the fore, that of morality rather than of the commodity. Within the law of non-pecuniary damages, courts monetized injury without commodifying it, a difference

---

[106] This likely troubled some injured plaintiffs as well. Barbara Welke has recently discussed aspects of non-pecuniary harms under the heading "owning hazard," as part of a broader discussion of law and risk in the American culture and economy. The term "owning hazard" indicates in part that injured people and their loved ones bear costs well beyond financial costs. These costs are not transferable, and so fit poorly within institutional responses to harm that are predicated on equivalency. See Barbara Young Welke, "The Cowboy Suit Tragedy: Spreading Risk, Owning Hazard in the Modern American Consumer Economy," *Journal of American History* 1, no. 1 (June 2014): 97–121, and Barbara Young Welke, "Owning Hazard: A Tragedy," *UC Irvine Law Review* 1, no. 3 (September, 2011): 693–771. The idea of owning hazard points out that nothing is fully monetizable in the sense that holding items, actions, experiences, or people to be equivalent always ignores important aspects of the things rendered equivalent. Equivalency exists only as a relationship, and whatever is related as equivalent is always more than that relationship: things, and especially people and their experiences, exceed their equivalency in a variety of ways. This also means that treating human losses through relationships of equivalence ultimately fall short of and perhaps even occlude and perpetuate those losses. The point also suggests a criticism of Karl Polanyi's distinction between fictional or artificial commodities and genuine commodities, because all commodification is fictive, in the sense of social artifice or construction. See Karl Polanyi, *The Great Transformation: The Political and Economic Origins of Our Time* (Boston: Beacon Press, 1944), 76, 79. For a similar distinction to Polanyi's, see Michel Aglietta, *A Theory of Capitalist Regulation: The U.S. Experience*, 2nd ed. (London: Verso, 2000), 31, and Sidney Mintz, *Sweetness and Power: The Place of Sugar in Modern History* (New York: Penguin, 1985), 43.

perhaps obscured behind the fact that damages were awarded as a single dollar amount.

CONCLUSION

The early twentieth-century US economy was rife with industrial violence. It harmed working-class people in a host of ways, physically and beyond, and the courts added additional harms and indignities, distributive and beyond. Public discussion would soon take up the issue of injury and its compensation, as the next chapter details. These critics eventually won out, creating compensation laws. The purpose of this chapter has been to set up the remainder of the book's inquiry into compensation laws.[107] I aim to show these laws in a new light, by showing both differences and continuities between compensation laws and the moment that preceded them. The point is not to defend the tyranny of the trial but to help analyze the two systems of employee injury law, and dramatize the shortcomings of each. To be very clear, the court-based system of injury law was cruel and unjust – hence the term "tyranny of the trial." The rest of this book will investigate the shortcomings of the new system of

---

[107] This chapter has proceeded in a somewhat synchronic in character, focusing on the legal moment from which compensation laws emerged and to which those laws were a response. In the rest of this book I tack back and forth between synchronic and diachronic. I know there are costs to this approach, but there are good works treating the origin of compensation laws diachronically. That approach, and that phrasing, is inspired by Walter Johnson's *Soul by Soul: Life Inside the Antebellum Slave Market* (Cambridge, MA: Harvard University Press, 1999). For another work combining synchronic and diachronic, see Daniel LaChance, *Executing Freedom: The Cultural Life of Capital Punishment in the United States* (Chicago: University of Chicago Press, 2016.) I am aware that my approach has limitations in terms of understanding the court-based system of employee injury law. There are excellent works that deal with elements of that system. See Paul Bellamy, "From Court Room to Board Room: Immigration, Juries, Corporations and the Creation of an American Proletariat: A History of Workmen's Compensation, 1898–1915" (PhD diss., Case Western Reserve University, 1994); Lawrence M. Friedman, "Civil Wrongs: Personal Injury Law in the Late 19th Century," *American Bar Foundation Research Journal* 12, nos. 2–3 (Spring–Summer 1987): 351–378; Donald Rogers, *Making Capitalism Safe: Work Safety and Health Regulation in America, 1880–1940* (Urbana: University of Illinois Press, 2009); James D. Schmidt, *Industrial Violence and the Legal Origins of Child Labor* (New York: Cambridge University Press, 2010); and Tomlins, *Law, Labor and Ideology*. Still, we lack a study that focuses centrally on that system, a strange absence given the importance of injury and employee injury law in U.S. working-class history. See Gerald Markowitz and David Rosner "Death and Disease in the House of Labor," *Labor History* 30, no. 1 (1989): 113–117, calling for occupational health and safety to be placed at the center of labor history and our understanding of class.

employee injury law that I have called the "tyranny of the table." The next chapter turns to early twentieth-century critics of the tyranny of the trial. As we will see, those critics made points that echoed the two logics present in the court system, sometimes making moral arguments and sometimes treating working-class people as economic objects. Critics of the courts created a set of representations of injury and law which was incompletely commodified, with commodity and non-commodity forms of valuation initially co-existing.

Historian James Schmidt characterizes injured plaintiffs and their families in this era as coming to court "with a desire to talk about the miseries that had befallen them." He calls the resulting legal proceedings "judicial morality plays."[108] These morality plays involved public storytelling and moral argument in a way that co-existed uneasily with the economic logic of the law. As this chapter concludes, take a moment to consider what people like Nettie Blom and Marguerite Murray wanted from the uneasy coexistence of these morality plays and the economic logic of the law. The historical record does not clearly answer this question. Surely they wanted to win their lawsuits, but what did they want to win, what did winning mean to them? Money, to be sure, but money of what kind – fee or fine? Economic or symbolic? If they wanted justice, was it justice as distribution or justice as recognition? Perhaps both. The court system rarely provided either and regularly denied both. As later chapters detail, the tyranny of the trial within employee injury law soon ended. As we consider that history in the remaining chapters of this book, let us also continue to ask what exactly this brought to an end, and what continued. We can if necessary take comfort in the injustices that went away with the end of the tyranny of the trial. More pressing, however, is to attend to the injustices that remained or began with the introduction of the tyranny of the table.

---

[108] Schmidt, *Industrial Violence and the Legal Origins of Child Labor*, 219, 208.

2

Injury Impoverished

Crystal Eastman must have taken injury personally. She wrote as if she did. Eastman spent 1908 in the homes of people affected by employment injuries, speaking with "strong men just learning to face life maimed" and people who were still stunned by their loved ones' injuries or deaths.[1] Eastman's time in working-class homes was part of the research that led to her *Work-Accidents and the Law*. This 1910 book formed part of the Russell Sage Foundation's Pittsburgh Survey, a landmark multi-participant work of social investigation that resulted in multiple books and articles. In her 1909 article "The Temper of the Workers under Trial," Eastman reflected on her experience doing this research, or at least used a posture of reflection in order to lay out some of the arguments that would later appear in her book.[2] In the article, Eastman wrote that she was "haunt[ed]" by the "thin face" of a grieving woman whose teenage daughter had been killed at her job by a fall down an elevator shaft. Another parent, Eastman explained, found that above all it was not the lost income or the financial difficulties after an employed child's death that most mattered but "the emptiness" of life after the loss that was the real tragedy.[3]

In 1910, reformer and journalist William Hard published his book *Injured in the Course of Duty*. Like Eastman, Hard clearly took injury

---

[1] Crystal Eastman, *Work-Accidents and the Law* (New York: Russell Sage Foundation, 1910), 223.

[2] Crystal Eastman, "The Tempers of the Workers under Trial," in Eastman, *Work-Accidents and the Law*, 223–239. Originally published in *Charities and the Commons*, January 2, 1909.

[3] Eastman, "The Tempers of the Workers under Trial," 224.

personally, and urged readers to do so as well. He underscored that the accident problem was a matter of "the physical injury, the physical agony, of human beings."[4] In his treatment of employee injuries, Hard evoked concrete instances of injury in working-class people's lives, many of which, he noted, went unreported in any official figures.[5]

> For the agony of the crushed arm, for the torment of the scorched body, for the delirium of terror in the fall through endless hollow squares of steel beams down to the death-delaying construction planks of the rising skyscraper, for the thirst in the night of the hospital, for the sinking qualms of the march to the operating-table, for the perpetual ghostly consciousness of the missing limb – for these things and for the whole hideous host of things like them, following upon the half million accidents that happen to American workmen every year, there can be no compensation. Nor can there be compensation for what follows the telling of the tale by some fellow-workman at the door of his stricken comrade's home. There can be no compensation for the stretching out of a woman's hand in search of support against the door's swinging edge. That gesture cannot be paid for. And payment is beyond human power for the emptiness of a father's chair while the girl that was a baby is growing up.[6]

Hard continued, "We cannot translate into dollars and cents the infinite torture, physical and mental, of America's 500,000 annual industrial accidents. We cannot capitalize the anguished leap of the workman's nerves under boiling metal. We cannot set a price upon the horror in the widow's heart when she carries to burial an oblong block of cold iron."[7]

To further illustrate the horrors of employee injuries, Hard told the story of the Allen brothers. Newton Allen worked at the Illinois Steel Company's Chicago plant. On December 12, 1906, a pot full of molten iron fell from the crane Allen operated, spilling the liquid metal onto the floor below. Allen climbed down from the crane and found a man lying face down, writhing and screaming in the melted iron. As Hard put it, "he was being roasted by the slag that had poured out."[8] A few moments after turning the injured man over, Newton Allen realized he was looking at his

---

[4] William Hard, *Injured in the Course of Duty* (New York: Ridgway Company, 1910), 5.

[5] This fits with my personal experience. Both of my brothers and I have all been seriously injured in factory work and never reported the injuries. My father regularly came home from his job as an electrician with electrical tape wrapped around a split thumb or a burnt patch of skin. "You just tape it up and move on," he once said to me when I asked if he ever put antibiotic ointment and a Band Aid on it like my mother always did when I scraped my knees.

[6] Hard, *Injured in the Course of Duty*, 38.   [7] Hard, *Injured in the Course of Duty*, 39.

[8] Hard, *Injured in the Course of Duty*, 7.

brother, Ora. Ora Allen suffered third-degree burns to his foot, leg, arms, hands, neck, and face. Three days later, he died.[9]

LIMITED RECOGNITION

Eastman and Hard sought to make employee injury trouble readers. They wrote in the attempt to make the injury problem of greater concern within the US public sphere. Deliberation in the public sphere constitutes part of how governments "puzzle before they power." This phrase indicates that ruling over other people involves collective thought processes.[10]

---

[9] Hard, *Injured in the Course of Duty*, 6–8.

[10] As Hugh Heclo, has put it, "[g]overnments not only 'power' ... they also puzzle. Policy-making is a form of collective puzzlement" about how to turn priorities "into concrete collective action." Hugh Heclo, *Modern Social Politics in Britain and Sweden: From Relief to Income Maintenance* (New Haven: Yale University Press, 1974), 305. I became aware of Heclo's work via Margot Canaday's *The Straight State: Sexuality and Citizenship in Twentieth-Century America* (Princeton: Princeton University Press, 2009). I have found Canaday's use of this idea particularly insightful. The point extends beyond state power and into probably all forms of governing others. Governing people requires a variety of knowledge and thought with which to execute governance, and so requires processes through which collective thought and knowledge generation take place. I think of these collective thought processes as "puzzling power" or governing-knowledge. This kind of knowledge both draws from broader cultural contexts and intellectual history and is itself culturally constitutive: governing-knowledge can actively shape the cultural categories through which people think. Thus governing-knowledge is not entirely separate from and neutral with respect to the social situation which is known, but actively defines and constitutes that situation. As Eileen Boris has put it, "law creates categories and identities through which groups and individuals become known and know themselves." Eileen Boris, "Labor's Welfare State: Defining Workers, Constructing Citizens," in *The Cambridge History of Law in America, vol. 3: The Twentieth Century and After*, ed. Michael Grossberg and Christopher Tomlins (Cambridge: Cambridge University Press, 2008), 321. To quote Boris again: "Rather than a self-contained system, law is subject to social, ideological, gendered, and class assumptions. It is a product of its time" (p. 321). I think of the study of the kinds of processes Boris describes as studying the intellectual life of governance, bridging intellectual, cultural, and social history – simultaneously a history of cultural categories and of institutional power. I am, of course, far from the first historian to engage in this kind of scholarship. For some other examples, see Dan Bouk, *How Our Days Became Numbered: Risk and the Rise of the Statistical Individual* (Chicago: University of Chicago Press, 2015); Canaday, *The Straight State*; Caley Dawn Horan, "Actuarial Age: Insurance and the Emergence of Neoliberalism in the Postwar United States" (PhD diss., University of Minnesota, 2011); Jonathan Levy, *Freaks of Fortune: The Emerging World of Capitalism and Risk in America* (Cambridge, MA: Harvard University Press, 2012); James Schmidt, *Industrial Violence and the Legal Origins of Child Labor* (New York: Cambridge University Press, 2010); Amy Dru Stanley, *From Bondage to Contract: Wage Labor, Marriage and the Market in the Age of Slave Emancipation* (Cambridge: Cambridge University Press, 1998); Susan Schweik, *The Ugly Laws: Disability in Public* (New York: New York University Press, 2009);

The public conversation about injury law in this era included great masses of information and argument, created by people we can call social investigators. In addition to journalists like Hard and activist social scientists like Eastman, there were also factory inspectors, statisticians, attorneys, and academics like John R. Commons, the reform-oriented economist, and Charles Henderson, a University of Chicago sociologist who served on the Illinois Workingmen's Insurance Commission. These roles were in turn constituted by institutions – social reform-oriented magazines like *Everybody's*, for which Hard wrote; the Russell Sage Foundation, which funded Eastman's research; state departments of factory inspection and bureaus of labor statistics; universities; and organizations such as the American Economic Association and American Association for Labor Legislation. Within these institutions and networks, individual public intellectuals might move from academic to private social investigator to public employee and back again as in the case of Henderson's status as an academic and as a member of the Illinois commission. Similarly, Eastman, after working for the Russell Sage Foundation, went on to serve on the New York Employers' Liability Commission.[11]

Christopher Tomlins, *Law, Labor, and Ideology in the Early American Republic* (Cambridge: Cambridge University Press, 1993); Barbara Young Welke, *Law and the Borders of Belonging in the Long Nineteenth Century United States* (Cambridge: Cambridge University Press, 2010). Robert Gordon has written that J. Willard Hurst and scholars writing in the Hurstian mode understand law as "a general label for several species of applied social intelligence" the point of which "is to increase men's ability to achieve rational control over social change." Robert W. Gordon, "J. Willard Hurst and the Common Law Tradition in American Legal Historiography," *Law & Society Review* 10 (Fall 1975): 9–56, 45–46. I would argue that the scholars I have mentioned emphasize specifically the application of social intelligence to the control of some persons over others and analyze law's role in creating categories of social inclusion and exclusion.

[11] Three other kinds of actors and institutions bear mention as well: the public actuary, defined by the insurance company; the business leader, constituted by corporations and trade associations; and the union leader, constituted by the labor movement. I shall return to the former sooner, and the others later. Relatively speaking, union officials and the labor movement get the least treatment in my account. That is not because of a lack of interest or appreciation on my part when it comes to either the labor movement or labor history – indeed, I count myself among those who lament the declining fortunes of both. Rather, it comes from my assessment that the labor movement and its officials were largely sidelined within the process of injury law reform, and my emphasis here is on what I take to be the dominant kinds of approaches to injury and injury law reform. A fourth kind of actor and institution bears mention as well: socialist, syndicalist, and anarchist radicals, and their organizations and movements. These are essentially absent from my account. What I said about the labor movement goes doubly for those individuals and groups.

Injury law reform grew in part out of a large and varied process of knowledge-making, dedicated to defining, studying, and addressing the ills of the injury problem. State commissions played an important role in this process. These commissions, empaneled by governors and legislators and charged with investigating the injury problem, tended to be composed of a mix of actors such as Eastman, Henderson, and Commons. The commissions would produce new knowledge about society to add to public conversation, sift among existing knowledge to distill and add credence to certain understandings of the injury problem, and suggest ways to turn that knowledge into governmental action – to bridge puzzling into powering.

Within commissions that studied employee injury there co-existed multiple ways to construct and define the problem of injury, why it was a problem, and why that problem mattered, and different values informing various ways of framing the problem. Actors like Eastman and Hard largely wrote about working-class people for middle-class audiences and approached employee injury as a problem of (in)justice. They tended to emphasize issues of distributive (in)justice and primarily discussed justice as recognition through rhetorical flourishes.

Eastman was an attorney, sociologist, feminist, and socialist, the Vassar- and Columbia-educated child of two ministers. Hard was the child of missionaries, educated at a private school in India, at University College in London, and Northwestern University, where he briefly taught. For both Eastman and Hard, their time spent on the injury problem constituted what historian David Huyssen has called a class encounter, meaning an interaction between people across class lines.[12] Eastman's and Hard's class encounters with regard to injury had both vicarious and immediate elements. Eastman read extensively about the injury problem. She also spent many house face to face in their homes with steelworkers who had been injured and with the families of steelworkers who had been killed in work accidents. Both drew on sources more at a remove from the injured as well, including official injury reports, coroners' inquests, and statements by company physicians.

Eastman's and Hard's audiences undoubtedly needed to hear what they had to say. Their works must have provided a kind of vicarious class encounter for many readers. Some of that textually produced encounter foregrounded the losses working-class people suffered, inviting, or

[12] David Huyssen, *Progressive Inequality: Rich and Poor in New York, 1890–1920* (Cambridge, MA: Harvard University Press, 2014).

perhaps challenging, readers to recognize the humanity of the working-
class people affected by injury. In doing so, Eastman's and Hard's writing
momentarily touched on the assignment of appropriate meaning to
persons, and valuing persons according to appropriate standards of
valuation – that is, justice as recognition. Eastman and Hard attended
to the suffering of the injured; depicted the injured as embedded in social
meanings and relationships like that of father and daughter, husband and
wife, friend and co-worker; and treated losses as relatively singular, in the
sense of unique to the injured and affected. Eastman's and Hard's respective works conveyed at least some sense of the moral worth of the persons
injured and some of the pain endured by the injured and their loved ones.
Social justice and respect for victims of trauma involves having some
sense of suffering and of human singularity.[13]

Eastman practiced at least some degree of recognition when she noted
that she aspired to "reveal the spirit of the people who suffered."[14] That
aspiration manifested in her attention to the singularity of the people she
spent time with and the manifold human truths of injury in their lives:
"working people meet trouble," she wrote, "in all the ways there are."[15]
She detailed many of these different ways. Within that plurality she
emphasized that working-class people "know the deepest sorrow," as
was "obvious to one who has seen the loyalties and lasting affections
which make up so much of their lives." Sometimes, Eastman stressed,
there existed in working-class homes "between two family members, a
rare love, exclusive and complete, so that the death of one left the other in
an empty world."[16] Eastman thought she needed to state her discovery

---

[13] By "human singularity" I mean the individuality of a person, what is conveyed or at least
implied in the having of a face and a proper name. "Someone died today" and "Newton
found his brother Ora burning to death" are very different sentences; "human singularity" expresses at least some of that difference.

[14] Eastman, "The Tempers of the Workers under Trial," 239.

[15] Eastman, "The Tempers of the Workers under Trial," 238.

[16] Eastman, "The Tempers of the Workers under Trial," 239. Eastman wrote about these
facts of working-class life with a tone of surprise, which can be read as evincing a kind of
failure of recognition. To put it reductively, Eastman made the paradigm-shifting social
science discovery that sometimes working-class people love each other and so as a result
they feel sad when they or their loved ones get hurt. I write sarcastically here because,
having grown up in a family where everyone did manual labor jobs, on my first reading
I felt genuinely astonished and, frankly, a little offended that Eastman even needed to say
this. There seems to me a question of the ethics of history writing implied here. E. P.
Thompson enjoined against the "enormous condescension of posterity," which is arguably what my reaction to Eastman expresses, while Eastman wrote in her era from the
enormous condescension of a privileged social stratum who viewed itself as the bearer of

for her audience, and it seems likely that she was right. This expresses something important about the context within which she wrote. As she put it, there was a widely prevailing "opinion many hold, that poor people do not feel their tragedies deeply."[17] Her effort to show working-class people's depth of feeling was a necessary response to that opinion within the time and circles within which she existed, however obvious and condescending it appears in a different time and different circles. To put it another way, Eastman's recognition of working-class humanity occurred in a context where that recognition was not widespread.

Eastman's and Hard's writings were akin to the court system in that, like legal actors in trials, they told moving stories of injury and loss as part of presenting morally charged arguments. The degree of recognition that Eastman and Hard expressed is to their credit, as is the degree to which their texts may have fostered a similar recognition on the part of their audience, which most likely consisted of non-working-class readers. Yet justice as recognition was not the primary goal of injury law reformers, including Eastman and Hard. It was not the main vision of justice that they drew on in their social criticism nor the sense of justice around which they formulated their policy goals. Justice as distribution was the main ground upon which they sought to try the court-based system of injury law in the court of public opinion, with their recourse to recognition being incidental or rhetorical.

In the court-based system of employee injury law, the injured and their attorneys sought to call attention to the injured and the full scope of their individual suffering and loss. They did so in an attempt to sway judges and juries. The court-based system of employee injury law staged multiple class encounters. Judges, employers, and attorneys had to face the injured employees, their families, and the suffering of all those harmed by injury. The injured witnessed the less than fully sympathetic response – or, to put it in the most charitable way possible, the mediation of sympathy via adversarial legal procedure – of judges, employers, and employers' attorneys. In their encounter with judges and juries, the injured also encountered the abstract persons of the law: the prudent, reasonable, responsible abstract person of the law against which actual persons were measured. This abstract person in a sense stood between the injured and their legal

---

a new future. See E. P. Thompson, *The Making of the English Working Class* (New York: Vintage, 1966), 12. Faced with a choice between two modes of enormous condescension I have attempted to choose neither.

[17] Eastman, "The Tempers of the Workers under Trial," 238–239.

opponents and reduced the degree to which other parties recognized those who suffered from injury. As I will detail below, reformers attacked that abstract person of the law due to its effects on injured people.

In their trial of the court system, reformers drew on their own abstract persons. The abstract persons that reformers enlisted helped them make their case against the court system and simultaneously reduced the degree of recognition present in reformers' class encounters around the injury problem. To put it another way, the abstract persons of reformers' texts helped reformers to make criticisms of injury law based on notions of distributive justice, rather than notions of justice as recognition. Eastman's and Hard's recognition of working-class people was in an important sense incidental to or at best secondary within their political project. To their credit, Eastman and Hard embedded recognition within the stories they told. Yet their critical projects were not above all centered on recognition. The primary goal, as Eastman put it, was to reveal the "dreary reoccurrence of the same kind of misfortune in home after home," in the hope to bring out "in the reader's mind a question, perhaps a protest." Eastman hoped that understanding how widespread working-class suffering was would lead readers to become "roused" to want social change.[18] There was within this emphasis a subtle shift in the definition and treatment of what the problem was, a shift that sat uneasily with recognition.

INJURY FREQUENCY AND DECLINING RECOGNITION

The text of Eastman's 1910 book *Work-Accidents and the Law* began with the heading "The Problem Stated" followed by four short accounts of injuries. "On December 4, 1906, James Brand, a young structural ironworker," began the first. Brand was on a scaffolding on the Walnut Street Bridge when he "fell to the ground and was killed." The next three vignettes had the same format, beginning with particularity – a specific date, proper name, demographic trait ("young," in Brand's case), the type of job held, and in a specific location. By providing specifics, these vignettes expressed a degree of recognition of the human side of injury. At the same time, they were meant as symbols. The book also included portraits of working-class men, taken by photographer Lewis Hine, a University of Chicago–educated sociologist, educator, and photographer.

---

[18] Eastman, "The Tempers of the Workers under Trial," 239. William Hard clearly wanted the same.

Hine was heavily involved in social reform efforts, not least through his social-realist photography.

Because of the singularity of the human face, the portraits in Eastman's book in one sense expressed individuality, the singularity of injury. And yet this singularity in the images was in tension with their captions. One was labeled simply "immigrant laborer – a slav," another "English-speaking miner."[19] Perhaps they were anonymized to protect them from their employer, though employers might also recognize their faces. The captions made the men into symbols – serving to concretize the problem of injury by underscoring to readers that the injury problem happens to real individual persons – without calling attention to the men as themselves individuals. Her discussions were not about those people as individuals but precisely as examples of a large-scale problem. The same is true of the anonymized persons and tropes in Hard's depiction: the generic widow, baby daughter, and fellow employee, like the "immigrant laborer" and "English-speaking miner," were not meant to be concrete individuals in their singularity, but abstract, generic persons.

Facing the title page to Eastman's book was a diagram labeled "Death Calendar in Industry for Allegheny County." The Death Calendar began in July 1906 and ended in June 1907. Each month consisted in a standard tabular calendar, seven days per week and so forth. Some of the days had one or more red Xs on them. At the bottom of each month was a number, again in red, tallying the Xs for the month. July, 35; August, 45; September, 37; and so on. The bottom of the image read: "Each red cross stands for a man killed at work, or for one who died as a direct result of an injury received in the course of his work."[20] The image is striking. The two lowest months, July and October 1906, both thirty-five Xs, show fewer days without an X than days with Xs, with nine X-free days in July and eight in October. What the image shows is the great frequency of injury, its "repetitive regularity," in Christopher Tomlins's words.[21] While I call the image striking, it is so only if one pauses and makes the effort to really reflect. As a device for showing injury's frequency, it is effective. At the same time there is something dull about the image, something bloodless. A death. Another death. Another. More. Still more. The level of compression in the image that usefully shows frequency also squeezes out a great

[19] Eastman, *Work-Accidents and the Law*, 88–89, 40–41.
[20] Eastman, *Work-Accidents and the Law*, n.p.
[21] Christopher Tomlins, "After Critical Legal History: Scope, Scale, Structure," *Annual Review of Law and Social Science* 8, no. 1 (December 2012): 31–68; 36.

deal of the human character of injury. The agony, torment, and "sinking qualms" that William Hard sought to conjure up are not depicted in the calendar. One can almost imagine the angel of history yawning.

Appropriate here is the quote, "Killing one man is murder. Killing millions is a statistic." A murder is a morally rich concept; a statistic is not.[22] Eastman's calendar showed the frequency of injuries and described those injuries thinly rather than thickly. It depicted injuries abstractly, as statistics rather than murder. The problem of injury as it happened to individuals was one kind of problem, depicted in one way, as with Hard's story about the Allen brothers. The problem of injury as a large-scale social problem happening over and over again, as with the Death Calendar, was another kind of problem, depicted in another way. This change of scale was bound up with different value judgments and definitions of what exactly the problem of injury was.

In the terse summaries of injury at the start of Eastman's prose and in the anonymized photo captions, injured persons were abstractions. In the Death Calendar, another kind of abstract person appeared: quantified, aggregated persons. The abstractions of the generic individual and of the aggregated mass of persons were in some ways useful or even necessary for adequately understanding the problem of injury. These abstractions helped answer the question of how many such harms happened and how often, certainly an important question to ask. Part of my point, however, is that these depictions answered a different question and did so in a way that expressed how reformers had changed what the question was that people ought to ask about injury. Each specific harm resulting from injury was in important respects an unpriceable trespass on the humanity of another person, involving losses unique to that person and others in their life. Those losses had some (and only some) possibility of being presented in the court-based system of employee injury law. Eastman and Hard clearly recognized these losses. But these losses easily disappeared in the aggregation of injuries into a mass. One injury was a single, singular tragedy to one person. Social investigators found that thousands of such singular tragedies occurred each year. This was information it was

---

[22] Clifford Geertz's writing on "thin" and "thick" description is instructive here as well. Clifford Geertz, "Thick Description: Toward an Interpretive Theory of Culture," in Geertz, *The Interpretation of Cultures* (New York: Basic Books, 1973), 3–32. Two accounts of the same incident illustrate the difference between thin and thick description: "one person's eyelid twitched, then another person's eyelid twitched," and "the young woman winked at her date, who winked back." The second contains much more information about social and cultural context as well as the causal connection between the two events.

certainly important to articulate, but it was quite difficult to square singularity with the abstractions required by emphasizing the scale and frequency of injury. In effect, investigations into injury in this era enlarged one facet of the law's social imagination of injury, but failed to enlarge and risked actively shrinking law's moral imagination.

To put it another way, injury law reformers like Eastman and Hard sometimes wrote a certain kind of sad story about injury, as in the story of the Allen brothers. These stories depicted injury in its particularity – this harm suffered by this person in this time and place, and the particular effects on this particular person and the others in this person's life. More frequently, though, reformers wrote another kind of sad story, in which they sought to emphasize the scale and the collective nature of the problem of injury. In the research for each kind of story they had different kinds of class encounters, and in telling each kind of story they produced different kinds of encounters for their readers, some more immediate and others at more of a remove. The more abstract approaches to injury involved a kind of encounter that was farther from the human singularity and suffering involved. This kind of story focused on statistical data, reports on aggregated quantities, and rates of injury. This depiction of injury treated injury in its generality and the injured as an abstraction: one thousand people injured this year, the average worker, and so on.

"In Chicago during the past year," wrote the *Chicago Daily News* in a 1906 editorial, "according to figures compiled by the Bridge and Structural Iron Workers' Union, 147 of its 1,358 members were either killed or disabled by accidents while at work. Thirty-four men lost their lives, thirteen were totally disabled, and 100 were partially disabled." This meant that approximately 11 percent of these construction workers suffered serious injury and just under 3 percent died in one year of normal work.[23] The *Chicago Daily News* took the structural ironworkers as symbolic of all workers. I say "all workers" deliberately, rather than "each worker." The conceptual unit here was a collective and large-scale one, distinct from the singular human individual emphasized in other kinds of accounts.

Injury rates for structural ironworkers were high but in keeping with employee injuries in the early twentieth century. The annual rate of workers killed on the job ranged from 1 in 1,000 to 1 in 300, with

---

[23] "Death as the Wages of Toil," reprinted in *Industrial Insurance: The Need of Providing Aid for Injured Workingmen and Their Dependent Families* (n.p., 1907). Originally printed in *Chicago Daily News*, November 21, 1906, 1.

non-fatal injury rates running substantially higher. Statistician Isaac Rubinow estimated that "there must be some 60,000 crippling injuries each year," such that a full 10 percent of the 18 million US wage earners "must sooner or later suffer not only bodily injury but even mutilation" during their working lives.[24] The point for Rubinow and others was to show that people who worked for wages put their bodies and lives on the line regularly in this era. James Harrington Boyd, a mathematician and attorney who was president of Ohio's Employers' Liability Commission, noted that "in 1870, 70 per cent of our population lived on the land and only 30 per cent in towns and cities. But today more than 65 per cent live in towns and cities and only 35 per cent live on the land."[25] As a result, more working people were exposed to industrial hazards and had fewer resources to provide for security in the event of calamity.[26]

BIOPOLITICS

In their attempts to show the scale of the injury problem, injury law reformers participated in a conceptual transformation in how to think about society and governance.[27] Injury law reformers, unlike the court

---

[24] Isaac Max Rubinow, *Social Insurance: With Special Reference to American Conditions* (New York: Holt, 1913), 61, 68. Rubinow noted that his figures included only those injuries that removed body parts from the injured person; the total number of injuries was even higher. That number amounted to one such injury every nine minutes, and Rubinow's estimate was likely low. The Massachusetts Industrial Accident Board reported a total of about 95,000 injuries to employees in 1915 in just that state alone. Massachusetts Industrial Accident Board, *Third Annual Report of the Industrial Accident Board* (Boston: Wright & Potter Printing Co., State Printers, 1916), 9.

[25] James Harrington Boyd, *Workmen's Compensation, or Insurance against Loss of Wages Arising out of Industrial Accidents* (Columbus: F. J. Heer Printing Co., 1911), 6.

[26] For a discussion of some of the ways wage earners sought security in the face of the hazards of their working lives, see Levy, *Freaks of Fortune*, 150–230, and John Fabian Witt, *The Accidental Republic: Crippled Workmen, Destitute Widows, and the Remaking of American Law* (Cambridge, MA: Harvard University Press, 2004), 71–102.

[27] They also participated in a change in American liberalism. Historian Alan Dawley has characterized the period from the opening of the twentieth century to the end of the 1930s as a gradual shift from ostensible laissez-faire to "liberalism with a social face." The key word to this new social liberalism in Dawley's view was "neither liberty nor equality, but security." Alan Dawley, *Struggles for Justice: Social Responsibility and the Liberal State* (Cambridge, MA: Harvard University Press, 1991), 4; see also 64, 163. Historian Mary O. Furner has similarly argued that there were conflicts between "two different conceptions of new liberalism" from the 1880s onward. Furner, "The Republican Tradition and the New Liberalism," in *The State and Social Investigation in Britain and the United States*, ed. Michael J. Lacey and Mary O. Furner (New York: Cambridge University Press, 1993), 171–241, 194. The shift within American liberalism involved conflict among

system they criticized, thought in a way that theorist Michel Foucault has called biopolitical. Biopolitics refers to a way of thinking about and organizing governance, centering on large social units over time. This involves concepts and social phenomena like rates, aggregates, populations, and averages. Foucault referred to this as a different "rationality of government." Biopolitical forms of power are directed at collective entities like populations. More specifically, they are aimed at managing uncertainty and probability within collective entities. Biopolitics deals with phenomena like rates of accidents, births, illness, and deaths.[28] For Foucault, biopolitics consists in efforts to create security in the face of uncertainty – including economic security – within the political-economic framework of liberalism and capitalism.[29]

As a rationality of government, biopolitics emphasizes collectivity. More specifically, a biopolitical perspective conceptualizes the social world through collectivity. It focuses on the group-ness to human groupings, rather than thinking of groups as consisting of many individual units. Furthermore, biopolitical approaches to government center on securing and maintaining populations – keeping living groups of persons at their most robust, specifically as a group. A biopolitical question takes the form of "What is good for this population as a whole? How can this group become a better group?," where "better" is understood as a quality of the collectivity. (Note here that a biopolitical collectivity is an object, not a collective subject.)

Security is often a keyword of biopolitical approaches to governance, as it was for injury law reformers. They sought to document the insecurity generated by the injury problem. Injury law reformers defined the problem of employee injury from a biopolitical perspective, and so called for laws that would create a specifically biopolitical solution to that problem: new security. That is to say, Hard and other reformers believed that the

various actors committed to different ideas about the role of law and the state in economic life.

[28] Michel Foucault, *"Society Must Be Defended": Lectures at the Collège de France, 1975–1976* (New York: Picador, 2003), 243–246. See also Michel Foucault, *Security, Territory, Population: Lectures at the Collège de France, 1977–78* (New York: Picador, 2004), 42, 79. I want to note here that statistical thinking tends to typify biopolitics, but the reverse is not necessarily true: not all use of statistics is necessarily biopolitical.

[29] Michel Foucault, *The Birth of Biopolitics: Lectures at the Collège de France, 1978–79* (New York: Picador, 2008), 65, 69. Foucault associated biopolitics with the rise of liberalism and more specifically with efforts to create security in the face of uncertainty, including economic security, in a way that was compatible with liberal and capitalist ideas and social practices.

problem of injury required a response that treated working-class people as aggregates and created aggregate security.

The biopolitical perspective injury law reformers displayed was, arguably, relatively new in the United States. It was certainly new within employee injury law. This perspective included an aggregating impulse. It drew on statistical knowledge, probabilistic understandings of predictability, and concepts drawn from insurance. In the United States in this era, the shift toward biopolitics in law was carried out through a change from an older worldview of contract to a new worldview of insurance. Commercial insurance was a response to market-generated insecurities, and it was a purchasable response. Sometimes the effects of markets could threaten people's lives or livelihoods. Insurance offered purchasable security to alleviate the financial effects of those threats. Insurers drew on statistical thinking to understand and manage risk more effectively, not least for the sake of their own profits and policy sales. When they sold customers insurance in the sense of financial security via risk-pooling, insurers also sold customers on insurance as a worldview. Insurers did cultural work, encouraging customers to understand themselves, their relationships, society around them, and their possible futures in new ways. In selling insurance, insurers spread ideas about society, security, and valuation, ideas embedded in collective practices of financially sharing risks.[30]

These new understandings informed injury law reform in the United States in important respects. Injury law reformers opted to insure injury

---

[30] This paragraph is informed by Levy, *Freaks of Fortune*; Bouk, *How Our Days Became Numbered*; Horan, "Actuarial Age"; Blumenthal, *Law and the Modern Mind*; and Welke, "The Cowboy Suit Tragedy." The rise of insurance as a worldview came amid, and largely in response to, what historian Jamie Pietruska has called a "crisis of certainty" in the late nineteenth-century United States. See Jamie L. Pietruska, *Looking Forward: Prediction and Uncertainty in Modern America* (Chicago: University of Chicago Press, 2017). Insurance became one of the key technologies and vocabularies for social management, and was especially important for employee injury. The rise of insurance built on and transformed earlier legal and economic developments. Specifically, during the late eighteenth- and early nineteenth-century United States, law rose to prominence among the institutions, vocabularies, and conceptual orders through which governance occurs. The prominence of law aided the rise of a market and liberal political economy. See Tomlins, *Law, Labor, and Ideology*. That legal, cultural, policy, and economic world became one in which labor was understood as free and employment was understood as a contractual affair. With the end of slavery and the further spread of waged labor, contract as a legal doctrine and as a worldview spread further. Contract and free labor were bound up closely with ideas of freedom and selfhood; to be truly free was to be a self-owning male, and to interact with others was to contract with them freely. See Stanley, *From Bondage to Contract*. I would argue that insurance concepts within employee injury law in turn drew on and revised concepts of contract.

risk through policy, following on the German model of compensation law. In doing so they opted not to pursue the British model, which kept a more important role for courts.[31] Reformers thus framed the specific policy choice as, in part, one between courts and insurance, implying that a biopolitical social vision like the new social viewpoint could not be instantiated through courts. People who took up an insurance worldview in pursuit of social reforms did so in response to the growing economic and social uncertainty of the late nineteenth century. This period was the era of "the emergence of corporate capitalism," writes historian David Berman.[32] With that emergence, argues historian Jackson Lears, "daily life became more subject to the systematic demands of the modern corporation."[33] That subjection generated new uncertainty, one element of which was the threat of injury. The new insurance worldview informed legal and policy changes, which in turn helped spread insurance as a worldview.[34]

Reformers used statistical rhetoric repeatedly in their treatment of the injury problem. "I believe in statistics just as firmly as I believe in revolutions," Crystal Eastman wrote in 1911. Eastman declared her commitment to both statistical reasoning and socialism, both of which she understood as contributions to human progress. Furthermore, she believed in a connection between the two, adding, "what is more, I believe statistics are good stuff to start a revolution with."[35] Reformers used statistics and statistical

[31] See Daniel Rodgers, *Atlantic Crossings: Social Politics in a Progressive Age* (Cambridge, MA: Harvard University Press, 1998), for more on connections between US and British social policy. See also John M. Kleeberg, "From Strict Liability to Workers' Compensation: The Prussian Railroad Law, the German Liability Act, and the Introduction of Bismarck's Accident Insurance in Germany, 1838–1844," *New York University Journal of International Law and Politics* 36, no. 1 (Fall 2003): 53–132.

[32] David Berman, *Politics, Labor, and the War on Big Business: The Path of Reform in Arizona, 1890–1920* (Boulder: University Press of Colorado, 2012), xi.

[33] Jackson Lears, *Rebirth of a Nation: The Making of Modern America, 1877–1920* (New York: Harpers, 2009), 1.

[34] Witt, *The Accidental Republic*, 126–151; Levy, *Freaks of Fortune*, 1–6, 191–230. Insurance constituted a mutation in the market as site of veridiction, to use Foucault's term. See Foucault, *The Birth of Biopolitics*, 31. Courts' use of insurance tables in employee injury suits helps demonstrate that insurance as a new kind of market veridiction was present in both the court-based system of employee injury law and compensation laws, but it was differently present in each. In the court-based system of employee injury law, insurance could inform the monetization and commodification of individuals but that system did not generally think biopolitically. With compensation laws, employee injury law commodified in a specifically biopolitical fashion.

[35] Crystal Eastman, "The Three Essentials for Accident Prevention," *Annals of the American Academy of Political and Social Science* 38 (June 1911): 99.

vocabulary to make their claims and voice their criticisms of the court-based system of injury law. This vocabulary gave their claims the garb of science and progress. It made their biopolitical approach to injury appear as not merely a difference of perspective but as an advance over the more individually focused perspective implicit in the court-based system of employee injury law. Reformers sought to change the rules of the market through legislation. They wanted to replace the court-based system of employee injury law with an insurance-based administrative system. They hoped this change would write into law new social liberal principles they saw as more in step with their times.

FROM PUZZLE TO POWER

In July of 1909 the Minnesota Employees' Compensation Commission organized a national conference held in Atlantic City. The conference brought together twenty-four people from the several state commissions then studying the problem of employee injury.[36] The 1909 conference helped move workmen's compensation from an idea reformers raised in publications to a fleshed-out policy proposal that could appear on the floor of state legislatures. The conference helped connect reformers and policy-makers in multiple states, making the creation of compensation laws a decentralized but still a single national process of policy formation. Conference attendees displayed many of the animating concerns informing compensation laws and expressed biopolitical perspectives, seeking state legislation to secure aggregated social entities like labor markets.

---

[36] *Report of Atlantic City Conference on Workmen's Compensation Acts, held at Atlantic City, N.J., July 29–31, 1909* (n.p., 1909). Accident and liability commissions shared the same tripartite structure common in commissions of this era, with a representative of business, labor, and the public, with an attorney generally serving as the public's representative. Price Fishback and Shawn Everett Kantor, *A Prelude to the Welfare State: The Origins of Workers' Compensation* (Chicago: University of Chicago Press, 2000), 132. The point of these commissions, like that of collective bargaining–oriented commissions, whether conducted under the auspices of private actors like the National Civic Federation or through public bodies, was to harmonize conflicting interests through representation, in service of society as a whole. See Richard A. Greenwald, *The Triangle Fire, the Protocols of Peace, and Industrial Democracy in Progressive Era* (Philadelphia: Temple University Press, 2005). After the creation of workmen's compensation laws, injury law came to center on administrative agencies, largely abandoning the tripartite commissions. The same occurred in collective bargaining in the 1930s, suggesting a general turn toward administration in both employment and labor law. See also Mark Aldrich, *Safety First: Technology, Labor, and Business in the Building of American Work Safety* (Baltimore: Johns Hopkins University Press, 1997), 93.

In the conference's opening discussion, Miles Dawson argued that the court-based system of handling employee injuries was wasteful. Dawson was an actuary and an attorney active in the American Association for Labor Legislation who later in 1909 would volunteer his legal services to the International Ladies Garment Workers Union during the garment workers' strikes.[37] Part of the source of waste in the law, Dawson argued, was that a "sharp lawyer" knew how to evoke "a great deal of sympathy on the part of the jury by exhibiting the widow and minor children, aiming to get a large verdict."[38] In Dawson's view removing this narrative and rhetorical component of the law, and the power of the jury, would result in a much less wasteful system for handling workplace injuries. Dawson particularly decried the immoral "ambulance chaser," suggesting that these attorneys preyed on helpless workers and bereaved families.[39]

Several conference attendees challenged Dawson on this point. George Gillette, of the Minnesota commission, argued that lawyers were often the "only friend" of injured workers and their families.[40] Charles Neill, US Commissioner of Labor, told a story about a friend who worked as an attorney in New York and who took on personal injury cases "as a matter of sentiment." This unnamed attorney had taken an injury suit for a fee of half the verdict, and expended more than $3,000 in pursuing the case. When the court awarded the plaintiff $6,000, the attorney found the case a net loss. John Blaine, an attorney who served on the Wisconsin Industrial Commission, argued similarly that while he was not specifically an injury lawyer, in his experience "a majority of attorneys who take these negligence cases are men of high standing in their profession and as citizens in their respective communities."[41] Rather than attack lawyers who represented the injured, Blaine argued, Dawson should criticize insurance agents who pressured grieving families and injured workers to accept low settlements that they never would accept if they "had time to consult a reputable attorney."

---

[37] The conference proceedings do not list the institutional affiliation of three of the attendees. Ten were members of state committees and agencies studying the accident problem in different parts of the country. Eleven worked for insurance companies. Here and elsewhere, insurance company personnel, insurance as a metaphor, and insurance-derived terms and concepts shaped the public and policy discussion of the problem of employee injury and its possible solutions. See David A. Moss, *Socializing Security: Progressive Era Economists and the Origins of American Social Policy* (Cambridge, MA: Harvard University Press, 1996), 80.

[38] *Report of Atlantic City Conference*, 26.   [39] *Report of Atlantic City Conference*, 16.

[40] *Report of Atlantic City Conference*, 266.   [41] *Report of Atlantic City Conference*, 38.

Blaine defined the problem of injury as one of working-class families suffering the loss of "the benefit of [men's] employment." That loss in turn helped push working-class children out of schools and, thus, out of their chance for "social betterment."[42] This social loss, Blaine suggested, was encouraged by insurance companies and settlements. The problem as Blaine posed it was that market actors' thoughts were too short-term, acting in ways that benefited them in immediate transactions but which in the long term threatened to undermine the conditions of economic life. The so-called invisible hand of the market did not really work, and the end result, without intervention, would ultimately be bad for businesses.

Lee Frankel, an official at the Metropolitan Life Insurance Company, commended Blaine's speech and expanded on Blaine's points. Frankel began by declaring that a new social understanding of poverty should inform policy. While "the conception in the English poor law [was] that a man who becomes impoverished is responsible for his condition," recent social science research had found the opposite: "The poor are not responsible for their condition."[43] Rather, recent studies of poverty had found that "[t]he large bulk of pauperism is primarily due to the bad environment of the individual, and is a result in part of our so-called employers' liability legislation." Frankel here expressed a relatively recent transformation in conceptions of poverty – from being understood as the result of the actions of impoverished persons to being understood as the result of social circumstances – which was of a piece with reformers' efforts on institutional reform. Conceptions of poverty's origins tracked with different notions of how to intervene to alleviate poverty. These conceptions tracked as well with the question of whether or not to intervene at all: if the poor were in their circumstances due to their own actions, perhaps they deserved it, some might reason. On other hand, if society inflicted poverty, then poverty was unjust and remediable.

When "[t]he father or the mother or the brother is killed or become [*sic*] incapacitated" by injury, Frankel elaborated, "the family, which has been self-sustaining and respectable, has to go to the wall perforce, because no provision is at present made by our legislation for its care, maintenance and support.... And we have the resulting condition that the family goes to pieces, falls by the wayside, becomes dependent on the

---

[42] *Report of Atlantic City Conference*, 39.
[43] *Report of Atlantic City Conference*, 45. For more on Frankel, see Nikki Mandell, *The Corporation as Family: The Gendering of Corporate Welfare, 1890 to 1930* (Chapel Hill: University of North Carolina Press, 2002), 12.

public purse simply because in this horrible crush to get ahead, in this desire to make profits, the individual laborer ... suffers the loss and bears the entire responsibility."[44] Frankel added that "we are no longer in an industrial age" and so the United States needed a new perspective, a "social viewpoint." For Frankel this social viewpoint meant government should intervene within the workings of business.

Wallace Ingalls of the Wisconsin Industrial Commission noted that the instantiation of what Frankel had called a "social viewpoint" via workmen's compensation was quite different from the old individualist perspective that had informed the court-based system of injury law. The social viewpoint, Ingalls said, represented "a move to revolutionize a [legal] system which has existed for over a century." This legal revolution involved "a destruction of the will of the individual, in a sense" and as such would face serious legal challenges from ideologically laissez-faire or individualist liberals who opposed the new social liberalism.[45]

Echoing Frankel's emphasis on society as a whole, Hugh Mercer of the Minnesota commission gave a compressed account of US intellectual and commercial history as part of presenting the legal basis for compensation laws. Mercer argued that early in US history "[t]he best thought of the best minds of this new and ambitious country was devoted to the essential features of both private and public law" and questions of government more generally.[46] After the Civil War, "the great minds in America" had turned to matters of business and industry; the success of those great minds had transformed the American economy. Economic expansion and industrialization brought new risks into Americans' lives. To manage these risks, Americans turned to new mechanisms including life insurance, fire insurance, and agricultural securities exchanges. American institutions had not, however, kept pace with the new risks of industrial accidents.[47] Mercer suggested that he and his fellow commission members were the latest actors at the end of this series of transformations. Their task was to fill a gap in American risk management institutions: "This is a

---

[44] *Report of Atlantic City Conference*, 47.   [45] *Report of Atlantic City Conference*, 288.
[46] *Report of Atlantic City Conference*, 158.
[47] *Report of Atlantic City Conference*, 162–163. On the history of the police power in the United States, see William J. Novak. *The People's Welfare: Law and Regulation in Nineteenth-Century America* (Chapel Hill: University of North Carolina Press, 1996); William J. Novak, "The Myth of the 'Weak' American State," *American Historical Review* 113, no. 3 (June 2008): 752–772; Christopher Tomlins, "Necessities of State: Police, Sovereignty, and the Constitution," *Journal of Policy History* 20, no. 1 (January 2008): 47–63.

risk; it really is an insurance problem and as such must be treated."[48]
Mercer's remarks further show the centrality of insurance to the new way
of conceptualizing and governing injury.

Mercer emphasized the history of fire insurance regulation as an
analogy to justify his call for the state to provide industrial accident
insurance. The state had both an interest and the legal right, based in
the police power, to intervene to regulate fire insurance. The state had "the
power to protect the public interests in all controversies between individuals." This power was "a condition precedent to all contracts" and "a
safety valve for all action." "[A]ll property is held subject to [this] power of
reasonable regulation and control."[49] Given the social effects of high rates
of injuries and low rates of compensation, there was a clear public interest
in state intervention on the question of industrial accident compensation:
"provision for mechanics and artisans and protection for their employers
is ... necessary to the people and ... an obligation of the state."[50]

Crystal Eastman spoke at the 1910 compensation conference. Eastman
noted that the New York State Labor Department's investigation into
"the loss of income to the man injured" and "the effect of the accident
upon his family" allowed the New York Employers' Liability Commission to get a sense of "the economic cost of work accidents."[51] Eastman
here used "economic" in an expanded sense to include financial costs as
well as the stability of working-class families. In her book, Eastman
argued that the annual cost of workplace injuries in just one county in
Pennsylvania was $5 million per year. Eastman noted that while these
injury costs were paid, they were unfairly paid by the wrong people.[52]
Specifically, working-class people paid these costs, compounding the
harm that employees and their families suffered.

To put it in economistic terms, employees and their families paid for
the costs of injury at the cost of their future human capital. The Illinois
Employers' Liability Commission decried "the evils of the present situation" with regard to employee injury and the law thereof. To dramatize
these evils, the Commission detailed how in the aftermath of fatal injuries
the families of the deceased often "had disintegrated or moved away."
A "persevering investigator" employed by the commission, however, had

---

[48] *Report of Atlantic City Conference*, 195.   [49] *Report of Atlantic City Conference*, 206.
[50] *Report of Atlantic City Conference*, 211.
[51] *Proceedings: Third National Conference, Workmen's Compensation for Industrial Accidents, Chicago, June 10–11, 1910* (n.p., n.d.), 15.
[52] Eastman, *Work-Accidents and the Law*, 317.

managed to follow "the available clews [*sic*] and found that a widow, left helpless by the killing of her husband, had been driven into a life of immorality." The Commission editorialized that "[t]he industry which took her husband's life took … a great deal more" as the widowed woman "was keeping her four little girls on the wages received for the sale of her person."[53] With similarly persistent research, the Commission suggested, similar instances might be found, and out of 1,000 cases found "hundreds of families became broken up and migratory." With the above story of family income replaced by a turn to prostitution, the Commission helped frame a call for "a reform of the evils" of the present system of workplace injury in order to formulate a system of "adequate support for the families deprived by industry of their bread winners."[54] Inadequate financial compensation of injuries could lead to social evils; thus, compensation must be made adequate.[55]

---

[53] *Report of the Employers' Liability Commission of the State of Illinois* (Chicago: Stromberg, Allen, & Co., n.d.), 10.

[54] *Report of the Employers' Liability Commission of the State of Illinois*, 11. In its research, the Illinois Commission assembled a list of 5,000 recent workplace injury legal cases, with approximately 1,000 involving fatal injuries. The commission ran into great difficulties in its effort to learn about the aftermath of those fatal injuries because of the dislocation that resulted: the effects of injuries themselves were an obstacle to efforts to produce knowledge about those effects.

[55] This account of social evils centered on the family, women, and gender. The commission here framed the sale of sex as a moral wrong, and one that resulted from interrupted income due to injury. The commission bundled together morally charged notions of gender roles and sexuality as well as the relationship between income and social reproduction. Some means of reproducing families were moral – such as waged manual labor by male heads of household – while others – such as waged sexual labor by female heads of household – were immoral. For a discussion of prostitution and market society in US history, see Stanley, *From Bondage to Contract*, 218–263. In the culture of the late nineteenth century, and this culture no doubt still existed in the 1910s, women engaging in extramarital sex were out of bounds according to prevailing morality. Economic arrangements helping create prostitution thus reflected poorly on those arrangements in that, according to the dominant perspective, sex was to take place for non-instrumental reasons rather than as instrumentalized market exchange. These attitudes toward sex for sale intersected with attitudes toward sex, gender, and morality more generally, many of which were most certainly not emancipatory for women. There are anti-market notions premised on values and notions of social organization which we should reject; criticisms of markets matter only when they are informed by emancipatory values. Nancy Fraser has written illuminatingly on oppressive versions of recognition that are sometimes opposed to markets, and argued that the harms of market-dominated society tend to give rise to those oppressive anti-market ideologies founded in a reactionary version of recognition. Those ideologies, in turn, help run ideological cover for policies and political outlooks that impose markets while voicing opposition to oppressive forms of recognition. Nancy Fraser, "From Progressive Neoliberalism to Trump – And Beyond," *American Affairs* 1, no. 4 (Winter 2017): 46–64.

Joseph Parks of the Massachusetts Commission on Employers' Liability and Workmen's Compensation underscored the importance of family
maintenance: "The operatives do not care much about the loss of a finger
or the loss of beauty, or any such thing as that," Parks asserted. "The
particular thing that the operative is interested in is, if he is a man of
family, how his family is going to make out while he is on a sickbed and
unable to work."[56] While Parks overstated the degree to which working-
class people were unconcerned over lost fingers and disfigurement, there is
no doubt that many working-class people did worry a great deal about
the welfare of their loved ones in the event of injury-induced financial
catastrophe.

Illinois State Senator Edward J. Glackin's treatment of the injury
problem centered on family breakdown as well. After injury, ironworkers – intended as a symbol for all workers – were regularly "brought
home crippled and unable to care for" their financial dependents because
their wages "stop the moment the accident occurs," leading to tremendous disruptions in their and their families' lives. Glackin framed the
problem of injury as a matter of income disruption and the effects of that
disruption on families.[57] The problem of employee injury remained
one freighted with moral ramifications – reformers still thought about
justice – but the focus became centered on distributive injustices and
social consequences flowing out of the financial effects of injury.

LOSS OF SINGULARITY

Injury law reformers, then, wanted government protection against the
negative effects of injury. Those effects were above all understood as
economic in nature. What injury law reformers focused on was protection
of working-class people from market-imposed effects of injuries. I noted
above that Eastman and Hard did exhibit an important attention to
justice as recognition, in the sense of awareness of singularity and
suffering. Overall, however, individuals, as concrete, specific, singular
persons, do not fit easily within the kinds of abstractions that characterize
biopolitical thinking. Biopolitics is in tension with those aspects of recognition that attend to singularity. This is part of why recognition largely

---

[56] *Proceedings: Third National Conference*, 29.
[57] Edward J. Glackin, "Life and Limb Too Cheap," reprinted in *Industrial Insurance: The
Need of Providing Aid for Injured Workingmen and Their Dependent Families* (n.p.,
1907), 2–3. Originally printed in *Chicago Daily News*, December 10, 1906, 2.

fell out of the reformers' treatment of injury. Along these lines, at the 1910 compensation conference Edwin Wright, the president of the Illinois Federation of Labor and secretary of the Illinois Employers' Liability Commission, sounded a warning about the limitations built into aggregate-centered forms of thinking about the injury problem. It was important, he said,

[to] understand the real meaning of all these figures in these reports. It is one thing to publish column after column of figures which nobody reads and nobody pays any attention to, but it is an entirely different proposition to get back of those columns of figures and see what they stand for. Those columns of figures stand for men's lives and they stand for the happiness of the family.[58]

That said, there was some room for recognition in reformer rhetoric, as can be seen in one of William Hard's uses of statistics to discuss injury. Hard drew on German statistical data to speculate about injury rates in the U.S. steel industry: "for every man killed in Germany there were eight who suffered a permanent disability of either a partial or a total character. It further appears that for every man killed, four were disabled temporarily, which, in the German statistics, means for at least thirteen weeks." Hard speculated that "[i]f the law of averages is the same in Chicago as it is in Berlin (and there is no reason to suppose that it isn't)," then he could derive an estimate of injuries at U.S. Steel's South Chicago plant. He estimated that with forty-six workers killed, then there were likely 184 disabled for thirteen weeks or more, and 368 disabled permanently in accidents.[59] Hard pointed out that "it should be remembered that the estimate here given does not include any of those men who suffered injuries which disabled them for a period of less than the thirteen weeks," injuries that were much more numerous. He estimated that "at least 1,200 men ... were involved in accidents of all kinds" at that plant.

Doctors who have been employed in the hospital of the Illinois Steel Company place the number even higher. They have said that there are at least 2,000 accidents every year. But many of these accidents extend only to the painful

---

[58] *Proceedings: Third National Conference*, 25–26. He sought to square that with mutual economic benefit, adding "yes, and they stand for the prosperity of the employer as well." By that year, the national conference had grown to become an organization: the National Conference on Workmen's Compensation for Industrial Accidents. The third national meeting, and the National Conference's first as a formal organization, took place in Chicago in June of 1910. About seventy people attended this meeting, including government officials, insurance company personnel, and labor union officials. Officials from the compensation and liability commissions of seven different states spoke at the conference.

[59] Hard, *Injured in the Course of Duty*, 4.

scorching of a leg. If the figure be kept at 1,200, it will be a conservative estimate, including only those injuries that may be legitimately regarded as being of material consequence.

Hard stressed that the Illinois Steel Company was not exceptional but rather exemplary. Hard's talk of "the painful scorching of a leg" implied some sense of the suffering of injury, mixed with his attempt to show injury as a large-scale problem. That pain, however, was not "legitimately regarded as being of material consequence." Suffering is immaterial, literally so in its intangible human qualities, and metaphorically so in that it was simply not Hard's real object of analysis or his real complaint about injury law. His recognition of suffering was attenuated.

Hard continued:

Here then, is the record of one American industrial establishment for one year! It is not an establishment that enjoys any preeminence in heartlessness. If it were, there would be no use in writing an article about it. The exceptional proves nothing. But the plant in South Chicago is just an American plant, conducted according to American ideals. Its officials are men whom one is glad to meet and proud to know. And yet in the course of one year in their plant they had at least 1,200 accidents that resulted in the physical injury, the physical agony, of human beings.[60]

With his numbers Hard sought to show the frequency of injury, the large scale of the injury problem. He sought to integrate his depiction of injury in the aggregate as a social problem with some sense of the individual, singular suffering of the people involved, through his references to physical agony and to employers not being heartless. That integration of perspectives was at best only ever partially achieved among employee injury law reformers.

Recognition was partially present within reformers' biopolitical understanding of injury in a second manner, as a matter of civic obligation. Civic obligation meant understanding another person as a member of a polity to which one had some kind of duty. This was a limited recognition of the other person, if not in their human singularity at least as a fellow civic actor. In his 1910 book *History of Labor Legislation in Iowa* actuary E. H. Downey wrote that "[t]he annual reports of deaths and injuries from industrial accidents read like the returns of a great battle."[61]

---

[60] Hard, *Injured in the Course of Duty*, 5.
[61] E. H. Downey, *History of Labor Legislation in Iowa* (Iowa City: State Historical Society of Iowa, 1910), 183.

That same year, in a speech, James Harrington Boyd of Ohio's Employers' Liability Commission, said that

the best estimate of the number of persons injured and killed in industrial accidents in 1909 is 536,000 people. What does this mean? Let us see. In the battle of
Gettysburg, which lasted three days of actual fighting, there were killed, wounded,
and missing 43,500 soldiers. If therefore you were to have a battle of Gettysburg
in one of each of twelve divisions of the United States ... you would not create
quite the damage and destruction which takes place yearly in the industrial activity
of the United States.[62]

William Hard similarly wrote that "the record of the long battle in the
cave of smoke on the north bank of the Calumet River for the year
1906 would therefore present 59 killed and wounded men to the consideration of a public which would be appalled by the news of the loss of an
equal number of men in a battle in the Philippines." As he more bluntly
described conditions at the Illinois Steel Company: "Steel is War."[63]
Charles Henderson used similar terms to describe watching a library
being built. Seeing

the men climb up along those iron structures ... made me shiver when I thought of
the possibility of their falling. But such men never quail; they go right on, and that
is why they are called reckless. But of what value is a railroad man who is always
watching to see that he does not get his fingers pinched, or that he does not lose his
limb? Of what use is a soldier in battle who is looking for a safe place? All these
men are engaged in battle, the battle against starvation; and they must be brave
men; so, let us do with them as we have done with our veteran soldiers; let them be
as careful as they can; but when they fall in this struggle for our wealth, let us take
care of them.[64]

Comparisons with war helped reformers like Hard and Boyd to dramatize
the severity and gravity of the problem of injury and compensation. Like
war, the economy killed many. The comparisons also invoked multiple

---

[62] Boyd, *Workmen's Compensation, or Insurance against Loss of Wages Arising out of Industrial Accidents*, 24.

[63] Hard, *Injured in the Course of Duty*, 18.

[64] Charles Henderson, *"Compensation or Insurance versus Employers' Liability": Address at the Sixteenth Annual Meeting of the Central Supply Association* (n.p., 1910), 59. The editors of *Domestic Engineering* described the members of the association (representatives of multiple Midwestern manufacturing companies including Kohler, Crane, Youngs-
town Sheet and Tube), as listening with "rapt attention" to Henderson and viewing his
speech as "one of the strongest and most timely presentations ever made before the
Association." See "Proceedings of the Sixteenth Annual Meeting of the Central Supply
Association," *Domestic Engineering* 53, no. 5 (October 29, 1910): 120–121.

important values. Dead and injured employees, like soldiers, met their fate bravely (as manly men, was the implication); they acted out of duty to the nation and afterward they or their loved ones were owed a reciprocal duty by the nation.

The editors of the *Chicago Daily News* had taken structural ironworkers and their families as symbols of the injury problem.[65] Edward Glackin similarly invoked structural ironworkers and their injuries. He emphasized that the ironworkers "risk[ed] their lives for the people" by building the infrastructure required by American industry and society.[66] Glackin painted their activity as public service. The activity they performed was necessary for the national community. Because society needed them to run these risks, he implied, when they got hurt society had an obligation to these men.

Through comparisons with the military, depictions of virtuously manly risk-taking, and claims as to the public nature of infrastructure building, reformers not only showed the scale of the injury problem but also expressed certain values. They presented injury as a problem that good social governance and civic obligation needed to respond to. While some aspects of justice as recognition fit into this framing of the injury problem, individual dignity, vulnerability, and singularity did not. There was, then, some possibility for thinking biopolitically about injury and also doing justice in terms of recognition to those affected by injury. It remains the case, however, that justice as recognition was not an animating concern of injury law reformers. They cared about it, but did not write policy for it. Biopolitics admits of room for expression of recognition, and that certainly matters, but it is unclear if biopolitical and distributive reasoning are suited to meeting recognition-centered goals.

ATTACKING THE COURTS

The court-based system of employee injury law dramatically fell short when it came to distributive justice. The courts imposed economic harms on top of the other harms suffered by those affected by injury. Reformers were right about this and to that extent their efforts are morally laudable.

[65] *Chicago Daily News*, "Death as the Wages of Toil," 1.
[66] Glackin, "Life and Limb Too Cheap," 2.

Their criticisms in large part amounted to redefining the criteria by which employee injury was a social problem. Through these criticisms, reformers sought to show that courts were hopelessly out of step with new and pressing social realities, and that this lag had tremendous consequences.

Reformers emphasized that many injuries seemed to be no one's fault. As James Harrington Boyd put it, "cases in which the employer is negligent ... do not exceed twenty per cent of all injuries."[67] William Hard similarly estimated that between 80 and 90 percent of work accidents were not due to fault.[68] Eastman found a lower but still high rate of no-fault injuries, with 117, or 23 percent, of the 501 accidents she investigated involving no clear fault.[69] She argued that these rates were likely not exceptional and that overall a significant proportion of injuries were no one's fault. In 1910 economist E. H. Downey argued that the US experience likely paralleled the picture painted by statistics from the German Imperial Insurance Office, which found that more than 40 percent of employee injuries were "due to inevitable accidents connected with employment."[70] The emphasis on no-fault injuries mattered, because in Downey's words, "unless the master is remiss ... the servant will have no ground of action against him. For without breach of duty there is no negligence, and without negligence there is no liability."[71] Crystal Eastman similarly wrote that "[i]t is a fundamental doctrine of the civil law that if a loss is to be suffered he who is at fault shall suffer it, in order to both secure justice between individuals and to prevent future faults of the same kind."

The centrality to the law of concepts of fault and negligence, reformers argued, created the situation reformers decried, where injured employees and their families rarely won their injury lawsuits.[72] As Eastman noted in

[67] Boyd, *Workmen's Compensation, or Insurance against Loss of Wages Arising out of Industrial Accidents*, 24.
[68] Hard, *Injured in the Course of Duty*, 54.
[69] Eastman, *Work-Accidents and the Law*, 86.
[70] Downey, *History of Labor Legislation in Iowa*, 183.
[71] Downey, *History of Labor Legislation in Iowa*, 155.
[72] Historian Paul Bellamy has argued that too many historians have taken reformers at their word and characterized courts in the same way. He argues that at least in some locales, there was in fact quite a lot of compensation happening via courts. My sense is that both Bellamy and those he criticizes are right. I suspect that there was a great deal more compensation happening than critics contended, and yet injury went uncompensated far too often. Paul Bellamy, "From Court Room to Board Room: Immigration, Juries, Corporations and the Creation of an American Proletariat: A History of Workmen's Compensation, 1898–1915" (PhD diss., Case Western Reserve University, 1994), v–x.

1910, a recent survey of New York Labor Department data on 902 accidents resulting in disability found that "only a small proportion of the workmen injured by accident of employment get substantial compensation."[73] In her own survey of injury cases, Eastman found that 53 percent of fatal workplace accidents went uncompensated.[74] Boyd similarly found that "the common law does not presume to furnish any relief for something like from sixty to eighty per cent of all persons injured in the United States."[75] Hard reported that out of a study of 241 workplace accidents, 194 went uncompensated.[76] Overall, reformers argued, the court system offloaded the costs of the US economy onto working-class people.

Furthermore, the courts could not meaningfully do otherwise. Any negligence-based system of employee injury compensation would leave some injured wage earners without compensation. Downey said that the fact that "[f]or most of these deaths and injuries [arising out of employment] our law affords no remedy" constituted an "indictment of the Common Law of employers' liability."[77] It was "clear that a rule which permits recovery only for the negligence of the master ... throws the chief burden of industrial accidents upon those least able to bear it themselves or to shift it to others."[78] Downey and other injury law reformers rejected this arrangement as morally unacceptable, hence the need to abandon courts and embrace insurance.

In industrial workplaces, everyone could do their duty and someone might still be disabled or killed. In the face of that reality, the law's emphasis on individual fault resulted in losses being suffered by faultless actors. As such, in Eastman's words, the law helped neither to "secure justice" nor to "prevent future faults."[79] Charles Henderson argued that the emphasis on fault made the court-based system of injury compensation outmoded in the contemporary American industrial economy. He said, "I have never known a man who wanted to injure or poison one of his workingmen; but nevertheless these things occur, and the employers'

---

[73] Eastman, *Work-Accidents and the Law*, 271.
[74] Eastman, *Work-Accidents and the Law*, 121.
[75] James Harrington Boyd, *Workmen's Compensation and Industrial Insurance under Modern Conditions* (Indianapolis: Bobbs-Merrill, 1913), 77.
[76] Hard, *Injured in the Course of Duty*, 66.
[77] Downey, *History of Labor Legislation in Iowa*, 183.
[78] Downey, *History of Labor Legislation in Iowa*, 183
[79] Eastman, *Work-Accidents and the Law*, 5.

liability law renders conditions worse, for it assumes someone has done intentional wrong. That fundamental falsehood is at the heart of our present law."[80] The US Industrial Commission similarly suggested that employers' legal defenses were a holdover from a "lower stage of civilization" in which injuries arose from "personal carelessness on the part of the workers." In more recent conditions, however, each worker was "but a single private in an army," working "in a great institution, over the conditions of which he has little control." Machines used motor power of their own and working conditions were "chiefly determined by his employer and his fellow-workmen."[81] Under these conditions, individual workers could no longer control working conditions nor avoid injury by being prudent. There had been a kind of aggregation or collectivization in social practice, the Industrial Commission suggested, in which many employees became subsumed within the machinery of large-scale industry. This practice of economic and social aggregation had analogs in the aggregating forms of reason that reformers used.

For injury law reformers, the issue of wage earners' injuries needed to be removed from courts entirely because the courts were incapable of governing injuries in the way that the problem of injury demanded. As William Hard put it, "the deep-down vice of our present system of awarding compensation for accidents is that it depends on litigation."[82] Hard's emphasis on litigation expressed a sense among reformers that the problem with injury law was not actually existing courts, but any possible courts. Any litigation-based system of injury law, the argument went, would be inadequate and unjust. Overall, reformers brought to bear all of their ingenuity and conceptual innovation to make their case against the court-based system. They drew on a limited appeal to recognition, a sustained appeal to distributive justice, and new concepts of poverty and state responsibility that reflected a turn to biopolitical rationality (via insurance). They expressed similarly biopolitical concerns over family breakdown and, as a result, loss of human capital that would cost both working-class people and the state. They used these conceptual tools to describe the present as afflicted with unacceptable ills, ills that could be avoided if employee injury ceased to be handled by lawsuit.

---

[80] Henderson, *Compensation or Insurance versus Employers' Liability*, 57.
[81] US Industrial Commission, *Final Report of the Industrial Commission* (Washington: Government Printing Office, 1902), 893–894.
[82] Hard, *Injured in the Course of Duty*, 61.

Policymakers would soon pass workmen's compensation laws along the lines of what reformers like Hard and Eastman called for, ending the tyranny of the trial and replacing it with the tyranny of the table. In this chapter, I have emphasized the notions of justice present in those calls, in order to assess those calls and the resulting legislation. I have suggested that distributive justice came to predominate in a way that left less room for justice as recognition. Reformers' primary concern with regard to injury and justice was that employee injury law unfairly inflicted poverty: injury impoverished. This was, to be sure, an important criticism, but the relative lack of attention to justice as recognition expresses what was itself an impoverished understanding of injury and its effects. It should be no surprise, then, that the law that satisfied reformers' criticisms became itself morally impoverished.

Appeals to distributive justice were part of how injury law reformers politicized the interruption of wages that law made result from injury. This approach defined injury as a financial problem, and therefore a problem remediable with money: hence, compensation laws. Reformers documented and dramatized a host of what they took to be good reasons for that policy. They no doubt understood the real human suffering involved in these aspects of injury, especially those reformers like Eastman who spent time in the homes of working-class people. At the same time, a host of other aspects of injury fell out in the process. Injury law reformers politicized some aspects of the injury problem and depoliticized others. They took it as a given that markets would remain compulsory, that firms would operate in the ways that created injuries and, therefore, that injury would persist. Injury rates might be reduced by incentive – by appeal to the instrumental self-interest of firms – but only reduced, not eliminated. The economy would continue to kill, and those deaths would be impersonally conceptualized: merely unfortunate, no one's fault, and inevitable. Injury law reformers like Hard and Eastman called on their readers to demand more distributive justice for injured people. At the same time, they did so in a way that accidentally encouraged their readers to restrict their imaginations. Reformers implicitly, and despite themselves, urged readers to settle for laws that largely abandoned justice recognition and to settle for labor practices and class relationships that killed and maimed working-class people. Worse still, they implicitly encouraged readers not to realize they were settling for less. Reformers helped create a kind of institutional opening, pointing out shortcomings of the tyranny of the trial and proposing a policy solution, and they did so in a way that kept that opening small. They thus expressed both outrage and complacency, hope and resignation.[83] Other reformers, as the next chapter details, sought to address employee injury in a way that allowed even less space for justice.

[83] Political theorist Goran Therborn has written that "[r]esignation, like fear, derives from consideration of what is possible in the given situation. But whereas obedience out of fear is contingent upon the presently prevailing constellation of force and is quite compatible with maintaining a belief in the possibility of a better alternative in the future, resignation has more deep-seated connotations. It connotes a more profoundly pessimistic view of the possibilities of change." Resignation, Therborn argued, designates "obedience that derives from conceptions of the practical impossibility of a better alternative." The resigned neither cower in fear nor consent to their fate, but see the fate to which they are consigned as both unacceptable and inevitable. Resignation helps secure institutional arrangements and social orders in a way that in a sense produces legitimacy, but a different kind of legitimacy than one premised on any facets of the current situation other than the situation's real existence. That there is no alternative possibility is in important respects a different kind of justification for a situation than consenting to that situation – how can one withhold consent to something that is the only thing possible? One does not consent to gravity, one accommodates to it. Goran Therborn, *The Ideology of Power and the Power of Ideology* (London: Verso, 1980), 99. In my view the limits of injury law reformers are especially salient given that there was in this era a widespread conversation in parts of the working class and the labor movement about taking much more aggressive steps to attenuate market dependency, including public ownership of enterprise and a right to a job, and in some cases, among parts of the socialist and revolutionary left, ending market-dependency altogether as part of ending capitalism. That is to say, injury law reformers wrote about injury not just in a way that falls short of the abstract concepts of justice I have articulated retroactively, but which was in contrast to much more thorough-going social criticism by some of these reformers' contemporaries. See, for example, Jeffrey A. Johnson, *"They Are All Red out Here": Socialist Politics in the Pacific Northwest, 1895–1925* (Norman: University of Oklahoma Press, 2009), and Salvatore Salerno, *Red November, Black November: Culture and Community in the Industrial Workers of the World* (Albany: State University of the New York Press, 1989). For an overview of some of the recent literature on radicalism in the Progressive Era, in the context of the broader historiography of the period, see Adam Quinn, "Reforming History: Contemporary Scholarship on the Progressive Era," H-SHGAPE, May 9, 2017, https://networks.h-net.org/node/20317/discussions/179222/reforming-history-con temporary-scholarship-progressive-era, accessed June 15, 2017. I am unable to give those criticisms serious attention here due to limits of space, but also because my emphasis is not on subordinate or alternative perspectives so much as on those perspectives which became dominant and informed the operations of state and employer power.

3

Suffering and the Price of Life and Limb

"While awaiting justice the widow and orphans suffer," Illinois Senator Edward Glackin wrote in the final line of his 1906 editorial calling for workmen's compensation. He immediately added, "and the state suffers, from the very fact that it must take care of those who are unable to care for themselves." Those rendered destitute due to the slow workings of the court system sometimes received charitable support, which came out of government funds or from society's resources, the efficient use of which were ultimately the state's responsibility. Glackin did not directly argue that these forms of suffering were the same or were morally equivalent, though the placement of the state's suffering within a position of emphasis in the article's final sentence did serve to call attention to the importance of the "suffering" the state endured due to the economic losses of injury. Glackin's expressed concern for a third suffering as well. Both the "employer and the employe," he wrote, "are suffering from the ill effects of the common law." Hence compensation laws that removed courts from the handling of employee injury would be "a great benefit" and "satisfactory to both."[1]

Glackin's concern that "the state suffers" and that "the employer" was "suffering" because of the tyranny of the trial exemplify two of the main objects of analysis for this chapter. This chapter uses the terms "instrumental-reform perspective," "business-protection perspective," and "social-justice reform perspective" to distinguish three different

---

[1] Edward J. Glackin, "Life and Limb Too Cheap," reprinted in *Industrial Insurance: The Need of Providing Aid for Injured Workingmen and Their Dependent Families* (n.p., 1907), 2–3. Originally printed in *Chicago Daily News*, December 10, 1906, 2.

approaches to the problems of employee injury law. These perspectives were conceptually distinct but were often braided together, as in Glackin's editorial. Glackin believed that different perspectives on employee injury law and different social interests could be harmonized: policy could be a benefit "satisfactory to both" employees and employers. Glackin did not address whether these different perspectives and interests would find compensation laws equally satisfactory, let alone equally beneficial.

Indeed, these different perspectives were often incompatible. Within the instrumental-reform perspective and business-protection perspective, as this chapter emphasizes, working-class people were abstract economic objects for instrumental use, a perspective that allowed no space for recognition of working-class humanity. This chapter concludes with a return to commodification, a theme implicit in the title of Glackin's editorial: "Life and Limb Too Cheap." Injury, under the tyranny of the table, would have a proper and easily determinable price, deepening the poverty of the law's notion of injury.

THE STATE SUFFERS

The state "suffered" due to the effects of injury- and law-induced financial hardships on working-class families. The state suffered from the "fact that it must take care of those who are unable to care for themselves," Glackin wrote. This statement expressed a biopolitical notion of the state, the state as caregiver for the population. Again, Glackin was in the company of Eastman and Hard and others discussed in Chapter 2 in his biopolitical outlook. The concern with the state's well-being specifically, however, rather than the well-being of the population as an end in itself, marks a difference between the approach to biopolitics within the social-justice reform perspective and the instrumental-reform perspective. These perspectives converged on the point that injury impoverished, but differed as to why poverty was a problem. The instrumental-reform perspective took injury- and law-induced poverty as a problem for social stability. Lurking within that understanding was another sense of working-class people again as abstract objects, specifically as objects of instrumental use.

In his speech to the 1909 national compensation conference, Miles Dawson voiced concern for how the state suffered biopolitically. Dawson argued that the problem of employee injury needed to be approached from what he called "a general economic standpoint," as distinct from "the standpoint of the interests of the workingmen themselves, and their families." This was not a position partisan to any particular class, for the general standpoint "includes the employers' position."[2] Dawson argued this perspective should inform state policy. Government should provide for the health of the economy as a whole in a way that individual economic actors could not. This view took working-class well-being as important because it was instrumentally valuable to the economy and society as a whole.[3]

Attendees at the 1909 compensation conference repeatedly returned to the theme of the state–economy–population nexus, discussing the relationships between economy and society, between the market and social reproduction, and between economic rationality and other forms of rationality. George Gillette of the Minnesota Commission on Employers' Liability said that compensation laws must be "approached both from the standpoint of the employer and the employee, with a spirit of compromising and doing that which will accomplish the greatest good." For Gillette, the problem of injury was a political problem to be navigated in light of the greater good. The state had to think economically, but it had to do so in a way that constituted and maintained the economy itself, which was different from the way that interested actors situated within the economy thought. Market actors served their own interests within the context of the market.

---

[2] *Report of Atlantic City Conference on Workmen's Compensation Acts, July 1909* (n.p., n.d.), 13. See also David A. Moss, *Socializing Security: Progressive Era Economists and the Origins of American Social Policy* (Cambridge, MA: Harvard University Press, 1996), 80.

[3] Later in 1909 and in early 1910, Dawson would serve as legal counsel to striking garment workers. Dawson most certainly sought to help the strikers win. At the same time, that service can be understood in multiple ways. It can be thought of as straightforward partisanship, one interest group over another, and it can be thought of as in service to society's higher principles – such as that of equal treatment before the law – against those who might infringe on that principle. Or both. Lawyers in service of causes often live in that conceptual overlap, representing individuals and groups with interests but who are also denied their access to what everyone already ought to have. This latter sense of lawyers as representatives of the general interest was apparent in economic and employment-related commissions much of the time in this era. Often one or more business owners and union leaders would sit as representatives of their specific interest groups, accompanied by one or more lawyers as representatives of the general public and the general interest. Dawson had a second relationship to the general interest than that of his legal training, namely, his actuarial training. If as a lawyer Dawson should have understood the rights and obligations of individuals and sought to foster rule of law, as an actuary Dawson would have understood statistical averages and the laws of large numbers and of economic forces, which both shaped and were shaped by law in the judicial and legislative sense of the term. See Laura Bufano Edge, *We Stand as One: The International Ladies Garment Workers' Strike, New York 1909* (Minneapolis: Twenty First Century Books, 2011), 77, and Richard A. Greenwald, *The Triangle Fire, the Protocols of Peace, and Industrial Democracy in Progressive Era* (Philadelphia: Temple University Press, 2005), 45.

The state should act to shape and, by doing so, preserve the market as a whole in ways that market actors could not adequately do.[4]

The instrumental-reform perspective and the social-justice reform perspective overlapped in the view that the state needed to act biopolitically; they shared a sense that markets were of limited use in coordinating and steering society when it came to working-class health. These perspectives differed, however, on the purposes of state intervention. The social justice perspective emphasized working-class well-being as an end in itself, notwithstanding some differences of emphasis on justice as distribution or as recognition. The instrumental-reform perspective focused less on justice of any sort and more on social order: the state should protect the economy by preventing the economy from using up human raw material at an unsustainably fast pace.[5]

Concerns over recognition were especially hard to mesh with the instrumental perspective. Indeed, some statements of the instrumental-reform perspective explicitly stated a need to set aside recognition. Fred Gray, an insurance company official, argued that "[e]ndeavor as we may to keep before us [the] human aspects" of the problem of workplace injury, "the whole problem is necessarily an economic one and in its final analysis we must count the cost."[6] Making the "human aspects" less of a priority amounted to saying that justice as recognition needed to be bracketed. What he did not say was that this approach set aside distributive justice as well, substituting instead a notion of working-class people as objects of instrumental use. James Harrington Boyd similarly set aside what Gray called the "human aspects" of injury when he declared that in an era that had become newly sensitive to the need for conservation of natural resources, Americans were insufficiently aware of the need for "the conservation of the human being, the conservation of the working man, who is the corner-stone of the state."[7]

---

[4] Michel Aglietta, "Capitalism at the Turn of the Century: Regulation Theory and the Challenge of Social Change," *New Left Review*, no. 232 (1998): 41–90.

[5] I do not mean to suggest here that biopolitics always or only serves the market. Rather, my point is that one strand of biopolitics in capitalist societies is devoted to the long-term needs of capitalism. Biopolitical projects are an understandable response on the part of some people to problems predictably generated by capitalism. This response and attempt at problem solving is not an automatic process, nor is it a foregone conclusion that all biopolitics would be pro-market. Christopher Tomlins's remarks on the explanatory limits of "the needs of capital" are salient here. Christopher Tomlins, *Law, Labor and Ideology in the Early American Republic* (Cambridge: Cambridge University Press, 1993), 294.

[6] *Report of Atlantic City Conference*, 315.

[7] James Harrington Boyd, *Workmen's Compensation, or Insurance against Loss of Wages Arising out of Industrial Accidents* (Columbus: F. J. Heer Printing Co., 1911), 5.

Like Boyd, Charles Henderson, a sociologist who served on the Illinois
Workingmen's Insurance Commission, argued that there was a desperate
need for "human conservation." Henderson worried that the rate of
consumption of workers was so high that industry would use up so many
workers that there wouldn't be enough left to do business. In a public
speech, he said:

> Economists show that there are two prime sources of wealth. One of these is the
> material of nature ... and the other is labor ... and health of workmen, regarded
> merely as a simple instrument, is vital for the production of wealth.... We should
> conserve our labor power more than anything else, and we are destroying it
> through negligence, not criminal intent but by criminal neglect.[8]

The "simple instrument" of working-class health needed to be managed carefully so as to allow continued "production of wealth." For
Henderson this management had important political stakes, namely, that
of protecting the nation, a notion that took an ugly eugenic overtone.
Henderson argued for compensation laws in part because, he believed,
"we are producing a new set of degenerates" as a result of employee
injuries. These "degenerates" needed to be "segregated" from the rest of
the population in order "to protect the future race," in Henderson's view.
After segregation, he said, these accident-created degenerates, like all
others, should be eliminated: "what we ought to do is to establish a
system in which the State takes those persons who are unfit for propaga-
tion and isolates them; then our philanthropy during the next forty or fifty
years would segregate the unfit in places where they would be treated
humanely but not permitted to propagate. This would, in turn, help to rid
society of an endless load and without suffering." Using a eugenics-
derived vocabulary of the fit and unfit, Henderson warned that
working-class people's working conditions and the results of accidents
affected future generations of working-class people. These conditions
could mean that "the children of laboring men" would grow up "unfit
for use in our community industries, and for parenthood." As result the
United States would have to "constantly import larger and larger
numbers of men from other countries." If that happened, Henderson

---

[8] Charles Henderson, *Compensation or Insurance versus Employers' Liability: Address at
the Sixteenth Annual Meeting of the Central Supply Association* (n.p., 1910), 54. Marian
Moser Jones has noted that American Red Cross officials in this era similarly discussed
their efforts as a form of conservation of human resources. See Marian Moser Jones, *The
American Red Cross from Clara Barton to the New Deal* (Baltimore: Johns Hopkins
University Press, 2013), 146–147, 154.

warned, "[t]his will retard our civilization."[9] In calling for compensation laws, Henderson articulated an economic view within which working-class people were a valuable raw material to use in a sensible economic fashion. Mingled with that view was a eugenic, nationalist, and xenophobic political concern for what Henderson saw as a need to protect the nation.[10] Both of these views treated working-class people as objects "fit for use" instrumentally.

Judge Nathaniel French spoke in a similar spirit to the Iowa Employers' Liability Commission:

The workman, now almost always an employe, is an essential factor of society. An adequate supply of workmen, and the more skillful the better, is of untold economic value to the state. The supply will be most adequate, other things being equal, in the state which protects them so far as may be from accidents, and which compensates them for the injury when the misfortune of an accident befalls them.[11]

We find here no human aspects, no concern to alleviate poverty because poverty was wrong. Instead, the only concern was careful management of "essential factors" to be kept in "adequate supply" for the sake of "economic value."

TOO CHEAP

By the late nineteenth century, some political economists had begun to theorize the role of the working-class family in capitalist society. Some of

---

[9] Henderson, *Compensation or Insurance versus Employers' Liability*, 54–56. Henderson serves as an example of the lethal potential that is the flip side of biopolitical conservation of life.

[10] To be categorized as unfit has often meant to be subject to terrible oppression and denial of recognition. See Susan M. Schweik, *The Ugly Laws: Disability in Public* (New York: New York University Press, 2009). On the other hand, without wishing to minimize the violence that has gone with being consigned to "unfit," the implied opposite of Henderson's "unfit for use" is "fit for use," hardly a beacon of freedom and recognition. The fit outrank the unfit, but at least in Henderson's phrasing neither were conceptualized as humans with dignity. They were both objects to be sorted instrumentally into those it was convenient to use and those it was not. The latter sensibility, that of seeing some people as unfit, has been largely discredited by subsequent social changes. The former, that of seeing some people as fitted well to instrumental use by others, has continued or even proliferated further. See Christopher Tomlins, "'Those Who Are Used': A Commentary on *The Employee: A Political History*, by Jean-Christian Vinel," *Labor History* 59, no. 2 (2018): 255–263. See also Chris O'Kane, "'Society Maintains Itself Despite All the Catastrophes That May Eventuate': Critical Theory, Negative Totality, and Crisis," *Constellations* 25, no. 2 (2018): 287–301.

[11] Iowa Employers' Liability and Workmen's Compensation Commission, *Report of Employers' Liability Commission*, 246.

these political economists understood working-class families as important for the reproduction of the economy and understood that families require income in order to play this role. Economic disruption of working-class family income was thus a kind of self-sabotage by the market.[12] Political economists' writing was part of the broader intellectual and cultural context within which injury law reform occurred. This writing can also help analytically clarify some of the issues involved in the relationship between family and economy, issues to which compensation laws responded. "Work is to the workman that which is necessary for the maintenance of himself and of his family," wrote Matteo Liberatore in *Principles of Political Economy* in 1889. Since work provided wages used to purchase the necessities of life, loss of access to income could disrupt families' "maintenance."[13]

Liberatore began *Principles of Political Economy* with an exercise in word origins which linked economy with family: "Economy is a Greek word, from *oikos*, house, and *nomos*, distribution; and according to this etymology it was at first used to signify domestic administration.... From the family this word was afterwards extended to the city or State (in Greek *polis*), as referring to the property of a whole people, under the name of social or public wealth."[14] Liberatore did not point out that the Greek *nomos* also has overtones of law and authority as well.[15] From early on, economy, family, and law were interwoven both in etymology and in social practice.

---

[12] Nancy Fraser and Rahel Jaeggi discuss the potential for capitalism to pose this kind of threat to itself in terms of what they call a crisis of social reproduction. They argue that all versions of capitalism will have a tendency toward social reproduction crisis, along with other tendencies toward crisis. See Nancy Fraser and Rahel Jaeggi, *Capitalism: A Conversation in Critical Theory* (Cambridge: Polity, 2018). I find their analysis of social reproduction crises illuminating but I am skeptical of their implication that in a crisis capitalism becomes especially vulnerable and thus more subject to being replaced by a new social system. I suspect that capitalism actually reproduces itself through crises, such that a period of greater frequency of crisis is one in which society is even more likely to remain capitalist.

[13] Matteo Liberatore, *Principles of Political Economy* (New York: Benziger and Co., 1891), i. Liberatore's book was written in 1889 but published in English in 1891.

[14] Liberatore, *Principles of Political Economy*, i. See also Christopher Tomlins's discussion of *oikos* in early America: *Freedom Bound: Law, Labor, and Civic Identity in Colonizing English America, 1580–1865* (New York: Cambridge University Press, 2010), 376–400.

[15] Classics scholars Stephen Todd and Paul Millett refer to the "meeting of law, society and politics in the idea of *nomos*." Stephen Todd and Paul Millett, "Law, Society, and Athens," in *Nomos: Essays in Athenian Law, Politics and Society*, ed. Paul Cartledge, Paul Millett, and Stephen Todd (Cambridge: Cambridge University Press, 1990), 1–19; 12.

In defining political economy as "the science of public wealth," Liberatore equivocated on the role of family. He noted that "public wealth" was distinct from "private economy, which belongs to the private person or the family."[16] Thus the family was outside political economy. And yet, he wrote, "the concrete man either is the father of a family or belongs to a family; and as such he should be considered."[17] Thus to think about actual persons, political economy had to consider the family. Some other late nineteenth- and early twentieth-century economists recognized the importance of the family to the capitalist economy as well. As Richard Ely put it, "The Family is to be kept in view as the true social unit in all economic discussion."[18]

Alfred Marshall argued that "[t]he most valuable of all capital is that invested in human beings," adding that "the most precious part is the result of the care and influence of the mother." Thus, "in estimating the cost of production of efficient labour, we must often take as our unit the family."[19] In his 1888 *Economic Studies*, Walter Bagehot wrote that "a good mother of a family causes more wealth than half the men, for she trains the beginning boys to be fit for the world, and to make wealth; and if she fails at that beginning the boys will be worse gold finders all their lives."[20] Families produced future wage earners – sellers of labor power – and future unwaged mothers – unwaged producers of labor power. Both were required for the continuation of the economy.

Working-class families required incomes in order to play their role in reproducing society and economy. If working-class families were deprived of income, working-class women would have to spend more time on securing monetary income in the form of wages and less time investing "capital" in children by "training" them to be future workers. William Jevons wrote, "Economists have supposed that there must be some amount of wages which is the least that a working man can live upon and rear a family so as to maintain the support of labour."[21] Liberatore agreed: "the natural price of a man's labour is the price which, inclusive of the wife's earnings . . . will suffice to maintain him and her and two or

[16] Liberatore, *Principles of Political Economy*, xvii.
[17] Liberatore, *Principles of Political Economy*, 290.
[18] Richard Theodore Ely, *An Introduction to Political Economy* (New York: Hunt & Eaton, 1893), 261.
[19] Alfred Marshall, *Principles of Economics*, vol. 1 (London: Macmillan, 1898), 647.
[20] Walter Bagehot, *Economic Studies* (London: Longman, Green, 1888), 173.
[21] William Stanley Jevons, *The Principles of Economics: A Fragment of a Treatise on the Industrial Mechanism of Society* (London: Macmillan, 1905), 233.

three little children." If wage earners received income below this "natural price," "they will not answer the intentions of nature."[22] That is to say, below a certain income threshold, wages became less able to serve a role in the maintenance of working-class families and the bearing and raising of children. If the economy did not provide families with sufficient income, the "unnatural" result would be greater scarcity of labor power and reduced social production of wealth. These economic theories implied that allocating resources to preserving working-class families was a good investment by the state, because it helped those families continue to raise the labor power for sale within labor markets and upon which capitalism rested. This perspective differed qualitatively from the call to help working-class families for reasons of justice. These theories conceptualized working-class people as objects for instrumental use, specifically as commodities. Families became productive units. Raising children became the use of capital investments to produce objects for sale on the market. Human beings became those objects, "efficient labor" with costs of production and prices.[23]

Compensation laws can be seen as operating in the spirit of these theories.[24] Injuries reduced employees' income below the so-called

---

[22] Liberatore, *Principles of Political Economy*, 181.

[23] Some might object that the people were not commodified; their labor or labor power was. That is a fiction that helps avoid the reality of human commodification. Every thing or being in which someone is instrumentally interested has qualities that go beyond that instrumental interest, qualities toward which that instrumental interest is indifferent. That employers are interested only in working-class people as labor power is an expression of that indifference. Hired hands may be for an employer merely hands, with the person to which they are appendages a matter of indifference. That person is still there, subject to that hiring and that indifference. That a process of commodification picks out only some qualities of a person as the economically valuable aspect does not mean that the person is not commodified. It means that parts of that person are discarded within the process of commodification.

[24] Marxist feminists later made somewhat similar claims, as part of criticisms of both capitalism and patriarchy, with the crucial exception that Marxist feminists wrote in protest against the organization of society around instrumentalizing human beings. Jeanne Boydston's *Home and Work* historicizes the relationship between work and wages in the United States. Male wage earners in the nineteenth century began to claim that their waged work supported families, in the attempt to claim greater status and dignity as well as to prop up their demands for higher wages from employers. Rhetorical emphasis on the fact that wages matter to wage earners' households transformed into the notion that working-class households' economic lives are reducible to waged income, thus obfuscating the importance of unwaged activities in households and in the economy as a whole. This obfuscation erased feminized labors and highlighted masculinized labors. Jeanne Boydston, *Home and Work: Housework, Wages, and the Ideology of Labor in the Early Republic* (New York: Oxford University Press, 1990). As Michael Hardt and Antonio

natural price of labor power, meaning the level at which working-class people's families can subsist in a way that is conducive to social and economic stability. Furthermore, these discussions presumed that working-class people were knowable as objects with monetary value – that is, prices. Employee injury law reform was in some respects a conversation about how to best institutionalize that pricing, rooted in a complaint that courts were pricing injury in an irrational fashion.

OPEN TO ATTACK

The social-justice reform perspectives viewed the common law of employee injury as causing suffering for working-class people (often specifically suffering via poverty, as Chapter 2 discussed). Glackin expressed an instrumental-reform perspective when he worried that "the state suffer[ed]" from the socioeconomic effects of the law. Despite their important differences, these perspectives overlapped in a focus on non-payment: the problem of employee injury was largely that courts compensated too little for injury. This line of reform thinking fits with legal scholar Lawrence Friedman's assessment that the court-based system of injury law in the late nineteenth century was characterized by non-compensation.[25]

From the business-protection perspective, however, the problem was a different one. As Glackin expressed it, the "employer is open to attack from the unscrupulous lawyer and in many cases is compelled to insure in a casualty company in order to protect himself against such attacks."[26] Miles Dawson argued similarly in his remarks at the 1909 compensation conference when he said that "sharp lawyer[s]" knew how to use moving stories of injury against employers.[27] In Dawson's view, workmen's

Negri have written, the definition of labor "always depends on the existing values of a given social and historical context" and so "is not given or fixed, but rather historically and socially determined." Michael Hardt and Antonio Negri, *Labor of Dionysus: A Critique of the State-Form* (Minneapolis: University of Minnesota Press, 1994), 8. See also Mariarosa Dalla Costa and Selma James, *The Power of Women and the Subversion of the Community* (Bristol: Falling Wall Press, 1972); Silvia Federici, *Caliban and the Witch: Women, the Body and Primitive Accumulation* (New York: Autonomedia, 2004); and Leopoldina Fortunati, *The Arcane of Reproduction* (New York: Autonomedia, 1995).

[25] See Lawrence M. Friedman, "Civil Wrongs: Personal Injury Law in the Late 19th Century," *American Bar Foundation Research Journal* 12, nos. 2–3 (Spring–Summer 1987): 351–378.

[26] Glackin, "Life and Limb Too Cheap," 2.   [27] *Report of Atlantic City Conference*, 26.

compensation laws would remove the narrative and rhetorical component of employee injury law and sidestep the power of juries. The result would be a system for handling employee injuries as "a purely business matter."[28] Employee injury law reform is a "business proposition," Hugh Mercer argued similarly at the 1910 national compensation conference, adding that workmen's compensation is "good business for the business men."[29]

Dawson and Mercer voiced a complaint different from that of lack of compensation. If anything, this line of thinking went, compensation was too frequent and too high. That the tyranny of the trial compensated too little and too infrequently and that it compensated too much and too often were opposite in emphasis, but both could be true. Each in a sense was true to a social position. The handling of injury by courts could be simultaneously so infrequent and meager that it was a distributive injustice inflicted on working-class people and a potential threat to labor reproduction and socioeconomic stability, and yet also so frequent and in high enough amounts that it threatened businesses.

Each assessment reflected a different aspect of the challenges of market dependency as those challenges manifested in the lives of people in different social positions. Working-class people needed money to get goods and services. When deprived of money those families faced deprivation. The population in the aggregate was at risk as a result because families facing deprivation might not serve their role in stocking the labor markets of tomorrow with human commodities. These dangers came from low, delayed, or infrequent injury compensation.

Marguerite Murray's case helps demonstrate the truth of these assessments. Her lawsuit, including two appeals, took five years. At her weekly wage of five dollars per week, she lost roughly $1,300 over the duration of the appeal process. Murray eventually won her suit, and her employer was ordered to pay $15,000 (adjusted for inflation, equivalent to nearly $400,000), a large sum for an unbudgeted expense. Thus, courts could be both too uncertain and slow to meet the obligations of either justice for working-class people or social stability, and yet award plaintiffs money at high enough levels to crimp businesses' ability to remain competitive and profitable.

---

[28] *Report of Atlantic City Conference*, 16.
[29] *Proceedings: Third National Conference*, 118.

The business-protection perspective emphasized the latter, the threat to businesses, as Glackin and Dawson voiced.[30] Another key element of the business-protection perspective was that the legal situation was not static but was progressively inflicting more financial "suffering" on employers. Employee injury lawsuits seem to have been rising in frequency, such that employers were losing more and more often, with damage awards against businesses rising as well. We do not have a precise tally of how often plaintiffs in employee injury lawsuits won or lost, but existing historical scholarship supports the business-protection view of what was happening in courts. By 1910 half of all court cases in Washington State were employee injury suits.[31] Historian Paul Bellamy analyzed the records of courts in Cuyahoga County, Ohio, and found that the American Steel and Wire Company, a U.S. Steel subsidiary based in Cleveland, lost every one of the 127 lawsuits brought by injured employees between 1898 and 1915. Based on this analysis, Bellamy argues that there was in fact in this era a court-based system of injury compensation, rather than non-compensation.[32]

For an example of increased frequency of injury suits, between 1867 and 1899, the Minnesota Supreme Court heard 275 appeals in employee injury lawsuits. From 1900 to 1913, the Court heard 487 such cases. In every year from 1900 through 1913 the Minnesota Supreme Court was more likely to find in favor of an employee than an employer in an injury suit. The vast majority of suits were brought as appeals by employers, and yet employers' chances of winning their suits was quite low – on average, employers had less than a one in five chance of winning. These odds seemed to be getting

---

[30] Dawson also implied that the goals emphasized within the business-protection perspective related harmoniously to the goals of the instrumental perspective, by arguing that the court system was a wasteful and inefficient use of society's resources.

[31] Joseph Tripp, "An Instance of Labor and Business Cooperation: Workmen's Compensation in Washington State," *Labor History*, 17, no. 4 (1976): 530–550, 537.

[32] Paul Bellamy, "From Court Room to Board Room: Immigration, Juries, Corporations and the Creation of an American Proletariat: A History of Workmen's Compensation, 1898–1915" (PhD diss., Case Western Reserve University, 1994), Bellamy further argues that compensation laws stripped working-class people of their right to trial, which was a downgrading in their citizenship. To underscore this loss of rights, Bellamy refers to compensation laws as turning US working-class people into a proletariat, in the sense of people without rights. Bellamy's remarks recall Marx's description of the working class as free and rightless. Marx meant free in the sense of free to enter the market, an ironic point on Marx's part intended to point out that the working class is in fact compelled to be in the market. That freedom is in a sense the flip side of proletarian rightlessness: calling the market voluntary serves to minimize rights claims by working-class people.

worse for employers over time as well.[33] At the national level, economists Price Fishback and Shawn Kantor count 154 state supreme court cases dealing with workplace injury in 1900. This number rose every year until 1909, when there were 484 such cases. [34]

Injury suit frequency seems to have been an important factor in the creation of compensation laws, as does the win rate of plaintiffs. Early adoption of compensation laws correlated with high numbers of employee injury–related state supreme court cases. All states saw rises in these kinds of cases. As Fishback and Kantor put it, the crucial factor in the creation of compensation laws was a sharp "increase [in] the uncertainty of the negligence liability system" for employers.[35] Employers and trade associations responded to this increasing uncertainty with growing support for the creation of compensation laws.[36]

One measure of growing uncertainty for employers – which is to say, the growing shift from non-compensation to court-based compensation – is employers' liability insurance. Both Glackin and Dawson highlighted the rise of employers' liability insurance as a problem facing businesses. In 1887 employers' liability insurance companies collected more than $200,000 in premiums across the United States (equivalent to more than $5 million today). By 1908, employers' liability insurance premiums had grown to $28 million per year (equivalent to more than $700 million today).[37] By 1912 employers' liability insurance premiums in the United States had risen to $35 million (equivalent to almost $830 million today).[38]

---

[33] This paragraph is based on my count using the *Minnesota Digest, 1851 to Date* (St. Paul: West Publishing Co., 1988). State Supreme Court cases have limitations as a source but they provide some sense of trends in this era, and employers, especially large companies operating on a national scale, would have paid attention to such cases.

[34] Price Fishback and Shawn Everett Kantor, *A Prelude to the Welfare State: The Origins of Workers' Compensation* (Chicago: University of Chicago Press, 2000), 95. My point is not that the court system worked for working-class people – after all, a long delay due to appeals could be punitive and harmful to an injured employee; clearly workers' well-being was not served by the process. Rather, my point is that the court system had ceased to work for the employing class.

[35] Fishback and Kantor, *A Prelude to the Welfare State*, 88; see generally 88–113.

[36] See James Weinstein, "Big Business and the Origins of Workmen's Compensation," *Labor History* 8 (Spring 1967): 156–174, and Paul Bellamy, "From Court Room to Board Room."

[37] David A. Moss, *When All Else Fails: Government as the Ultimate Risk Manager* (Cambridge, MA: Harvard University Press, 2002), 164. Inflation adjustment calculated via inflation calculator at www.westegg.com/inflation/, accessed January 7, 2018.

[38] Roy Lubove, *The Struggle for Social Security 1900–1935* (Cambridge, MA: Harvard University Press, 1968), 261.

The increase in premiums can be attributed to two causes. More employers purchased insurance in this era, seeking control over the employer-side financial risks of employee injury. The increase also reflects the rise in the cost of liability insurance. In Washington State, for example, between 1905 and 1910, employers' liability insurance rates rose from $0.45 per $100 of payroll to $1.50, an increase of over 300 percent.[39] Rising premiums meant that employers' liability insurance was an increasing cost, itself thus a source of uncertainty for employers, albeit a lower uncertainty than that of being uninsured.

Insurers exiting certain markets threatened employers further by reducing employers' ability to manage risk. Courts could sometimes become so unpredictable, and payments for plaintiffs so high, that some insurance companies stopped offering employers' liability policies altogether in certain jurisdictions.[40] That loss of insurance options both exposed employers to more risk and signaled to employers the generally uncertain character of their legal and economic situation with regard to employee injury.

While employers' liability insurance premiums were straightforward costs for employers, they also were evidence that the problem of employers' liability costs in court was not only unresolved, but worsening. In both facets, increasing liability insurance premiums likely encouraged employers to favor compensation laws. Insurance provided a mechanism to restore some certainty to employers, but only some. The accident problem threatened to overwhelm insurers' risk management capacity because that capacity needed to be profitable.

One source of the growing uncertainty that courts posed for employers came from within the courts themselves. Legal historian Peter Karsten argues that late nineteenth-century courts developed an increasing willingness to compensate injured plaintiffs for pain and suffering, which increased damage awards.[41] Karsten attributes this change in part to

---

[39] Tripp, "An Instance of Labor and Business Cooperation," 537.

[40] Fishback and Kantor, *A Prelude to the Welfare State*, 97. Fishback and Kantor found that legally and legislatively generated uncertainty for businesses was a significant factor in the passage of compensation laws, as were insurance premiums that rose in response to those same factors.

[41] Peter Karsten, *Heart versus Head: Judge-Made Law in Nineteenth-Century America* (Chapel Hill: University of North Carolina Press, 1997), 276–290. See also the discussion on pain and suffering in Barbara Young Welke, *Recasting American Liberty: Gender, Race, Law, and the Railroad Revolution, 1865–1920* (New York: Cambridge University Press, 2001), 125–136. For an account of employers' liability law earlier in the nineteenth century, see Tomlins, *Law, Labor and Ideology*, 372–381.

changes in political perspectives tied to the rise of Populism and the election of judges. One crucial component to this perspective was skepticism or even outright hostility toward big businesses. As Karsten puts it, "as soon as careless corporations appeared on the scene, they were sent signals about accountability and carefulness via their 'pocket nerve.' These signals were sensitive to the pocket's contents: The individual who assailed paid less than the doctor who delicted, who paid less than the careless city, which paid less than the reckless railroad" or other big business.[42]

Another source of growing legal uncertainty for businesses came from legislation. In an early wave of reform, numerous states passed legislation designed to open some gaps or to lower the wall of employers' legal defenses. By 1901 seven states had created such legislation, making it easier for workers to win injury lawsuits. By 1910, twenty-three states had such laws. Many more states had similar laws applicable only to specific industries viewed as especially dangerous, such as mining.[43] These laws made it easier for employees to win their suits and so increased the threat of employer "suffering" of the kind Glackin worried about.

Retaining the trial as the means for handling employee injuries meant that employers' liability laws left open the possibility for Glackin's other worries, that of working-class people's suffering and the "suffering" of the state. Courts might still move too slowly and find against plaintiffs in employee injury suits often enough that suits would foster working-class poverty. This meant that liability laws were inadequate from the social-justice reform perspective, the instrumental-reform perspective, and the business-protection perspective. Thus, the different reform perspectives converged on compensation laws.

THE EMPLOYER SUFFERS

As noted above, one way to understand the differences among the social-justice reform perspective, the instrumental-reform perspective, and the business-protection perspective is to see them as emphasizing the needs of

---

[42] Karsten, *Heart versus Head*, 288–290. In addition to the sympathetic emotional and political responses that Karsten credits, it is also possible that judges were interested in preserving the role of courts in the governance of injury. This could be understood cynically in the sense of judges not wanting to lose social prestige by having their institutions demoted, or as judges wanting to keep themselves in business, but it could also be understood more charitably: at least some legal professionals likely believed in courts as important for the good of society and as good institutions of governance.

[43] See Fishback and Kantor, *A Prelude to the Welfare State*, 95.

different constituencies: the needs of the working class, the needs of capitalist society, or the needs of actually existing capitalists. These needs do not always align. Reformers such as Charles Henderson, voicing the instrumental-reform perspective, argued that compensation laws were in the interest of US society and the economy as a whole; capitalism needed these changes, he thought. While Henderson thought US capitalism needed compensation laws, what capitalism needs is not sufficient as an explanation as to why compensation laws succeeded. Capitalism does not always get what it needs, including from capitalists, because capitalists do not necessarily do what capitalist society needs. Hence the needs of capitalism do not explain the actions of capitalists. Capitalists are not capitalism; they are themselves market-dependent actors within – which is to say, subject to – capitalism. This means in part that the needs of capitalism are a concept of limited explanatory power: needs can go unmet, breakdown is possible.[44] "Interests," as the economic sociologist Karl Polanyi explained, "like intents, remain platonic unless they are translated into politics by the means of some social instrumentality."[45] That is to say, how social needs are met is itself in need of explanation. That meeting of needs is heavily constrained by the weight of history and social forces – path dependency is real; people do not make history in the manner of their own choosing. At the same time, whether or not capitalism's needs are met is in important respects a contingent outcome, taking place in historical time through the behavior of contending social actors – people do make history, using partial, situated, and fallible knowledge.[46] In the case of employee injury laws, a key reason why US capitalism got the policies that it needed was that in this case capitalism's needs lined up with what many actually existing capitalists needed.

Compensation laws offered something particularly valuable to large, early twentieth-century companies: greater predictability. These laws

---

[44] On the explanatory limits of the needs of capitalism, see Tomlins, *Law, Labor*, 28 and 294. On capitalism having unmet needs that lead to crisis, see Fraser and Jaeggi, *Capitalism: A Conversation in Critical Theory.*

[45] Karl Polanyi, *The Great Transformation: The Political and Economic Origins of Our Time* (Boston: Beacon Press, 1944), 8.

[46] I am here alluding to Karl Marx's famous remark that people "make their own history, but they do not make it as they please; they do not make it under self-selected circumstances, but under circumstances existing already, given and transmitted from the past." Karl Marx, "The Eighteenth Brumaire of Louis Bonaparte," *Die Revolution*, 1852, www.marxists.org/archive/marx/works/1852/18th-brumaire/, accessed October 15, 2018. On the usefulness of Marx's ideas for historical analysis, see Walter Johnson, "On Agency," *Journal of Social History* 37, no. 1 (Autumn 2003): 113–124.

promised to make injury into an expense for which employers could insure and budget. Manufacturing firms in this era tended to be relatively fixed-capital-intensive. Expenditures for material like machinery and company infrastructure are relatively fixed costs regardless of the rate of production. A machinery-intensive firm faces a large set of costs due to depreciation and any debt on the machinery, regardless of whether production is high or low. In addition, the cost to increase production per unit is relatively low compared with less machinery-intensive firms.[47] This often led to economic crises in the late nineteenth century, as some firms responded to pressures to keep up outputs by cutting prices, eventually dropping prices below the cost of production.[48] Through their internal structures and their co-existence in competitive markets, fixed-capital-intensive firms generated their own kind of risk of uncertainty for their owners and managers. These developments occurred in the context of a larger cultural ferment about certainty and unpredictability. In the words of historian Jamie Pietruska, in this era "Americans confronted a future more difficult but seemingly more crucial to anticipate."[49]

Many business people responded to problems of uncertainty, unpredictability, and interruptions to profit by restructuring and merging their companies.[50] These efforts can be seen as a business-side attempt to

[47] See Naomi R. Lamoreaux, *The Great Merger Movement in American Business, 1895–1904* (Cambridge: Cambridge University Press, 1985), 31–38, for a discussion of these dynamics in American industry, with an emphasis on fixed-capital-intensive companies' drive to maximize output and increase the pace of production. See also Alfred Chandler on what he calls "economies of speed": Alfred Chandler, *The Visible Hand: The Managerial Revolution in American Business* (Cambridge, MA: Belknap Press of Harvard University Press, 1977), 281–283. This speeding up of production was likely a factor in the rise of the accident crisis in the first place. For a discussion of the relationship between injury and "the political economy of speed" in the nineteenth-century United States, see Tomlins *Law, Labor, and Ideology*, 322–326.

[48] See Michael Perelman, *Railroading Economics: The Creation of the Free Market Mythology* (New York: Monthly Review Press, 2006).

[49] Jamie L. Pietruska, *Looking Forward: Prediction and Uncertainty in Modern America* (Chicago: University of Chicago Press, 2017), 2.

[50] Lamoreaux, *The Great Merger Movement*. William Roy cites the economic depression of 1893 as an important factor in the growth of large industrial corporations, because the collapse of many companies freed up capital later put to use in industrial corporations. The memory of this depression likely shaped the behavior of business personnel as well. William G. Roy, *Socializing Capital: The Rise of the Large Industrial Corporation in America* (Princeton: Princeton University Press, 1997), 223. For another account of the merger movement and public and private business efforts to reduce economic uncertainty, including a discussion of the relationship between mergers and investor confidence, see Stanely Buder, *Capitalizing on Change: A Social History of American Business* (Chapel

control or abandon markets as a way to meet firms' production needs.[51] Restructuring and merging were responses to how market imperatives manifested in the specific social position of the large firm within capitalist society, and were efforts to mitigate or escape those imperatives.[52]

The late nineteenth-century merger wave was so great a transformation that financier and industrialist George Perkins, an insurance executive who later came to play key roles in the growth of U.S. Steel and International Harvester, described the new corporate economy as a kind of socialism.[53] Perkins and other corporate leaders sought to create a reorganized capitalism that would help free capital accumulation and

---

Hill: University of North Carolina Press, 2009), 119–233. See also James Livingston, *Origins of the Federal Reserve System, 1890–1913* (Ithaca: Cornell University Press, 1986), 27; Martin Sklar, *The Corporate Reconstruction of American Capitalism, 1890–1916* (Cambridge: Cambridge University Press, 1988), 1–40; James Livingston, *Pragmatism and the Political Economy of Cultural Revolution, 1850–1940* (Chapel Hill: University of North Carolina Press, 1994), 84–98; Perelman, *Railroading Economics*; Harland Prechel, *Big Business and the State: Historical Transitions and Corporate Transformation, 1880s–1990s* (Albany: State University of New York Press, 2000).

[51] Marc Eisner identifies corporations as having "internalize[d] many functions previously accomplished through market transactions." Marc Allen Eisner, *Regulatory Politics in Transition* (Baltimore: Johns Hopkins University Press, 1993), 4. Scholarship on economic policy and regulation in this era also shows an attempt to minimize economic uncertainty as well. Morton Keller, *Regulating a New Economy: Public Policy and Economic Change in America, 1900–1933* (Cambridge, MA: Harvard University Press, 1994). On greater economic and political stability as a goal of workmen's compensation, see Donald Rogers, *Making Capitalism Safe: Work Safety and Health Regulation in America, 1880–1940* (Urbana: University of Illinois Press, 2009), 33; Moss, *When All Else Fails*, 7–14; James Weinstein, *The Corporate Ideal in the Liberal State, 1900–1918* (Boston: Beacon Press, 1968), 40–61. See also Jennifer Alexander, *The Mantra of Efficiency: From Waterwheel to Social Control* (Baltimore: Johns Hopkins University Press, 2008), 52–100.

[52] Those imperatives could be quite troublesome for employers. As James Livingston has written, the late nineteenth century was, "[f]rom the standpoint of capital … more nightmare than golden age," characterized by conflict, uncertainty and limited ability to exercise social control. James Livingston, *Pragmatism and the Political Economy of Cultural Revolution, 1850–1940*, 41.

[53] On Perkins, see Jonathan Levy, *Freaks of Fortune: The Emerging World of Capitalism and Risk in America* (Cambridge, MA: Harvard University Press, 2012), 264–307. Raniero Panzieri has pointed out that this view was common among Marxists in the early twentieth century: planning and risk reduction were seen as antithetical to capitalism, such that any forms of capital accumulation involving economic planning and reduction of the use of markets were seen as inherently steps toward socialism, rather than being a matter of variants of capitalism. Raniero Panzieri, "Surplus Value and Planning: Notes on the Reading of Capital," in *The Labour Process and Class Strategies*, ed. Conference of Socialist Economists (London: Conference of Socialist Economists, 1976), 4–25.

society more broadly from market-produced risks. Within this "socialist" corporatized economy the link between risk avoidance and corporations was so great that some commentators, such as early twentieth-century economist John Bates Clark, took risk reduction as the defining task and role of corporate managers.[54]

Given their aversion to uncertainty, it is unsurprising that many employers sought insurance against the risk of employers' liability lawsuits, as reflected in the increase in employers' liability payments discussed above. Insurance was another risk-control measure akin to corporate merger, another attempt to manage the market imperatives to which businesses were subject. Private insurance was (and is) a response to the kinds of insecurities generated by market dependency, a purchasable response. The rule of society by commodification creates problems that specific commodities can mitigate, for those able to afford it.

Employers' liability insurance companies themselves generally favored workmen's compensation laws. Insurers preferred these laws over employers' liability reforms that kept courts as the main institutions for handling lawsuits, because the wide variation in courts' behavior made it difficult to calculate predictable insurance rates.[55] Private liability insurance, then, served employers as an only partially reliable stopgap. Furthermore, it served as a stopgap that reminded employers that the underlying problem had not been solved.

Big businesses had another reason to worry about employee injury lawsuits: the law of large numbers. If a given industry had an injury rate of one worker in 300 killed each year, a firm employing thirty people might go ten years without a fatal accident. A firm employing 3,000 people would likely have about ten such fatal injuries per year. That is to say, given employer practices that exposed employees to dangers predictably, and given that businesses were employing larger and larger numbers of people, employee injury eventually ceased to be a matter of chance and became a certainty. Thus, large firms could expect their employees to face injuries regularly, which in turn means these firms had a greater interest in a more

---

[54] Levy, *Freaks of Fortune*, 281.
[55] Joseph L. Castrovinci, "Prelude to Welfare Capitalism: The Role of Business in the Enactment of Workmen's Compensation Legislation in Illinois, 1905–12," *Social Service Review* 50, no. 1 (March 1976): 80–102, 89. Unsurprisingly, insurers did not support compensation measures that would replace private insurers with public insurance plans. See, for example, Robert Asher, "Radicalism and Reform: State Insurance of Workmen's Compensation in Minnesota, 1910–1933," *Labor History*, no. 14 (1973): 19–41; and Lubove, *The Struggle for Social Security 1900–1935*, 261.

predictable body of employee injury law. Corporate mergers were a response to the specific problems that market dependency posed for fixed-capital-intensive companies in competitive environments. Mergers resulted in larger companies, which in turn created new problems, in that risk of employee injury had become a certainty with an unknown delivery date – a question of when, not if.

Business corporations and their leaders had another good reason to fear the court-based system of employee injury law – and not a narrowly financial one. Specifically, dealing with injuries through the courts seemed to have the potential to create industrial strife, because of the adversarial character of the US legal system.[56] As historian Robert Asher puts it, business leaders believed lawsuits "bred antagonism between employers and their employees," a concern Asher places in the context of "alarm of employers, politicians, and community leaders at the growth of domestic political radicalism and labor militancy and violence."[57] Asher argues that this was an important factor in employer support for compensation laws. Alarm over class tensions made business and political officials "particularly receptive to programs and proposals that promised to mitigate class strife," as Asher put it. Compensation laws appealed to employers in part because by "reduc[ing] friction and ill feeling between employers and employees" they might reduce "labor militancy and the need for unions."[58] Historian Joseph Tripp similarly argues that one of the main goals of compensation laws was "to improve labor relations."[59]

Business leaders such as George Perkins, an executive at both International Harvester and U.S. Steel, similarly supported compensation laws because of the prospects of fostering cooperative relationships between employers and employees.[60] Employer–employee cooperation,

---

[56] Mark Aldrich, *Safety First: Technology, Labor, and Business in the Building of American Work Safety* (Baltimore: Johns Hopkins University Press, 1997), 95.

[57] Asher, "Business and Workers' Welfare," 463, 453–54. Joseph Tripp argues that the threat of political radicalism helped build business support for progressive reforms, and that those reforms in turn helped diffuse radical social movements. Tripp, "An Instance of Labor and Business Cooperation."

[58] Asher, "Business and Workers' Welfare," 454. See also Lubove, *The Struggle for Social Security 1900–1935*, 264–265.

[59] Tripp, "An Instance of Labor and Business Cooperation," 531–532.

[60] Weinstein, *The Corporate Ideal in the Liberal State*, 45. On Perkins and more broadly on cooperation and hierarchy, see Levy, *Freaks of Fortune*, 264–307. Large companies like U.S. Steel and International Harvester were able to implement voluntary compensation programs much more than small companies, due to financial resources as well as greater in-house administrative expertise.

Perkins argued, could be more profitable for business than conflict. In keeping with this vision, many companies implemented voluntary accident relief plans that anticipated compensation legislation. This notion of employer–employee cooperation was intended to preserve employer authority while reducing the likelihood that workers would engage in class conflict. U.S. Steel's plan was modeled on the plans required under Germany's compensation laws.[61] German compensation laws, in turn, were passed as anti-socialist measures, aimed at mitigating the threat of radicalism by easing the social tensions that helped give radicals' claims more legitimacy.[62] The adversarial nature of the courts meant that lawsuits over injury were conflictual affairs, even more so given the highly charged kinds of issues raised, as Chapter 1 discussed. In injury lawsuits, employers' attorneys sought to deny vulnerable people much needed money and often blamed the injured for their own accidents, likely feeding notions of employer indifference to employee suffering. Both the proceedings and the results of employee injury lawsuits threatened to foster discontent, by raising questions of values and justice, and airing highly emotionally charged accounts of human loss that resulted from injury. It is understandable how this scenario would unsettle employers worried about class conflict.[63]

[61] Weinstein, *The Corporate Ideal in the Liberal State*, 46. For more on Germany's compensation laws, see Daniel Rodgers, *Atlantic Crossings: Social Politics in a Progressive Age* (Cambridge, MA: Harvard University Press, 1998), and John M. Kleeberg, "From Strict Liability to Workers' Compensation: The Prussian Railroad Law, the German Liability Act, and the Introduction of Bismarck's Accident Insurance in Germany, 1838–1844," *New York University Journal of International Law and Politics* 36, no. 1 (Fall 2003): 53–132. For useful studies of Canada and Britain, respectively, see Eric Tucker, *Administering Danger in the Workplace: The Law and Politics of Occupational Health and Safety in Ontario, 1850–1914* (Toronto: University of Toronto Press, 1990), and Jamie Bronstein, *Caught in the Machinery: Workplace Accidents and Injured Workers in Nineteenth-Century Britain* (Stanford: Stanford University Press, 2007).

[62] See Frederick L. Hoffman, "Some Lessons of the German Failure in Compulsory Health Insurance," in Hoffman, *Health Insurance Addresses, 1916–21* (Newark: Prudential Press, 1921), 181–190; 181. "Otto von Bismarck, German Chancellor 1862–1890," Social Security Administration hwww.ssa.gov/history/ottob.html, accessed February 12, 2018; Jonathan Steinberg, *Bismarck: A Life* (Oxford: Oxford University Press, 2011), 12, 417.

[63] Concern over class conflict may explain why businesses tended to support compensation laws before the labor movement did. Until 1909, US unions tended to oppose workmen's compensation laws in favor of legislation further expanding employers' liability in court. Lubove, *The Struggle for Social Security*, 56–57; William Forbath, *Law and the Shaping of the American Labor Movement* (Cambridge, MA: Harvard University Press, 1991), 51–52; Jennifer Klein, *For All These Rights: Business, Labor, and the Shaping of America's Public* (Princeton: Princeton University Press, 2003), 21–22. Historians have often

Fears of courts stoking class conflict occurred within a larger context of sociopolitical uncertainty. It was plausible in the early twentieth century to think that capitalism might be unraveling. Socialism, anarchism, and revolution were widespread keywords in US culture: political violence stalked the headlines, and strikes were frequent.[64] Strikes could easily break out into violence between employers and employees as well, and that violence in turn could threaten to spill beyond violent conduct of industrial relations into more widely directed political violence. In 1907, William D. Haywood, a leader in the radical Industrial Workers of the World, the Western Federation of Miners, and the Socialist Party, stood trial accused of the murder by bomb of Idaho's governor. That murder, in turn, was bound up with a long history of state and employer violence against unionists, and unions' retaliatory violence.[65] That same year, members of the Buffalo, New York, business community, having recently broken a strike of the Iron Molders' Union, commissioned a statue to

discussed US unions as being suspicious of the state and so as preferring to resolve problems themselves without state intervention, a trait historians call voluntarism. Unions' opposition to workmen's compensation laws could be seen as union voluntarism, but it is important to note that this opposition to compensation legislation was not a rejection of state intervention in the economy as such. Rather, it was a preference for economic intervention by one kind of state entity over another: unions preferred injuries to be governed by courts rather than administrative agencies. Furthermore, unions' preferences for courts over compensation legislation was tied to the active pursuit of employer' liability legislation which competed with compensation legislation. Both kinds of legislation were state intervention. Alice Kessler-Harris argues that the American Federation of Labor was voluntarist due largely to a preference for a kind of masculine collective action and to a vision of men as civically engaged citizens. Alice Kessler-Harris, *In Pursuit of Equity: Women, Men, and the Pursuit of Economic Citizenship in 20th-Century America* (Oxford: Oxford University Press, 2001), 67. It could be that the American Federation of Labor's preference for a modified court-based system of injury law over workmen's compensation as an insurance-based administrative system was the result of a social vision of men as having a right to file suits in courts as part of their being men and citizens.

[64] On strikes in this era, see Christopher Tomlins, *The State and the Unions: Labor Relations, Law, and the Organized Labor Movement in America, 1880–1960* (Cambridge: Cambridge University Press, 1985), 11–20; Bruno Ramirez, *When Workers Fight: The Politics of Industrial Relations in the Progressive Era, 1898–1916* (Westport: Greenwood, 1978), 9, 134–137.

[65] See Jeffrey A. Johnson, *"They Are All Red Out Here": Socialist Politics in the Pacific Northwest, 1895–1925* (Norman: University of Oklahoma Press, 2009), 73–75. See also, more generally, Louis Adamic, *Dynamite: A Century of Class Violence in America, 1830–1930* (New York: Viking, 1934), on violence in this era. Andrews's *Killing for Coal* covers the Ludlow Massacre, a few years later, but still speaks to class tensions in this era, as does David Huyssen, *Progressive Inequality: Rich and Poor in New York, 1890–1920* (Cambridge, MA: Harvard University Press, 2014).

commemorate President McKinley, murdered by an anarchist only six years earlier in their city.[66]

The class line in this era threatened to become, in the words of political theorist Carl Schmitt, a "friend–enemy distinction," wherein classes formed imagined communities to which people belonged, akin to nations, with people in other classes seen as members of foreign and hostile nations.[67] "The working class and the employing class have nothing in common," as the Industrial Workers of the World famously declared. Class tensions were exacerbated by the differences in the makeup of the two classes: foreign-born workers who did not speak English were easier for employers to see as other than themselves rather than members of a shared imagined community, and vice versa. Furthermore, the conduct of the judiciary and the police within violent conflicts threatened to undermine the legitimacy of both institutions, by appearing not as representatives of the public's general interest but as partisans acting to defend specific interest groups – employers – against unions and the working class. Employers who sought to maintain the status quo risked winning battles in a way that would lead to their eventually losing the class war altogether.[68] These concerns about class conflict were in the background amid employers' approach to the problem of employee injury. From a perspective centered either on social harmony and stability or on the well-being of individual businesses, class conflict promised to be at best expensive to manage and at worst a serious threat of personal harm and loss of social position as a result of revolution.

The notion that courts fed class conflict may explain why employers accepted or even embraced compensation laws while rejecting some other changes to the construction of the employment relationship. Employers in this era tended to be virulently anti-union and opposed to any form of state disciplining of employers' behavior in labor–management relationships. Of course, employers were less troubled by, and often even demanded,

---

[66] Chad Pearson, *Reform or Repression: Organizing America's Anti-Union Movement* (Philadelphia: University of Pennsylvania Press, 2016), 221.

[67] See Carl Schmitt, *The Concept of the Political* (Chicago: University of Chicago Press, 2007.) The term "imagined communities" comes from Benedict Anderson, *Imagined Communities: Reflections on the Origin and Spread of Nationalism* (London: Verso, 2006).

[68] William Forbath has argued that unions' frustrations with judges' issuing injunctions and overturning or taking the teeth out of pro-labor legislation encouraged unions to seek to resolve their disputes with employers via direct economic conflict rather than relying on state institutions. Lurking here was an important degree of delegitimation of the law in the eyes of the labor movement. Forbath, *Law and the Shaping of the American Labor Movement*. See also Tomlins, *The State and the Unions*, 61–67.

the use of state repressive power against workers, and the state often complied, intervening on management's behalf within industrial relations. This is easy to see as simple hypocrisy, wherein Janus-faced employers spoke against government involvement while also demanding it, but the reality is complex: employment was ideologically coded as private, not subject to state involvement, and an employer's enterprise was private property. What capitalists called for was specifically state repressive force against employees' collective attempts to trespass on private property.

Unions fought in a sense to politicize employment, against the rhetorical or ideological treating of property and employment as depoliticized. Employers did fight against unions for the sake of profits or specific managerial prerogatives, but also, or perhaps above all, they fought to keep employment private and depoliticized, such that it would remain subject to employers' general prerogatives and not subject to negotiation or justice claims by employees. Workers' compensation was a significant legal reform, but it was not one that threatened to change any of the above: compensation laws did not shift power to employees, nor did they depict employment as a governance – which is to say, political – relationship between unequal parties. Compensation laws kept all of those elements fixed, while changing costs.[69]

[69] In light of the above, we should understand compensation laws as part of the history of employment law, as distinct from labor law. The difference between labor law and employment law can be understood as simply a matter of administrative jurisdiction, at least in the United States after the 1930s. Labor law is the purview of the federal National Labor Relations Board and similar bodies, which govern collective bargaining between employers and organizations of employees. Employment law is the purview of the federal Department of Labor and its state-level analogs, administering laws like the Fair Labor Standards Act and workmen's compensation. For an overview of law and labor in US history, see Eileen Boris, "Labor's Welfare State: Defining Workers, Constructing Citizens," in *The Cambridge History of Law in America, vol. 3: The Twentieth Century and After*, ed. Michael Grossberg and Christopher Tomlins (Cambridge: Cambridge University Press, 2008). For an older but still relevant overview of labor and employment law history and their differences, see Christopher Tomlins, "How Who Rides Whom: Recent 'New' Histories of American Labour Law and What They May Signify," *Social History* 20, no. 1 (1995): 1–21. Boris's work shows the benefits to studying commonalities between labor and employment law in different periods, an approach that might open toward a broader synthesis of the role of law and the state in class relations. Tomlins has gestured toward such a synthesis, centering on the relationship between law, production, and reproduction. See Christopher Tomlins, "Subordination, Authority, Law: Subjects in Labor History," *International Labor and Working-Class History*, no. 47 (Spring 1995): 56–90, and more recently Christopher L. Tomlins, "The State, the Unions, and the Critical Synthesis in Labor Law History," *Labor History* 54, no. 2 (May 2013): 208–221. Understood in this way, to call compensation laws "employment law" can be seen as anachronistically projecting backward a subsequent distinction. Employment law

EMPLOYERS' PUZZLING POWER

While reformers presented compensation laws as necessary for social purposes, it was at least equally important to the passage of compensation laws that those laws lined up with what actually existing capitalists needed. But how did businesses know what they needed? Some business knowledge of the injury problem must have arisen from simply paying attention: reformers sought to publicize the injury problem; business personnel may have read those works or reports on them, and understood how they related to businesses' own interest. Another source of business knowledge was baked into the corporation as a type of organization. Corporate mergers were risk management strategies, as noted above, and were shepherded consciously by risk management professionals from financial circles. They brought new finance-derived concepts of risk into corporate management.[70] The risk management professionals involved in these efforts in the corporate reorganization of industry helped bring what historian Paul Bellamy has called "actuarial self-awareness" into manufacturing.[71] This is similar to what I have called insurance as a worldview, at the level of individual firms. This self-awareness was a matter of both new cultural perspectives on risk and new institutional innovations wherein companies employed new knowledge-producing personnel such as those in early human resources and medical departments. This meant that the large corporations of the late nineteenth and early

and labor law can also be understood, however, as two different kinds of state management of different facets of capitalist society, kinds of management with their own ways of thinking about and representing working-class people. These different approaches to state management of class relationships do not have to map onto difference in institutional jurisdiction. Indeed, both forms of management overlapped in US industrial relations institutions prior to the National Labors Relations Act. See Greenwald, *The Triangle Fire, the Protocols of Peace, and Industrial Democracy in Progressive Era*. Labor law constitutes and regulates the official politics of class, the power relationships between employers and employees, which areas of economic life are subject to formal collective negotiation, and what conduct is allowable in that negotiation. Labor law is state regulation of conflicts between capital and labor as relatively self-conscious collective actors, setting the terms for legitimate and illegitimate forms of conflict between groups of employees and employers, and policing behavior accordingly. Employment law, on the other hand, sets the terms for legitimate employment practices outside periods of collective conflict. My suspicion is that in different ways both labor and employment law normalize and reify class, by ideologically establishing or maintaining different aspects of employment as normal and ostensibly apolitical.

70 See Levy, *Freaks of Fortune*, 264–316.
71 See Bellamy, "From Court Room to Board Room," xiii.

twentieth century were not simply bigger versions of earlier small busi-nesses, but possessed new capacities for knowing about and responding to their own enterprises and thus to the injury problem. They had a greater institutional capacity, in Hugh Heclo's words, to "puzzle" in order more effectively to "power."[72] To use a biological metaphor: corporations were both larger and more complex social organisms with more developed nervous systems.

The business corporation was an organism with a complex nervous system. It was a relatively social organism as well, in that businesses became aware of their needs through trade and civic associations. These associations also helped make that knowledge politically efficacious via lobbying and propagandizing. Labor and working-class historians have extensively addressed the agency and collective action of working-class people. To the degree that working-class people can be said to have interests defined by their class position, they can act on those interests in different ways and in greater degrees when acting in concert rather than individually. Likewise, collectivity shapes worldview and self-understanding. The same is true for the capitalist class, though in relation to different organizations.[73] For capitalists in the early twentieth century, trade associations were especially important in these processes.[74]

---

[72] Hugh Heclo, *Modern Social Politics in Britain and Sweden: From Relief to Income Maintenance* (New Haven: Yale University Press, 1974), 305.

[73] See Ira Katznelson and Aristide R. Zolberg, eds., *Working-Class Formation: Nineteenth Century Patterns in Western Europe and the United States* (Princeton: Princeton University Press, 1986), for a discussion of how different meanings of the word "class" relate to each other and map onto different social realities of class. See also Erik Olin Wright, *Understanding Class* (London: Verso, 2015). See Livingston, *Origins of the Federal Reserve System, 1890–1913*, for both a theoretical account of the consciousness and organization of the capitalist class and an account of capitalists acting consciously to shape capitalism through policy in the early twentieth century. See also Sven Beckert, *The Monied Metropolis: New York City and the Consolidation of the American Bourgeoisie, 1850–1896* (New York: Cambridge University Press, 2001), on the US capitalist class becoming class-conscious. Beckert's analysis could be described in Katznelson's terms as articulating the relationships between social structural position, economic development, and national culture in the making of class organization, disposition, and subjectivity. See Ira Katznelson, "Working-Class Formation: Constructing Cases and Comparisons," in Katznelson and Zolberg, *Working Class Formation*, 3–41. My analysis in this book is centered more on the role of law in constructing class as a structural position. These are complementary approaches, though I would argue that specifically structural elements of class have been relatively neglected in recent history.

[74] On the early twentieth century, see Pearson, *Reform or Repression*. Arguably, insurance can be understood as an alternative kind of class formation. Insurance involves creating collectivity – a risk pool – with practices of sharing and coordination among members of

The Illinois Manufacturers' Association, representing about 1,000 large businesses, began calling for reform to employee injury law in 1905, and by 1909 favored compensation laws specifically.[75] In 1910 the National Association of Manufacturers (NAM) surveyed 25,000 employers and found that 95 percent supported compensation for employees' injuries via insurance methods, but many felt they could not afford to set up such policies on their own.[76] The survey reflected the fact that workmen's compensation emerged as the primary business-supported policy proposal for the accident problem.[77] The National Metal Trades Association and the National Civic Federation, the employer-heavy civic association, joined the NAM members in supporting an insurance-based approach to injury law.[78] Employers supported

the pool organized by the insurance company's personnel. An insurance company risk pool is thus a kind of passive collectivity under the governance of the company. To the degree that this meets members' needs and shapes their outlook, it could be all members need – or it could crowd out other potential kinds of collectivity, both ideologically and practically. On other working-class mutual security and solidarity measures, see John Fabian Witt, *The Accidental Republic: Crippled Workmen, Destitute Widows, and the Remaking of American Law* (Cambridge, MA: Harvard University Press, 2004), 71–102, and Levy, *Freaks of Fortune*, 191–230.

[75] Castrovinci, "Prelude to Welfare Capitalism," 88.

[76] Weinstein, *The Corporate Ideal in the Liberal State*, 47.

[77] Fishback and Kantor, *A Prelude to the Welfare State*, 93–102. Weinstein, *The Corporate Ideal in the Liberal State, 1900–1918*, 45. For a discussion of the alternatives to workmen's compensation, see Witt, *The Accidental Republic*.

[78] Aldrich, *Safety First*, 94. On the National Association of Manufacturers' response to compensation laws, see Weinstein, *The Corporate Ideal in the Liberal State*, 47. The National Civic Federation was made up of what Alan Dawley has called "a tripartite structure of capital, labor, and the public that would bargain as corporate entities to resolve their differences peaceably within the overarching solidarity of the nation." Social liberal organizations like the NCF proposed to "ride herd on social forces, so that America's destiny ... would be in the hands of social organizations that were conscious and purposive expressions of human will." Alan Dawley, *Struggles for Justice: Social Responsibility and the Liberal State* (Cambridge, MA: Harvard University Press, 1991), 114. The need for someone to "ride herd" in this way arose from a sense of crisis or potential catastrophe. As President Theodore Roosevelt explained his involvement in resolving the massive and bitter 1902 anthracite coal strike, "I was anxious to save the great coal operators and all of the class of big propertied men, of which they were members, from the dreadful punishment which their own folly would have brought on them if I had not acted." Dawley, *Struggles for Justice*, 134. Roosevelt here expressed a relatively new sensibility within efforts to regulate employment from the late nineteenth century through the Second World War. Employment is a relationship; regulating employment means governing multiple actors in that relationship – employers, employees, and, in the case of compensation laws, working-class families. For much of the nineteenth century, legal regulation of employment centered on regulating employees and unions. Toward the end of the nineteenth century and over the early twentieth

compensation laws in part because legislation promised to organize industry. By getting most businesses to operate similarly, legislation might mitigate downward pressures on safety as a result of competition, pressures that, in a time of expanding legal liability, would have increased liability costs.[79]

A STABLE PRICE FOR LIFE AND LIMB

And so compensation laws came, written into legislation by policymakers drawing on and responding to the range of views and forces described in this chapter, bringing about the shift from the tyranny of the trial to the tyranny of the table. By 1911, nine states had such laws on the books. Other states rapidly followed suit, with forty states having such laws by 1920.[80] In the new normal brought by these laws, employers would carry part of the financial cost of injury. While the particulars varied by state, generally, injured persons got a weekly payment under compensation laws. The more severe the injury, the longer the number of weeks of payments. For the loss of one hand, for example, a person would likely get 100 weeks of payments, slightly less than two years. For the loss of both hands, a person would likely get 400 weeks of payments, slightly less

century, government came increasingly to regulate employers, driven in part by the view that without governing both sides, class conflict would become heated and ultimately harmful to capitalism. See Tomlins, *The State and the Unions*, 89, 99–247. See also Richard Greenwald's analysis of the involvement of Robert Wagner and Frances Perkins in industrial relations policy in New York in the 1910s prior to their role in shaping federal policy in the 1930s. Greenwald, *The Triangle Fire, the Protocols of Peace, and Industrial Democracy in Progressive Era New York*. See also Dawley, *Struggles for Justice*, 154–155. The NCF played a role in particular in building labor movement support for the employer-preferred option of compensation laws, with Samuel Gompers of the American Federation of Labor coming to support compensation laws by 1909. Weinstein, *The Corporate Ideal in the Liberal State*, 48–51. The debate in the NCF then shifted toward the specifics of how to achieve security of payment for injury compensation, a debate predicated on agreement over the importance of compensation laws. Business leaders generally preferred private insurance, while labor leaders generally preferred state monopoly insurance, a preference hard to square with some scholars' characterization of unions as voluntarist.

[79] Historian James Livingston has argued that financial policy in the turn of the twentieth century is best understood as part of a process of class formation among US capitalists. See Livingston, *Origins of the Federal Reserve System, 1890–1913*. Employer support for compensation laws can be seen in a similar light.

[80] Price Fishback, "Workers' Compensation," in Robert Whaple, ed., *EH.Net Encyclopedia*, March 26, 2008, http://eh.net/encyclopedia/article/fishback.workers.compensation, accessed April 1, 2013.

than eight years. Often, 400 weeks was the statutory maximum duration of compensation.

The amount of the weekly payment for injury was usually set at a minimum of five dollars per week and a maximum of ten dollars per week. The exact amount would be equal to some percentage of the injured person's pre-injury wage. Depending on the state the person lived in, they (or their surviving family in the event of death) would get half or two-thirds of the pre-injury weekly wage. Thus, a person paid twelve dollars per week would get an injury payment of six to eight dollars per week. The remaining costs of injury, such as the half or one-third of wages not included in the employer's payment, or wages lost beyond the statutory maximum duration, would remain a cost borne by employees, coded implicitly as an acceptable loss within the law. Under these laws, injury was routinized conceptually, rendered easily knowable and valuable in dollars. The value of injury was defined by the going price for labor power on the labor market. Payment for injury would become as regular, brisk, and business-like as the ongoing maiming and killing of employees.

Glackin's editorial can stand as a kind of tableau of the conceptual world of injury law reform, showing in miniature many of the concerns and conceptualizations in that world. The title forms a key element of that tableau: "Life and Limb Too Cheap." Notions of justice certainly appear here. In the phrase "life and limb" there was some implicit awareness that injuries hurt individual human beings, and in his discussion of families Glackin expressed some sense of those humans being as embedded in value-laden interpersonal relationships. There was then some element of justice as recognition and some sense of suffering and singularity. As with Crystal Eastman and William Hard, however, Glackin focused primarily on concerns about distributive justice. He spent much of his editorial on the low wages of working-class people, in a way that made his disapproval apparent. "Too cheap" can be read in a distributive light, as an expression of low payment. It can also be read as implying a relationship between distribution and recognition, that payments can be so low as to serve as a denial of recognition.[81] On the other hand, the phrase also

---

[81] At least at the low end, the social phenomena that we can call distributive injustices are themselves also unjust denials of recognition: poverty consigns people to suffering which is not entirely thinkable in distributive terms. Anyone who has worked for minimum wage may have experienced how pay can be so low as to feel like a disregarding of one's humanity. I once worked a low-paying canvassing job where two co-workers of mine were homeless and sleeping in a public park. A supervisor who knew this fired one of

implies an opposite, that there is life and limb too expensive, which was the complaint of Glackin and others about the "suffering" of businesses at the hands of lawyers. Between too cheap and too expensive sits just right, injury properly priced. While this is admittedly an uncharitable reading, it highlights some themes within the injury law reform milieu that gave rise to workmen's compensation laws, which in turn sheds light on those laws. The overly narrow and exclusively distributive perspective written into those laws is inattentive to recognition and bound up with – or at least uncomfortably close to – commodification.

The tyranny of the table administered commodification in two senses. Compensation laws regulated the prices of injuries to prevent labor power from falling below what Matteo Liberatore called its natural price, to avoid family disruption and the resulting social disorder that could follow. These laws carried out this function by administering commodification in a second sense, by valuing the lives and limbs of injured persons according to those people's pre-injury wages, that is, according to the labor market. In doing so, compensation laws took the collective (even if not consciously coordinated) pricing of labor power practiced by employers via the labor market and made it into the state's measure of the value of injury and injured persons. While of course we can and should criticize low payments for injury, in doing so we must not miss the underlying choice to treat employees' lives and limbs as economic objects. Injuries, suffering, deaths, body parts, lives, human beings – these all are in one respect priceless, yet the tyranny of the table treated them exclusively through monetary equivalence. The value of an arm? A face? A life? These became simple, knowable quantities, defined by labor market prices.

Waged labor is deeply inegalitarian: people were (and are) paid massively disparate wages. We are often encouraged to see these disparities as reflecting value judgments when doing so justifies those disparities – wage differences attract the best talent – but we are also discouraged from thinking of differences in wages as judgments of difference in the underlying value of the humans who are, by virtue of income disparities, consigned to fates with vastly different qualities of life. Compensation laws made those varying, inegalitarian wages into the legal measure of the

them after she failed to meet our daily fundraising quota for three days in a row. My co-workers and I talked a great deal about this, and while we did not use these terms it certainly felt like a denial of or indifference to her humanity. We saw that supervisor in a new light afterward. What we missed in our conversations was that the supervisor was only the tip of the iceberg, or one small cog in a large machine, when it comes to both distributive injustice and unjust denial of recognition.

value of human lives and body parts. In effect, under the tyranny of the table the law came to answer the question of "What is the value of my body, or of my life?" with "Well, how much are you paid at your job?" States and businesses both puzzle before they power.[82] Part of the power of the tyranny of the table was that it rendered economic valuations for human lives no longer puzzling. Compensation legislation wrote a commodifying perspective on human beings into the fundamental outlook through which injury law puzzles through what to do about the ongoing harm to persons within the economy, and this legislation did not write into law any non-commodifying ways of valuing human beings.

Legal theorist Margaret Radin has identified what she calls the "four indicia" of commodification conceptually speaking: objectification, fungibility, commensurability, and monetary equivalence. By objectification Radin means "status as a thing in the Kantian sense of something that is manipulable at the will of persons." By fungibility Radin means "things are fully interchangeable with no effect on value": one thing is essentially replaceable with another without any important difference. Commensurability means that the objects have comparable and rankable value. Monetary equivalence means that money is the medium for that comparison and ranking. These four indicia function metaphorically like stairs. A person standing on the fourth step of a staircase is also standing atop the first three steps. Thus, where there is fungibility, there is also objectification. Where there is commensuration, there is fungibility. Where there is monetary equivalence, there is commensuration. Thus, practices of monetary equivalence, widespread in capitalist society, have woven into them the other three indicia as constituent elements of that equivalence.[83]

Radin's analysis helps make clear the ways in which commodification requires mental or cultural work.[84] Commodification is an activity. It is so common and taken for granted in capitalist society that it can be forgotten that commodification is a practice, and status as a commodity is the result of that practice. To put it another way, we do well to think of the word "commodity" as a synonym for "commodified," the past tense of a verb, indicating prior activity. Commodification is in a sense analogous to

---

[82] Heclo, *Modern Social Politics in Britain and Sweden*, 305.

[83] Margaret Jane Radin, *Contested Commodities: The Trouble with Trade in Sex, Children, Body Parts, and Other Things* (Cambridge, MA: Harvard University Press, 2001), 118.

[84] See also Stephanie Smallwood, "Commodified Freedom: Interrogating the Limits of Anti-Slavery Ideology in the Early Republic," *Journal of the Early Republic*, no. 24 (Summer 2004): 289–298.

catching a baseball, wherein a host of muscles contract and neurons fire. The act is extraordinarily complex and involves many component processes performed simultaneously, and it is often done without conscious awareness of that complexity. Part of the value in Radin's categories lies in making visible those constituent parts and that complexity.

Radin's concepts are suggestive as well for how different kinds of abstractions relate to each other. Chapter 2 argued that people voicing the social-justice reform perspective sometimes focused on distributive justice in a way that treated working-class people as objects and as abstract in the sense of interchangeable, as with the impersonal anecdotes that opened Crystal Eastman's book and captioned the book's photos of workers. In Radin's terms, here were two of the four indicia of commodification: objectification and fungibility. Social-justice reformers like Eastman and Hard sometimes treated working-class people abstractly, but they did not commodify them. In their abstractions, however, they did some of the conceptual work necessary for commodification. They walked partway down the road, so to speak, and so shared some degree of affinity with the more fully commodifying treatments of working-class people by the instrumentally focused reformers and by businesses.

Discussion of injury through economic metaphors, as within the instrumental-reform perspective, carried out the conceptual commodification of working-class people and sought to make that commodification into the practice of government via policy. Representing working people as costs and factors of production was of a piece with framing injuries as an issue of economic efficiency and rational cost allocation. Compensation legislation was a shift in law to a new, specifically biopolitical practice of commodifying working-class people. The tyranny of the table standardized injury values in service of protecting large-scale social entities like the market and its resource, the aggregate population.

MORAL THINNING AND IMPOVERISHED INJURY

In order to standardize payments and thus create predictability for employers, compensation laws removed from the law arguments about injustice and narration of the individual effects of injury. This loss of deliberation changed the ethical grammar of the law, so to speak, deepening the eclipse of recognition, further impoverishing injury. The human meaning of injury had no place in the law. I call this phenomenon moral thinning: from murder to statistics.[85] Non-financial harms also had no place under compensation laws. Pain and loss became newly worthless as the law provided no more space for people to narrate what it meant to lose a limb or a family member in an industrial accident. Injured wage earners became conceptually disembedded from their social and interpersonal contexts.

There is an element of moral thinning involved whenever the commodification of persons begins to occur, because commodification must ignore differences and particularities, setting aside whatever is unique or nonequivalent about them. Commodification tramples on singularity.[86] This makes no difference when singularity makes no difference: the uniqueness of my morning cup of coffee does not matter; what matters is its instrumental use in my struggle toward wakefulness. The uniqueness of human beings, however, does matter: the reduction of human beings to abstract instrumental objects should trouble us. Recognition and commodification co-exist at best uneasily.

The moral thinning of injury under the tyranny of the table is more apparent when juxtaposed to the tyranny of the trial. Despite the many limits of the court-based system of employee injury law, that system did allow some space for fragments of the experiential truths of injury, which made possible elements of justice as recognition. As historian Kimberly Welch has put it, "[s]torytelling is omnipresent in human discourse.... Telling stories in court is an attempt to organize, interpret, and direct the world in which one lives, and the stories told in adversarial processes signal the narrator's interpretation of how the world ought to operate."[87] The contending oughts embedded in legal stories made courts into places of normative deliberation, places where the contest of stories had explicitly moral and political stakes.

---

[85] Morally thick vocabularies are not always or necessarily better than morally thin vocabularies. Recognition can be oppressive. See Nancy Fraser, "From Progressive Neoliberalism to Trump – And Beyond," *American Affairs* 1, no. 4 (Winter 2017): 46–64, for examples of negative versions of recognition. That said, in the specific case of employee injury law, the loss of legal capacity for recognition, the change I have called moral thinning, was an injustice.

[86] See Barbara Young Welke, "The Cowboy Suit Tragedy: Spreading Risk, Owning Hazard in the Modern American Consumer Economy," *Journal of American History* 1, no. 1 (June 2014): 97–121, for an exploration of the ways that aspects of human experiences of injury cannot be rendered as financial equivalents, and how the formatting of injury experience into money occludes those non-monetizable aspects of injury.

[87] Kimberley M. Welch, *Black Litigants in the Antebellum American South* (Chapel Hill: University of North Carolina Press, 2018), 28.

Access to that site of deliberation, and the recognition that came through that access, is likely part of what working-class people wanted from the court-based system of employee injury law. As historian James Schmidt has put it, injured plaintiffs and their families "came to court with a desire to talk about the miseries that had befallen them."[88] That telling intersected with other actors in court to produce what Schmidt calls "judicial morality plays." Going to court was one kind of ritual through which people processed and, in important respects, produced the meaning of what Schmidt rightly calls industrial violence. There was, then, some space for this ritual use of law under the tyranny of the trial. With compensation laws, employee injury law was deritualized, no longer made available to working-class people in the same way.[89]

To be clear, compensation laws never said that no other framework for valuing human beings existed in society, but these laws did not allow any other such framework to touch the legal response to employee injury. In the court system multiple systems of valuation could intersect, while under compensation laws non-pecuniary valuations of people, their experiences, their relationships, and their bodies had no legal space. The point is absolutely not to celebrate the tyranny of the trial, but to use the courts' narrative and value plurality to highlight the moral thinning of injury under the tyranny of the table. In the court-based system of injury

---

[88] James D. Schmidt, *Industrial Violence and the Legal Origins of Child Labor* (New York: Cambridge University Press, 2010), 219.

[89] Schmidt, *Industrial Violence and the Legal Origins of Child Labor*, 208. My use of the term "ritual" here is influenced by Michael K. Rosenow, *Death and Dying in the Working Class, 1865–1920* (Chicago: University of Illinois Press, 2015). Rosenow writes that working-class people "developed specific rituals and attitudes" toward injury and death, rituals that "could reflect, solidify, or challenge prevailing sentiments and social order" (p. 3.) Schmidt and Rosenow's books are in important respects in the Thompsonian tradition of labor history, showing what working-class people did and made of themselves. Thompsonian labor history remains vitally important, but that is not what I am doing in this book. My primary object is less working-class people's ideas and culture and more the legal ideas and culture to which working-class people were subjected. I see my work as also Thompsonian but in a different sense, less Thompson the analyst of working-class culture and agency and more Thompson the critic of what working-class people are subjected to. In my view this difference of emphasis between working-class agency and working-class subjection is one useful way to parse the some-times justifiably blurry line between labor history and the history of capitalism, historical subfields that should be seen as complementary and perhaps even interdependent. In important respects Schmidt's book is more than Thompsonian, emphasizing the cultur-ally constitutive power of the law in society. He argues that lawsuits over injuries to child laborers shaped ideas about child labor. I am convinced of the culture-shaping power of law, but am not here making such an argument.

law at least it was possible to pose the questions of whether or not an injury was a wrong, and what it meant in the lives of the persons affected. There was no more space for these questions or for the answering stories of injury and its effects under the tyranny of the table.

CONCLUSION

As Fred Gray put it at the 1909 compensation conference, the "human aspects" of injury do not fit within an economic perspective on injury. The degree that concerns over distributive justice took that economic perspective was the degree to which those concerns were incapable of attending to justice as recognition. As we have seen, other concerns with employee injury did not attend to distributive justice. Distributive justice divorced from concern with justice as recognition lined up with other perspectives that were much less concerned with justice. And as we will see, compensation laws would soon help give rise to new distributive injustices and a lack of real commitment to what Glackin called an obligation to "take care of those who are unable to care for themselves."

Let us pause a moment, however, before turning to those matters. Arguably, this book has followed historical actors into a sky clouded with abstractions. In the attempt to think past those abstractions and back into the concrete realities of injuries to singular humans, let us picture Walter Benjamin's angel of history, suspended in mid-air over a small mining village in Illinois, once again unable to look away as human lives were reduced to rubble.

Interlude

Tramped-on and Trampler in the Cherry Mine Fire

Samuel Howard thought he was going to die. The twenty-year-old worked at the St. Paul Coal Company's mine in Cherry, Illinois. On Saturday, November 13, 1909, a fire broke out in the mine. Howard, his fifteen-year-old brother Alfred, and many others became trapped deep underground. Howard kept a diary of his ordeal. In the diary, he worried about what would happen to his family. "The only thing I regret is that my brother is here, and cannot help my mother out after I am dead and gone," he wrote.[1] In the end, the fire in the Cherry mine killed 259 people. These deaths cut off the incomes for more than 500 people, mostly women and children. Among them was Salina Howard, and her four other children, who had relied financially on Samuel and Alfred's income.

Local humanitarians and state officials echoed Howard's worries. As an Illinois Bureau of Labor Statistics report asked, "What is to become of the widows and orphans?"[2] Providing income to the people rendered

---

[1] "Dying Miner's Diary Details His Fight for Life," *Chicago Daily Tribune*, November 24, 1909, 4. The full text of Howard's diary was published in *The Engineering and Mining Journal*, December 11, 1909, 1173. For letters to their families by survivors of Cherry Mine disaster prior to their rescue, see Edith Wyatt, "Heroes of the Cherry Mine," *McClure's Magazine* 34, no. 5 (March 1910): 473–492.

[2] "Ask State to Fix Fault for Horror," *Chicago Daily Tribune*, November 16, 1909, 3. See also "1909 Cherry Mine Fire," in Ballard C. Campbell, *Disasters, Accidents, and Crises in American History: A Reference Guide to the Nation's Most Catastrophic Events* (New York: Facts on File, 2008), 1909. Illinois Bureau of Labor Statistics, State Board of Commissioners of Labor, *Report of the Cherry Mine Disaster* (Springfield: State Printer, 1910), 65. The miners killed at Cherry left behind "159 widows, 38 children 14 years of age or upward, and 352 children under 14" as well as many "aged parents, young brothers

newly destitute was a task taken up by the Cherry Relief Commission, made up of personnel from the Red Cross, the United Mine Workers, the Coal Operators' Association of Illinois, the Illinois state government, and local volunteers. The commission received donations from individuals and fraternal associations eager to help the afflicted, and from the Illinois government.[3]

The relief commission stepped into the gap between the immediacy of the Cherry survivors' need for money and the slow, delay-prone legal process. The fund stepped into a second gap as well: it was not clear if the St. Paul Coal Company actually had enough money to support the survivors. Women whose husbands died in the mine learned this two months after the fire, on Saturday, January 16, at a meeting with officers from the relief commission. Meeting attendees learning that many families of people killed in the fire had filed lawsuits against the coal company and that the total damages sought in these suits added up to $3 million. Yet the St. Paul Coal Company's capital was only worth $350,000. Even if the company were put out of business entirely, with all of its assets liquidated and all of that money turned over to the victims' families, the claimants would receive only about one-tenth of the damages sought in lawsuits.[4] Looking that financial picture in the face, many of the survivors agreed to attempt to negotiate, and so to lower the amount of money they demanded. They empowered a committee to act on their behalf and to approach the St. Paul Coal Company's sole customer, the Chicago, Milwaukee and St. Paul Railroad Company, asking it for help. Whether this meeting generated that plan or ratified a pre-existing plan for a settlement is unclear.

John Williams, a former coal miner turned business owner, played an especially important role in this plan. Williams wrote to Albert J. Earling, president of the Chicago, Milwaukee and St. Paul Railway, asking for money. In Williams's words, the "the principle of the proposal" he made

---

or sisters, or other near relatives," according to the American Red Cross. US House, *Sixth Annual Report* of the American National Red Cross, 61st Cong., 3rd sess., February 21, 1911, H. Doc. 1399, 20.

[3] Shortly after the fire, Illinois's Governor Charles Deneen called a special legislative session, in which, at his urging, the Illinois General Assembly allocated $100,000 to the relief fund. "New Date of Extra Session," *Chicago Daily Tribune*, November 30, 1909, 5. *Journals of the Senate and House of Representatives: Special Session of the 46th General Assembly of the State of Illinois* (Springfield: State of Illinois, 1910), 13.

[4] "Cherry Disaster Claims," *The Black Diamond* 44, no. 4 (January 22, 1910): 18. There were initially 113 such lawsuits. *Coal Age* 2, no. 14 (October 5, 1912): 474.

to Earling was "the principle of the English law" of workmen's compensation: "for each accidental death the equivalent of three years' earnings."[5] In Cherry this meant $1,800 per family financially affected by the fire.[6] Providing each family with that much money, Williams estimated, meant that the relief commission needed half a million dollars more than the donations they had received. Earling agreed that his company would cover the $500,000 and framed his decision as a matter of justice. "I hope no question more appalling or more difficult to solve will ever come to any corporation than that involved in doing justice to the survivors at Cherry," he wrote in a letter to Williams. Earling defined survivors expansively. "There were two survivors of that disaster, the bereaved and stricken people, and the ravaged corporation." Earling wished to do justice to both kinds of survivors, expressing a desire to provide for the financial security of families who lost their income and to make sure that this security provision was compatible with the financial security of business.

The Cherry relief effort was widely praised in the fire's aftermath. *The Open Court* magazine called the effort "very satisfactory all around."[7] Sarah Barnwell Elliott, writing in *The Forensic Quarterly*, went further, calling it an "epoch making settlement between labor and capital." Elliott argued that the Cherry Relief Commission's pension plan led International Harvester to adopt a similar plan, giving the families of employees killed three years of payments at the employee's pre-injury wage.[8]

Elliott expanded on her assessment of the epochal quality of the events in Cherry, borrowing a phrase from literary scholar R. W. Church in order to characterize the Cherry relief effort as "one of those solemn moments [that] had just passed when men see before them the source of the world turned one way, when it might have been turned another." Elliott attributed not only historical but existential significance to the relief effort. Often, she wrote, in the face of "the titanic movements of the universe ... our world seems very diminutive," leading people to feel "anxiously insignificant." In the face of "solemn moments" like the Cherry relief effort, however, "a sense as of greatness comes over us," that countered those anxieties and feelings of smallness.[9]

Elliott set what was in her view the relief effort's deep significance against a long temporal view and a religiously inflected sense of how society worked: "Down to that Spring day outside the walls of Jerusalem,

---

[5] *Report of the Cherry Mine Disaster*, 74.   [6] *Report of the Cherry Mine Disaster*, 85, 88.
[7] *The Open Court*, September 1910, 575–576.
[8] *The Forensic Quarterly*, June 1910, 129.   [9] *The Forensic Quarterly*, June 1910, 129.

when the Sacrifice of the World was offered up, there had been but two classes – the Tramped-on and the Trampler."[10] Elliott here expressed in Christian idiom a point that would have been at home alongside Marx and Engels's famous slogan that "the history of all hitherto existing society is the history of class struggles."[11] Marx and Engels, however, looked forward to the eventual end of class struggle through dismantling the social structures of class, while Elliott hoped for the end of class struggle by looking back to a version of Christ as a mediator who reduced friction among the persons consigned to different social classes. Mediating disputes called on all people to love one another "as thyself," Elliott wrote, and through that notion to mediate the relationships between the "Tramped-on and the Trampler." Elliott attributed this view to John Williams. In doing so she portrayed him as both inspired by Christian values and himself a Christ figure, offering the world an opportunity to embrace the call to love one another. And, she concluded, the government needed to follow suit, making sure that this principle "shall become the law of the land."[12]

The Cherry relief effort gave more energy and a new rhetorical reference point to calls for workmen's compensation to "become the law of the land."[13] Thomas Burke, editor of the *Plumbers, Gas and Steam*

---

[10] *The Forensic Quarterly*, June 1910, 144.

[11] Karl Marx and Friedrich Engels, *The Communist Manifesto: A Modern Edition* (London: Verso, 2012), 34.

[12] *The Forensic Quarterly*, June 1910, 144.

[13] Historians have emphasized the role of New England states in compensation laws and in the history of occupational safety and health. See, for example, John Fabian Witt, *The Accidental Republic: Crippled Workingmen, Destitute Widows, and the Remaking of American Law* (Cambridge, MA: Harvard University Press, 2004), and Richard A. Greenwald, *The Triangle Fire, the Protocols of Peace, and Industrial Democracy in Progressive Era* (Philadelphia: Temple University Press, 2005). While there were important developments in those states and those developments played important roles in the evolving national conversation about compensation laws, the same is true of the Midwestern states. Indeed, the Minnesota accident commission organized the first national conference on compensation laws. Wisconsin-based economist and accident commissioner John R. Commons played a key role in that conference, as discussed in David A. Moss, *Socializing Security: Progressive-Èra Economists and the Origins of American Social Policy* (Cambridge, MA: Harvard University Press, 1996). See Donald Rogers's account of the importance of nineteenth-century safety law innovations in Wisconsin: Donald Rogers, *Making Capitalism Safe: Work Safety and Health Regulation in America, 1880–1940* (Urbana: University of Illinois Press, 2009). See also Paul Bellamy's analysis of events in Ohio: Paul Bellamy, "From Court Room to Board Room: Immigration, Juries, Corporations and the Creation of an American Proletariat: A History of Workmen's Compensation, 1898–1915" (PhD diss., Case Western Reserve University, 1994).

Fitters Journal, called for "universal laws to provide adequate care and compensation for the victims of industrial accidents and those dependent on them. A disaster like that of the Cherry mine loses some of its appalling horror when it is known that the widows and helpless children are to be provided for by the state mandate, and not to be plunged into the class of public charges – paupers in one day."[14] The Illinois Bureau of Labor Statistics (BLS) prepared a special report on the Cherry fire, which included a section calling for workmen's compensation legislation. It noted that the American Mining Congress, an organization of coal mine operators, had recently come to support compensation laws, perhaps in part due to the Cherry mine settlement, which allowed the St. Paul Coal Company to avoid many lawsuits. The BLS report used rhetoric in keeping with that discussed in Chapters 2 and 3. The report praised the coal operators' humanitarianism and "their business sense," as expressed "in an organized effort to dispense with the unjustifiable waste that marks every attempt to adjudicate accident claims under existing law." The report lauded the effort to replace the court-based system of injury law with a plan that was "inexpensive and easy of enforcement."[15]

The report lamented that Americans were late in adopting "the most important conservation movement," workmen's compensation, pointing out that twenty-one other countries had already done so. The United States was "the only civilized nation in this respect that persists in its adherence to an out-grown, obsolete legal policy."[16] The BLS report said that workmen's compensation was "based on the sound economic theory that the losses sustained by workmen from accidents received in the line of their employment is a legitimate tax upon the industry" that should be "charged against the business in the same manner as breakages, depreciation of plants and other unavoidable costs of production."[17] The report also noted that these and similar costs were already paid, just in an inefficient and unpredictable manner, adding that an unnamed manufacturer had found he paid in liability insurance five times the cost he would pay for all his injured workers' costs under workmen's compensation laws.[18]

---

[14] *Plumbers', Gas and Steam Fitters' Journal* 16, no. 4 (April 1911): 35.
[15] *Report of the Cherry Mine Disaster*, 81.   [16] *Report of the Cherry Mine Disaster*, 81.
[17] *Report of the Cherry Mine Disaster*, 83.
[18] *Report of the Cherry Mine Disaster*, 84. The Bureau of Labor Statistics report also reprinted an article by Sherman Kingsley of the United Charities of Chicago, which called for workmen's compensation and noted that US manufacturers had recently paid $95 million in liability insurance premiums, of which only about $30 million wound up in the hands of injured employees and their families. *Report of the Cherry Mine Disaster*, 90.

The Missouri Division of Mine Inspections referenced the Cherry disaster in a call for compensation laws as well, writing that with the "horrors of the Cherry mine disaster ... still fresh in the minds of everyone," state legislatures needed to enact "an equitable liability and compensation law that will protect the laborer and those depending upon him."[19]

The Cherry Relief Commission gave more support to calls for workmen's compensation not least because, as Iowa Industrial Commissioner Warren Garst said, the Commission provided a practical example of how to administer funds for the families of the miners, based "on the general plan of the English Compensation Act." The Commission was in effect a locally instituted workmen's compensation program, providing a concrete working example of workmen's compensation in action in the United States. The Commission's actions demonstrated that workmen's compensation laws would more equitably distribute funds than lawsuits would. Garst pointed to "comparison between fifty families at Cherry so quickly relieved under the new plan, and fifty representative families in various cities east and west who had recently lost their breadwinners in industrial accidents but were left dependent on lawsuits and haphazard charity for relief in the old way."[20] Garst argued that 90 percent of the money collected went to people affected by the Cherry disaster, thus an average of $1,800 for each of the fifty families, compared with a total of $9,149 for the fifty families who sought compensation through the courts, an average of less than $200 each.[21] Garst likely approved of the spirit behind the Cherry settlement as well. He praised the relief effort for operating by what he called "the cardinal rules" of "[r]elief by schedule, aid for all, revenge for none."[22]

Harry Frederick Ward of the Methodist Federation for Social Service drew similar comparisons in his book *The Social Creed of the Churches*. Ward pointed to 526 people killed on the job in Pennsylvania, where more than half of the fatalities went completely uncompensated. Out of 236 workplace fatalities investigated by the New York accident commission, half received only funeral expenses. In Wisconsin, only one-third of fifty-one fatalities resulted in payments higher than $500. Compared with these examples, Ward wrote, "[t]he compensation paid to the victims of the Cherry mine disaster comes like an oasis in a dry desert." Ward

[19] *Bureau of Mines, Mining and Mine Inspection of the State of Missouri*, 12.
[20] Warren Garst, *First Biennial Report of the Iowa Industrial Commissioner to the Governor of the State of Iowa for the Period Ending June 30, 1914* (Des Moines: State of Iowa, 1914), 28.
[21] Garst, *First Biennial Report*, 29.   [22] Garst, *First Biennial Report*, 28.

asserted as well that under many European countries' compensation laws, even the comparatively well-compensated Cherry claimants would have received twice as much.[23] The Cherry relief effort certainly served the financial well-being of the families of the dead miners better than the courts would have. And it served the businesses involved as well, in that the families that got money from the relief fund agreed to drop their lawsuits, rendering the process much more predictable.[24] Williams stated explicitly that part of the success of his "efforts of mediation" between businesses and the families of victims in Cherry was "preventing a lawsuit involving a great number of claims."[25] *The Open Court* magazine praised the relief effort, going beyond financial stakes to emphasize the effort as both morally and politically significant. The magazine praised Williams in particular for transforming "the destroying fire" of the mine disaster into "a 'Refiner's fire,' where the dross of all evil contentions, all bitterness was burned away and only the pure gold of loving-kindness, of Christ-like compassion was left."[26] The families got money and businesses reduced costs, in a policy informed by compassion and love.

Compassion, love, and power: control over another person's access to money offers a significant form and degree of authority over that person. The Cherry Relief Commission, by becoming the source of the newly widowed women's access to money, took on the power to discipline women. In 1911 the Cherry Relief Commission exercised that power over Maria Guglielmi, suspending her support payments after discovering that she was living in a saloon and that her two children were living in Italy. Eighteen months later when the commission found that Guglielmi and her children were cohabitating with a man to whom Guglielmi was not married, the commission began to discuss having her children removed from her custody.[27] Had Guglielmi married the man, she would have lost the pension she received for the death of her husband.

[23] Harry Frederick Ward, *The Social Creed of the Churches* (New York: Abingdon Press, 1914), 99.

[24] *Coal Age* 2, no. 14 (October 5, 1912): 474.

[25] US Congress, Senate, Commission on Industrial Relations, *Final Report and Testimony*, vol.1, 710.

[26] *The Open Court*, September 1910, 576.

[27] See Marian Moser Jones, *The American Red Cross from Clara Barton to the New Deal* (Baltimore: Johns Hopkins University Press, 2013), 153. Jones notes that the American Red Cross took its efforts in Cherry as the template for future relief work in industrial disasters.

The relief commission likewise exercised power over the families based on age: pension payments ended when children turned fourteen. Ernest Bickle, national director of the American Red Cross and a member of the Cherry Relief Commission, described the "chief feature" of the relief commission's plan as "a system of pensions to be paid to widows with young children until the children are old enough to legally take wage-earning employment." The relief commission defined this age as fourteen years old. Families with multiple children would lose their funding when the oldest child became fourteen. Financial responsibility for the household's income would then transfer from the relief fund to that child. The policy was a decision to financially force children into labor markets at fourteen.[28] Withdrawing someone's access to money is a form of control. So is not granting access to money in the first place. Mamie Robinson, for instance, did not get any money for Samuel Howard's death. Had the fire been a few weeks later, she would have been compensated as a widow, as she and Howard had planned to marry on Christmas Day.[29] Howard had written about Robinson in his diary. Sunday, November 14, 1909, was the day when Howard had planned to give Robinson the engagement ring engraved with her initials. On that day, after a full day trapped underground, he wrote, "if I am dead, give my diamond ring to Mamie Robinson. The ring is at the post office. I had it sent there."[30] The decision to fund widows involved a decision to allocate money based on a notion of family more narrow than the actual kinship structures lived out by working-class people.

Robinson's losses, like Salina Howard's and so many others, went beyond the monetary.[31] At least some of the women whose husbands died in the mine wanted things that the tyranny of the table could not

---

[28] State of Illinois Board of Administration, *Fourth Annual Report* (Springfield: Illinois State Journal Co., State Printers, 1915), 86.

[29] Wyatt, "Heroes of the Cherry Mine," 490.

[30] "Dying Miner's Diary Details His Fight for Life," 4.

[31] The point is not to romanticize working-class families. Families vary widely and have historically (and still today) included a great deal that feminists have rightly objected to. Working-class people are by the fact of their social position subject to an injustice, but that is not a synonym for being morally laudable: oppressed and subordinated people are as complex and morally flawed in the same degrees and frequency as anyone else. What Howard and Robinson's relationship shows, then, is not that working-class people were angels but that there were kinds of valuation within working-class family relationships that did not fit into financial calculations. These kinds of valuation had some space within non-pecuniary damages for injury, but no space under strictly pecuniary calculations of injury prices, like Williams's decision that each family of a dead miner would get $1,800.

provide, and for a moment that demand threatened to prevent the table from being implemented. Specifically, many of the Cherry widows demanded their husbands' bodies, so they could hold funerals. They made this demand at the very beginning of the negotiations with the Chicago, Milwaukee and St. Paul Railway, at the January 16, 1910, meeting. A group of women protested against the coal mine remaining sealed up, thus leaving the bodies of their loved ones in the mine. Before they would consider dropping their lawsuits or otherwise negotiating, the women insisted that a telegram be sent to the company demanding the opening of the mine so that their loved ones' bodies could be recovered for burial. Funerals, with their emotional and moral meanings, trumped negotiations or monetary settlements.[32]

Samuel Howard's diary reveals more that did not fit into the table. He recorded his physical suffering: "We are cold, hungry, weak, sick, and everything else."[33] He wrote as well of his emotional suffering, including both his worries about his mother and siblings, and the terrible, traumatic sights of the disaster: "A good many dead mules and men." "I tried to save some." "I tried my best to get out, but could not. I saw Jim Jamieson and Steve Timko lying dead along the road and could not stand it any longer. So what is a fellow going to do when he has done the best he can?" "It is something fierce to see men and mules lying down all over like that."

"We lost a couple of our group," Howard wrote, when two of the miners he was trapped with tried to make their way out and failed. The men likely succumbed to toxic gases in the mine known as blackdamp. Later Howard and the rest of the group he was with built fans for themselves to clear away the gas, and tried another escape. They got further than the men who had made the prior attempt, but still found the gas too thick. This deepened Howard's sense that his death was likely inevitable. "We gave up all hope. We have done all we could."

Part of why Howard wrote his diary was as an attempt to hold his experiences, thoughts, and fears at arm's length: "To keep me from thinking I thought I would write these few lines." Many of his diary entries contain only the time and the fact that he was alive, sometimes paired with expressions of fear and suffering.

---

[32] "Cherry Disaster Claims," 18. On working-class funerals and their meanings, see Michael K. Rosenow, *Death and Dying in the Working Class, 1865–1920* (Urbana: University of Illinois Press, 2015).

[33] For the full text of Howard's diary, see *The Engineering and Mining Journal*, December 11, 1909, 1173. All quotes from the diary in the rest of this section are from this source.

"14-1909. Alive at 10:30 o'clock yet." "10.45. 11 sharp."

"Half past 11.10 to 12 o'clock. 7 after 1 o'clock. 2 o'clock. 3 o'clock and poor air."

"7:50 o'clock – thirsty, hungry, and sleep [sic], but I could stand quite a bit of this if I could get out of this hole."

"25 after 10 a.m. Sunday. Still alive, that is, you will find me with the bunch. It is 11 a.m. There are six of us: Alfred Howard, Miller, Leyshon, Sam D. Howard, Steele, and Gus Francisco. We are still alive."

"I think I won't have the strength to write pretty soon. 15 after 12 p.m. Sunday." "14 after 2 a.m. Monday. Am still alive."

"9:15 a.m. Monday morning. Still breathing. Something better turn up soon or we will soon be gone. 11:15 a.m. Still alive at this time."

Howard's diary ended, "10 to 1 p.m. Monday. This [sic] lives are going out. I think this is our last. We are getting weak. Alfred Howard as well as all of us." The least horrific scenario imaginable here is that of both Howard brothers losing consciousness simultaneously, neither having to see the other pass.

Howard's diary depicted horrible events. Unrecorded but no less horrible events took place in the final moments of so many other miners. No less horrible would have been Mamie Robinson or Salina Howard reading the diary, if they did so, and the other families, knowing their loved ones endured something similar.[34] The point is to draw out the singularity, the human reality: harms are done to individual persons with lives, senses, feelings, hopes, frustrations, people as complex and important as anyone else but treated in our society as simplified and as insignificant, as mere objects. To add further insult to insulting injury, that simplification and consignment to insignificance is itself widely denied, as in the widespread acceptance of the term "human resources."

Samuel Howard. Alfred Howard. Salina Howard. Mamie Robinson. Each of these people was embedded within and constitutive of networks

---

[34] Samuel Howard's diary was printed in newspapers. Eight days after the fire, twenty men were found underground still alive. They were interviewed by journalists about their hunger, thirst, and days in the darkness. Wyatt, "Heroes of the Cherry Mine." This too would have meant that the families of the dead could have known in ghastly detail what their loved ones suffered underground. See also Antenore Quartaroli's account of being trapped underground, written in Italian and self-published in 1911: Antenore Quartaroli, *The Great Cherry Mine Disaster November 13th, 1909, Described by Antenore Quartaroli, One of the Survivors of the 21 Buried Alive for 8 Days in the Mine* (Chicago: La Parola Printing and Publishing House, 1910). For a discussion of Quartaroli's text, see Adria Bernardi, *Houses with Names: The Italian Immigrants of Highwood, Illinois* (Chicago: University of Illinois Press, 1989), 254, and Ilaria Serra, *The Value of Worthless Lives: Writing Italian American Immigrant Autobiographies* (New York: Fordham University Press, 2007), 21, 34.

of relationships; all people are. As social and relational beings we make each other who we are: my children make me a father, my friends make me a friend, my colleagues make me a scholar, my students make me a teacher. As individuals we both constitute and are constituted by various kinds of collectivities. For each person in the Cherry Mine there was some different but analogous network of mutually constitutive people and relationships in which – in whom – the fire blew holes. The mine burnt up, taking literal human lives, like the Howard brothers, and taking parts of the lives of the survivors.

While some of the people who died at Cherry died faster than others, few of them – probably none of them – died instantly. They did not all leave diaries, but it is likely that all of them endured a range of traumatic and terrible experiences like those Samuel Howard wrote about. I include below the names of everyone that the Illinois Bureau of Labor Statistics reported as killed in the Cherry fire.[35] Readers will understandably be tempted to see this list of names as a single mass of text and to skip or skim. I encourage readers to attempt to read every single name, perhaps out loud.

M. Adakosky. Foliani Agramanti. Joseph Alexius. Alfio Amider. Charles Armelani. Paul Armelani. G. Atalakis. Peter Atalakis. George Bakalar. Antone Barozzi. Mike Bastia. Milce Bauer. Frank Bawman. Lewis Bawman. Thomas Bayliff. J. Benossif. Charles Bernadini. Tonzothe Bertolioni. John Betot. Peter Bolla. Antonio Bolla. Joseph Bordesona. Alph Bosviel. Jerome Boucher. Oliver Brain. Peter Bredenci. John Brown. Thomas Brown. Edward Bruno. John Bruzis. Richard Buckels. Charles Budzon. Joseph Budzon. John Bundy. Joseph Burke. Clemento Burslie. August Butilla. John Cagoskey. Frank Camilli. Carivo Canov. Elfi Carlo. Dominick Casolari. Elizio Casolari. John Casserio. Chelsto Castoinelo. Charles Cavaglini. Joseph Chebubar. Peter Ciocci. Canical Ciocci. Mike Cipola. Robert Clark. Henry Cohard. John Compasso. Henry Conlon. Angelo Costi. Lewis Costi. John Davies. John Debulka. Fred Demesey. Francisco Denalfi. Victor Detourney. John Donaldson. Andrew Dovin. George Dovin. Leopold Dumont. John Dunko. Benjamin Durand. Andrew Durtlan. Miestre Elario. George Elko. Peter Eloses. Charles Erickson. Eric Erickson. Joseph Famashanski. John Farlo. Peter Fayen.

---

[35] The names of the dead are taken from Illinois Bureau of Labor Statistics, State Board of Commissioners of Labor, *Report of the Cherry Mine Disaster*, 36–45. I am grateful to Angelica Mortensen for pressing me on the point about not forgetting the names of the dead.

Joseph Finko. John Fluod. John Forgach. Dominick Formento. August Francisco. John Francisco. Ole Freebirg. John Garabelda. J. Garletti. John Garletti. Angone Gialcolzza. Lewis Gibbs. John Governer. Andrew Grehaski. Frank Grumeth. Peter Guglielmi. John Guidarini. Joseph Gulick. Jalindy Gwaltyeri. Steve Hadovski. August Hainant. Mike Halko. Dan Halofcak. Joseph Harpka. John Hertzel. Alfred Howard. Samuel Howard. John Hudar. William Hynds. Frank James. James Jamison. Joe Janavizza. John Kanz. John Kenig. John Klaeser. George Klemiar. Richard Klemiar. Thomas Klemiar. Dominick Kliklunas. John Kometz. Antone Korvonia. Joseph Korvonia. Frank Kovocivio. Alfred Krall. Henry Krall. Alex Kroll. Julius Kussner. Paul Kutz. Frank Lallie. Frank Leadache. James Leadache. Joseph Leadache. John Leptack. Isaac Lewis. Urban Leynaud. Charles Leyshon. Seicom Lonzetti. John Lonzotti. David Love. James Love. John Love. Morrison Love. Andrew Lukatchko. Mike Lurnas. John Maceoha. Joe Malinoski. Joseph Mani. Archie Marchiona. Frank Marchiona. Anton Masenetta. Frank Mayelemis. John Mayersky. John Mazenetto. Robert McCandless. John McCrudden. Peter McCrudden. J. McGill, Jr. George McMullen. Joseph Meicora. Tony Mekles. Arthur Merdior. Joseph Miller or Malner. Lewis Miller or Malner. Edward Miller. Arthur Mills. Edward Mills. John Mittle. James Mohahan. Joseph Mokos. Hasan Mumetich. Joseph Rimkus. Joseph Robeza. Frank Ruygiesi. Olaf Sandeen. Julius Sarbelle. August Sarginto. Edward Seitz. Paul Seitz. J. Semboa or Sereba. John Sestak. Antone Shermel. Andrew Siamon. John Smith. Cantina Sopko. James Speir. Antone Stam. Frank Stanchez. John Stark. Tony Saszeski. James Stearns. Peter Steele. Dominick Stefenelli. Harry Stettler. Harry Stewart. Charles Sublich. John Suffen. John Suhe. Mike Suhe. Joseph Sukitus. John Szabrinski, known as John Smith. Eugene Talioli. Pasquale Tamarri. George Teszone. Andrew Tinko. Joseph Tinko, Jr. Steve Tinko. Emilia Tonnelli. John Tonner. Frank Tosseth. Nocenti Turchi. Filippe Ugo. Charles Waite. Anthony Welkas. George White. William Wyatt. Frank Yacober. Frank Yagoginski. Peter Yannis. Joseph Yearley. Antone Yurcheck. Giatano Zacherria. Pat Zeikell. Joseph Zekuia. Thomas Zliegley.

Every person in that list lived a death, one that was both incomparable with any other and yet was similar to what is revealed in Howard's diary. Human deaths are as singular as human lives; each person has a unique life and death. Maintaining both the awareness of singularity and the awareness of quantity is incredibly difficult, akin to thinking of light as both wave and particle, or thinking of one's self as simultaneously grammatically and conceptually an "I" and a "me." It is easy to forget the

singularity of those harmed, to begin to see the injured dead as a homogeneous mass – 259 dead – rather than as a constellation of individuals
with names, faces, loved ones. The way the deaths in the Cherry fire were
reported by the Illinois Bureau of Labor Statistics and the Cherry Relief
Commission encouraged that forgetting. They were examples of the
tyranny of the table writ small. Soon afterward the forgetting of the dead
would become writ large in compensation laws.

Two years after the fire, the United Mine Workers of America erected a
monument dedicated "to the memory of the miners who lost their lives in
the Cherry mine disaster," and there have been subsequent plaques and
memorials.[36] One name that does not appear on any monument is that of
a woman who the *Bureau County Tribune* reported as dying of grief. In
its February 1912 article the *Tribune* referred to her as "Mrs. Thomas
Bailiff." The paper reported her death as "another death which may be
attributed to the awful Cherry disaster," writing that "the death of her
husband" in the mine fire was so shocking "that she never fully recovered.
Constant mental distress over the sad affair finally lead to illness which
resulted in her own death." She was undoubtedly a victim of the fire,
though she was not counted on any official list.[37]

The memory of the fire certainly must have never left the few people
who were trapped underground and lived, or the many who lost family
members. The memory of the fire remained as well in the town of Cherry
and in the United Mine Workers, in the form of the United Mine
Workers' monument and regular commemoration ceremonies. Overall,
however, the Cherry fire has disappeared from cultural memory. Cherry

---

[36] Kenneth E. Foote, *Shadowed Ground: America's Landscapes of Violence and Tragedy*
(Austin: University of Texas Press, 2003), 81–85.

[37] *Bureau County Tribune*, February 16, 1912. I am aware that some memory of the Cherry
dead remains, but that memory is dispersed and marginalized. That marginalization has
many factors and facets, only some of which are due to the legal handling of injury. My
point is not to blame the law as the sole or ultimate perpetrator, but to implicate the law
as a co-conspirator. I would be remiss if I did not comment as well on the erasure in the
naming of "Mrs. Thomas Bailiff." Here too law is co-conspirator in that patriarchal
convention. I have been unable to locate her first name. That is undoubtedly the result of
a confluence of factors, including sexism, and the relative lack of importance of rural,
Midwestern, and working-class people. Here too law was a co-conspirator. We can
imagine the angel of history as cursed with perpetual insomnia, perfect eyesight, and
the inability to forget. The angel of history, looking at the night sky, would see every star
in the universe, a multitude of singular points the quantity of which scientists have not
enumerated. Eyes downward, the angel of history similarly sees and remember lives,
deaths, and harms beyond what anyone has counted. One of those is the woman erased
under the name Mrs. Thomas Bailiff.

is, so to speak, nowhere. Flyover country. No one important lives there, judged according to hegemonic and appalling standards of importance and power. According to those standards, generally speaking, no one important dies of workplace injury. Charles Atherton, the manager of the mine, is a partial exception. On February 18, a miner named Milis Manditch, alias Peter Brown, shot Atherton while the bodies of miners were being removed from the mine. Atherton died three days later.[38] Some readers may balk at "no one important," insisting rightly that everyone is important, but such readers will surely understand that our society has rarely if ever actually lived up to that view. And so the dead, and the ongoing dying, are forgotten, over and over. "Even the dead will not be safe," as Walter Benjamin has put it, and this "has not ceased."[39]

---

[38] *Bureau County Tribune*, February 25, 1910. Atherton's death was legally quite important. It was considered murder. The deaths of the miners were an administrative matter, and the death of "Mrs. Thomas Bailiff" was hardly a legal matter at all. People on the socialist left briefly contested the meaning and categorization of the Cherry miners' deaths. J. O. Bentall, from the Illinois branch of the Socialist Party, called the deaths "wholesale murder." J. O. Bentall, "The Cherry Mine Murders," *International Socialist Review* 10, no. 7 (January 1910): 577–586, 586. Vincent St. John, of the socialist union the Industrial Workers of the World, called it "wanton slaughter" and the "Cherry holocaust." Vincent St. John, "The Brotherhood of Capital and Labor: Its Effect on Labor," *International Socialist Review* 10, no. 7 (January 1910): 587–593, 587. The *International Socialist Review*'s editors described the bereaved in Cherry as "unanimous in the opinion" that the deaths were "directly due to the action of the mine officials." People in Cherry, the editors claimed, were "filled with a desperate rage against the capitalist murderers – a rage that would wipe them off the earth if opportunity came." This was, the *Review* suggested, part of why soldiers had been deployed to keep order in Cherry. "The burning of these Illinois miners is one among the daily incidents of capitalist production." Indeed, the pages of Illinois newspapers from this era regularly reported deaths at work in Illinois and around the country. "Because hundreds on this occasion are sacrificed at one time and place," the *Review* continued, "the world stops for a moment to look and listen and shudder" (pp. 551–552). Calling the deaths murder was an attempt to extend the moment, deepen the looking and listening, and intensify the shuddering in service of transformation. Then the world moved on.

[39] Walter Benjamin, "Theses on the Philosophy of History," in *Illuminations: Essays and Reflections*, ed. Hannah Arendt (New York: Harcourt, 1968), 253–264, 255. For an example of a kind of forgetting of the dead, or at least a forgetting that they died as a result of violence, consider a remark in a contemporary Bureau of Labor Statistics' Census of Fatal Occupational Injuries. The BLS noted that there were 5,915 people killed in employee accidents in 2001. The reported added in a footnote that "[t]otals for 2001 exclude fatalities resulting from the September 11 terrorist attacks." United States Bureau of Labor Statistics, "1992–2002 Census of Fatal Occupational Injuries," "Census of Fatal Occupational Injuries (CFOI) – Current and Revised Data," www.bls.gov/iif/oshcfoi1.htm, accessed April 3, 2014. There is something disconcerting in the colorless terminology "fatalities resulting from" when juxtaposed to "the September 11 terrorist attacks." The degree to which this language is not disconcerting when applied to

The angel of history has read William Blake and, suspended in the air above the grain of sand that was Cherry, looked down and saw a whole world, a world not entirely legible to itself. When looking through the lenses of the tyranny of the table people like those who praised the Cherry settlement forgot that in touching one another they held "infinity in the palm," forgot that the suffering and dying lived "eternity in an hour." So much did not fit into standardized dollar amounts, so much went unrecognized in the new language of the law. The angel of history cannot have been surprised at what came after the shift from trial to table, after having seen these and so many similar events in the long history of the relationships between "the Tramped-on and the Trampler." As we will see, with the transition from trial to table there was not so much a cessation as a reorganization of that trampling.

[handwritten margin note: — Concept of grief in dollar amounts or weight in the law]

---

workplace deaths is the degree to which the character of industrial violence as violence has been forgotten. This forgetting is bound up with notions of historical progress, as if "employment is less dangerous today" is the final word. As historian Walter Johnson has put it, that kind of narrative of progress establishes "a closed circuit by which historians and their audience together share in the knowledge that they have transcended the past," representing the present as "washed clean of the sins of the past (rather than doggedly implicated in them)." Walter Johnson, "On Agency," *Journal of Social History* 37, no. 1 (Autumn 2003): 113–124; 120–121.

PART II

NEW MACHINERIES OF INJUSTICE

The crisis in Cherry did not so much end as recede into the shadows. The dead remained dead. The bereaved remained bereaved. The powerful remained forgetful. Meanwhile, injury law reformers won their battles in the public arena. They delegitimized the court system, helping to bring about the replacement of the court system by compensation laws, the shift from the tyranny of the trial to the tyranny of the table. Compensation laws alleviated the threat that employee injury might create a crisis for powerful people in early twentieth-century US capitalism. In doing so this legislation brought about a new legal world within employee injury law and a new economic environment for businesses.

Within this new legal world, justice became less of a legal concern, commodification extended its reach, and new forms of exclusion proliferated. These changes were the result of a sequence of actions by interlocking institutions. As Part I detailed, when the twentieth century opened, injuries were a problem handed to courts. Courts often threw that problem back in the faces of the injured, but occasionally gave out large awards. This handling of injuries eventually became unsatisfactory to many people who in effect pressed the problem onto government commissions and policymakers, who enacted compensation laws.

Part II continues to follow the links in the institutional chain. Legislatures passing compensation laws did not so much solve the employee injury problem as create new problems. One such problem, discussed in Chapter 4, was what should happen when an already disabled person suffered a further disabling injury. This problem pushed injury back into courts, forcing courts to do some epistemological work, refining the definition of disability and the allocation of injury's financial costs.

Another such problem was how employers could best insure their ability to pay for injury liability; this problem, as Chapter 5 shows, had important ramifications in terms of distributive injustice. A third problem was how employers could keep costs down by identifying employees who might be expensive to insure. As Chapter 6 examines, this became the purview of the new field of industrial medicine. Industrial physicians stood as the penultimate link in the chain of institutional changes under the tyranny of the table. They came to use their medical knowledge not to provide medical care but to reduce employer-side financial risk.

Eventually, the problems of injury were largely solved, insofar as employee injury and employee injury law came to be no longer a crisis for anyone except for working-class people themselves, the final link in the chain. Employers continued to pass costs downward to vulnerable employees. Ultimately, the reformers' victories against the tyranny of the trial created new potentials for injury and injury law to create crises in working-class lives, new distributive injustices, and a continuing lack of recognition.

4

The Disabling Power of Law and Market

In the early twentieth-century United States, wealth concentrated upward while costs flowed downward. Like many other working-class people, Charles Weaver wore a share of those costs on his body and his person. In 1906, while working in a dye factory, Weaver suffered an accident that blinded his right eye. Seven years later, on July 3, 1913, while working at a Detroit auto plant, Weaver was struck by a crowbar in his left eye, blinding that eye. For the latter injury, Weaver filed a claim under Michigan's recently created workmen's compensation law.[1]

Weaver was relatively typical of working-class people in the early twentieth-century United States: in his having been injured, in that he was an employed person with a condition we would today call a disability, and in his making a legal claim. His employer contested that claim, resulting in a lawsuit. That lawsuit, and others like it, formed a process of legal remaking of the distribution of costs in the early twentieth-century US economy, and a remaking of who would count as an acceptable employee. Compensation laws were supposed to be a sea change in the institutional response to employee injuries providing, as detailed in previous chapters, new distributive justice, social stability, and predictability for business. In Weaver's case none of that happened, least of all justice. In the aftermath of Weaver's and similar cases, law adjusted the ongoing distribution of wealth upward and harm downward. The tyranny of the table brought improvements in terms

---

[1] *Weaver v. Maxwell Motor Co.*, 152 N.W. 993 (Mich. 1915). Weaver's 1906 injury occurred when Michigan still had a court-based system of employee injury law. I have not been able to locate any information about Weaver's 1906 eye injury. I do not know if he took any legal action or received any compensation.

of aggregate social stability and business predictability, while distributive justice was replaced with redistributed injustice.

DISABLED EMPLOYEES

With so many people suffering injuries in the course of their employment, that people with conditions we would today consider to be disabilities were often employed should be no surprise.[2] Yet for many able-bodied people it is nonetheless a surprise to learn about disabled people's employment. When I first encountered lawsuits brought by injured employees, I read them making claims that due to their new disabilities they would never be employed again. This seemed obvious to me, because of what was to me an intuitive and hence unexamined link between disability and unemployment. In this intuitive conception, which is widespread in the early twenty-first-century United States, there are two conceptual slippages. The first equates disability with unemployment, while the second equates unemployment with incapacity. Often today disability is equated with inability to work, which implies that disabled people deserve unemployment. In this conception, the condition of individual persons explains those persons' social circumstance. Here, as in many other circumstances, interpreting the past requires us to step outside part of our contemporary conceptual framework. The primary reason people are unemployed is that employers have opted not to hire them, a choice that is not always and only made based on an accurate judgment about ability to perform labor.

The above makes it worth underscoring the fact of disabled people's waged workforce participation prior to workmen's compensation. Charles Weaver was in one sense disabled by his 1906 loss of an eye, yet he continued to be employed. People with physical conditions that likely would be considered disabilities today seem to have been employed across the economy in the early twentieth-century United States. This is not a particularly well-documented phenomenon, likely because people with physical impairments were employed often enough that their presence in waged workplaces was unremarkable.[3]

---

[2] Isaac Max Rubinow, *Social Insurance: With Special Reference to American Conditions* (New York: Holt, 1913), 61, 68; Massachusetts Industrial Accident Board, *Third Annual Report of the Industrial Accident Board* (Boston: Wright & Potter Printing Co., State Printers, 1916), 9.

[3] It is likely that conditions that would today be called disabilities were ubiquitous in working-class life in the early twentieth century, especially given the prevalence of injury. On disability as a category for labor and working-class history, see Sarah Rose,

In her fictionalized account of her experience working briefly at an industrial laundry, social reformer Dorothy Richardson recounted that on her first day at work, a co-worker asked, "Ever worked at this job before?" Richardson said, "No. Have you?" Her co-worker "replied with a sharp laugh, and flinging back the sleeve of her kimono, thrust out the stump of wrist," saying, "It happens every wunst [*sic*] in a while, when you was running the mangle and was tired. That's the way it was with me: I was clean done out, one Saturday night, and I just couldn't see no more; and first thing I know – Wo-o-ow! and that hand went right straight clean into the rollers."[4] Richardson did not present her co-worker's injury as a rare occurrence; the women's crushed hand was a symbol of the horrors of industrial work generally. Whatever liberties Richardson may have taken with actual conversations she had with co-workers, her choice to include this anecdote demonstrates something Richardson did not foreground: workers who suffered disabling injuries sometimes returned to work.[5]

In her 1914 study, "Care and Education of Crippled Children in the United States," Edith Reeves argued in favor of vocational education for children with disabilities. Reeves appealed to the power of waged work to uplift: "the cripple of wage-earning age takes great strides toward a normal point of view when he finds himself actually doing useful work ... such work may partially bridge the gap between them and the

---

"'Crippled' Hands: Disability in Labor and Working-Class History," *Labor: Studies in Working-Class History of the Americas* 2 (2005): 27–54, and Sarah F. Rose, *No Right to Be Idle: The Invention of Disability, 1840s–1930s* (Chapel Hill: University of North Carolina Press, 2017). John Williams-Searle's work also integrates disability and gender into the study of labor history. See John Williams-Searle, "Broken Brothers and Soldiers of Capital: Disability, Manliness, and Safety on the Rails, 1863–1908" (PhD diss, University of Iowa, 2005); John Williams-Searle, "Courting Risk: Disability, Masculinity, and Liability on Iowa's Railroads, 1868–1900," *The Annals of Iowa*, no. 58 (Winter 1999): 27–77; and John Williams-Searle, "Cold Charity: Manhood, Brotherhood, and the Transformation of Disability, 1870–1900," in *The New Disability History*, ed. Paul Longmore and Lauri Umansky (New York: New York University Press, 2001), 157–186. See also Kim E. Nielsen, *A Disability History of the United States*, (Boston: Beacon Press, 2012). On disability and class in Britain, see David M. Turner and Daniel Blackie, *Disability in the Industrial Revolution: Physical Impairment in British Coalmining, 1780–1880* (Manchester: Manchester University Press, 2018).

4 Dorothy Richardson, *The Long Day: The Story of a New York Working Girl* (Charlottesville: University Press of Virginia, 1990), 233–234.

5 For other examples of people returning to waged work after disabling injuries, see United States Senate, *Report on Condition of Woman and Child Wage-Earners in the United States, vol. 12: Employment of Women in Laundries* (Washington: Government Printing Office, 1911), 52, 54; and Crystal Eastman, *Work-Accidents and the Law* (New York: Russell Sage Foundation, 1910), 227.

outer world, and so increase their happiness." This perspective relied on the possibilities of disabled people actually finding employment. Reeves believed this was possible: "many crippled children who would otherwise be entirely dependent can be taught occupations by which they can earn part of their own support.... It may be said in general that there are many occupations open to cripples whose hands are in good condition, and also that the loss or disablement of one arm is by no means a barrier to choice among a considerable number of employments." Reeves cited a 1911 census of Birmingham, England, which found that just over 21 percent of "cripples" there were able to work "under ordinary conditions" and that almost 27 percent could do work at home or in a workshop for disabled workers.[6]

In 1915, the Welfare Federation of Cleveland conducted a survey based on "a house-to-house canvass and visits to 150,000 families" that found "4,186 persons [who] were reported by themselves or their families as physically handicapped." Out of 3,250 people of working age, 59 percent were employed, or 1,912 people employed and 1,338 unemployed.[7] The Welfare Federation was surprised by this finding, writing that "one of the most interesting and valuable points about this Survey is the distinction between the definition of 'cripple' adopted at the start and the one actually used as a working basis by the Cleveland Committee." The committee had begun by defining a disabled person as one "whose (muscular) movements are so far restricted by accident or disease as to affect his capacity for self-support." The Cleveland Committee found, however, that the same physical condition could be "a measurable economic handicap in one case and apparently none at all in another."[8] The above sources are not an exhaustive document of disabled people's employment, but they do demonstrate that people with disabilities often worked for wages in the early twentieth century.

LEGAL ANOMALY AND THE PRIOR NORMAL

Even though the employment of people with physical impairments was widespread in the early twentieth century, compensation laws assumed an

[6] Edith Reeves, *Care and Education of Crippled Children in the United States* (New York: Survey Associates, 1914), 64, 67.

[7] Welfare Federation of Cleveland, *Education and Occupations of Cripples Juvenile and Adult: A Survey of All the Cripples of Cleveland, Ohio, in 1916* (Cleveland: Welfare Federation of Cleveland, 1916), 50.

[8] Welfare Federation of Cleveland, *Education and Occupations*, 12.

unimpaired worker. These laws were written for able-bodied workers who became disabled, not for disabled workers who suffered further disabling injury. As the Iowa Supreme Court put it, "[o]ur state legislature seems to have fixed the basis of compensation, having in its legislative mind a standard or normal man with a body and all members thereof in a serviceable condition."[9] This observation was generally true of other states' workmen's compensation laws as well. Compensation laws' assumption that the normal worker was able-bodied meant that injuries to already impaired people like Weaver did not fit neatly into the categories of the law. That left Weaver's injury legally ambiguous, and so created room for Weaver's employer to contest his compensation claim.

In Michigan, as in many states, the workmen's compensation law stipulated that injured people receive weekly payments for injury. The amount for the weekly payment was 50 percent of the employee's pre-injury wages, an easily budgetable sum for employers. The Michigan law set three different kinds of caps on injury payments: a weekly payment maximum, a maximum quantity of weeks, and a maximum total dollar amount. The weekly maximum payment was ten dollars per week. Payments would never be ordered for longer than 500 weeks, and the total injury compensation maximum was $4,000.

The Michigan compensation board initially granted Weaver's compensation, ordering his employer to pay the statutory maximum of payments, ten dollars per week, up to the maximum total dollar amount, $4,000, thus 400 weeks. The amount was based on Weaver's pre-injury wage of 37.5 cents per hour, or $21.50 per week. That means his payment of ten dollars per week was not quite 50 percent of his pre-injury wage. Under the law, in Weaver's case as in any such injury, the effects of the financial hardship involved in losing more than half of his income were Weaver's private problem. Once the payments ran out, what Weaver did was his private problem as well. Inflicting distributive injustice on people in the aftermath of injury was built into the law. This means that even had Weaver's compensation claim been treated as normal, in important respects the employer had already in effect won, while Weaver lost financially, bodily, personally – a great deal. The legal contest would be about the further extent of this winning and losing.

Weaver's employer did not challenge the weekly payment, but rather the number of weeks of payments, arguing that they should only pay

---

[9] *Pappas v. N. Iowa Brick & Tile Co.*, 206 N.W. 146 (Iowa 1925).

100 weeks of compensation, for a total of about $1,100.[10] The two sides
in Weaver's case offered in a sense two worldviews on injury, disability,
and labor power. The employer-side brief described Weaver's blindness as
"not due independently to the accident that he sustained at the time of his
later injury. It was due partially to other causes." That is, multiple events
had conspired to cause Weaver's blindness, and only some of the events
were his current employer's problem. Parsing the injury into multiple
causes allowed the attorney to claim that the Maxwell Motor Company
was responsible for only some of those causes, and so should not be liable
for the total result. The brief added that it was unknown if Weaver had
already been paid for his earlier injuries, speculating that "[i]f he did he is
now recovering double damages."[11] The implication here was that
Weaver might be trying to get more than he deserved, and that this was
unfair to his employer.

The brief continued, invoking fairness to the employer explicitly: "it
would be unfair and inequitable to charge the cost of the plaintiff's first
injury to the employer at the time of the second injury and to permit the
plaintiff to receive compensation, from the later employer, for the loss of
sight of both eyes. If the plaintiff is to receive compensation for the loss
of the sight of the eye that was first injured, a claim therefore should be
made against the employer for whom he was working at that time."[12]
There was an appeal here to the moral notion of fairness, a version of
distributive justice reduced to not being double billed.[13]

In his brief, Weaver's attorney described Weaver's blindness differently, offering a different worldview on injury and disability. Weaver's
vision prior to his injury at the Maxwell Motor Company "was sufficient
for him to properly and satisfactorily perform his work for them. His total

---

[10] Adjusted for inflation, Weaver's initial compensation award was to be about $276 per
week in today's dollars, for a total cost to his employer of almost $103,000. The lower
compensation level his employer sought would be about $28,000 in inflation adjusted
dollars. His wages adjusted for inflation would be about ten dollars per hour and $553
per week. Inflation adjustment via the Bureau of Labor Statistics Inflation Calculator,
https://data.bls.gov/cgi-bin/cpicalc.pl, accessed July 15, 2018.

[11] *Weaver v. Maxwell Motor Co.*, Appellant's Brief, 4, State Law Library at the Library of
Michigan, Lansing, MI. For an illuminating discussion of legal ideas about causality, see
John Fabian Witt, *The Accidental Republic: Crippled Workmen, Destitute Widows, and
the Remaking of American Law* (Cambridge, MA: Harvard University Press, 2004),
152–186.

[12] *Weaver v. Maxwell Motor Co.*, Appellant's Brief, 4.

[13] For a similar reduction, see the discussion of the concept of equity in the life insurance
industry in this era in Dan Bouk, *How Our Days Became Numbered: Risk and the Rise of
the Statistical Individual* (Chicago: University of Chicago Press, 2015), 4–19.

vision consisted of that one eye.... That vision was so complete that the defendant never discovered that he was lacking in any of his vision, nor was the claimant hampered or handicapped in any way in doing his work." Weaver could do the work with the capacity he had. "1. Is Mr. Weaver entitled to loss of total vision, even though that consist of the loss of but one eye? Or, 2. Is Mr. Weaver entitled to compensation for but the loss of one eye from the injury while in the employ of the Maxwell Motor Company, and therefore entitled to compensation limited to one hundred weeks? Or, 3. ... does the act warrant a construction that the Legislature intended in a case such as this, to grant a compensation equivalent to the differences between the compensation fixed for the loss of one eye and compensation fixed for the loss of two eyes, or three hundred weeks?" "It must be borne in mind," he added, that the compensation act "was passed for the purpose of protecting and compensating the workman for such loss as he actually sustained ... The very evident theory of the act is to reimburse for the loss of compensation, not merely to pay so much per finger, per arm, per leg or per eye, that might be lost."[14] Loss of compensation here referred to loss of earnings or earning capacity due to injury. Weaver had lost all of his earning capacity: "He can now do nothing that he could immediately do before the injury to this one eye. Before the injury he had full capacity to do his work; after the injury he had no capacity." "With his one eye he did all the work. Without his one eye, he can do no work. It seems, therefore, an irresistible conclusion that his present total incapacity for work resulted from the injury received on the 3d day of July, 1913."[15]

The dispute in this case was over legal responsibility, with a large sum of money hanging in the balance, and also was a kind of meta-dispute over the terms in which injury would be conceptualized: Was injury a matter of bodily quantity or of capacity? This was a dispute, that is, about determining the fate of concrete persons, a dispute conducted through rhetorical abstractions about capacity and fairness; it was also a dispute about the concepts and vocabulary in which the dispute would be conducted.

Weaver's attorney focused on capacity, arguing that Weaver previously had sufficient capacity to do his job, and that his 1913 injury destroyed all of that capacity. This focus on capacity made his prior

---

[14] *Weaver v. Maxwell Motor Co.*, Appellee's Brief, 4–5, State Law Library at the Library of Michigan, Lansing, MI.
[15] *Weaver v. Maxwell Motor Co.*, Appellee's Brief, 6.

injury irrelevant, and made the causality no longer parse-able into a set of multiple events. "The objection is made that Mr. Weaver, having lost one eye some years previously, it would be unfair to penalize the Maxwell Motor Company as for the loss of both eyes, when, in fact, he lost only one while working for them. This might be true if the test of the act is purely the number of eyes which a man can lose, but if the test of the act is, as we stated in the beginning of this brief, the injury actually suffered by the man in his vision, then we find that he lost his total vision."[16] There had been no prior court cases on this, but the compensation boards of Ohio, Washington, and Massachusetts had ruled similarly to the Michigan board. The brief quoted a member of the Massachusetts board: "To that man, that one eye was invaluable. If he was rendering good service with that one eye to the industry in which he was employed, and that one eye was as good as two eyes, and you take away his one eye so that he is absolutely sightless, the same as though the accident had destroyed both eyes, why should he not be compensated?"[17]

In these two arguments, the lawyers framed Weaver's injuries as having two distinct kinds of effects: loss of some quantity of body (one eye) or loss of some quantity of capacity (some proportion of a person's sight). As Iowa Supreme Court Justice William D. Evans would later put it, the dispute was over whether compensation laws set "a fixed value for the loss of one eye, regardless of whether the eye thus lost is the only eye of the injured party."[18] These different framings had consequences in terms of liability and who got how much money. Bodily quantum arguments leaned toward lower payments: Weaver had lost only one eye, so he should be paid only for the part of his body he had given up. In this framing the law put the pound of flesh on the scale and weighed it. Capacity arguments leaned toward higher payments: Weaver had lost all of his sight, so he should be paid for being rendered blind. In this framing the law considered the marginal utility of the loss, so to speak, in light of the likely (in)hospitability of the labor market to the injured person's future employment.

In June 1915 the Michigan Supreme Court ruled against Weaver. In that decision the court seemed to split the difference between the arguments by the two attorneys. The decision treated Weaver's loss not only as the loss of an eye but also as a loss of capacity. But it treated Weaver's

---

[16] *Weaver v. Maxwell Motor Co.*, Appellee's Brief, 15.
[17] *Weaver v. Maxwell Motor Co.*, Appellee's Brief, 16.
[18] *Jennings v. Mason City Sewer Pipe Co.*, 174 N.W. 785 (Iowa 1919).

injuries as two distinct partially disabling injuries, accepting the framework of the employer's attorney in which Weaver's blindness was parsed causally and temporally. Implied here was an important difference in how to treat disabled people under compensation law. Weaver's lawyer had argued that compensation laws required employers to pay employees for the degree of loss of capacity that an employee suffered due to an injury on the job. That is, the standard was to be the total condition after the injury. This framing meant that disabled people possessed the capacity that they had, and that capacity was to be valued according to the wages they earned, just as with able-bodied persons. If disabled people lost all the capacity they had, that lost capacity was just as valuable as the capacity of able-bodied persons. In this framing, employees owned property in their labor power and that property was to be equally valued in the law. The framing by the employer's attorney implied that a disabled person entered employment with already reduced capacity, and so had labor power that was legally worth less than that of an able-bodied person.[19]

The Michigan Supreme Court endorsed the latter view in its decision:

The loss of the second eye, standing by itself, was also a partial disability, and of itself did not occasion the total disability. It required that, in addition to the results of the disability occasioned by the accident of seven years ago, there should be added the results of the partial disability of the recent accident to produce the total disability. The absence of either accident would have left the claimant partially incapacitated. We think it clear the total incapacity cannot be entirely attributed to the last accident. It follows that the compensation should be based upon partial incapacity.[20]

Weaver's second accident had caused him to go from a condition in which he was sighted, and sufficiently so to work for the auto company, to a condition of blindness, a condition in which employers were unwilling to hire him. He was thus genuinely incapacitated and out of work as a result of his second injury. But the court took each injury in isolation as partially disabling, two partial disabilities adding up to a total disability. Since only one of those disabilities had happened at his 1913 job, the court reasoned, the auto company was liable for only one of Weaver's

---

[19] This was in addition to any differences in wages paid. My earlier statements in this paragraph, that disabled people were to be "just as valuable" and "equally valued," need to be qualified by adding "relatively speaking." The argument by Weaver's attorney amounted to saying that the capacity of a disabled person should be valued at the same number of weeks of pay as an able-bodied person. This leaves aside the lower pay rates employers sometimes paid to disabled employees.

[20] *Weaver v. Maxwell Motor Co.*, 152 N.W. 994 (Mich. 1915).

disabling injuries. The additional incapacity above the partial disability caused by Weaver's second injury was privatized, rendered Weaver's individual burden.

The Michigan court believed this was the first appellate case dealing with the issue of injury to an already disabled individual. It noted that Minnesota had had a similar case, that of John Garwin. In 1915, the Minnesota Supreme Court ruled that John Garwin's loss of his only eye did not count as permanent total disability. The Minnesota court's decision was easier than the decisions of other courts, because Minnesota's workmen's compensation law stated: "If an employee receives an injury, which, of itself, would only cause permanent partial disability, but which, combined with a previous disability, does in fact cause permanent total disability, the employer shall only be liable for the permanent partial disability caused by the subsequent injury." Therefore, the Minnesota court held that Garwin's blinding was, for the purposes of the law, a partial disability. Garwin's blindness was a total disability in fact, but a partial disability at law.[21]

In 1919, the Iowa Supreme Court issued a ruling in response to an injury to a man named I. B. Jennings. The Iowa court drew on multiple kinds of reasoning about injury, liability, disability, and justice, combining them into an odd patchwork.[22] In 1915, Jennings fell from a wagon while at work at a sewer pipe factory. He tumbled twenty feet down a steep, rocky embankment, and suffered injuries that blinded his left eye. Jennings was already blind in his right eye, such that he was left fully blind by his 1915 injury. He had filed a compensation claim and won. As with Weaver's case, Jennings's employer contested his claim. Iowa's Industrial Commissioner found in favor of Jennings and editorialized that ruling "compensation for the second eye, as contended by defendants, should be upon the basis of loss of a single eye, is so unjust and unreasonable as to establish its own denial. It is only reasonable to conclude the Legislature

---

[21] *State ex rel. Garwin v. District Court of Cass County*, 151 N.W. 910 (Minn. 1915). Minnesota was one of a sizable minority of states with provisions to this effect. As of 1921, other states with these provisions included Alabama, Georgia, Indiana, Missouri, Nebraska, New Mexico, Tennessee, Texas, and Wyoming. See F. Robertson Jones, *Digest of Workmen's Compensation Laws in the United States and Territories, with Annotations*, 21, 73, 106, 188, 201, 228, 307, 315, and 373, respectively.

[22] *Jennings v. Mason City Sewer Pipe Co.*, 174 N.W. 785 (Iowa 1919). The Iowa court's reasoning largely follows that suggested by Iowa's Attorney General Henry Sampson in 1914. See "Iowa Confronted by Problem of the One Eyed Workman," *National Compensation Journal* 1, no. 8 (August 1914): 3–4; 3. It is reasonable to assume that the Iowa Court was familiar with and convinced by Sampson's arguments.

had in mind, in providing 100 weeks of compensation, a situation where the workman still had one eye remaining."[23] Jennings's employer appealed and lost. The Iowa Supreme Court argued in its decision in *Jennings v. Mason City Sewer Pipe Co.* that Jennings clearly could not be counted as only partially disabled. The court wrote that doing so would give Jennings only 100 weeks of compensation, and that to grant

[o]ne hundred weeks of compensation to a man condemned to grope in darkness the rest of his natural life is so grossly inadequate to the loss he has sustained as to make such settlement nothing less than monstrous. It seems impossible that any legislature in the United States should have ever intended to countenance such dealing with the unfortunate victim of industrial accident had it anticipated the effect.[24]

In this assessment the Iowa court invoked an implied notion of justice that while murky was clearly present, as displayed by the rhetoric.[25] Even though the Iowa court did not think 100 weeks of compensation was enough, at the same time the court argued that Jennings should not receive the full compensation that workers compensation law stipulated for permanent total disability, 400 weeks of payments. To give Jennings 400 weeks of payment, the court held, would be to hold his employer unfairly liable for the loss of both of Jennings's eyes. In the end, the Iowa court split the difference. The court took the statutorily stipulated compensation for blindness and other forms of permanent total disability, 400 weeks of payments, and subtracted the value of loss of one eye, 100 weeks of payments. The court thus decided to give Jennings 300 weeks of payments, a ruling somewhere between partial and total disability. Since Jennings was blinded by the loss of one eye, the court allocated Jennings more compensation than the norm for the loss of one eye and less compensation than the norm for blinding. The Iowa ruling for Jennings was different insofar as the financial fates of the individual men involved: Weaver got less money than Jennings. The rulings were similar in another sense, however, in that each ruling continued the old normal of subordinated inclusion and devaluation for people with disabilities.

---

[23] *State of Iowa Report of the Workmen's Compensation Service for the Biennial Period Ending June 30, 1918* (Des Moines, 1918), 27.

[24] Michigan and Minnesota had both made precisely this monstrous choice. *Jennings v. Mason City Sewer Pipe Co.*, 174 N.W. 785 (Iowa 1919).

[25] Judges were in effect part of a kind of moral economy of injury, however attenuated. See E. P. Thompson, "The Moral Economy of the English Crowed in the Eighteenth Century," in Thompson, *Customs in Common: Studies in Traditional Popular Culture* (London: Merlin Press, 1991), 185–258, and "The Moral Economy Reviewed," also in *Customs in Common*, 259–351.

Under these decisions, able-bodied people would receive money equal to the legal measure of the full capacity they lost in their injury. Disabled people who suffered an employee injury would receive the amount of money their injury would cause to an able-bodied person, and any additional lost capacity would be left on the injured individual and their support system. Weaver was compensated as if he had two eyes and lost only one of them. The additional costs to Weaver of his condition were his problem. Jennings was treated more generously, but he still received less than a two-eyed person who was blinded. These decisions amounted to a two-tiered system of injury valuation, one in which blinding a one-eyed person was cheaper and less important than blinding a two-eyed person. The same principle applied broadly to other matters of disabling injuries to already impaired persons. This was a clear distributive injustice visited on disabled people.

The legal fate of these men illustrates multiple facets of compensation laws. The law was ableist in such a way that rendered disabled people anomalous in the law. This meant that disabled people were in important respects left out of the new right to file a claim. Compensation laws that rendered disabled people legally anomalous left them to the tyranny of the trial. The resolution of these case ended that condition in their respective states. After that resolution, disabled people in Michigan, Minnesota, and Iowa were under different legal particulars, but they all shared a subordinate, second-class status, with their injuries worth less legally than injuries to able-bodied people. Disabled people were legally categorized as having reduced capacity and that capacity was legally worth less than the capacity of able-bodied people. It was doubly devalued. Disabled people could be legally paid lower wages due to their disabilities, and their injuries and the capacity damaged by those injuries could be further devalued under the law.

These outcomes were in keeping with long-standing patterns of the subordination of and social disrespect to disabled people, which were typical in the United States for many years – the "old normal." The supreme courts of Michigan, Minnesota, and Iowa ruled that their states' compensation laws would remain artifacts of the old normal in which disabled people were subordinated, second-class persons. At most, these decisions created innovations within (and which preserved) the old normal.

It bears mention here that within the old normal, disabled people's lower social status was reflected in markets. Social disrespect for disabled people, in the form of the long-standing assumption that disabled people were worth less and were less capable than able-bodied people, meant lower wages. This was in effect extra-economic values shaping the (de) valuation of disabled people within markets. This was a social world like that of the court system prior to compensation laws, where economic values in a narrow sense co-existed with other values, a condition Margaret Radin has called incomplete commodification. In this sense, then, labor markets were embedded in or enmeshed with the social norms of the time – which is not at all to defend those norms.[26]

INFLICTING DISABILITY

While disability is often considered a condition inhering in a person individually, it can instead be considered a social condition and a power relationship. Disability is itself a kind of abstraction organizing society. In this perspective, a disabled person is someone who is, in specific times and places, consigned to the social status of being disabled. To put it another way, disable is a verb; institutions and actions disable people in the sense of putting people in social positions of disability. "Is this person disabled?" is a question more complex to answer than might first appear, requiring that the response be "when, where, by what standards, and with what consequences?"

All of this means disability is best understood in historical terms. As scholars of disability history have argued, disability should be considered as a social and historical phenomenon, rather than an exclusively medical, personal, and individual matter. That is, disability is a social relationship and a power relationship. People with disabilities, write Catherine Kudlick and Paul Longmore, should be considered as a "historically excluded minority."[27] This means, in the words of Paul Longmore and Lauri Umansky, that "the social marginalization and economic deprivation of

[26] Margaret Jane Radin, *Contested Commodities: The Trouble with Trade in Sex, Children, Body Parts, and Other Things* (Cambridge, MA: Harvard University Press, 2001). While I am critical of commodification in this book I want to note that social practices that are relatively noncommodified or shaped by cultural patterns that originate outside the market can be quite oppressive. This point is made forcefully in Nancy Fraser, "Behind Marx's Hidden Abode: For an Expanded Conception of Capitalism," *New Left Review* 2, no. 86 (2014): 56, and Nancy Fraser and Rahel Jaeggi, *Capitalism: A Conversation in Critical Theory* (Cambridge: Polity, 2018). Fraser and Jaeggi also make the important argument that systematic non-commodification of some areas of life and society is part of capitalism.

[27] Catherine Kudlick and Paul Longmore, "Disability and the Transformation of Historians' Public Sphere," *Perspectives on History* 44, no. 8 (November 2006), www.historians.org/publications-and-directories/perspectives-on-history/november-2006/disability-and-the-transformation-of-historians-public-sphere, accessed January 15, 2014.

many people with disabilities" should be thought of as political and as historically produced, rather than as natural or explained by physical condition.[28] Historian Sarah Rose demonstrates that experiences of disability – including injury, occupational disease, and disabled people's marginalization – have been central to work and to working-class life in the United States in ways that have not been sufficiently recognized.[29]

Borrowing from theorist Rosemary Garland-Thompson, literary scholar Susan Schweik discusses the construction of what she calls "the normate." The normate is the social figure of a normal person at any given time and place – the type of human being that is normalized. Successfully portraying one's self as normal, as meeting the standards required to be considered normate, or failing to successfully portray one's self as such, has serious consequences. The standards of normate status tend to vary by institutional location – the waged workplace versus the asylum versus the border – as do the consequences of being judged as not meeting those standards. Disability should be understood as a process of defining a normate as a certain type of person, judging who does and does not meet that definition, and creating a set of consequences for being judged non-normate. These processes are specific to, and change over, time and place.[30] Historian Kim Nielsen has advocated for disability

---

[28] Longmore and Umansky, *The New Disability History*, 12. Barbara Welke has argued that US law has long assumed persons to be able-bodied white males. Law both reflects and creates disability as subordination and exclusion, and shapes how disability interacts with other kinds of subordination and exclusion. See Barbara Young Welke, *Law and the Borders of Belonging in the Long Nineteenth Century United States* (Cambridge: Cambridge University Press, 2010). See also Douglas Baynton, "Disability and the Justification of Inequality in American History," in Longmore and Umansky, *New Disability History*, 33–57; Rose, "'Crippled' Hands" and *No Right to Be Idle*; Williams-Searle, "Courting Risk" and "Broken Brothers and Soldiers of Capital."

[29] Rose, *No Right to Be Idle*. As Rosemary Garland Thomson has put it, "[h]istorically, disabled people have for the most part been segregated either as individuals or in groups ... enclosed, excluded, and regulated.... Perhaps the most enduring form of segregation has been economic." Rosemarie Garland Thomson, *Extraordinary Bodies: Figuring Physical Disability in American Culture and Literature* (New York: Columbia University Press, 1997), 35. The point is not that disability is above all economic, but rather that economic marginalization is one frequent and important facet of disability. See also Turner and Blackie, *Disability in the Industrial Revolution*, 4–8, criticizing Garland Thomson and other disability scholars for overestimating the importance of industrialization in marginalizing disabled people. I would argue that it was not industrial production as such that marginalized disabled people, but legally structured incentives. That is, exclusion resulted not from technical factors but from political economy.

[30] Susan Schweik, *The Ugly Laws: Disability in Public* (New York: New York University Press, 2009).

history as the history of the "definitions of 'fit' and 'unfit' bodies," which means examining "how politics, culture, economics, and larger ideological notions of normality define who is and who is not disabled; or conversely, who is and who is not normal."[31] This kind of history analyzes "the power to define bodies as disabled" and to shape the consequences of being so defined.[32] That power has often rested with judges, as demonstrated in cases like Weaver's. Discrimination against disabled people in the form of lower wages shows how that power also rested – with law's approval – with employers.

Weaver and people like him lived within one set of definitions of disability and its consequences. Initially, Weaver believed he was included in compensation laws, and so sought to file a claim when he was injured. Yet because of the assumption of ableness in compensation laws, he was not legally included. This fact fits with what Barbara Welke has called the abled character of US law generally, which means that the normative legal person, the person assumed by law, is able-bodied.[33]

While left out of legal rhetoric, disabled people like Weaver had access to employment. As such they were in a sense socially included. Inclusion in employment is not equality, however, because employment itself is hierarchical. Disabled people's relative social inclusion in employment was further hierarchical in that disabled people tended to be pressed lower in the labor market and valued less than able-bodied people. Historian Sarah Rose has argued that people we would today call disabled were once relatively integrated into economic life, though in a subordinated position.[34] The subordinated inclusion of people with disabilities in employment often meant lower pay. Wage discrimination

---

[31] Kim E. Nielsen, "Historical Thinking and Disability History," *Disability Studies Quarterly* 28, no. 3 (Summer 2008), http://dsq-sds.org/article/view/107/107, accessed January 15, 2014; Kim E. Nielsen, *The Radical Lives of Helen Keller* (New York: New York University Press, 2004), 3.

[32] Nielsen, *A Disability History of the United States*, 182.

[33] Welke, *Law and the Borders of Belonging*. The abled character of the law under the tyranny of the trial seems to have worked differently. It included the openness of trial proceedings to cultural assumptions about disability and the lower financial valuation of disabled people legally and by employers. It is likely that these aspects of court proceedings not only reflected but actively helped construct disability in their day. For a study of the role of trials in constructing the meaning of work, childhood, injury, and child labor, see James Schmidt, *Industrial Violence and the Legal Origins of Child Labor* (Cambridge: Cambridge University Press, 2010).

[34] Rose argues in addition that both disability and productivity were conceptualized as a continuum. Later a binary emerged between able/disabled and productive/unproductive, as well as an association between the pairings, with able and productive being treated as

against people with disabilities was legally permissible and probably widespread in the early twentieth century. At the start of the twentieth century, then, it was relatively normal for physically impaired people to be included in waged work, but often at a lower standard of pay.[35]

In their claims-making, Weaver and people like him demanded in effect a new normal of equal status for disabled people. Instead, they were subjected to long-standing versions of disability – the old normal. In other states, however, the old normal – in employee injury law and in employment – would soon be transformed and in some settings even replaced by a new normal for disability.

FAIRNESS TO INDIVIDUALS AND A NEW NORMAL

In 1910 at a Massachusetts bobbin factory a bobbin broke and a piece of flying debris struck Eugene Branconnier in his right eye. The injury would lead to the loss of that eye. On January 18, 1915, at the same factory, another airborne fragment struck Branconnier in his left eye. After Branconnier left work, Branconnier's wife put bread and milk on the injury to try to reduce the inflammation, but the injury would lead to loss of sight in the eye. Like Weaver, Garwin, and Jennings, Branconnier's two injuries occurred under different legal frameworks, with the second falling under the Massachusetts compensation law. Branconnier too filed a compensation claim, which his employer contested. Branconnier's legal fate differed from that of the others discussed above. Taken together, the legal processes in cases like Branconnier's case would come to reshape the legal and economic fate of disabled people.

The compensation commission granted Branconnier compensation for total disability.[36] Pointing to the decision in Weaver's case, Branconnier's employer contested this decision. As in Weaver's case, the employer's

synonyms, and disabled and unproductive as likewise synonyms. See Rose, *No Right to Be Idle*, and Schweik, *Ugly Laws*. Over time, across different institutional locations, there seems to be a trend in the United States toward normate and non-normate being constructed as a binary rather than a continuum, with regard to race, gender, and sexuality in addition to disability. See Margot Canaday, *The Straight State: Sexuality and Citizenship in Twentieth-Century America* (Princeton: Princeton University Press, 2009), and Ian Haney López, *White by Law: The Legal Construction of Race*, revised ed. (New York: New York University Press, 2006).

[35] See *Schwab v. Emporium Forestry*, 153 N.Y. Supp. 234 (1915) for legal approval of wage discrimination against the disabled.

[36] Branconnier's Case (223 Mass. 273), Record on Appeal, 4, in the collection of the Social Law Library, Boston, Massachusetts.

attorney tried to segment the causality of Branconnier's blindness into two events, with the employer responsible for only one such event. The employer should not, the attorney argued, "be called upon to pay compensation based upon the total disability of an employee which is made up of two different elements," namely, the 1910 and 1915 injuries. The employer "should not be required to pay the same compensation as it would had the injury destroyed the sight of both eyes."[37]

The Massachusetts Industrial Commission had stated in its ruling on Branconnier's injury that the fact that Branconnier had previously lost his right eye in an injury did not "prejudice his rights" under the compensation law

any more than are prejudiced the rights of an employee whose previously diseased or dormant condition is aggravated or accelerated to the point that he is compelled to leave his employment and by reason of an injury is rendered unfit for the performance of any work. The law provides for the payment of compensation to an injured employee on the basis of his ability to earn wages after he receives a personal injury which arises out of and in the course of employment.... This holds true, whether the employee, having but one eye, or one leg, or one hand, or dormant disease, is rendered sightless, legless, armless, or helpless, by reasons of a personal injury occasioned by and arising out of his employment. Prior to the injury, his earning capacity was secure; thereafter it became insecure, with little or no promise of future ability to earn.[38]

The commission added that prior to his 1915 injury Branconnier had been able to earn wages, while after that injury he was left "unable to earn any wages; therefore the said employee's total incapacity" was a new condition attributable to that 1915 injury.[39]

The Massachusetts court ruled in favor of Branconnier in 1916, finding that Branconnier had been blinded by the loss of his only eye. Since Branconnier had lost all of his ability to see, he ought to be considered totally disabled and his employer ought to be liable for Branconnier's blindness.[40] In its decision for Branconnier, the Massachusetts court cited a decision by the New York Court of Appeals in favor of a man named Jacob Schwab. In 1914 Schwab lost his right hand in a workplace accident. The 1914 accident left him handless, since Schwab had lost his

---

[37] Branconnier's Case (223 Mass. 273), Defendant's Brief, 1, in the collection of the Social Law Library, Boston, Massachusetts.
[38] Branconnier's Case (223 Mass. 273), Record on Appeal, 4.
[39] Branconnier's Case (223 Mass. 273), Record on Appeal, 4.
[40] Branconnier's Case (223 Mass. 273).

left hand in 1892.[41] The 1915 decision of the New York Court of Appeals held that Schwab should be compensated for his total post-injury condition – his being rendered handless – rather than the loss of one hand. The court thus considered him permanently totally disabled. The basic point was that in cases of compensation for workplace injuries employers should be liable for the total post-injury condition of the injured. These decisions, like Weaver's lawyer, conceptualized injuries in terms of loss of capacity, rather than loss of quantity of body parts.

In an important sense, the legal decisions in Michigan, Minnesota, and Iowa were less just than the decisions in Massachusetts and New York. Weaver, Garwin, and Jennings were treated worse than Branconnier and Schwab. Furthermore, the Massachusetts and New York courts were in important respects a departure from the old normal of disabled people's explicit second-class status in the law. The decisions for Branconnier and Schwab made employee injury law in Massachusetts and New York somewhat less ableist and thus more formally egalitarian. That said, on closer scrutiny it is hard to consider any of these courts as enacting justice for disabled people. They braided together older patterns of subordination and devaluation of disabled people with new ones.

Elements of the old normal of disabled people's inclusion while subordinated and devalued explicitly informed the legal reasoning of the Massachusetts court. The court said Branconnier, on beginning work,

had that degree of capacity which enabled him to do the work for which he was hired. That was his capacity. It was impaired capacity as compared with the normal capacity of a healthy man in possession of all his faculties. But nevertheless it was the employee's capacity. It enabled him to earn the wages he received.... The total capacity of this employee was not so great as it would have been if he had had two sound eyes. His total capacity was thus only part of that of the normal man. But that capacity, which was all he had, has been transformed into a total incapacity by reason of the injury.[42]

The Massachusetts court's argument about capacity had involved the claim that Branconnier had lower than normal ability. It further implied, without disapproval, that his wages reflected this condition. It thus expressed elements of what I have called the old normal, disabled people's subordinated inclusion.

[41] *Schwab v. Emporium Forestry*, 153 N.Y. Supp. 234 (N.Y. App. Div. 1915).
[42] Quoted in William R. Schneider, *The Law of Workmen's Compensation: Rules of Procedure, Tables, Forms, Synopses of Acts*, vol. 2 (St. Louis: Thomas Law Book Company, 1922), 1069.

The old normal figured importantly in the New York court's decision in favor of Jacob Schwab as well. A central presupposition to the New York court's reasoning was that a one-handed worker would provide "less efficient service" and thus receive lower wages. The court compared two hypothetical workers. If a two-handed worker earned twenty dollars per week, then the loss of a hand would have been worth more than $3,500, because "[t]he method of payment of compensation for the loss of one hand [was] to allow sixty-six and two-thirds per centum of the salary which the injured party was earning for 244 weeks." Conversely, the court presumed its hypothetical one-handed worker to earn "say $10 a week." Such a worker on losing the sole remaining hand would receive under the same formula only around $1,600. A one-handed person's hand should be more than doubly valuable, not half as valuable, the New York court reasoned. To say otherwise would be an "anomalous result" that obviously "the Legislature could not so have intended."

"If a man has two hands," the opinion in Schwab reads, "he is presumably a more efficient worker and can receive higher wages than if crippled by the loss of one hand."[43] The court assumed that a one-handed worker's single hand would be more valuable to that worker, and that that worker would be less efficient and thus receive lower wages than a two-handed worker. If the one-handed worker lost his remaining hand, then the doubly valuable hand would be compensated at half the value of one hand belonging to a previously two-handed worker. The court found that conclusion unacceptable, because the discrepancy was too great. The New York court's arguments explicitly began from a working assumption of wage inequalities for disabled workers. Furthermore, the court appears to have found the practice of wage inequality legitimate, since the court used wage differentials between the disabled and the able-bodied in order to make its arguments. The court thus understood and contributed to the old normal of disabled people's subordinated inclusion in labor markets.

The court's decision underscores elements of the old normal present in compensation laws as well. The New York court reasoned that an injury that left someone with no hands rendered that person totally disabled under the law. At the same time, a person who lost two hands would receive more money than a person who lost their one and only hand. The difference in payment was not due to a notion of greater injury severity but to differences in pre-injury wages. As the New York Court of Appeals

[43] *Schwab v. Emporium Forestry.*

put it, "the man with one hand is presumably earning less wages than a man with two hands."[44] The court took for granted that employers would see the labor power of disabled workers as worth less money.

The rulings in favor of Jacob Schwab and Eugene Branconnier awarded greater compensation to an individual disabled person through a process of reasoning that affirmed elements of employment discrimination against disabled people under the old normal. That said, they were in important respects more generous, and arguably more just, toward the injured plaintiffs. Furthermore, under these decisions, there was an important new normal for disabled people. In New York and Massachusetts, disabled people were not to be legally second class within employee injury law. Their injuries would be treated through the same framework, allowing disabled people a measure of legal equality.

The apparently more unjust courts that upheld the old normal thought about legal equality for disabled people as well. The Iowa court based part of its decision in I. B. Jennings's case on the theory that counting Jennings's employer as liable for his full disability would

place a serious handicap upon the defective workman in search of employment, for while an employer might be willing to compensate him for more than 100 weeks, due to the fact that his taking from the workman a member which represents total eye-sight and which is therefore more valuable than one eye, yet he would certainly not be willing to employ him if it might mean that he must pay for two eyes though he took but one.[45]

The Minnesota court similarly commented on the Minnesota legislation that required that John Garwin's blinding count for purposes of legal liability as only a partial disability. The court said:

The employer accepts in his service a disabled employee, knowing of the disability and with the knowledge that under the compensation statute he is liable for accidental injuries to such employee while engaged in his service, but to couple the prior disability with one suffered while in his service and make the employer liable for both, would seem a hardship the legislature intended to avoid.

What is more, the court added, if employers were responsible for the entire disability resulting from injuries to disabled workers, it "would tend only to embarrass partially disabled laborers from securing employment, for employers would be reluctant to engage them if there was a contingent liability to make compensation for injuries previously suffered by them."[46]

[44] *Schwab v. Emporium Forestry.*   [45] *Jennings v. Mason City Sewer Pipe.*
[46] *Garwin v. District Court.*

The Pennsylvania Supreme Court reasoned similarly. On September 13, 1920, Antonio Lente was digging a ditch while in the employ of Frank Lucci. A wheelbarrow fell and hit Lente in the temple. The injury caused a detached retina in his left and only eye. Lente ended up in court. In the end of his legal story, the Pennsylvania Supreme Court found against Lente, awarding him compensation for only the loss of sight in a single eye. The court wrote in its decision that while the fate of an injured individual bore "strongly on the sympathies of the Court," awarding more compensation to Lente "would mean that thousands of men employed in this Commonwealth who have only one leg, one arm or one eye would be subjected to a very great handicap in the field of labor." If the court found for Lente, "it will surely follow [that] these men will lose their employment. No one will employ such a man when another, without handicap, equally good, can be secured. Unless the legislature directs it, we must not create such conditions merely to recompense this man, even if it is a distressing case of total blindness."[47]

Weaver's lawyer had been aware of this possibility, and even welcomed it. "We are not unmindful of the economic results" of finding in favor of Weaver, he had written in Weaver's case. "It would probably follow that either the law would be specifically amended to meet such cases, or employers will not hire men with only one eye, leg, or arm." The resulting exclusion "would be a good solution, as it is axiomatic that a man with only one eye, one arm, or one leg, should not be engaged in such work as would make him totally disabled or a public charge if he lost that sole remaining member because of being in that particular employment."[48] Weaver's lawyer, like the judges in all of these cases, weighed lives against lives.

The courts that handled already disabled individuals' injury lawsuits in an apparently more parsimonious manner displayed concern for the welfare of disabled people as a population. These courts practiced a kind of judicial biopolitics that considered the ramifications of legal equality for social practice. In these decisions, the Minnesota and Iowa courts made their decisions, or at least justified their decisions, in terms of the relationships between individuals and aggregates. Concerns for people with physical impairments as a population justified lower injury compensation for injured individuals. Higher compensation for injured individuals based on their greater individual injury risk, these courts reasoned, would result in a

---

[47] *Lente v. Lucci* (275 Pa. 217).   [48] *Weaver v. Maxwell Motor Co.*, Appellee's Brief, 15.

new unemployment risk for people with disabilities in the aggregate. This demonstrates that courts too could manage risk and think in aggregates. This also demonstrates that the management of one sort of risk could cause the proliferation of other risks. The judicial biopolitics of these courts was an attempt to stave off the threat of a new normal wherein disability would disqualify people from employment.

The rulings in New York and Massachusetts in favor of Schwab and Branconnier in a sense treated those individuals more justly in a distributive sense. They also treated people with disabilities as a group more justly in terms of recognition, in that these rulings meant that workers with disabilities were to be treated the same as able-bodied workers, in that all employees were entitled to compensation for their total condition after injury. These decisions made the tyranny of the table became more formally inclusive in the sense of making fewer legal distinctions between able-bodied and disabled people.

In cases like those of Weaver and Branconnier, courts decided to abandon the old legal normal for disabled people in favor of a new normal involving greater formal equality for disabled people. These courts believed that the new status of disabled people within employee injury law would change economic practice. A new legal normal for disabled people would produce new incentives for employers to exclude disabled people from employment in new ways. In effect, these courts speculated that they were enacting distributive justice for individuals and greater recognition for disabled people and doing so at the expense of creating new exclusion of disabled people from employment.

RISK AVOIDANCE AT PULLMAN

It is a mistake to assume without evidence that a possible incentive actually shapes behavior. In this instance, however, judges' concerns proved well-founded: employers did begin to discriminate in precisely the way judges discussed. The Pullman Corporation illustrates the point. In 1915 J. A. Rittenhouse, the superintendent of Pullman's Pennsylvania district, suggested in an internal memo that he had been "trying to work out some plan by which we would avoid getting cripples in the service." Doing so "would be economy on the part of the company" because the company "seemed to be constantly getting into trouble" because of the costs for employees' injuries. Employees "in the service a short time [were] coming to us and claiming that on account of hernia or kindred disease, they could not work … and it often developed that they had this trouble before they came into the service but had been aggravated by the strain" of work.[49] By 1922, Pullman had stopped hiring one-eyed applicants.[50]

In a company memo to lower management in 1923, Pullman management repeated the policy to its supervisory employees, literally underscoring that the company would not hire people with one eye. "Do not accept one-eyed men," the memo underlined those words, and placed one-eyed applicants first in a list including "men with badly defective eyes and ears, with organic heart disease, with suspected tuberculosis, with nephritis, with mental infirmities, with major deformities, or men who are much undernourished and manifestly below par physically."[51] The ramifications of physical condition for employment arose out of the company's financial priorities in response to their changing legal-economic environment.

Initially the prevailing attitude among Pullman officials was to avoid hiring one-eyed applicants but to retain employees who lost an eye after being hired at Pullman. Officials believed the company ought to retain employees who became one-eyed in a work accident and to accept the increased risk that went with retaining these employees. This likely expressed some minimal sense that the employment relationship involved an element of obligation to employees beyond narrowly financial concerns. That obligation was one the company no longer wished to enter into with disabled people because of the greater cost of injuries to disabled people. Thus, while an element of non-financial relationship likely existed at least in vestigial form at Pullman, the company used financial reasoning to decide whether or not to enter into that relationship with people. In 1925 the company undertook "a canvas ... to determine the number of

[49] J. A. Rittenhouse to T. R. Crowder, July 7, 1915. Administrative Subject Files, 1905–1968, Pullman Corporation Records, Box 1, Folder 14, Employee and Labor Relations, Medicine and Sanitation, Pullman Corporation Records, Newberry Library, Chicago, IL.

[50] Memo from H. Guilbert to E. F. Carry, March 25, 1925. Employee and Labor Relations, Safety and Compensation, Administrative Files, 1927–1968, Pullman Corporation Records, Newberry Library, Chicago, IL. This policy remained in force for at least twenty years. Letter, June 29, 1943, Graham to J. M. Carry, Employee and Labor Relations, Safety and Compensation, Administrative Files, 1927–1968, Pullman Corporation Records, Newberry Library, Chicago, IL.

[51] Memo from Thomas Crowder to all medical examiners, May 29, 1923. Employee and Labor Relations Medicine and Sanitation, Administrative Subject Files, 1905–1968; Labor Relations 1942–1964; Medical Examinations, Truck Drivers, and Chauffeurs, 1956–1961, Pullman Corporation Records, Newberry Library, Chicago, IL.

one-eyed employes now in the service."[52] That study found eighty-eight one-eyed Pullman employees.[53]

Pullman employed approximately 35,000 people at this time, but Pullman's safety director, Harry Guilbert, still displayed a great deal of concern for the small number with one eye.[54] The internal study of one-eyed employees "found that a great number of these people entered the service after having lost the use of one eye." The memo reminded Pullman managers and supervisors that "a person with only one good eye is necessarily handicapped so far as usefulness is concerned, and, in view of the hazard connected with work ... the employment of such persons should be avoided." The memo went on to name the one-eyed employees under the supervisor being written to. "As to those already in service, they should be required to wear goggles while on duty and instructed to exercise every precaution to protect their one good eye at all times."[55]

The requirement to wear goggles became a serious disciplinary issue at Pullman, one involving the highest level of management. In 1925 Guilbert and J. A. Rittenhouse, by now the superintendent of the Pullman repair shop in Mott Haven, New York, corresponded about Jerry Murphy, a supervisory employee with one eye. Murphy was the head mechanic at the Mott Haven facility and had worked for Pullman for thirty-five years. He had repeatedly been found not wearing goggles as ordered. Guilbert complained to Pullman's vice president and general manager, L. S. Hungerford, that various managers and supervisors "have talked to [Murphy] repeatedly without very much success. It costs $3300 for an eye in the State of New York. Should Murphy lose his remaining optic,

---

[52] Memo from unknown official to agents and supervisors, July 30, 1925. Employee and Labor Relations, General Labor Files, Pullman Corporation Records, Newberry Library, Chicago, IL.

[53] Memo from H. Guilbert to H. P. Walden, June 11, 1925. Guilbert first wrote to Pullman supervisors requesting the numbers of one-eyed employees in March of 1925. Guilbert to all supervisors, March 31, 1925. Employee and Labor Relations, Safety and Compensation, Administrative Files, 1927–1968, Eyes – One Eyed Employees. Pullman Corporation Records, Newberry Library, Chicago, IL.

[54] In 1923 Pullman employed 35,825 people. Document, "Labor Turnover, 1923," Employee and Labor Relations Medicine and Sanitation, Administrative Subject Files, 1905–1968; Labor Relations 1942–1964; Medical Examinations, Truck Drivers, and Chauffeurs, 1956–1961, Pullman Corporation Records, Newberry Library, Chicago, IL.

[55] Memo from unknown official to agents and supervisors, July 30, 1925. Employee and Labor Relations, General Labor Files, Pullman Corporation Records, Newberry Library, Chicago, IL.

chances are we will be compelled to pay for total blindness."[56] Hungerford replied that Murphy must "take every precaution to safeguard his
remaining good eye . . . not only for his own sake but in view of the liability
that would probably attach to the company if that good eye should be
injured while Murphy was on duty."[57] Rittenhouse wrote again, saying
that Murphy had "shown rather an independent spirit on the question of
wearing goggles, claiming they did him more harm than good, that they
weakened his one eye, through the heat created by the goggle and frames."
Murphy was probably right, as he would have been best placed to know
what the goggles meant for his work and his eyesight, but Pullman
management's primary concern was with the company's liability. Rittenhouse asked for advice on disciplining Murphy.[58] Ultimately, the company
decided to lay him off for a week without pay, "and if necessary longer" in
order to "teach Head Mechanic Murphy that the President's orders will be
obeyed explicitly."[59] Murphy's understanding of his own safety and comfort at work was to be subordinated to his bosses' understanding of what
might expose the company to injury costs.

The attention to one-eyed employees at Pullman, and the exclusion of
one-eyed applicants, happened in large part because of Pullman officials'
awareness of and concern over liability for injuries to those employees.
Pullman officials worried that given the law and the company's dangerous
labor practices, some employees' physical condition might pose a financial threat to the company. Pullman also worried about a continued
evolution of legal rules creating additional financial risks. Pullman

---

[56] Guilbert to Hungerford, August 2, 1926, Employee and Labor Relations, General Labor
Files, Pullman Corporation Records, Newberry Library, Chicago, IL. That Pullman did
not simply fire Murphy is curious. This is likely due to his status as head mechanic, which
gave him valuable skills that would have made him expensive to replace. The company
was at the time quite concerned about the costs of employee turnover. Crawford to
Crowder, December 29, 1923, Employee and Labor Relations Medicine and Sanitation,
Administrative Subject Files, 1905–1968, Pullman Corporation Records, Newberry
Library, Chicago, IL. More generally on turnover in this era, see "History of Labor
Turnover in the U.S.," Laura Owen, http://eh.net/encyclopedia/article/owen.turnover,
accessed February 20, 2014. See also Laura J. Owen, "Worker Turnover in the 1920s:
The Role of Changing Employment Policies," *Industrial and Corporate Change* 4, no. 3
(1995): 499–530; and Jay L. Zagorsky, "Job Vacancies in the United States: 1923 to
1994," *Review of Economics and Statistics* 80, no. 2 (May 1998): 338–345.
[57] Hungerford to Tull, August 8, 1926, Employee and Labor Relations, General Labor Files,
Pullman Corporation Records, Newberry Library, Chicago, IL.
[58] Rittenhouse to Tully, August 23, 1926, Employee and Labor Relations, General Labor
Files, Pullman Corporation Records, Newberry Library, Chicago, IL.
[59] Tully to Rittenhouse, August 18, 1928, Employee and Labor Relations, General Labor
Files, Pullman Corporation Records, Newberry Library, Chicago, IL.

officials collected information on legal rulings about one-eyed employees and workplace injury law. The company's safety files included an August 10, 1925, article from the *Insurance Press* arguing that "serious eye accidents are likely to occur where men, women and children are employed. There is not any such thing as a really non-hazardous occupation." The company's safety files included another August 10, 1925, article from the *Chicago Journal of Commerce* titled "Illinois Ruling on Injury to Impaired Eye." The article noted that a recent Illinois Supreme Court decision provided compensation for the loss of employees' eyes without requiring that "the eye must have been perfect" and without any provision "for reducing the amount of compensation in proportion to the defect in vision. The same compensation is due whether the eye lost is one with perfect vision or imperfect vision by reason of natural defects or previous injury." Another undated article from the *Underwriters Report*, marked with a handwritten note in the margin, warned employers of "Full Liability Awarded on Loss of Second Eye." The article discussed a "decision affecting the application of the employer's liability law in Alaska," decided by the US Circuit Court of Appeals in San Francisco, "wherein it is ruled that a one-eyed man who loses the remaining eye is entitled to full disability rating." Thomas Scott, the plaintiff in *Thomas D. Scott v. Killisnoo Packing Company of Alaska,*

had only one eye when he went to work for the firm, but the evidence showed that he performed the same work as men with two good eyes, so that when he lost his remaining eye it was contended that he had really suffered complete disability. Scott sued the company under the Alaska employers' liability law. The Court held that if Scott, with one eye, was able to perform the work of men with two eyes, the loss of one eye in his case constituted total disability within the meaning of the law.

In 1927 Guilbert wrote to Pullman's president, E. F. Carry, about a California Supreme Court decision in favor of an injured man named John Liptak. This case was similar to Branconnier's case in that it ruled that in California employers were liable for full blindness in the event of a one-eyed person losing their only working eye. "This is another reason why one-eyed men should be compelled to wear goggles all the time while on duty," Guilbert wrote. This incident illustrates that Pullman officials paid attention to legal developments across the country. Developments in specific states shaped company policy in its operations across the country. Professionals like Guilbert had a unique role within the new corporate political economy. By producing knowledge about the companies' business and legal environment, they enabled their employers to adjust more quickly to that environment. That knowledge-making capacity created managerial awareness of the threat that compensation laws might change in the future in a way that would cost Pullman more money. That threat provided a kind of encouragement – a notional incentive – to discriminate in advance of an incentive involving actual, non-notional costs.

Carry replied with an even stronger statement, saying, "Your note . . . in regard to full liability in the loss of the remaining eye by a one-eyed man, emphasizes the necessity of getting rid of all one-eyed men and not employing them."[60] Carry here suggested that Pullman cease to consider itself obligated to its already one-eyed employees. It is important to note here that a policy of firing employees with a pre-existing physical impairment would amount to a policy of firing an employee who became impaired in an accident.

One-eyed employees and their legal liabilities remained the topic of managerial discussion at Pullman for some years. In March of 1928, an employee named Gisalle Kopitar filed a compensation claim, arguing that the infection that took the sight in one of her eyes was the result of her work as a car cleaner at Pullman. In discussing her situation, a Pullman official said that since "one-eyed employes are much more liable to injury than those possessing both eyes . . . it may prove necessary to dispense with her service at a later date after the case receives a hearing. In any event, she would be dismissed if she failed to wear goggles and safeguard the vision of the other eye."[61] Kopitar lost her compensation claim. By December of 1928, company records listed her as "resigned and is now out of service and will not be re-employed."[62] Whether she resigned under pressure is unclear, but presumably her filing and losing a compensation claim was a factor in this outcome.

A 1929 article in the *Bulletin of the United States Bureau of Labor Statistics* helps explain some of Pullman's attention to the problem of

---

[60] Guilbert to Carry, January 3, 1927, and Carry to Guilbert, no date, Employee and Labor Relations, Safety and Compensation, Administrative Files, 1927–1968, Eyes – One Eyed Employees, Pullman Corporation Records, Newberry Library, Chicago, IL. A year later Guilbert reported to Carry that twenty employees of the New York Central Railroad had lost an eye. In 1927 the number was twenty-eight, with fifty-two employees at the Pennsylvania Railroad losing eyes. Guilbert to Carry, November 26, 1928, Pullman Corporation Records.

[61] Guilbert to Tully, March 22, 1928, Employee and Labor Relations, General Labor Files, Pullman Corporation Records, Newberry Library, Chicago, IL.

[62] Tully to Guilbert, December 3, 1928, Employee and Labor Relations, General Labor Files, Pullman Corporation Records, Newberry Library, Chicago, IL. I have not found records detailing how Kopitar left her employment at Pullman.

one-eyed employees despite the relatively minor nature of the problem from an aggregate perspective. The article, "Eye Conservation through Compulsory Use of Goggles in Workshops," focused on safety efforts at the Pullman company, with an emphasis on eye injuries. The article's author, Carl Hookstadt, an actuary employed by the Bureau of Labor Statistics, argued that these efforts had saved "the eyes of approximately a thousand of their men" at Pullman. Thus the increased risk due to one-eyed employees' injury costs prompted policy changes at Pullman directed toward injury prevention, in line with the theory that compensation laws incentivized safety. Pullman officials estimated the cost of an eye at $3,300, which would make this a savings of more than $3 million. The article cited Pullman officials' reasons for the goggle requirement as "the experience of Pennsylvania and New York in recent years ... In Pennsylvania up to October, 1927, the sight of 6,842 eyes had been completely destroyed in industrial accidents since 1916, while from January 1, 1927, 383 eyes had been made sightless."[63] Eye injuries seemed quite common, and Pullman officials worried about their frequency – especially in light of their potential cost to the company. In just one year, compensation paid for eye injuries in Pennsylvania ran to more than $800,000, "representing an estimated total economic loss of $5,000,000." Compensation for eye injuries in New York was even higher: $1.7 million. "According to the National Safety Council's estimate that the total cost of industrial accidents is five times the amount of the compensation payments, this class of accidents cost the workers, the employers, and the public more than $8,000,000 in the single year."[64]

Though upper management worried that some one-eyed applicants had been hired, internal correspondence at Pullman did not indicate how many one-eyed employees had been hired in that condition and how many had become one-eyed while working at the company. In 1931 Pullman officials were again trying to determine how many one-eyed employees there were and whether or not they were suffering injuries. F. R. Callahan, superintendent of Pullman's repair facilities, wrote to

---

[63] "Eye Conservation through Compulsory Use of Goggles in Workshops," in *Bulletin of the United States Bureau of Labor Statistics* 491 (Washington, DC: United States Government Printing Office, 1929), 280–281, 280.

[64] "Eye Conservation through Compulsory Use of Goggles in Workshops," 281. This is another example of the moral thinning of injury, in that eye injuries were valued in terms of dollars, as opposed to the variety of values and meaning which people gave to their bodies and injuries.

lower managers asking for "report of injury to any employe having but one eye."[65] Another official replied, "Every district in this service and I think every General Foreman in the service, understand [*sic*] that men with one eye, arm, or crippled in any way should not be employed."[66] Another added, "It is understood by all concerned that employes with defective vision or but one eye should not be employed, under any circumstances." The company's internal survey turned up only eight one-eyed employees. Of these, at least one had definitely become one-eyed due to an injury at Pullman, and five were longtime Pullman employees.[67] This means Pullman had eighty-eight one-eyed employees in 1925 and eight in 1931.[68] Some of this decrease can likely be attributed to firings. That is, the company had likely begun to act on Carry's idea that the company not only should turn away disabled applicants but should fire disabled people who were found to be in the company's employ. That suggests that the non-financial sense of obligation to the company's employees became attenuated at Pullman over time, at least for disabled employees. Again, it is important to note that all employees were subject to becoming disabled due to injury at any moment during their time on the clock because of dangers built into the labor process. The loss of a single eye in an accident could become, in terms of employment prospects, a total disability whether the injured person had two eyes or one.

In 1934, company president David Crawford argued for continuing and expanding employment discrimination at Pullman. Crawford took one-eyed individuals as symbols of employees whose unacceptability was now established, saying that the company should now begin discriminating against workers with illnesses. "I am very strongly of the opinion that we should take all steps to prevent physical crooks from getting on the employment list," wrote Crawford, adding, "there is just as good reason for not employing a man with a bad heart or bad arteries as there

[65] F. R. Callahan to Rittenhouse, Ransom, et al., March 3, 1931, Employee and Labor Relations, General Labor Files, Pullman Corporation Records, Newberry Library, Chicago, IL.

[66] Ransom to Callahan, March 5, 1931, Employee and Labor Relations, General Labor Files, Pullman Corporation Records, Newberry Library, Chicago, IL.

[67] Rittenhouse to Callahan, March 19, 1931; Dunn to Callahan, March 9, 1931; Vallette to Callahan March 9, 1931, Employee and Labor Relations, General Labor Files, Pullman Corporation Records, Newberry Library, Chicago, IL.

[68] I have not found dismissal records, but it seems highly improbable that all of those eighty missing employees left of their own accord.

is for not taking on a new one-eyed man."[69] Avoiding these "physical crooks," Crawford said, would involve some supervisory costs, but "it is enlightened expenditure to see that we do not take in risks that are fundamentally poor at the start, especially when the times are such that we can afford to wait for men that are not physically below par before we hire them."[70] This expenditure was enlightened in the sense of spending money to save even more money. While the high unemployment of the early 1930s was a problem for working-class people, it offered Pullman an opportunity to become more selective in employment and thus reduce liability costs. Crawford's "enlightened expenditure" echoed Rittenhouse's reasoning in his original proposal in 1915 to avoid hiring "cripples." Both men approved of excluding disabled people from employment because doing so saved money. That exclusion was conceptualized via the abstractions of the labels "cripple" and "physical crook" and the category "economy." Both involved a denial of recognition of the human beings excluded and a lack of concern for the consequences of that exclusion on those people. The company's primary concern was that compensation laws made so-called cripples into a new kind of problem, an unacceptable financial risk. Pullman continued to not hire one-eyed applicants until at least 1943. Crawford wrote in 1943, "We of course cannot avoid the risk of the one-eyed people that we already have or those who lost their eye in our service, but I would say we would do better to do without."[71]

---

[69] Memo from D. A. Crawford to L. S. Hungerford, May 31, 1934. Employee and Labor Relations, Medicine and Sanitation, Administrative Subject Files, Pullman Corporation Records, Newberry Library, Chicago, IL.

[70] D. A. Crawford to L. S. Hungerford, May 31, 1934, Employee and Labor Relations, Medicine and Sanitation, Administrative Subject Files, Pullman Corporation Records, Newberry Library, Chicago, IL.

[71] Crawford to Carry, May 13, 1943, Employee and Labor Relations, General Labor Files, Pullman Corporation Records, Newberry Library, Chicago, IL. See also replied May 13, 1943, see also Crowder to Callahan Employee and Labor Relations Medicine and Sanitation, Administrative Subject Files, 1905–1968; Labor Relations 1942–1964; Medical Examinations, Truck Drivers, and Chauffeurs, 1956–1961, Pullman Corporation Records. The marginalization of people with disabilities as practiced by executives like Crawford was financially motivated, a matter of indifference rather than conscious antipathy toward people with disabilities. Lizabeth Cohen narrates a similar financial incentive toward discrimination by white homeowners against African American would-be homeowners in the mid-twentieth century. Cohen quotes a white homeowner opposed to his new black neighbor: "He's probably a nice guy, but every time I look at him I see $2000 drop off the value of my house." Lizabeth Cohen, *A Consumers' Republic: The Politics of Mass Consumption in Postwar America* (New York: Knopf, 2003), 217. As David Freund has put it, state policy "racially structured the market for residential property." David M. P. Freund, *Colored Property: State Policy and White Racial Politics in Suburban*

RISK-AVERSE EMPLOYERS

Pullman was not exceptional; it was exemplary. In 1915, the same year that Rittenhouse was puzzling out how to best practice profitable employment discrimination, workers and unions repeatedly spoke out about compensation laws, "emphasiz[ing] especially the danger of loss of employment in the case of men having only one eye. Persons so afflicted are often just as capable as ever to earn full wages, but as they have only one eye remaining they are peculiarly exposed to complete blindness."[72]

The Welfare Federation of Cleveland conducted its "Survey of All the Cripples of Cleveland" in 1915 as well.[73] The Cleveland Committee found that the same physical condition could be "a measurable economic handicap in one case and apparently none at all in another." What constituted "a measurable economic handicap" was an artifact of employer decisions. Compensation laws changed the economic environment employers responded to and so shaped their decisions, turning more physical conditions into "economic handicaps." As the report noted, "the development of Workmen's Compensation and Employers' Liability Acts" had begun to worsen employment prospects for people with disabilities. "Employers will not stand for the employment of handicapped labor if it increases insurance rates or their liability for compensation in case of accident – especially if the handicapped workman did not meet with his original disability in their employ."[74] The report argued that "[t]he increased care with which, under existing [compensation] laws, employers tend to avoid the added risks of liability in employing physically handicapped labor, place[s] the handicapped, however competent

---

America (Chicago: University of Chicago Press, 2007), 321. Under this kind of arrangement, a white person would likely have to be actively opposed to racism and committed to equality in order to not oppose housing integration. Similarly, with the extension of injury liability, businesses would have had to have been actively committed to equality for people with disabilities, committed to such a degree that they were willing to face lower profits, in order to avoid acting in line with the incentives to discriminate.

[72] Warren Garst, *First Biennial Report of the Iowa Industrial Commissioner to the Governor of the State of Iowa for the Period Ending June 30, 1914* (Des Moines: State of Iowa, 1914), 7.

[73] Welfare Federation of Cleveland, *Education and Occupations*, 50. Having said that Pullman was not exceptional, it bears mention that Ford seems to have been exceptional in its treatment of disabled people, due to a surprising ideological commitment to disabled people's employment on the part of Henry Ford. See Rose, *No Right to Be Idle*, 111–136.

[74] Welfare Federation of Cleveland, *Education and Occupations*, 15.

they may be, at an increasing disadvantage except at times and places where other labor is difficult or impossible to secure."[75]

In some instances, the exclusion of people with disabilities from employment explicitly received public written approval. An unsigned editorial in 1914 in the *Railway Age Gazette* explicitly commended employment discrimination under compensation laws. The editorial, titled "Corporation Eugenics," wrote that General Electric's decision to employ only unimpaired people "should operate to improve the efficiency of the employees by serving as an inducement to them to keep in good physical condition. There is nothing the average American is so prodigal of as his health. If he knows that his job depends on his keeping fit, there will be the strongest possible incentive for him to safeguard himself against disease." General Electric was motivated not by eugenic concerns but rather by market concerns, the editorial argued, and yet the changes in injury law meant that the company, by pursuing success in the market, had produced what the editorial considered to be positive eugenic outcomes: "The company is obviously inspired by a desire to reduce its liability under the compensation law; but the rule may prove a benefit to the men, as have the rules against drinking, enforced by the railroads. Perhaps in the end the corporations will do more for practical eugenics than the legislatures."[76] This was a kind of biopolitical argument in favor of employment discrimination, in which the exclusion of the disabled would make the able-bodied into more responsible subjects out of the fear of being consigned to greater poverty. The editorial writer expressed no concerns for the disabled human beings who would be hurt by this policy.

In his 1920 survey of workmen's compensation laws, actuary Carl Hookstadt noted that discrimination was a widespread problem. "When a one-eyed workman loses the second eye in an industrial accident," Hookstadt wrote,

he will be totally disabled for life. If the employer is required, under the law, to pay compensation for permanent total disability in such cases he will feel considerable apprehension about employing such men. On the other hand, if the employee is to receive compensation for the loss of one eye only, regardless

---

[75] Welfare Federation of Cleveland, *Education and Occupations*, 19–20.
[76] "Corporation Eugenics," *Railway Age Gazette* 57, no. 8 (August 21, 1914): 334. For a discussion of eugenics within early twentieth-century US legal thought more broadly, see Herbert Hovenkamp, *The Opening of American Law: Neoclassical Legal Thought, 1870–1970* (Oxford: Oxford University Press, 2015), 36–74.

of the resulting disability and loss of earning capacity, he will be inadequately compensated and the purpose of the compensation act will be partially defeated.[77]

Again, one-eyed employees were exemplary, the paradigm case for what compensation laws meant for all "physically defective workers." Hookstadt noted that injuries to employees who already had physical impairments were "infinitesimally small," statistically speaking. He cited an unnamed statistical study that found that "of all the employees under the compensation act in the State of Wisconsin who had lost a hand, an arm, a foot, a leg, or an eye, only one would sustain a second major injury in any given year."[78] Hookstadt said that even under the assumption that "all second major permanent disabilities would result in permanent total disability" – that is, assuming that all injuries to already disabled employees removed all of those employees' remaining capacity to work – "the increased compensation cost of such accidents would probably in the aggregate not exceed three-tenths of 1 per cent of the total compensation costs for all accidents." Statistically speaking, in the aggregate, injuries to employees with disabilities were minuscule in occurrence and cost. And yet "an individual employer is not particularly concerned with the fact that 'in the aggregate' the increased cost of second disabilities is insignificant," wrote Hookstadt. "When a crippled workman in his employ sustains second major disability the increased cost to him is much greater than the cost of a similar disability to a normal worker would be, and this notwithstanding the fact that the increased aggregate cost is negligible."[79] Even if injuries to one-eyed employees were rare and relatively inexpensive in the aggregate, individual firms like Pullman did not act in response to aggregates; they acted to minimize their own individual share of total costs.

In 1925, the Oklahoma Supreme Court heard *Nease v. Hughes Stone* and, using reasoning like that of the New York and Massachusetts courts, ruled that W. A. Nease had been blinded by the loss of his only eye. His employer was thus responsible for the full costs of his post-injury condition.[80] I. K. Huber, an official of the Oklahoma-based Empire

---

[77] Carl Hookstadt, "Comparison of Workmen's Compensation Laws of the United States and Canada up to January 1, 1920," *Bulletin of the United States Bureau of Labor Statistics* 275, 71.
[78] Hookstadt, "Comparison of Workmen's Compensation Laws," 73.
[79] Hookstadt, "Comparison of Workmen's Compensation Laws," 74.
[80] *Nease v. Hughes Stone*, 114 Okla. 170 (1925)

Companies, argued that as a result "thousands of one-eyed, one-legged, one-armed, one-handed men in the State of Oklahoma were let out and can not get employment under the workmen's compensation law of Oklahoma."[81] As courts across the country reasoned like the Massachusetts and New York courts, firms across the country acted like Pullman in response. In the words of Fred Wilcox of the Wisconsin Industrial Commission,

> We allowed the employee who lost his second eye to have twice as much compensation for the loss of the second eye as for the loss of the first eye. But what about it? Did anyone ever get any compensation for the loss of a second eye? No; he never got a job. He never got a chance to lose his second eye in industry – to be blunt in stating the facts, employers would not hire him, because they would take on twice as much liability as they had before.[82]

Once pushed out of waged labor, people with disabilities had less access to money and so less access to goods and services. Decreased access to wages was thus an important change in the relationship between physically impaired individuals and social reproduction.

Across the developments discussed in this chapter were two basic trends in the social and legal fate of disabled people. On the one hand, there was what I have called the old normal, wherein disabled people

---

[81] United States Bureau of Labor Statistics, *Bulletin of the Bureau of Labor Statistics* 536 (1931): 268. Huber's comments are important for indicating that at least some business officials had moral reservations about the exclusion of people with disabilities. Historian Sarah Rose places compensation laws in the context of longer changes over time in the meanings of and relationships among class, disability, and economy in the United States. Rose argues that these laws contributed to a conceptual shift away from older notions of disability and toward disability as exclusion from economic life, making the exclusion of people with disabilities in response to workmen's compensation a formative episode in creating disability as inability to work in modern American culture. Rose traces the development of the category of disability in social policy, and the social and cultural effects of the changes in that category. Prior to compensation laws, people who suffered disabling injuries tended to continue to work. After compensation laws, people with disabilities faced much more inhospitable labor markets. Rose also points out that disabled workers were not accounted for within the damage award schedules set up by compensation laws, frequently resulting in lengthy lawsuits when disabled workers suffered injuries. Disabled workers were effectively left out of the improvements made by workmen's compensation. Furthermore, the economic exclusion of these people contributed to the development of the idea that disability means inability to work, such that laws meant to respond to the problem of workplace injury ultimately rendered people with disabilities newly and increasingly dependent. Rose, *No Right to Be Idle*.

[82] Quoted in *Lawson v. Suwanee Fruit and Steamship Co.*, 336 U.S. 198 (1949). The original remark appears in United States Bureau of Labor Statistics, *Bulletin of the Bureau of Labor Statistics* 577 (1933): 157, 158.

were included but subordinated. On the other hand, there was the new normal, composed of two elements: legal equality and economic exclusion. Wilcox's state of Wisconsin introduced a variation on the new and old normal. In effect the state passed on to disabled people the ugly choice of whether to reside in the new normal of being the bearer of the legal right to compensation – rights that employers took as grounds to exclude a disabled person from hiring – or to remain in the old normal by waiving their rights to compensation for their full disability. The waiver amounted to requiring disabled people to select between two kinds of discrimination, as the story of Clarence Fors illustrates.

In 1931, a representative of the Wisconsin River Paper and Pulp Company wrote to the Wisconsin Industrial Commission about an employee named Clarence Fors, who had a liver and heart condition.[83] Fors had become the growing object of concern for the company because "[t]he danger of something happening to him has been increasing as his condition has been steadily getting worse." Wisconsin River Paper said that Fors was "incapable of doing even the light work we have given him" and that the company kept him on only because his father had worked for the company for more than thirty years. Noting that Fors had a wife and child to support, and that his condition would not allow him to find a new job, the company said they were willing to keep him on provided that it could be released from liability for any injuries Fors might incur at work. The Wisconsin Industrial Commission replied, suggesting that Fors might elect to voluntarily waive his right to come under the workmen's compensation law. Since the law forbade employers from soliciting non-election, the commission offered to write to Fors "and suggest that he make application to you [the employer] for work under a non-election on his part." The commission requested that the company provide Fors's mailing address for this purpose. Wisconsin River Paper supplied Fors's address; the Industrial Commission wrote to Fors; and Fors agreed to waive his right to be covered by the workmen's compensation law.[84] Clarence Fors kept his job by agreeing to accept all of the risk of work.

---

[83] Wisconsin Industrial Commission Correspondence File E1747, Correspondence between Wisconsin River Paper and Pulp Company and Wisconsin Industrial Commission, Correspondence and forms, 1912–1954, Workmen's Compensation Division records, Wisconsin Historical Society, Madison, WI.

[84] Wisconsin Industrial Commission Correspondence File E1747, Correspondence between Wisconsin River Paper and Pulp Company and Wisconsin Industrial Commission, Correspondence and forms, 1912–1954, Workmen's Compensation Division records, Wisconsin Historical Society, Madison, WI.

Fors's situation illustrated a dynamic that Iowa Industrial Commissioner Garst had pointed out more than a decade earlier: one downside of the compensation law was that "a crippled man has to reject its project or lose his protection."[85] Under waivers as in Wisconsin, disabled people were forced into a terrible choice: the old normal, which allowed continued access to employment at the cost of second-class status, or the new normal of greater civic equality and security in the event of injury, at the expense of the threat of employment discrimination.

CONCLUSION

Disabled employees like Weaver and Branconnier assumed that compensation laws applied to them, so when injured they sought compensation. Yet they soon found that they were within an interregnum wherein the tyranny of the trial remained for disabled people, because compensation laws often made them legally anomalous. As courts heard lawsuits arising from these injury claims, judges had to determine what was compensated: loss of body parts, or loss of capacity. In the aftermath of compensation laws as interpreted by courts, in some states disabled people faced the old normal of subordinated inclusion preserved through change, remade in some of its details but not unmade; in other states they faced the new normal of legal equality and financially driven economic exclusion.

The new legal normal of formal equality for disabled people resulted in a less abled law. That new legal normal existed in an institutional context where compensation laws distributed greater costs to employers based on that new legal normal. That, in turn, intersected with other forms of knowledge in large manufacturing companies, including the expertise of their medical departments and hiring departments. In response to these new market pressures, employers exercised their authority in ways that created a new economic normal. Rather than disabled people being subordinated while included in employment, disabled people would be increasingly excluded from employment. This new exclusion was distinctly impersonal, driven by concerns over liability costs rather than

---

[85] "New Law Reducing Accidents," *Correctionville News*, October 15, 1914. In his talk at the meeting of the International Association of Accident Boards and Commissioners, Frank Pedley stated that in 1930 there were twelve US states that placed the burden of additional risks on disabled people in this way. United States Bureau of Labor Statistics, *Bulletin of the Bureau of Labor Statistics* 536 (1931): 250. People with disabilities had to elect not to fall under the protection of workmen's compensation if they wished to be employed, and in many states they did not have this limited choice.

conscious stigma about disabled people as disabled. The result was new financially incentivized and legally constructed employment discrimination against people based on physical conditions. Physically impaired people became disabled in a new way, socially and economically. To use Edward Glackin's words, compensation laws had fixed the problem of "life and limb" being "too cheap" in a way that made many employers come to see hiring people with disabilities as too expensive, thus rendering those people's labor power worth less on the labor market and consigning them to greater poverty as a result.

Within these changes, the relationship between law, culture, and economy transformed.[86] Narrowly economic or financial concerns, within a new legal distribution of expenses, generated incentives to exclude disabled people from employment. Law became more marketized, so to speak, approximating more closely what Margaret Radin has called universal commodification. Other forms of valuation were crowded out.[87] A cousin to that crowding-out is what earlier chapters called moral thinning or the impoverishment of injury. What did it mean to Weaver, Branconnier, and others to be rendered blind? The answer did not appear in their suits. While these men were forced by law back to the tyranny of the trial, their lawsuits were really about the allocation of money within the tyranny of the table. These suits centered entirely on money and had nothing to say about the human meaning of injury beyond costs measured in dollars. Their suits occurred within the morally thin framework of workmen's compensation laws, which permitted little space for recognition of suffering and singularity – little space for the human truths of injury – in keeping with the general retraction of meaning involved in the transition to the tyranny of the table, as earlier chapters discussed. Under compensation laws injuries had become narrowly pecuniary. Left out were all the ways in which people's bodies are more than just ways to earn money, such that destruction of someone's body is more than just a

---

[86] Law forms a variety of social knowledge that helps define the world. As Ian Haney Lopez has put it, law is both a system of behavioral control and a system of ideological representations. Lopez, *White by Law*, 81–87. As Christopher Tomlins has written, law "authorizes and inscribes" our society's "relations of production and reproduction ... on people ... Such authorizations, such naming, are the law's business." Law composes what counts as the "facts of life." Christopher Tomlins, *Law, Labor, and Ideology in the Early American Republic* (Cambridge: Cambridge University Press, 1993), 16. Changes in employee injury law inscribed employees' physical conditions into the facts of economic life in a different way.

[87] See Radin, *Contested Commodities*, and Michael J. Sandel, *What Money Can't Buy: The Moral Limits of Markets* (New York: Farrar, Strauss and Giroux, 2012).

financial expense. The other kinds of losses involved in injury had no place in the institutions that governed injury under workmen's compensation laws. Law is a genre of social knowledge, and yet compensation laws offered a quite narrow scope through which to know the human truths of injury. Disabled people were subjected to both distributive injustice and unjust denial of recognition. Meanwhile, the harm to persons through industrial accidents continued. Injury compounded. From the view of Benjamin's angel of history, all of these outcomes were elements of the social storm that produces variations on human catastrophe.

5

Insuring Injustice

The tyranny of the table visited an ensemble of old and new injustices on disabled people, as illustrated by the stories of people like Charles Weaver. Some of these injustices originated in society and culture outside of law and the economy and were taken up into law, making compensation laws artifacts of and a continuation of long-standing oppression. Compensation laws created an innovation within the power relations visited on – resting on the lives and built from the labor of – working-class people.[1] That innovation partially redistributed the financial costs of injury, resulting in a rearrangement of market imperatives. Companies responded with exclusion.

The new market-generated injustices had everything to do with insurance. Compensation laws made employers into guarantors of risk pools, and employers responded like insurers, by gatekeeping the boundaries of their risk pools. Insurance also provided a vocabulary for explaining and justifying employer actions, and for leaving unaddressed the human consequences of injury and exclusion. Insurance was peculiarly suited to inflict both distributive injustice and unjust denial of recognition on people.

---

[1] I have found Erik Olin Wright's writing on the differences between Durkheimian, Weberian, and Marxian analyses of class illuminating for explaining what kind of change compensation laws were and were not. Wright points to the difference between deciding between two moves permitted within the rules of a game, two proposed changes to the rules of a game, and two different games a group might play. Compensation laws changed a few of U.S. capitalism's rules. The game remained the same, as did the patterns in who won and lost. See Erik Olin Wright, *Understanding Class* (London: Verso, 2015), x–xi and 118–125. For my gloss on his analysis, see Nate Holdren, "Moral Economy as Structurally Recurrent Interpellation: Reading Thompson Pessimistically," forthcoming in the *Elgar Research Handbook on Law and Marxism*.

Actuary Edward Bunnell Phelps worried about some of these injust-ices, asking what he called "Certain Grave Questions" about workmen's compensation, namely, "Will it lead to discrimination against married men and slightly impaired lives?"[2] Phelps answered in the affirmative. So did Iowa Industrial Commissioner and former governor Warren Garst. In 1914, the same year that Phelps posed his questions, Garst argued that there were "classes of employes who though good workers" were becom-ing newly unemployable because they were "as the insurance interests term them, 'impaired risks.'"[3]

The use of terms like "impairment" and "risk" illustrates how actors increasingly used insurance terms in the aftermath of compensation laws. Compensation laws partially redistributed the financial risks of employee injury, and spread insurance as a worldview. Risk and impair-ment were technical terms from the insurance industry. Impairment was the life insurance industry's term for a condition that created a greater chance of dying, something life insurers sought to identify in order to avoid selling insurance policies to people who were likely to die sooner rather than later. That is, impairment was a term through which insurers decided who to exclude. A risk was a threat of financial insecurity – a chance of losing money.[4] The degree to which discrimination and

---

[2] Edward Bunnell Phelps, "Certain Grave Questions of Workmen's Compensation: Will It Lead to Discrimination against Married Men and Slightly Impaired Lives?," *The American Underwriter Magazine and Insurance Review* 42, no. 1 (July 1914): 1–10, 3.

[3] Warren Garst, *First Biennial Report of the Iowa Industrial Commissioner to the Governor of the State of Iowa for the Period Ending June 30, 1914* (Des Moines: State of Iowa, 1914), 8–9. Iowa labor union officials concurred, declaring the existence of "a class of persons who are discriminated against" and "los[ing] their employment because they are poor risks." J. J. Johnston and C. A. McClure to Governor Clarke, December 31, 1914, Multiple Governors Correspondence, Box 21, Folder "Correspondence – State Officers, Boards, & Depts: Veterinary Surgeons (3) – Workmen's Compensation," Multiple Gov-ernors Correspondence: State Officers, Boards and Departments, State Historical Society of Iowa, Des Moines, Iowa.

[4] On the category of impairment, see Dan Bouk, *How Our Days Became Numbered: Risk and the Rise of the Statistical Individual* (Chicago: University of Chicago Press, 2015), 85–86. The concept of impairment and its use evolved within the insurance industry from impairment as ground for exclusion from insurance to impairment as source of higher policy premiums to impairments as possibly correctible conditions. Phelps and Garst responded to the early stages of compensation laws bringing insurance concepts into employers' hiring decisions. They worried about the first sense of impairment, impairment as grounds for exclusion. Like impairment, the word "risk" too originated as a technical term. According to historian Jonathan Levy, the word first came into English from maritime shipping. Merchants sold shares called "risks" in order to offset the cost of the loss of vessels and cargo at sea. In contemporary terms, they created risk pools to gain more financial security, spreading out the losses and the profits of maritime commerce.

insurance were braided together in the law or might be pulled apart would soon become a matter of debate, as Phelps's and Garst's remarks demonstrate. In the end, the hopes that distributive justice-focused reformers like Crystal Eastman had for compensation laws foundered as the abstractions of insurance helped organize new injustices. Insurance terms reflected and helped create not only distributive injustice but also a continued loss of recognition. Garst argued that there was a serious threat that employers would begin to "weed out the aged, the married, and the partly incapacitated" due to compensation laws.[5] To borrow Garst's metaphor, compensation laws had suddenly turned some previously acceptable populations into so-called weeds to be removed without concern for the ramifications of that removal for those human weeds. Insurance terminology, insurance as a worldview, facilitated that lack of concern.

OTHER GRAVE QUESTIONS

Phelps limited his grave questions to the fate of men – implicitly, white men – and so neglected the ways in which compensation laws had grave consequences for women and African Americans. Compensation laws continued old patterns of subordination for disabled people, patterns Chapter 4 referred to as the "old normal." These laws also continued the old normal for race and gender, in two ways: limits on where compensation laws applied and devaluation within compensation laws.

In 1910, more than half of wage-earning women worked in agriculture and domestic services. Over four-fifths of wage-earning African Americans worked in these areas of the economy. By 1920, these employment sectors had fallen in proportion for both groups, but still accounted for almost two-fifths of wage-earning women and almost two-thirds of wage-earning African Americans.[6] Compensation laws regularly excluded both domestic

Over the course of the nineteenth century, risk spread from sea to land and from commerce to the rest of culture, becoming a term, concept, and practice through which people began to understand and organize their lives. Jonathan Levy, *Freaks of Fortune: The Emerging World of Capitalism and Risk in America* (Cambridge, MA: Harvard University Press, 2012), 3.

[5] Garst, *First Biennial Report*, 11.

[6] The figures for African Americans' employment come from Lorenzo J. Greene and Carter G. Woodson, *The Negro Wage Earner* (Washington, DC: Association for the Study of Negro Life and History, 1920), 204, table 34. The figures for women's employment come from Matthew Sobek, "Major Industrial Groups of Labor Force Participants – Females: 1910–1990," table Ba688–705 in *Historical Statistics of the United States, Earliest Times*

and agricultural workers and thus excluded many women and African Americans.[7] In that regard, compensation laws continued the old gender and racial normal of second-class status.

Many other women and African Americans, however, were employed in places where compensation laws did apply. For example, in 1910 and 1920, roughly 20 percent of wage-earning women, between one and two million women, were employed in manufacturing.[8] Between 1900 and 1910, African American employment in industry more than doubled, and that trend accelerated after 1914. By 1920, nearly a million and a half African Americans were employed in manufacturing, construction, and transportation.[9] Women and African Americans employed in these areas were regularly subject to employment discrimination in the form of lower wages. African Americans in waged labor were regularly subject to racialized pay scales. African Americans were paid as little as a quarter of their white co-workers' pay in some instances.[10] Women were

---

to the Present: Millennial Edition, ed. Susan B. Carter, Scott Sigmund Gartner, Michael R. Haines, Alan L. Olmstead, Richard Sutch, and Gavin Wright (New York: Cambridge University Press, 2006).

[7] While the gist of this book is critical of the shortcomings of compensation laws, it remains the case that exclusion from access to these laws was significant and unjust. On the exclusion of domestic and agricultural employment from compensation laws, see Price Fishback and Shawn Everett Kantor, *A Prelude to the Welfare State: The Origins of Workers' Compensation* (Chicago: University of Chicago Press, 2000), 125, 135. The exclusion of domestics likely resulted from long-standing notions that labors in the home were not "work," a staple of both patriarchal and middle-class values. See Vanessa H. May, *Unprotected Labor: Household Workers, Politics, and Middle-Class Reform in New York, 1870–1940* (Chapel Hill: University of North Carolina Press, 2011); Lara Vapnek, *Breadwinners: Working Women and Economic Independence, 1865–1920* (Champaign: University of Illinois Press, 2009). In the early twentieth century, African Americans were geographically concentrated in the South or, rather, confined there as a result of oppressive measures to restrict black people's mobility. Risa Goluboff, *The Lost Promise of Civil Rights* (Cambridge, MA: Harvard University Press, 2007). See Thomas N. Maloney, "African Americans in the Twentieth Century," tables 2 and 3. https://eh .net/encyclopedia/african-americans-in-the-twentieth-century/. Southern states tended to adopt compensation laws relatively later than other states. This provided another way in which African Americans were largely not allowed into the new arrangement that compensation laws brought about. For state adoptions of compensation laws by year, see Fishback and Kantor, *A Prelude to the Welfare State*, 103–104.

[8] Matthew Sobek, "Major Industrial Groups of Labor Force Participants – Females: 1910–1990."

[9] Greene and Woodson, *The Negro Wage Earner*, 204, table 34; see also 337–344.

[10] Greene and Woodson, *The Negro Wage Earner*, 302. It is worth noting as well the persistence of bound labor, distinct from chattel slavery but approximating some of its characteristics, forced onto African Americans by extra-market means after the official end of slavery. See Goluboff, *The Lost Promise of Civil Rights*.

regularly paid lower wages than men in this era as well.[11] That inequality in the labor market became, under workmen's compensation, inequality within the law.

Women and African Americans who fell under compensation laws were subjected to lower values for their injuries. Compensation laws made pre-injury wages into the measure of the value of people's injuries. The wage is a hierarchical social institution, expressing the relative (de)valuation of subordinates by their superiors.[12] That hierarchy in turn creates other hierarchies in the form of higher and lower wages for some people, including discrimination in pay for women, racialized minorities, and disabled people. By making wages the sole measure of injuries' values, compensation laws imported the hierarchies of the labor market into the law. Patterns of low pay became patterns of low value for a person in the event of injury.[13] Because compensation laws expressed valuation in money, they stood as both a disrespect and a distributive injustice, one visited on people already vulnerable due to injury.

RISKY COMMODITIES

Phelps and Garst did not seem especially worried about compensation laws continuing old inequality for already subordinated populations. Rather, their primary concern was about the threat of discrimination

---

[11] Women's weekly earnings in manufacturing in 1914 were about 57 percent that of men's. This figure fluctuated through 1930 but never went over 62 percent. Robert A. Margo, "Female-to-Male Earnings Ratios: 1815–1987," table Ba4224–4233 in *Historical Statistics of the United States*. See also Alice Kessler-Harris, *A Woman's Wage: Historical Meanings and Social Consequences* (Lexington: University of Kentucky Press), 1990.

[12] Often in the United States people to try to avoid or, rather, to obfuscate, the implication that those dollar valuations reflect other non-monetary valuations. But differences in access to money are differences in access to different kinds and qualities of life, and different prices for labor power do reflect differences in esteem. This is part of why pervasive disrespect for a demographic group tends to go in tandem with lower pay.

[13] One argument made in this era in support of compensation laws was that these laws would reduce women's employment. In 1917 Mary Conyngton appealed to what I have called the old normal in support of compensation laws. Conyngton, a statistician employed by the federal Bureau of Labor Statistics, argued that a major virtue of the new compensation legislation was that it reduced incidents of widowed mothers working for money after industrial accidents killed their husbands. Mary K. Conyngton, "Effects of Workmen's Compensation Laws in Diminishing the Necessity of Employment of Women and Children," *Bulletin of the United States Bureau of Labor Statistics* 217 (December 1917).

against older, able-bodied, married men – most likely, white men.[14] Chapter 4 discussed the growth of incentives to discriminate based on physical condition, under the term "the new normal." The threat of discrimination against older, married white men was a newer kind of threat, both for the population threatened and for the social logic behind that threat. Compensation laws turned employees into a newly predictable source of financial risk for employers. In deciding whether or not to hire, employers began new calculations of risk and reward: Was the chance of profit to be had by setting the employee to work greater than the risk of cost for injury? This led to exclusion not based on consideration of social disrespect – as with the old normal for gender, race, and ability – but rather based on financial considerations.[15]

[14] On white men as the normative center in US law and much of US culture, see Barbara Young Welke, *Law and the Borders of Belonging in the Long Nineteenth Century United States* (Cambridge: Cambridge University Press, 2010), and Ian Haney López, *White by Law: The Legal Construction of Race*, revised ed. (New York: New York University Press, 2006).

[15] My point in distinguishing social disrespect from financial considerations is that there are animus-based forms of oppression that are in a sense about a subordinate group, and there are forms of oppression that involve indifference to the subordinated group. See López, *White by Law*. The reduction of human beings to objects and the subjection of human well-being to instrumental considerations like those involved in financial cost/benefit analyses is itself a form of social disrespect. This is a different sort of disrespect, however, than animus toward a group. Two points made by the Scottish comedian and commentator Frankie Boyle are salient here. Boyle polemically claimed that the 2015 electoral victory of the Conservatives meant that Scotland was doomed, because the Conservatives hated the Scots. The comedian Katherine Ryan replied, "I think you might have mistaken apathy for hatred. It's not that Westminster wishes you any specific harm, they just couldn't give a fuck about you." Boyle responded, "I think what we're arguing about here is the definition of hatred." Boyle's point is that indifference to other human beings approximates to a species of hatred. *Frankie Boyle's Election Autopsy 2015*, 21:35–23:25, www.youtube.com/watch?v=5bJVoDR-als, accessed June 15, 2019. In June of 2017, Boyle made a similar point in response to the deadly fire that month at Grenfell Tower, a public housing building. Public housing residents and advocates in England had said for many years previously that there was a risk of fire that went unaddressed by the government. Boyle argued that the fire and the lack of action to prevent it demonstrated that the deaths of ordinary people were viewed casually by British elites. "I think there's a genuine moral thing, so [British MP] John McDonnell was in trouble for saying oh this was like social murder or whatever the phrase was, I think it's worse than that, because if you set out to murder someone in a moment of passion that's one thing, if you set up a whole series of circumstances that will probably lead to people dying and you just let them die like bugs on your windshield that's a different level of immorality." *Frankie Boyle's New World Order*, season one, episode three, June 2017, 12:26–12:51, www.youtube.com/watch?v=IcRD_zEUt8M, accessed June 15, 2019. That kind of indifference is not exceptional but endemic to capitalist societies, even if institutional and situational specifics express this indifference in different ways over time and place.

Compensation laws created incentives for discrimination against married employees in particular because of differentials in death benefits. When an employer's business operations killed an employee, it cost the employer more money if the employee was married rather than unmarried. Typically, in the event of death at work, if the deceased had no dependents, employers paid funeral expenses, a cost that tended to run in the low hundreds of dollars. If the person had dependents, however, the employer had to pay compensation to the family for the lost income, which could run into thousands of dollars.[16]

Delegates at a convention of the American Federation of Labor argued that "the most conspicuous achievement of the New York compensation law has been to force married men and heads of families out of their positions because employers fear to risk losses in indemnity to widows and orphans."[17] A committee of the New York State Federation of Labor said that "[w]e should speak out in thunderous tones our severest condemnation of employers who are attempting to nullify the act by discrimination against the married man."[18] Unions were not the only people to raise concerns over married men and workmen's compensation–related employment discrimination. An insurance industry trade journal wrote that after New York created its compensation law "numerous complaints [were] made that some large employers of labor have discharged or threatened to discharge married employees, attempting to justify their action on the ground that the Compensation Law imposes a greater burden on industry where such men and women are employed than it does in the case of unmarried employees."[19] Fred Mason, an executive with the Shredded Wheat Company, said that the "workmen's compensation law ... is so severe that in case an employe with a large family is hurt the responsibility of the employer is tremendously heavy. This has had the effect of throwing out of work men with large families."[20] The New York Workmen's Compensation Commission complained that the compensation law gave an employer "strong incentive and temptation to

[16] *Workmen's Compensation Law of the State of Iowa* (New York: Robertson Jones, 1914). Adjusted for inflation, $1,000 in the early twentieth century would be equivalent to about $75,000 today. See the Bureau of Labor Statistics Consumer Price Index Inflation Calculator, https://data.bls.gov/cgi-bin/cpicalc.pl.
[17] *Insurance Monitor* 62, no. 1 (January 1914): 602.
[18] *The Bulletin of the General Contractors Association* 5, no. 9 (September 1914): 278.
[19] *The Week*, August 8, 1914, 826.
[20] *Brotherhood of Locomotive Firemen and Enginemen's Magazine*, 57, no. 1 (July 1914): 187.

lighten his burden under the act by discharging or refusing to employ married men."[21] The New York Labor Commissioner reported that New York Labor Department inspectors had found "discrimination by employers against married men and those physically disabled" as a result of workmen's compensation.[22]

Critics identified workmen's compensation as a source of insecurity for older workers as well. To be sure, age discrimination pre-dated workmen's compensation, as part of the old normal for age. That discrimination often took the form of reduced pay rather than exclusion from employment altogether. Workmen's compensation, however, changed the form of employment discrimination against older workers, helping create a new normal for age. It reduced the possibilities for inclusion in a subordinated position and increased pressures toward exclusion from employment.[23] Age discrimination under the new normal was in tension with previous norms of age, gender, and class. Thomas R. Cole has argued that in the nineteenth century the normative notion of old age became one of "healthy, productive independence."[24] The normative

---

[21] *The Standard*, August 15, 1914, 175.

[22] James Lynch, *Fourteenth Annual Report of the Commissioner of Labor for the Twelve Months Ended September 30, 1914* (Albany: State Department of Labor, 1915), 18. The threat of discrimination against married men cut against the goal of securing working-class reproduction, discussed in Chapter 2. Wage-earning male heads of household were supposed to be the conduit through which wages flowed into working-class families in order to facilitate those families playing their role of maintaining the current population of employees and producing future generations of employees.

[23] Demographers Roger L. Ransom and Richard Sutch argue that late nineteenth-century US wage earners often experienced declining wages late in life. Roger L. Ransom and Richard Sutch, "The Impact of Aging on the Employment of Men in American Working-Class Communities at the End of the Nineteenth Century," in *Aging in the Past: Demography, Society, and Old Age*, ed. David I. Kertzer and Peter Laslett (Berkeley: University of California Press, 1995), 303–327; 305. Disability and age are overlapping categories. In some respects, age is constituted by disability, with younger people often being considered incapable and older people aging back into that status, and with real corporeal changes related to age as well. It bears mention that compensation laws may have also shifted the line defining the numerical age at which workers were counted as old.

[24] Thomas R. Cole, *The Journey of Life: A Cultural History of Aging in America* (Cambridge: Cambridge University Press, 1992), 146. As Cole notes, many people did not live out this normative ideal; it was primarily a white, masculine, middle- and upper-class phenomenon. Ability to live out this ideal was predicated in part on access to income, a portion of which could be saved for old age. Ransom and Sutch argue that voluntary "[r]etirement was not unusual at the turn of the century; in 1900 the probability of eventual retirement for a 32-year-old man was more than 35 percent." While this does support the authors' contention that retirement was prevalent, this also means that almost two-thirds of male wage earners in their early thirties could expect not to retire voluntarily. Ransom and Sutch examined waged labor force participation for men over sixty and

ideal that Cole identified changed through compensation laws and employers' responses to old age as physical vulnerability and unsuitability for employment due to the employer's potential expenses because of that vulnerability. In the new normal, working-class people increasingly aged into being a population surplus to economic requirements – people to be discarded.[25]

Maurice Low reported that in the British case "since the enactment [of compensation legislation] there has been a tendency among employers not to employ men who have passed their prime."[26] Low added that "one of the effects of the law is to make it more difficult for elderly men" because a "workman past his prime is more likely to become injured than one younger and more alert, and as the law imposes severe liabilities on the employer he will naturally take every precaution to minimize his risk." The 1904 British Departmental Committee report offered similar conclusions as Low, noting that "diseased, weak or partially maimed persons" were particularly subject to employment discrimination under workmen's compensation.[27]

The same pattern played out in the United States. In his 1914 report Warren Garst quoted a letter from a lawyer well placed "to forecast the effect of the present insurance methods in causing loss of employment" because he represented large corporate clients. The lawyer told Garst that "the old man is carrying a heavier weight than he ever carried before."[28]

found participation rates that ranged from about 64 to 67 percent from 1890 to 1910. This suggests that the expected norm for working-class men was waged work well into what was considered to be old age. Those men who did manage to retire did so by saving wages earned earlier in life. Ransom and Sutch, "The Impact of Aging on the Employment of Men in American Working-Class Communities," 303–305.

[25] Gregory Wood argues that employers in the early twentieth century associated youth with the capacity to do the new, faster work demanded by pressures on workers to speed up in industrial settings. Gregory Wood, *Retiring Men: Manhood, Labor, and Growing Old in America, 1900–1960* (Lanham: University Press of America, 2012), 24–25.

[26] Low, "The British Workmen's Compensation Act and Its Operation," 117–118. On relative surplus population – surplus to the needs of employers and the economy in general – see Karl Marx, *Capital: A Critique of Political Economy*, vol. 1 (London: Penguin, 1990), 762–801. The writing and editorial collective Endnotes, and their journal of the same name, *Endnotes*, has done a great deal of work to point out the usefulness of this category to understanding capitalism.

[27] Garst, *First Biennial Report*, 9.

[28] Garst, *First Biennial Report*, 6–7. The new inequality resulting from compensation laws caught some early twentieth-century Americans by surprise. The Massachusetts Industrial Board, for example, characterized new incentives to restrict hiring as "[o]ne of the logical but most unexpected developments of the Workmen's Compensation Act." Massachusetts Industrial Accident Board, *First Annual Report* (Boston: Wright and Potter Printing

Also in 1914, an Iowa labor assembly called for the government to "look after the welfare of its aged and partially incapacitated workers" by amending the law in some way so as to eliminate the incentives for employers to discriminate.[29]

The Massachusetts Industrial Board similarly argued that the Workmen's Compensation Act had resulted in "the throwing of aged and infirm employees out of industry."[30] The Board reported that "almost immediately" after workmen's compensation laws were implemented that "[o]ne company in Massachusetts ... discharged twenty-two employes, who were either aged or under par physically, within a few weeks after the act went into effect."[31] It is important to note that what defined "par," to use the Massachusetts Industrial Board's term, had been redefined by employers' new financial concerns under the revised rules of injury liability. The definition of an acceptable body had changed because of new buyer-side liabilities bundled by law into the purchase of labor power. Workers in Los Angeles agreed, voicing concerns over age discrimination. In 1917 the *Los Angeles Times* reported that older workers believed workmen's compensation created age discrimination

Co., State Printers, 1914), 44. That compensation laws could create exclusion was foreseen and circulated in at least some American reformer circles. In 1901 the Department of Labor published a report by social investigator A. Maurice Low on Britain's 1897 workmen's compensation law. Low argued that "[o]ne of the results which might have been naturally anticipated from the passage of the law was that it would lead the employers to be more careful in their selection of workmen." A. Maurice Low, "The British Workmen's Compensation Act and Its Operation," *Bulletin of the Department of Labor* 6, no. 32 (January 1901): 103–132, 117–118. Low presented similar material at the 37th Annual Meeting of the American Social Science Association in 1902. Samuel Gompers of the American Federation of Labor was a discussant on Low's paper, though he made no comment about discrimination. Low's report was republished in 1903 by the Massachusetts Committee on Relations between Employer and Employee and was discussed in the insurance industry: *Insurance Monitor* 55, no. 1 (January 1907): 297. A 1904 British government report widely circulated in social reform circles in the United States reached similar conclusions to Low. This information appears to have made no difference to how compensation laws and employers' discriminatory responses to these laws played out. For a further discussion of transatlantic dialogue among policymakers concerning workers' compensation, see Daniel T. Rodgers, *Atlantic Crossings: Social Politics in a Progressive Age* (Cambridge, MA: Harvard University Press, 1998), 209–265.

[29] Geo. C. Campbell to Governor Clarke, December 31, 1914, Multiple Governors Correspondence, Box 21, Folder "Correspondence – State Officers, Boards, & Depts: Veterinary Surgeons (3) – Workmen's Compensation," Multiple Governors Correspondence: State Officers, Boards and Departments, State Historical Society of Iowa, Des Moines, Iowa.

[30] Massachusetts Industrial Accident Board, *First Annual Report*, 44.

[31] Garst, *First Biennial Report*, 8.

against people over the age of forty-five. Workers planned to march carrying signs reading "The Compensation Law Put Us Out of Work." "[T]heir famous law has thrown thousands of us out of jobs," said one worker.[32]

The specter of employment discrimination against "men who were good workers," in Garst's words, must have been worrying.[33] These new reasons for discrimination had until recently been qualifications: marriage connoted stability and maturity; minor physical conditions meant men who had worked enough to wear work's effects on their bodies; age showed experience and often loyalty of service. Garst quoted an employer who worried that some older and work-worn physically impaired employees – "good, faithful men" – were newly undesirable. The employer wanted to reward their loyalty with ongoing employment, but not at the risk of greater cost for employee injury.[34] For employers, what had been markers of reliability had suddenly become signs of dangerous financial liability. The employers Garst quoted invoked values such as productivity, seniority, trustworthiness, and loyalty – all of which were in conflict with the new financial valuation of injury risk that came in the wake of compensation laws. The financial valuation took priority as employers, however regretfully, fired these "good, faithful" employees.

THE SOURCE OF DISCRIMINATION

What was the exact source of the incentive to discriminate in response to compensation laws? Did the transfer of risk itself create such incentives? Or did the problem lie in the particular ways in which employers secured their compensation liabilities? That is, would all workmen's compensation incentivize employment discrimination, or could changes in the particular form of compensation insurance solve the problem? Observers and critics like Warren Garst and Edward Phelps asked these questions, and answered them in different ways. Their disagreements centered on how deeply discrimination was woven into compensation laws.

In addition to making employers newly liable for employees' injuries, compensation laws required employers to have the financial means to meet this liability. Often employers secured their ability to pay for employees' injury costs via insurance. Many employers enrolled in

---

[32] *Los Angeles Times*, February 11, 1917, 18.   [33] Garst, *First Biennial Report*, 9.
[34] Garst, *First Biennial Report*, 6.

employers' mutual insurance programs, purchased a policy from a private insurance company, or, in states where such an option existed, enrolled in a state-provided insurance plan.[35] All of these methods involved multiple employers pooling their accident liability risks together with the risks of other enterprises, thus transferring part of their responsibility to provide financial security for injured employees to some collective entity. These methods were in keeping with the aggregating aspect of insurance as risk management. Other employers decided to forgo insurance, carrying their own risk via savings, a practice known as self-insurance. Many states allowed large companies to self-insure if the company proved to the state's insurance commission that it had sufficient funds set aside dedicated to meeting its liability for workplace accidents. Self-insuring employers were responsible for the aggregated risk of their workforce, but they did not share that responsibility with other enterprises. They were guarantors of a risk pool – a collective entity – but they still acted in keeping with a different, individualizing logic of risk.[36] They remained individualized at the level of the enterprise, rather than joining together with other employers to share risks across enterprises.

Warren Garst thought compensation laws could be shorn of incentives to discriminate if private insurers were removed from the handling of employee injuries. Garst quoted a letter from an employer who said that due to higher insurance rates he planned to fire three long-standing aged and partially disabled employees "unless there is some way in which we can be released of the extraordinary hazard" posed by employing the three because they "will not be accepted by the insurance companies."[37] Garst quoted another letter blaming inspectors from workmen's compensation insurance companies. If the inspector "sees the one-eyed man, the man with the wooden leg, the man with the varicose veins, and the old man, he will tell you that each and all of these make your rate higher and that your insurance rate will be reduced if you do not have these employes the next time he comes around."[38] Some labor union officials similarly attributed discrimination to "private insurance companies" who raised the premiums of employers who hired "poor risks" like older and

---

[35] Seven states had mandatory and exclusive state insurance funds for workmen's compensation risk. David A. Moss, *When All Else Fails: Government as the Ultimate Risk Manager* (Cambridge, MA: Harvard University Press, 2004), 168.

[36] For a discussion of how risks and statistics created new ways people could be collectivized or aggregated and new ways people could be individualized, see Bouk, *How Our Days Became Numbered.*

[37] Garst, *First Biennial Report*, 6.   [38] Garst, *First Biennial Report*, 6–7.

physically impaired workers.[39] The New York Workmen's Compensation Commission also placed the blame on private insurers. The insurance companies "may attempt to reduce their compensation payments by encouraging or instructing employers" to fire or refuse to hire married or physically impaired individuals.[40]

For critics like Garst, the solution was to secure employers' ability to pay for their share of employee injury costs through state monopoly insurance. Unsurprisingly, this proposal was unpopular with insurance companies, as it threatened to close them out of employers' liability insurance markets.[41] An insurance industry publication expressed concern over complaints that insurers were causing workers to be "thrown out of work by their employers," noting that some government and union officials had "threatened to start an agitation for state insurance if these complaints are found to be well grounded."[42]

Insurance companies pushed back on two fronts, arguing first that their critics lacked evidence because insurers simply were not recommending discrimination to the companies they insured. They agreed that there were discriminatory incentives built into workmen's compensation as legislators had crafted it, but they attributed this to a need for more, not less involvement of insurance companies. Albert W. Whitney, an executive with an insurance industry body called the Workmen's Compensation Service Bureau, wrote a reply to Garst that the Insurance Federation of Iowa reprinted as a pamphlet. Whitney accused Garst of "disregard of the difference between theory and practice. In theory there is, to be sure, some chance for discrimination," but "in practice it is insignificant."[43] Whitney further claimed that investigations by Deputy

---

[39] The Ottumwa Trades and Labor Assembly likewise feared discrimination against "persons that private insurance companies would object to." See J. J. Johnston and C. A. McClure, J. J. Johnston and C. A. McClure to Governor Clarke, December 31, 1914, and Ottumwa Trades and Labor Assembly to Governor Clarke, December 31, 1914, Multiple Governors Correspondence, Box 21, Folder "Correspondence – State Officers, Boards, & Depts: Veterinary Surgeons (3) – Workmen's Compensation," Multiple Governors Correspondence: State Officers, Boards and Departments, State Historical Society of Iowa, Des Moines, Iowa.

[40] *The Standard*, August 15, 1914, 175.

[41] One Iowa newspaper reported that insurance companies did discriminate but that they had stopped doing so in response to calls for a state-monopoly insurance program. *The Perry Daily Chief*, October 22, 1914.

[42] *The Indicator*, January 1914, 341.

[43] Insurance Federation of Iowa, *Shall the State of Iowa Experiment with So-Called "State" Insurance?* (Des Moines, 1914), 32.

Commissioner Phillips of the New York Workmen's Compensation Commission and one of the co-sponsors of the original New York compensation act found "not only that there is no discrimination against married men but that employers prefer married men because of their greater steadiness." Whitney said he had never heard of a case where "the physical condition of the employes" led an insurer to forgo insuring an employer.[44]

The Travelers Insurance Company wrote a reply to Garst as well, which was similarly reprinted in pamphlet form. Travelers argued that insurance companies were removed from hiring and firing such that there was "no occasion for interfering with [employment decisions] or making any suggestion in respect to it." Furthermore, insurance companies operated "under analytical schedules" for setting insurance rates, schedules that were

available to the public and there cannot be found in them any provision respecting the change of rate either upward or downward because of the presence or absence of those who are physically incapacitated or impaired. We can speak with absolute confidence for our own company when we say never in all our experience in compensation matters and our preceding experience in liability matters have we sought to influence or even suggest the dismissal of any man or woman because of existing physical impairment. This is absolutely unknown in our practice.... We do not believe a single case can be found ... where a physically impaired man has been dismissed from service because of his impairment upon the suggestion of any insurance company.[45]

A construction industry trade publication similarly argued that "with respect to the rejection or discharge of married men we find that this complaint has very slight foundation ... There may have been, probably have been some cases in which men known to have large families have been denied work of a particularly hazardous nature," but, the article argued, this was a rare occurrence.[46] The *Indicator*, an insurance trade publication, stated: "There have been no complaints in Iowa ... in regard to married men having been discriminated against."[47] The Insurance Federation of Iowa similarly argued that the claim that "the

[44] Insurance Federation of Iowa, *Shall the State of Iowa Experiment with So-Called "State" Insurance?*, 32.

[45] Insurance Federation of Iowa, *Shall the State of Iowa Experiment with So-Called "State" Insurance?*, 44–45.

[46] *The Bulletin of the General Contractors Association* 5, no. 9 (September 1914): 279.

[47] *The Indicator*, January 5, 1915, 341.

insurance companies discriminate against sub-standard risks to the serious detriment of the working classes of Iowa" had been "amply and repeatedly disproved."[48] They added that this charge was "wholly unsupported by evidence."[49]

Not only did insurance officials deny making recommendations in favor of discrimination, they also argued that a state monopoly insurance fund would not eliminate any existing incentives to discriminate. In his argument against Garst, Whitney pointed out that insurance company actuaries set rates using state-provided accident statistics. Private insurers could set rates scientifically, at "exactly the same rate" as any publicly provided fund.[50] As such, a state fund would improve nothing. Furthermore, Whitney added, insurance rates were "made absolutely without reference either to marital condition or physical condition"; therefore, insurers could not be blamed and a state monopoly fund would not help prevent discrimination. He added, "The only opportunity for discrimination by the Insurance Companies would lie in their selection of business."[51]

The Travelers Insurance Company agreed that workmen's compensation "in practice does place a handicap upon a physically impaired workman," but blamed this on how legislators had written the laws. Compensation laws individualized costs to firms in such a way that a company with more injuries or more expensive injuries would pay more than a company with fewer or cheaper injuries. This was a good thing insofar as it could incentivize safety improvements. Economist John R. Commons argued that if employers were required "to pay accident compensation" by law, then it would create "an inducement to accident prevention."[52] The inducement, however, was to save money, with

---

[48] Insurance Federation of Iowa, *Shall the State of Iowa Experiment with So-Called "State" Insurance?*, 6.

[49] Insurance Federation of Iowa, *Shall the State of Iowa Experiment with So-Called "State" Insurance?*, 7.

[50] Insurance Federation of Iowa, *Shall the State of Iowa Experiment with So-Called "State" Insurance?*, 29.

[51] Insurance Federation of Iowa, *Shall the State of Iowa Experiment with So-Called "State" Insurance?*, 32.

[52] David A. Moss, *Socializing Security: Progressive Era Economists and the Origins of American Social Policy* (Cambridge, MA: Harvard University Press, 1996), 69. See also Leon Fink's discussion of the University of Wisconsin, where Commons spent most of his career. Leon Fink, *The Long Gilded Age: American Capitalism and the Lessons of a New World Order* (Philadelphia: University of Pennsylvania Press, 2014). While the policy particulars of workmen's compensation in its early years varied by state, the kind of incentive Commons identified was present in some form in nearly every US state's

accident prevention a mere side benefit. Employers could respond to the same structure of financial incentives by introducing safety improvements or new exclusionary hiring policies. By holding employers liable for a greater amount in the event of injuries to the already disabled, workmen's compensation laws placed a "very heavy burden upon the employer of those who have suffered serious physical impairment." When older or already disabled employees suffered injuries, they would be more impaired afterward, and hence their injuries were more expensive. These more expensive injuries would raise employers' insurance premiums, incentivizing discrimination. "That employers, mindful of their own hazard" had sometimes responded by refusing to hire these workers "is doubtless true," but, Travelers Insurance added, insurers had nothing to do with this.[53] The company argued that any incentives to discrimination that might exist under private insurance would also exist under a state monopoly insurance plan because state fund premiums, like private insurance premiums, would be higher for employers whose employees suffered more expensive injuries. Travelers added that discriminatory incentives would be greater, not lesser, under state monopoly insurance because the risk pools insured by state monopoly insurance funds were smaller than the large, multistate private insurers' risk pool.

If anything, Travelers argued, insurance companies mitigated incentives to discriminate because they dealt with aggregates and risk pools larger than individual states and much larger than companies' employment rolls. Since insurance companies handled such a large volume of policies and premiums, incidents of injury to elderly and disabled workers would be "absolutely lost in the operation of the law of average."[54] Individuals were minuscule within the aggregated risk that insurance companies spread across risk pools consisting of numerous firms.

---

compensation legislation, in that all states individualized employers' costs for employee injuries to some extent. For example, while Ohio, Oregon, Virginia, and Washington had state monopoly insurance plans, Ohio and Virginia permitted self-insurance and Washington and Oregon experience-rated employers' premiums. For a concise summary of the differences between different states' compensation laws in the early years of workmen's compensation, see Fishback and Kantor, *A Prelude to the Welfare State*, 103–104. For a very detailed treatment of the specifics of these laws, see Barbara Armstrong, *Insuring the Essentials* (New York: Macmillan, 1932), 251–281.

[53] Insurance Federation of Iowa, *Shall the State of Iowa Experiment with So-Called "State" Insurance?*, 45.

[54] Insurance Federation of Iowa, *Shall the State of Iowa Experiment with So-Called "State" Insurance?*, 45.

A smaller risk pool meant less spreading of the increased injury risk due to injuries to married, older, or physically impaired employees. The smaller the risk pool, the larger the relative cost of each individual injury within the pool. Hence discrimination would be more likely under any pool smaller than that of private insurance, Travelers suggested.[55] The solution, they argued, lay in larger numbers and bigger pools.

SELF-INSURANCE

Travelers leveraged the point about the size of risk pools into an argument against self-insurance, arguing that self-insurance made companies especially likely to practice discrimination. "If any discrimination exists in this state against aged, married, or physically imperfect workmen, it will, in our judgment, be found only in concerns where the Industrial Commissioner has permitted self-insurance: it will not be found in risks which are regularly insured" via a for-profit insurance company.[56]

In attacking self-insurance, the Travelers Insurance Company criticized the business practices of many of the largest businesses in the United States and the global economy in the early twentieth century. Seven of the ten largest firms in the world in this era became self-insurers under US workmen's compensation laws: American Tobacco, General

---

[55] The Iowa Employers' Liability Commission argued for a different policy, but similarly emphasized the importance of the size of risk pools. The Commission implied that the combination of state and market-based insurance had particularly problematic results for the law of averages. The Commission said that the state of Massachusetts made a mistake by creating a state-provided workplace injury insurance plan but allowing private insurers to compete with that plan. This was a mistake because the insurance "companies would seek the cream of the risks," meaning the companies with the lowest accident costs, while the state plan would be left with "the greater number of the most undesirable ones and in addition thereto reduce the number of patrons" of the state plan to such a degree that it would be unable "to obtain and apply the rule of average." This would render the state insurance plan ineffective, "it being a recognized established principle of insurance that unless you can obtain a sufficient number of employers having a sufficient number of employes, reaching to such number as will enable the making of estimates of rates upon a good general experience, that you cannot obtain a reasonable and satisfactory safe average to determine an equitable rate reasonably safe to meet the requirements without overburdening the industries coming within the limited scope." This fragmentation of risk pools and resulting problem of costs was an insuperable effect of the combination of public and private insurance, the Commission argued. Iowa Employers' Liability Commission, *Report of Employers' Liability Commission, Part I* (Des Moines: Emory H. English, State Printer, 1912), 9.

[56] Insurance Federation of Iowa, *Shall the State of Iowa Experiment with So-Called "State" Insurance?*, 13–14.

Electric, International Harvester, Pullman, Singer, Standard Oil, and U.S. Steel.[57] While the exact number is unknown, self-insurers were numerous, increased over time, and included among them many of the largest manufacturers.

The New York Self-Insurers' Association had sixty-two members in 1918.[58] In 1919 *The Standard* reported that "over 60 per cent. of

[57] On the size of these firms, see the work done by Alfred Chandler and Christopher Schmitz. Both created lists ranking US companies in the early twentieth century by size. Their lists offer the basis for a rough estimate of the importance of self-insuring companies in the economy in the early twentieth century. Out of the companies that Chandler listed as the twenty-five largest American companies in this era, twelve became self-insurers under workmen's compensation: American Smelting and Refining, American Tobacco, BF Goodrich, General Electric, International Harvester, Pullman, Singer, Standard Oil New Jersey, Standard Oil of New York, Swift, U.S. Steel, and Westinghouse Electric. Christopher Schmitz also counted these twelve companies in his list of the twenty-five largest American companies in 1912. Schmitz's list differs from Chandler's; seventeen companies on Schmitz's list soon became self-insurers under workers' compensation law. These companies included the companies already listed as well as American Can, American Car and Foundry, National Biscuit, Utah Copper, and Westinghouse Air Brake. Christopher Schmitz, "The Worlds Largest Industrial Companies of 1912," *Business History* 37, no. 4 (1995): 85–96. See also the appendices to Alfred D. Chandler, *Scale and Scope: The Dynamics of Industrial Capitalism* (Cambridge, MA: Belknap Press of Harvard University Press, 1990), and Alfred D. Chandler, *The Visible Hand: The Managerial Revolution in American Business* (Cambridge, MA: Belknap Press of Harvard University Press, 1977). My sources on the self-insured status of these companies are as follows. American Can: R. A. Mansfield Hobbs, "Self-Insurance," *The Spectator*, May 23, 1918, 79; American Car and Foundry: *The National Compensation Journal*, April 1914, 8–9; American Smelting and Refining: Industrial Commission of Colorado, *First Report of the Industrial Commission of Colorado*, 35; American Tobacco: Hobbs, "Self-Insurance," 79; BF Goodrich: Nebraska Department of Labor, *Second Biennial Report: Department of Compensation, 1917–1918*, 39; General Electric: Industrial Commission of Colorado, *Second Report of the Industrial Commission of Colorado*, 8; International Harvester: Nebraska Department of Labor, *Second Biennial Report: Department of Compensation, 1917–1918*, 39; National Biscuit: Industrial Commission of Colorado, *Fifth Annual Report*, 9; Pullman: H. F. Browne to F. L. Simmons, March 27, 1931, F. L. Simmons Administrative Files, 1918–1936 Box 3, Folder 64, Employee and Labor Relations, Medicine and Sanitation, Pullman Corporation Records, Newberry Library, Chicago, IL; Singer: Industrial Commission of Colorado, *Second Report of the Industrial Commission of Colorado*, 8; Standard Oil of New York: Industrial Commissioner of New York State, *The Industrial Bulletin*, May 1923, 189 (before self-insuring, Standard Oil of New York made headlines by first enrolling in New York's state insurance plan then pulling out of the state plan and insuring with the Travelers Insurance Company; see *The Spectator*, January 4, 1917, 6); Swift: Nebraska Department of Labor, *Second Biennial Report: Department of Compensation, 1917–1918*, 39; U.S. Steel: *The Spectator*, December 23, 1915, 397; Utah Copper: *Monthly Labor Review*, January 1921, 180; Westinghouse Air Brake: *The Spectator*, December 23, 1915, 397; Westinghouse Electric: *The Standard*, April 19, 1919, 427.

[58] Hobbs, "Self-Insurance," 77–81.

[Pennsylvania] manufacturers were covered by self-insurance" including "five hundred of the largest employers" in the state.[59] William H. Horner, director of the Workmen's Compensation Bureau of Pennsylvania, estimated that in 1920 self-insurers operating in Pennsylvania "employ more than 900,000 persons and pay a very large part of the compensation liability incurred in the State."[60] The 1920 census listed 3,426,359 people as gainfully employed in Pennsylvania, with 1,426,705 of them employed in manufacturing.[61] If self-insurers employed 900,000 people, then approximately 26 percent of Pennsylvania's employed population, and probably the majority of employees in manufacturing, worked for a self-insurer. *The Standard* estimated a 60 percent self-insurance rate among all Pennsylvania manufacturers. In 1921, New York Industrial Commissioner Henry D. Sayer reported that 380 New York employers had elected to become self-insurers. These 380 companies had deposited $8.25 million with the Industrial Commission as guarantee of their ability to pay for future injury liabilities. New York had 532 self-insurers by 1926.[62] Self-insurance grew in other states as well.[63] Self-insurance was even more widespread in terms of the numbers of employees exposed to the practice. In 1920, 67 percent of employed Americans, and 75 percent of American employed in manufacturing, worked in a state allowing self-insurance. States permitting self-insurance were home to 78 percent of US manufacturing capital.[64]

---

[59] *The Standard*, April 19, 1919, 427.

[60] Horner, "The Activities of the Workmen's Compensation Bureau," 293.

[61] US Department of Commerce, Bureau of the Census, *Abstract of the Fourteenth Census of the United States, 1920*, 500.

[62] Industrial Commissioner of New York State, *The Industrial Bulletin* 1, no. 2 (November, 1921): 24; Industrial Commissioner of New York State, *The Industrial Bulletin* 5, no. 9 (June 1926): 231.

[63] Carl Hookstadt, "Comparison of Workmen's Compensation Insurance and Administration," *Bulletin of the United States Bureau of Labor Statistics* 301 (April 1922). By Hookstadt's count, California had 221 self-insurers employing 204,802 people (pp. 157–158); Idaho had 46 self-insurers (p. 160); Illinois had 558 self-insurers (p. 164); Massachusetts had 120 self-insurers (p. 169); Ohio had 250 self-insurers (p. 104); Maryland had 300 self-insurers (p. 166); and Michigan had about 600 self-insurers (p. 167).

[64] There are no available figures for total numbers of self-insurers, but states with self-insurance were by far the majority, especially in terms of the numbers of resident employees, manufacturing employees, and capital investment in manufacture. The figures for numbers of employed persons in self-insuring states are drawn from calculations using the 1920 census. See US Department of Commerce, Bureau of the Census, *Fourteenth Census of the United States Taken in the Year 1920*, vol. 4: *Population, 1920, Occupations* (Washington, DC: Government Printing Office, 1923), 44. For the figures on numbers of wage earners and capital invested in manufacturing, see US Department of

TABLE 5.1 *Compensation laws and self-insurance, 1913–1922*

Year	States with compensation laws	States with self-insurance provisions	Percentage of compensation laws allowing self-insurance
1913	22	10	45
1916	32	19	59
1919	41	28	68
1922	42	30	71

The growth of self-insurance was in part a product of law. Legislative provisions for self-insurance of compensation risks were widespread from the beginning of compensation laws and increased over time. Table 5.1 shows the number of states with compensation laws and the number and percentage of those states permitting self-insurance for the years 1913–1922.[65]

The Standard magazine reported in 1918 that enough US states had self-insurance provisions in their workmen's compensation legislation that business owners in Massachusetts had begun to worry that they were at a competitive disadvantage because their state had not yet allowed manufacturers to self-insure.[66]

Commerce, Bureau of the Census, *Fourteenth Census of the United States Taken in the Year 1920, vol. 8: Manufactures, 1919, General Report and Analytical Tables* (Washington, DC: Government Printing Office, 1923), 296–297.

[65] States that did not allow self-insurance of compensation risks were also more likely to have been earlier adopters of compensation laws. By 1922, of the twelve states that had compensation laws but no self-insurance provisions, eight of them had adopted their laws between 1913 and 1915. The dates of states' adoption of compensation laws comes from Shawn Kantor and Price V. Fishback, "How Minnesota Adopted Workers' Compensation," *The Independent Review* 2, no. 4 (1998): 557–578. For the number of states per year with self-insurance provisions, see the following sources. For 1913, see *Workmen's Compensation: Report upon Operation of State Laws*, a report compiled by a joint commission of the American Federation of Labor and the National Civic Federation, United States Senate, Document 419, 63rd Congress, 2nd Session (Washington: Government Printing Office: 1914). For 1916, see "Workmen's Compensation Laws of the United States and Foreign Countries," *Bulletin of the United States Bureau of Labor Statistics*, no. 203 (January 1917). For 1919, see "Workmen's Compensation Acts in the United States: The Legal Phase," *National Industrial Conference Board Research Report* 1 (August 1919). For 1922, see William R. Schneider, *The Law of Workmen's Compensation: Rules of Procedure, Tables, Forms, Synopses of Acts*, vol. 2 (St. Louis: Thomas Law Book Company, 1922).

[66] *The Standard*, March 3, 1918, 231.

The main reason for a company to self-insure was to save money. As R. A. Mansfield Hobbs of the New York Self-Insurers Association put it, "[t]he principal argument in favor of carrying self-insurance is the question of expense – for instance, one of our membership, to carry its own risk in the state fund, at its rates, for the first year of the operation of the New York act, would have had to pay a premium in excess of $7,000,000 per annum" while its actual costs in its first year operating as a self-insurer were less than one-tenth of that cost. "None of the members [of the self-insurance association], it is believed, have exceeded a loss ratio greater than one-third of what it would cost to cover the risk in the state fund or straight line insurance." The savings came because self-insurers avoided "the burden of [paying for insurance companies'] profit or responsibility for other employers' losses, which other insurance carriers must figure upon."[67]

E. D. Alexander, an official at the American Car and Foundry Company, estimated that self-insurers in Detroit saved "from slightly to exceed fifty per cent to about seventy per cent of the insurance rate."[68] W. H. Burhop, the chief statistician at the Wisconsin Industrial Commission, estimated that self-insurers would have tripled their accident costs if they met their accident risks via purchasing insurance policies.[69] In the words of Henry Sayer from the New York Industrial Commission:

I like rather to think of self-insurance as furnishing compensation at actual cost, and as eliminating the high cost of insurance in the private companies.... The self-insurer finds that instead of paying large premiums for insurance some part of which goes to make up the losses of the less careful and less completely equipped employers, and some part to make up the high overhead expense of the carrier and its profits, he is paying exactly what his own accident experience requires. He does not get off any cheaper than the law requires, but he does not on the other hand have to pay anything more than the law demands.[70]

While large businesses saw self-insurance as a form of savings, some commentators argued that it was not in fact insurance and so was a departure from the effort to deal with the problem of injury via insurance principles. Henry Sayer argued that "self-insurance is a misnomer, for as

---

[67] Hobbs, "Self-Insurance," 79.
[68] E. D. Alexander, "Suggestions to Those Contemplating Self-Insurance," *National Compensation Journal* 1, no. 4 (April 1914): 8–9; 9.
[69] *Bulletin of the United States Bureau of Labor Statistics* 212 (June 1917): 167.
[70] Industrial Commissioner of New York State, *The Industrial Bulletin* 1, no. 2 (November 1921): 24.

we all know, it is not a form of insurance at all."[71] Statistician Isaac
Rubinow said that "self-insurance simply means relief from insurance
compulsion upon sufficient evidence of solvency."[72] Harwood E. Ryan,
an actuary with the New York State Insurance Department, said, "Self-
insurance is really non-insurance. The employer simply assumes his own
risk and obtains permission from the authorities to deal directly with his
employe-claimants or their dependents."[73]

Others argued that self-insurers still operated according to insurance
principles even if they did not purchase insurance enrolling them into a
larger risk pool. R. A. Mansfield Hobbs called self-insurance "the oldest
and purest method of insurance with which society is acquainted." All
insurance, Hobbs argued, was a form of "making financial provision
against certain risks." As such, self-insurance was not a misnomer, despite
what critics had said. "When prehistoric man seized a club, or built
himself a shelter from the weather, he unconsciously became a self-insurer
of his safety, his life and health and comfort."[74] In a sense both sides were
right: self-insurers were uninsured, and yet, because the law required them
to manage their risk pools, they faced pressures to act out the logic of
insurance – or rather, a logic of insurance. Insurance has a collectivizing
aspect and an individualizing aspect, an element of wealth redistribution
and an element of exclusion. Self-insurance encouraged the individualizing and exclusionary logic of insurance.

Travelers Insurance argued that self-insurers were particularly prone to
practice exclusionary hiring in response to their risks under workmen's
compensation because of the relatively small size of their risk pools. Self-
insurance was effectively vertical integration of the functions of insurance
companies. It was a partial refusal of the market. Self-insuring firms
essentially said, "Why buy what we can self-provide?" This vertical
integration was only partial, though, because of a peculiar quality of
insurance as a commodity. Insurance is an institution for spreading risks
over large populations. Risk spreading across multiple firms simply could
not be integrated into a single firm alone. For the purposes of risk

[71] Industrial Commissioner of New York State, *The Industrial Bulletin*, 1, no. 2 (November
1921): 24.
[72] Isaac Rubinow, *Standards of Health Insurance* (New York: H. Holt and Company,
1916), 179.
[73] Harwood E. Ryan, "Methods of Insuring Workmen's Compensation," *Annals of the
American Academy of Political and Social Science* 70, no. 15 (March 1917): 244–254,
251.
[74] Hobbs, "Self-Insurance," 77.

spreading, the larger the population in a risk pool, the better. Travelers Insurance argued that private insurance of accident risks removed incentives for employers to make changes in hiring practices. Once averaged into the larger number of people in a private insurance company's risk pool, any differences in injury costs in individual cases due to physical condition would be tiny. Larger risk pools, the argument went, would encourage the collectivizing logic of insurance and discourage the individualizing logic. Even though self-insurers were large employers relative to other companies, their employees formed a smaller risk pool compared with the number of people in the risk pools insured by insurance companies.[75] Individual employees thus formed a larger share of self-insurers' smaller risk pools, providing a greater incentive to keep out risky individuals. Because self-insurers opted not to pool their risks with other companies but instead faced their risks alone, self-insurers had more incentive to individualize and to practice gatekeeping.

Other critics concurred with Travelers Insurance that self-insurance was more likely than other ways of handling workplace accident risk to incentivize changed employment practices. In 1914 actuary Harwood E. Ryan said, "It has been argued that self-insurance will work to the disadvantage of labor. It is claimed that employers will apply strict standards in engaging employees, that the physically inferior and those with dependent families will be discriminated against."[76] The New York State Workmen's Compensation Commission argued that same year that a self-insurer was "subject to strong incentive and temptation to lighten his burden under the act by discharging or refusing to employ married men, and by instituting a rigorous physical examination of his employes."[77] New York Industrial Commissioner John Mitchell similarly argued that some self-insurers

discharge every man who shows physical defects – that is why we do not find the workingmen advocating self-insurance ... The premium rate is not affected, for employers who carry insurance with the casualty company or with the state fund, by the physical condition of their men. But the self-insured, because he himself

---

[75] Insurance Federation of Iowa, *Shall the State of Iowa Experiment with So-Called "State" Insurance?*, 13–14.

[76] Ryan, "Methods of Insuring Workmen's Compensation," 251. Some critics rejected both self-insurance and private insurance of employers' liabilities under compensation laws. For example, the Cigar Makers Journal called for the elimination of both, in order to do away with "all cause for physical examination of employees and for any discrimination against any class of employees." *Cigar Makers Journal* 38, no. 12 (December 1914): 12.

[77] *The Standard*, August 15, 1914, 175.

pays the money, does take this factor into account in many cases. He feels that by a physical examination and a dismissal of the man not physically fit – or not physically perfect – he may reduce his cost.[78]

Along similar lines, T. J. Duffy of the Ohio Industrial Commission wrote that "[e]mployers who are carrying their own risks," which is to say, self-insurers, were particularly prone to discriminate against those "people who have already lost an eye, a hand or some other member."[79] Delegates at the American Federation of Labor's 1914 convention similarly blamed self-insurers for discrimination. An AFL committee "appointed to consider compensation laws reported that the heart of the trouble is in the 'self-insurance' systems maintained by corporations, who institute their own indemnity funds."[80] The AFL delegates argued that "the privilege of employers being self-insurers" should be removed from the compensation law.[81]

Travelers Insurance noted that insurers had no control over hiring and firing decisions. Self-insuring companies, however, did have the power to practice exclusionary hiring and firing as well as an increased incentive to use that power. Actuary Carl Hookstadt pointed out that by combining employment with underwriting employees' risks, self-insurance was particularly subject to abuse because self-insuring employers handled both employment and injury in-house.

Probably the most important objection to self-insurance is that it makes the employer practically the final arbiter in the settlement of compensation cases. The unwillingness of the employees to antagonize their employer through fear of losing their jobs will many times prevent them from appealing to the industrial commission. This latent power of intimidation possessed by self-insured employers, though they may be entirely just, effectively inhibits injured workmen from seeking redress from the commission. The commission, moreover, since it obtains its information from the accident reports of the employer, is not in a position to judge of the merits of the case unless the injured employee brings the matter to its attention.[82]

---

[78] John Mitchell, "Operation of the New York Workmen's Compensation Law," *American Labor Legislation Review* 5, no. 1 (1915): 15–30, 21.

[79] *International Molders' Journal* 51, no. 1 (January 1915): 41–42.

[80] *Insurance Monitor* 62, no. 1 (January 1914): 602. See the *Weekly Underwriter* 31, no. 21 (November 21, 1914): 592.

[81] *The Spectator*, December 24, 1914, 356.

[82] Hookstadt, "Comparison of Workmen's Compensation Insurance and Administration," 65. It is possible that this power on the part of self-insuring employers discouraged employees from filing compensation claims when they could do so, out of fear of retaliation. For contemporary studies of the ongoing problem of retaliation, and the ways in which fear of retaliation discourages injured people from filing compensation claims, see

By being both employer and insurer of employees' risks, Hookstadt argued, self-insurers had a great deal of discretion and faced little over-sight. Companies that self-insured and discriminated in hiring acted in a locally or situationally rational manner in response to market impera-tives. Self-insuring reduced costs, and it made self-insuring firms especially sensitive to each instance of cost, each injury or threat of injury. They tended to respond in the direction incentivized by market imperatives, by restricting hiring and so passing the force of market imperatives down-ward to working-class people.

In 1914, the same year Phelps posed his grave questions, General Electric employees began to complain that their employer was firing workers at its plant in Schenectady, New York. Frank Dujay, president of a union federation in the plant, the Electrical Alliance, attributed the change to self-insurance: "[t]he General Electric Company carries its own insurance; that is, it pays benefits to injured workmen directly from its own treasury to the Workmen's Compensation Commission, and it is attempting to reduce the amount of benefits it will have to pay." Dujay called for the New York State Workmen's Compensation Commission to do something, but the Commission declared itself "powerless to prevent a self-insuring company from discriminating so long as it acts legally."[83]

Self-insurance was especially common among large manufacturers. The same aspects of large manufacturers that made compensation laws appealing to these companies as a response to the employer-side financial risks of employee injury also made discrimination appealing as a form of cost control. These companies were predisposed to try to avoid uncer-tainty and unpredictability, as Chapter 3 discussed, including the new financial risk posed by employees' injuries under the new allocation of costs brought about by compensation laws.

Both critics and defenders of self-insurance argued that self-insurers experienced their changed liabilities under workmen's compensation as providing particularly strong incentives to control costs, because self-insurers did not pool their compensation risks with other companies. Advocates of self-insurance agreed that self-insurers were subject to par-ticularly strong incentives to change their practices in order to reduce accident costs, but disagreed about how employers would respond to

Deborah Berkowitz, "Legislation to Protect Injured Workers in Massachusetts," National Employment Law Project Policy Brief, June 24, 2019, www.nelp.org/publication/legisla tion-protect-injured-workers-massachusetts/#_ednref4, accessed June 24, 2019.
[83] *New York Times*, August 12, 1914.

these incentives. These advocates emphasized that self-insurance could incentivize employer-sponsored safety measures. Hobbs argued that self-insurance made workplaces safer because "[w]hen the employer pays compensation out of his own pocket, he appreciates the value and necessity of safety devices."[84] Actuary Carl Hookstadt said in his report on workmen's compensation laws that "[p]robably the greatest social benefit derivable from self-insurance is the impetus it gives to accident prevention. Self-insured employers at least have a strong incentive to prevent accidents, because there exists a more direct relationship between their accidents and compensation costs."[85] Along similar lines, Henry Sayer suggested that self-insurers would be "inspire[d] to efforts to reduce accidents and lessen the effects of them" for both financial and moral reasons. Self-insurance would foster "great improvement in the physical aspect of industry." The improving effect of self-insurance in New York "has been splendid," said Sayer.[86] Robert McKeown of the Wisconsin Industrial Commission similarly said, "The self-insurer ... probably does realize more than those who not carry their own insurance, the cost of each individual accident, as it comes out of his own pocket directly and continues while the disability lasts."[87] These advocates of self-insurance on safety grounds conceded the point that self-insurers were particularly sensitive to incentives.

Arguments that self-insurance made work safer assumed employers were responsive to incentives. This assumption may have rested on a general world-view that all humans maximize self-interest.[88] Self-insurers'

---

[84] Hobbs, "Self-Insurance," 79.

[85] Hookstadt, "Comparison of Workmen's Compensation Insurance and Administration," 65.

[86] Industrial Commissioner of New York State, *The Industrial Bulletin* 1, no. 2 (November 1921): 24.

[87] Robert McKeown, "The Relation between Workmen's Compensation and Safety," in *Proceedings of the Sixth Annual Convention of the Association of Governmental Labor Officials of the United States and Canada* (Washington: Government Printing Office, 1920), 97–100; 99.

[88] The conditions under which people respond to economic incentives are themselves historically produced and ultimately contingent. Rational maximizing of self-interest is an effect rather than a cause of capitalist society. While the particulars vary, in general the institutions of capitalist society tend to take this assumption and make it prescriptive, rewarding some people who act in line with this norm and punishing others who do not act in line with this norm. Though the point is not posed this way, Rakesh Kurana offers an illuminating discussion of the role of business schools in educating people into becoming the kinds of people who respond to incentives in this fashion. Rakesh Kurana, "MBAs Gone Wild," *American Interest* (July–August 2009), www.the-american-interest .com/articles/2009/7/1/mbas-gone-wild/, accessed February 1, 2014. Furthermore, it is

responsiveness to the incentives built into compensation laws likely resulted as well from the economic or financial particulars of those firms. Self-insurance required that a company be large enough to self-insure, and self-insurance was especially common among manufacturers, and above all among large manufacturers. These companies were predisposed to try to avoid uncertainty, unpredictability, and interruptions to production in general, as discussed in Chapter 3.

In an important sense, "self-insurance" was a misnomer because it was not insurance at all. In another sense, however, self-insurance fit with the insurance goals of compensation laws.[89] Compensation laws aggregated some of the risks from each individual employee into a pool at a company and made employers financially responsible for that pool. Employers responded to being pressed into treating their labor force as risk pools by gatekeeping at the boundaries of those pools. This phenomenon was especially intense for self-insurers, but these pressures affected all employers under compensation laws.

DRIFT TOWARD SELECTION

Both Warren Garst and his insurance industry opponents expressed hope that compensation laws could be rendered non-discriminatory. They believed discrimination due to compensation laws could be eliminated by changing how individual employers' liability risks were secured: either through state-provided insurance, in Garst's case, or private insurance,

---

worth noting that self-interest is not a given but itself historically and socially constituted. For a critical account of why it is a mistake to take interests as given, see Goran Therborn, *The Ideology of Power and the Power of Ideology* (London: Verso, 1980), 4–5, 10.

[89] Self-insurance and employment discrimination represent two different but related versions of what insurance theorist Tom Baker has called a de-pooling effect. Insurance involves pooling risks, but it can also encourage people and institutions to avoid pooling. See Tom Baker, "Containing the Promise of Insurance: Adverse Selection and Risk Classification," in *Risk and Morality*, ed. Richard Victor Ericson and Aaron Doyle (Toronto: University of Toronto Press, 2003), 258–283; 259. Self-insurers de-pooled in that they did not share their risks because it was cheaper to self-insure than to pay for the costs of pooling their risks. Law allowed them to do this, and created the set of incentives in which this was the cheapest option. The specifics of the arrangements for securing ability to pay for the employer-side share of the financial costs of injury incentivized this de-pooling as well as discriminatory hiring as a specific practice of de-pooling. Self-insurance was itself a kind of risky behavior because of the lack of pooling. The reward for that risk was the cost savings that came by not paying insurance premiums. Self-insurers responded to their own risk-taking by becoming more risk averse in their hiring decisions.

for the insurance companies. Edward Phelps argued more pessimistically that any version of workmen's compensation would be insurance legislation, and insurance always produced discrimination. He speculated that employers had probably always preferred younger and less physically impaired applicants, but argued that workmen's compensation had given employers new reasons for this preference, what I have called a new normal. Phelps held that there was a "drift toward physical selection in the employment of wage-earners coming within the range of Workmen's Compensation protection," because of the nature of insurance institutions. The physical selection was at least equally financial selection. Compensation laws in a sense financialized employees' bodies for employers, rendering some employees newly risky hires.[90]

Regardless of how employers secured their ability to pay for injury liability, employers would face pressures to become more selective in hiring under workmen's compensation. This was, Phelps argued, because the "foundation of all forms of insurance ... the so-called 'law of average,' involves selection" of people for admission or exclusion. In Phelps's view, all insurance involved decisions about a minimum standard of risk, below which individuals could not gain entry to the risk pool in question. Guarantors of a risk pool, whether an insurance company or an employer, always evaluated risks and excluded some category of people who were judged as below the minimum standard. "[I]t is only a matter of academic detail, so to speak, whether the condition so operating is one of age, impairment, or multiplicity of benefit-sharing dependents on the part of the injured workmen." As such, Phelps argued, any system of insuring against workplace injuries would pressure employers to change whom they hired. Compensation laws could make the lives of some people more secure only at the expense of pushing others out of work. No matter the institutional particulars, for Phelps, "so long as insurance is conducted on a cold-blooded business basis," workmen's compensation of any kind would create new incentives for excluding some people from employment: "There would seem to be no room for difference of opinion on this matter-of-course proposition, and I can conceive of no reason why Workmen's Compensation should be exempted from this basic insurance principle."[91]

Phelps identified individualizing practices within compensation insurance. Insurance as risk sharing is a collectivizing practice, sheltering

90 Phelps, "Certain Grave Questions," 4.　　　　91 Phelps, "Certain Grave Questions," 4.

individuals from their risks by spreading them out across a pool. The idea that the insured party's premiums should reflect their losses, a practice known as experience rating, moved in the opposite direction, individualizing people as unacceptable risks, gatekeeping their entry to the risk pool in order to protect the pool from the individual. Experience rating meant that insurance premiums would tend to rise with payouts, such that companies with more accidents would pay more costs. Experience rating created financial incentive for employers to behave in less risky ways, using insurance as a tool to not only respond to behavior but to actively shape and govern behavior. Employers could respond to these incentives by either safety improvements or discrimination.[92]

---

[92] An important factor in employer ability to discriminate in hiring was the idea of at-will employment. At-will employees "have no enforceable claim to ongoing employment." Katherine V. W. Stone and Harry Arthurs, *Rethinking Workplace Regulation: Beyond the Standard Contract of Employment* (New York: Russell Sage Foundation, 2013), 368. See also Kenneth M. Casebeer, "At-Will Employment," in *Encyclopedia of United States Labor and Working-Class History*, ed. Eric Arnesen (New York: Routledge, 2007), 136. As Casebeer notes, the reasons for the rise of the doctrine of at-will employment are the subject of scholarly disagreement. At-will employment is a historically specific version of capitalist social relations, a particular manner of practicing the general pattern of commodifying labor power. Part of at-will employment, though not unique to it, is a picture of markets as practices of freedom, consensual and voluntary. Compensation laws required new terms to be written into most employment relationships. Depicting employment relationships as voluntary bargains emerging out of buyers and sellers meeting as equals in a freely entered market means employers merely opted not to purchase under the terms legally required. This image of markets depoliticizes and runs cover for a wide range of injustices. At-will employment forms the core of the institutional particulars through which employer control over the hiring and firing of waged workers has been organized in the United States from the late nineteenth century to the present. As such, at-will employment has been a shaping force in American labor relations and American capitalism. At-will employment also provides a good counterexample to the idea that law follows after the economy. For criticisms of that idea, see Robert Gordon, "Critical Legal Histories," *Stanford Law Review* 36, no. 57 (1984): 57–125, and Christopher Tomlins, *Law, Labor and Ideology in the Early American Republic,* (Cambridge: Cambridge University Press, 1993), 304. See also the symposium on "Critical Legal Histories" in *Law & Social Inquiry* 37, no. 1 (Winter 2012). As Tomlins puts it, law is a "modality of rule," a form of governance that shapes the meaning of and sets the rules for other social behaviors broadly, in economic life and beyond. Christopher Tomlins, *Law, Labor, and Ideology in the Early American Republic* (Cambridge: Cambridge University Press, 1993), 19–34. Rather than law being determined by the economy, law constitutes economic life not least because concepts and practices of property, money, and employment are simultaneously economic and legal. See Anne Fleming, "Legal History as Economic History," in *The Oxford Handbook of Legal History*, ed. Markus D. Dubber and Christopher Tomlins (Oxford: Oxford University Press, 2018). This is especially so if "economic life" is understood expansively so as to include class relationships, employers' directive authority, and the commodification of people. See Michael Heinrich,

Insurance secures some person or group against the financial effects of events. In market settings and in settings where insurance is not universal, insurance always draws some boundary line between persons, groups, or events that are or are not covered by insurance. Any "'risk sharing' arrangement," in the words of sociologist Ulrich Beck, involves "conventions and boundaries around a 'risk community' that shares the burden."[93] Changing the boundaries of a risk community tends to bring about consideration of changes in risk sharing, and, vice versa, changes in risk sharing tend to bring about consideration of a community's boundaries.[94] As Tom Baker has written, "all other things being equal, people behave differently when they bear the costs of their misfortunes than when they do not." At the very least, changed allocations of risk mean changed incentives for behavior. Political scientist Deborah Stone has described insurance as creating "communities of privilege" that are fragmented "into ever-smaller, more homogeneous groups."[95] Gatekeeping around risk pools creates and maintains these communities of privilege, and the corresponding populations of people disadvantaged and excluded. Compensation laws imported these dynamics into labor markets. Of course, the risk "communities" employers headed up were hierarchical ones, organized by employer power and centered on profit and accumulation. Thus, employers made the

Introduction to the Three Volumes of Karl Marx's Capital, trans. Alexander Locascio (New York: Monthly Review Press, 2012), 199–218.

[93] Ulrich Beck, *World Risk Society* (Cambridge: Polity Press, 1999), 16. See also François Ewald, "Insurance and Risk in Graham Burchell," in *The Foucault Effect: Studies in Governmentality*, ed. Colin Gordon and Peter Miller (Chicago: University of Chicago Press, 1991), 197–210.

[94] Tom Baker, "Risk, Insurance, and the Social Construction of Responsibility," in *Embracing Risk: The Changing Culture of Insurance and Responsibility*, ed. Tom Baker and Jonathan Simon (Chicago: University of Chicago Press, 2002), 33–51; 45. Insurers have long been aware of the tendency for insurance to change the behavior of the insured, a phenomenon typically discussed under the term "moral hazard," defined as "the effect of insurance on incentives." Baker and Simon, "Embracing Risk," in *Embracing Risk*, 15. Caley Horan points out that this change in behavior reflects the character of insurance as an institution of governance: to be an insurer is to govern the behavior of others, and to change how people are or are not insured is likely to change those people's behaviors. It is worth noting that changing incentives have effects not only on the insured but on the insuring as well. Insurance is collective; risk-sharing is a relationship. To change allocations of risk is to change relationships, which can affect the behavior of all parties involved, including, in the case of workmen's compensation, the behaviors of employers. Caley Horan, "Actuarial Age: Insurance and the Emergence of Neoliberalism in the Postwar United States" (PhD diss., University of Minnesota, 2011).

[95] Deborah A. Stone, "The Struggle for the Soul of Health Insurance," *Journal of Health Politics, Policy and Law* 18, no. 2 (June 1993): 287–317; 299, 290.

decisions to change their boundaries relatively unilaterally, based on concerns for the financial bottom line.

Workmen's compensation was insurance in the sense of risk pools managed with a dual logic of aggregation and individualization. As the construction industry employers' group the General Contractors Association put it, "workmen's compensation is nothing more nor less than life and accident insurance combined."[96] The dual logic of insurance introduced new gatekeeping to employment decisions, since hiring had become entry to the risk pool employers were required to guarantee. Without screening "at the entrance gate" of a risk pool, insurance theorist Henry Lipincott wrote in 1905, "the weakest and least desirable lives would be surest and soonest to come in," at the expense of the risk pool or the profits of the company securing the pool.[97] While Lipincott wrote about life insurance, this is what employers began to do in hiring and firing after compensation laws. They sought to select employees in the way life insurance companies selected policyholders, seeking to reduce the total risk in their pool. Compensation laws had grouped workers' injury risks together into pools. That aggregation introduced new forms of individualization – the "impaired" and "poor risk" – that provided new reasons to exclude some individuals from those pools, which under compensation laws meant exclusion from employment.

When insurance is organized for profit and insurers are allowed to exclude, they will do so. Because compensation laws made employment and risk pool membership come to overlap, employers who refused to take on a person's injury risk also refused to hire that person. Access to employment – the commodification of working-class people in the labor market – became newly distributed according to a logic of risk. Risk was not the only concern by which employers steered their hiring decisions, but it was an increasingly important one. Employers began to gatekeep

---

[96] *The Bulletin of the General Contractors Association*, September 1914, 278.

[97] Quoted in Baker, "Containing the Promise of Insurance," 261. This is known as the problem of adverse selection. The people who most need insurance are likely to claim resources from the risk pool, while the people who contribute most to a risk pool's security are people who are least likely to need insurance. Insurance is transfer of wealth. In insurance, large populations share their risks so that the people who need security at any moment are only a subset of the larger group. Everyone pays in some amount regularly, regardless of lack of momentary need, so that funds are available in moments of acute need. If at any moment the needs outstrip the available funds, the ability of the insurance to provide for people's needs breaks down. The larger the proportion of people in the pool likely to have acute needs relative to other people in the pool and to the pool's resources, the higher the risk and the lower the relative security of the risk pool.

access to employment in order to avoid hiring people who had become, under the new rules for injury liability, too risky to hire. The security that compensation laws provided for some came at the cost of new insecurity and distributive injustice for others.

While policy reformers had hoped for systemic improvements as a result of compensation laws, in their managerial decisions business personnel were not oriented toward these large-scale systemic goals. Market pressures meant that businesses had to pursue their own immediate interests. Companies would face penalties if they protected the well-being of employees and applicants over their financial bottom line. Employers thus made their choices in the face of structural pressures, as they were themselves actors situated within, and in important respects subject to, market imperatives. Seeking to reduce their individual share of workmen's compensation risk, they followed the pressures of those imperatives. In doing so they intensified the pressure of those imperatives on their social subordinates, their employees and job applicants.

Changed hiring practices at some companies could indirectly pressure other companies to make similar changes. The medical director for the Chicago-based Crane Company stated that Crane was "practically forced" to begin screening job applicants "because other industries were doing it and this company was hiring the rejected men." This had the potential to lead to a greater accumulation of higher-risk employees at Crane than at other companies, which would raise Crane's total cost for workplace injuries relative to its competitors. Crane officials felt that they had no choice but to implement medical examinations as a way to control employment risks, because other companies had done so.[98] Crane's medical director described a situation in which other companies acted in line with the incentive to restrict hiring such that it intensified that incentive for Crane. This situation was in keeping with the dynamics of commercial insurance identified by legal scholar Tom Baker: "identify[ing] and exclud[ing] high risks improves [a company's] competitive position in two ways: it lowers its average risk and, assuming the people it rejects go elsewhere, it increases the average risk of its competitors" as higher risk people move to other company's risk pools. When there are multiple pools competing with each other, gatekeeping is intensified, as insurers compete to have the

---

[98] H. Guilbert to E. F. Carry, April 29, 1924, Administrative Subject Files, Employee and Labor Relations, Medicine and Sanitation, Pullman Corporation Records, Box 1, Folder 14, Employee and Labor Relations, Medicine and Sanitation, Pullman Corporation Records, Newberry Library, Chicago, IL.

most favorable risk pool. Crane's medical director believed this pattern had occurred at Crane. Some companies restricted hiring, lowering their risks and raising risks for others, thus indirectly encouraging Crane to implement new gatekeeping measures.[99] Insurance logic became an increasingly important way in which market imperatives were organized – with discriminatory consequences.

COLD-BLOODED BUSINESS

Edward Phelps thought discrimination was irrevocably woven into insurance enterprises conducting themselves on the "cold-blooded business basis" typical of, and in important respects required of, businesses. The discrimination that followed in the wake of compensation laws had a distinctly impersonal or cold-blooded character, because it was rooted in the impersonal, cold-blooded political economy of corporate bureaucracies acting in response to market dependency.

Sociologist Max Weber argued that "without regard for persons" was "the watchword of the market and, in general, of all pursuits of naked economic interests." This "dehumanized" market rationality meant, Weber argued, that "if the principle of the free market is not at the same time restricted," domination of a distinctly impersonal kind would spread throughout society.[100] Compensation laws were,

[99] Baker, "Containing the Promise of Insurance," 261. Employers' changed hiring practices foregrounds the fact that employers govern a portion of social life delegated to them by law. See Christopher Tomlins, "How Who Rides Whom: Recent 'New' Histories of American Labour Law and What They May Signify," *Social History* 20, no. 1 (1995): 1–21; and Tomlins, *Law, Labor, and Ideology.* Historians have tended to focus on how individual employers govern their employees directly. Philosopher Elizabeth Anderson terms this power of employers over employees "private government." Elizabeth Anderson, *Private Government: How Employers Rule Our Lives (And Why We Don't Talk about It)* (Princeton: Princeton University Press, 2017) In the aggregate, employers also indirectly govern job-seekers and the unemployed through the decisions they make en route to their goals as businesses. The situation at Crane, like Baker's description of insurance companies, also points out the ways in which businesses govern each other indirectly through competition in the market. Compensation laws remade the mutual governance of employers over each other, via competition, and their shared governance over job-seekers and the unemployed. These are examples of additional forms of private government exercised by employer over employees, and to some extent over fellow employers. That this form of private government is often unconscious, with markets serving as the mechanism for coordination, makes it harder to address and to change. The current academic job market is a case in point.

[100] H. H. Gerth and C. Wright Mills, eds., *From Max Weber: Essays in Sociology* (Abingdon: Routledge, 1991), 215. Weber saw decision making "without regard to persons" as a key component of both legal and market rationality.

on the one hand, a restriction of that free market principle, imposing order on markets and on courts, requiring payments, and setting prices for injury. Yet these laws were, on the other hand, an extension of the market, subjecting more areas of life to market valuation "without regard for persons." The insurance character of compensation laws facilitated both facets of compensation laws, constraining and organizing the market, while also extending the reach of market valuations.[101]

Compensation laws brought a risk-driven and impersonal – cold-blooded, in Phelps's terms – form of boundary drawing into law and, via law, into labor markets. Some labor power – some people – became potentially financially dangerous for employers' purchase. These people were thus threatened with exclusion from access to wages. This new employment discrimination was not animus driven. It was not done out of any desire to exclude or subordinate the people targeted but rather was a matter of indifference. It was "cold-blooded" activity "without regard for persons." It grew out of the new corporate political economy, which was itself a response to market imperatives, as discussed in Chapter 3. An instrumental orientation to employment was fostered and rendered compulsory by capitalist labor practices or, rather, labor markets. Labor power was a commodity like any other, purchased for instrumental use – for consumption – by the purchaser. Employers did what many consumers did when prices and risks change: they changed their purchasing habits, rendering some things newly oversupplied. That those newly surplus things happened to be human beings was undoubtedly something some individual employers felt bad about – warm-blooded persons often regret their socially compelled cold-blooded actions – but in acting as they did, employers followed the imperatives of market dependency as newly mediated and channeled by compensation laws.

---

[101] The legal organization of the free market via compensation laws involved the crowding-out of other forms of valuation by instrumental rationality. This process can be characterized as a local version of the shift from formal subsumption to real subsumption. See Marx, *Capital*, vol. 1, 944–1046. The former refers to practices that pre-date capitalism becoming taken up into capitalist society and changed via their new social context. The latter, real subsumption, refers to a remaking of social practices due to market and commodity logics. See Fraser and Jaeggi, *Capitalism*, 26 and 37, and *Endnotes*, "The History of Subsumption," *Endnotes* 2, https://endnotes.org.uk/issues/2/en/endnotes-the-history-of-subsumption.

INSURING AND LEGITIMATING INEQUALITY

The discriminatory incentives under compensation laws sometimes became controversial, as the dispute between Garst and Travelers Insurance indicated. Insurance is an important respect political. As Deborah Stone has put it, "insurance underwriting, far from being a dry statistical exercise is a political exercise in drawing the boundaries of community membership."[102] Members of a risk pool have the ability to make a claim on resources to which they are entitled as a member of that pool. Determination of whether or not someone can become a member of a risk pool is in a sense political; it is a decision on belonging, access to resources, and ability to make claims, and a decision made about subordinates by superiors. Employment too is political in the same sense; arguably, all of economic life is. "An economic transaction is a solved political problem," as economist Abba Lerner has put it.[103] Insurance and employment are power relationships. They are political, yet often depoliticized through rhetoric of choice and freedom. In general, the economy under capitalism should be understood as a set of political relationships that are in contention as to whether or not they are political.[104]

Insurance served employers and managerial personnel with a rhetorical framework within which to depoliticize and legitimate discrimination, through recourse to a depoliticized notion of insurance. A dispute between New York Industrial Commissioner John Mitchell and the General Contractors Association illustrates this point. In 1914, Mitchell, a former official with the United Mine Workers of America, said he was "thoroughly opposed" to employers becoming more discriminatory in hiring as a result of workmen's compensation. Mitchell further argued that in the face of discriminatory incentives "a man dependent on his labor for a living had a right to conceal any physical defect that he might

---

[102] Stone, "The Struggle for the Soul of Health Insurance," 299, 290.
[103] Quoted in Samuel Bowles and Herbert Gintis, "Contested Exchange: New Microfoundations for the Political Economy of the Firm," in *The Economic Nature of the Firm: A Reader*, 2nd ed., ed. Randall S. Kroszner and Louis Putterman (Cambridge: Cambridge University Press, 1992), 217–232, 217.
[104] As right-wing political theorist Carl Schmitt once wrote, "Any decision about whether something is unpolitical is always a political decision, irrespective of who decides and what reasons are advanced." Carl Schmitt, *Political Theology: Four Chapters on the Concept of Sovereignty*, trans. George Schwab (Chicago: University of Chicago Press, 2005), 2.

have."[105] Mitchell implied that compensation laws might actively erode trust between employers and employees as working-class men sought to evade employer gatekeeping in order to get and remain on the payroll.[106] Furthermore, he actively approved of employee-side deception in light of that new condition. The General Contractors Association objected to Mitchell's statement. The Contractors Association drew an analogy to insurance to criticize Mitchell, saying that "false statements made in applications for life insurance render the policy void, and certainly an applicant who refused to submit himself to a medical examination could not expect the insurance company to issue him a policy." Matters should not be any different with employers under compensation laws, the Contractors Association suggested.[107]

In 1915 James Harrar, the medical director at the Lord and Taylor department store chain in New York, used a similar analogy. Employers' new practice of screening job applicants, Harrar stressed, was the same as in "an ordinary life insurance examination ... to weed out all impaired applicants from employment." Harrar admitted that in a sense "the procedure is a selfish one," but he defended the practice, arguing that "accident and health insurance companies ... will not accept an impaired risk if they have knowledge of it."[108] Lord and Taylor was only doing what insurers had already been doing. Harrar added that "every employer retains the privilege of not engaging the applicant who is stupid, careless, dirty, or ignorant; and there should be no reason why an employer has not the right to ask as well for average health in the applicant."[109] In effect,

---

[105] *New York Times*, August 12, 1914. What made a particular physical condition into a "defect" had changed. That change had everything to do with legal liability and cost allocation. A "defect" was a condition that would cost an employer more money under the new rules introduced by workmen's compensation legislation. The legal shaping of the meaning of defect is part of the broader role of law in the making of social and cultural categories. For more work along these lines, see Barbara Young Welke, *Law and the Borders of Belonging in the Long Nineteenth Century United States* (Cambridge: Cambridge University Press, 2010); Margot Canaday, *The Straight State: Sexuality and Citizenship in Twentieth-Century America* (Princeton: Princeton University Press, 2009); and Susan Schweik, *The Ugly Laws: Disability in Public* (New York: New York University Press, 2009).

[106] *New York Times*, August 12, 1914.

[107] *The Bulletin of the General Contractors Association*, September 1914, 278. On the history of workplace medical examinations, see Nugent, "Fit for Work."

[108] James Harrar, "How a Large Department Store Conserves the Health of Its Workpeople," *Safety: Bulletin of the American Museum of Safety* 3, no. 3 (March 1915): 67–71, 70.

[109] Harrar, "How a Large Department Store Conserves the Health of Its Workpeople," 69.

Harrar argued, Lord and Taylor adopted the same practice as insurers, screening applicants who sought entry to the company's risk pool, in order to manage the composition of the company's risk pools. Harrar and the Contractors Association reached for insurance as an analogy with which to offer a moral justification for their practices of discrimination. Lack of access to life insurance could have serious consequences, but insurers were still permitted to deny access to insurance. Furthermore, an insurer who did not gatekeep would quickly go out of business, resulting in no one benefiting from insurance. An employer who took on so-called poor risks might similarly face a competitive disadvantage.

The analogy with insurance helped corporate officials like Harrar to see employer practices as unobjectionable. Insurance was not morally objectionable, the argument went, and employers were merely doing what insurers already did. Using insurance as an analogy in this way in effect started the conversation downstream from several social and institutional processes that were taken as given and thus insulated from criticism. Employers were depicted as having no option, and, in a sense, the world was depicted as having no alternative. Analogies between insurance and employment reflected an ostensibly depoliticized market rationality that presented a host of social practices as self-evident and incontestable. In the aftermath of compensation laws, employers committed new injustices, and yet within the logic and rhetoric of insurance these injustices were represented as apolitical. The result was a kind of resignation, a throwing-up of the hands or shrugging: we all agree that this is unfortunate, but such is the way of the world.[110]

---

[110] As the philosopher Louis Althusser has put it, "it is characteristic of ideology to impose self-evident facts as self-evident facts (without in the least seeming to, since they are 'self-evident') which we cannot *not* recognize and before which we have the inevitable and eminently natural reaction of exclaiming (aloud or in 'the silence of consciousness'): 'That's obvious! That's right! That's true!'" Louis Althusser, *On the Reproduction of Capitalism: Ideology and Ideological State Apparatuses* (London: Verso, 2014), 189. Emphasis in original. I have found Goran Therborn's reformulation of Althusser especially illuminating. See Therborn, *The Ideology of Power and the Power of Ideology*. Law plays a particularly important role in the imposition of self-evident facts, constituting what are taken as the facts of social life by persuading people to take on specific understandings of the world as self-evident. See Tomlins, *Law, Labor and Ideology*, and López, *White by Law*. Insurance too helped create self-evident facts. In doing so, it served as a legitimating device. Harrar and insurance industry spokespeople, as users of that device, engaged in legitimation work. See Angelica Thumala, Benjamin Goold, and Ian Loader, "A Tainted Trade? Moral Ambivalence and Legitimation Work in the Private Security Industry," *British Journal of Sociology* 62, no. 2 (June 2011): 283;

INDIVIDUALIZING AND COST SHIFTING BY LAW

Warren Garst had feared insurance companies would pressure employers to discriminate in order to prevent more expensive injury claims; that is, he feared that insurance companies would encourage employers to practice the individualizing or depooling aspect of the logic of insurance. In reply to Garst, Travelers Insurance suggested that compensation laws made all employers subject to pressures to discriminate. Employers were made responsible for their labor forces as risk pools; that responsibility was defined in amoral and financial terms; therefore, they sought to make the financially wise decision to more tightly regulate entry to those pools. This version of insurance logic brought about distancing and division, a proliferation of borders and gatekeepers. Travelers argued, in my view

and Dominik Rueede and Karin Kreutzer, "Legitimation Work within a Cross-Sector Social Partnership," *Journal of Business Ethics* 128, no. 1 (April 2015): 39. I am grateful to Will Garriott for bringing the idea of legitimation work to my attention. This legitimation work operated differently in relation to different audiences, because legitimation is a relationship. That is, legitimation via insurance had social-position specific expression and effect: corporate executives, managers, supervisory employees, and front-line employees likely were affected by this activity in different ways. To put it differently, ideologies interpellate people, crafting different kinds of subjectivities and assigning people to those social positions. If we think of society as a kind of theater, ideologies are both playwrights and casting directors: they create a cast of characters that play out social scripts, then cast individuals to play specific characters. See Althusser, *On the Reproduction of Capitalism*, 188–199, 261–266. Those subjectivities are distributed within society differently depending on class position and position in chains of command, as well as race, gender, ability, citizenship status, and other social categories. The point is that legitimation is always specific to some population. For the populations hailed by remarks like those of Harrar and the insurance industry, one likely effect was to depict discrimination as at most unpleasant but not truly morally objectionable. Here insurance rhetoric helped create what Eugene Genovese described as key role for law: "The law acts hegemonically to assure people that their particular consciences can be subordinated – indeed, morally must be subordinated – to the collective judgment of society." Eugene D. Genovese, *Roll, Jordan, Roll* (New York: Random House, 1976), 27. Genovese's discussion of law and hegemony remains relevant and vibrant (pp. 25–48). Raymond Williams's understanding of hegemony is relevant as well. For Williams, hegemony is a "form of class rule which exists not only in political and economic institutions and relationships" but also in "ways of seeing the world," of "acceptance as 'normal reality' or 'commonsense'" social practices and institutions that are less likely to be challenged and remade because of their normalization. Insurance rhetoric likely had such an effect. Raymond Williams, *Keywords: A Vocabulary of Culture and Society*, revised ed. (New York: Oxford University Press, 1985), 145. In justifying discrimination in hiring, Harrar implicitly justified a host of labor practices and practices of commodification, or rather rhetorically placed those practices off the table as not subject to discussion.

convincingly, that commercial insurers, with their larger risk pools, would mitigate these pressures. That mitigation would occur through the other logic of insurance, that of collectivity and solidarity. What Travelers did not mention, however, was that insurers acted out the individualizing aspect of insurance in other ways, at the expense of working-class people.

One way was by underpayment of claims. In 1919, Jeremiah F. Connor conducted an investigation into the administration of workmen's compensation in New York, at the instruction of the state's governor. Connor examined 1,000 compensation claims and found that 11 percent were compensated below the amount awarded to the injured person. The average undercompensation was $450 per person, a total undercompensation – which is to say, transfer of wealth upward – of more than $50,000. Adjusted for inflation, this would be almost $6,900 per person, nearly $800,000 total in that year. Connor noted that there were 34,000 cases like the thousand he examined. If 11 percent of all cases involved undercompensation like Connor found, then the amount of unpaid compensation for the year 1919 alone would have been almost $1.7 million. Adjusted for inflation, this would be almost $26 million.[111] Of the 114 cases of underpayment that Connor found, in twenty-nine the employer was a self-insurer. The individualizing logic of insurance extended to cost reduction as shown by employers not paying what was legally owed to injured employees. Insurers underpaid as well. The number-one undercompensating company on Connor's list was Travelers Insurance, which was responsible for twenty of Connor's 114 cases of underpayment.[112]

---

[111] Jeremiah F. Conner, *Report of Investigation by Jeremiah F. Connor* (Albany: J. B. Lyon, 1919), 4–5.

[112] Conner, *Report*, 47–48. Aetna came second, being responsible for ten underpayment cases. Similar financial incentives to those behind injury undercompensation lie behind wage theft and uncompensated overtime in the twenty-first century. See Cynthia Estlund, *Regoverning the Workplace: From Self-regulation to Co-regulation* (New Haven: Yale University Press, 2010), 110–119; Kim Bobo, *Wage Theft in America: Why Millions of Working Americans Are Not Getting Paid – And What We Can Do about It* (New York: New Press, 2009). This phenomenon dates back to at least the mid-nineteenth century. In *Capital*, Marx quoted English factory inspectors and employees who referred to employers making employees work a few minutes during their lunch hours as "petty pilferings of minutes" and "nibbling and cribbling at meal-times." Those small thefts added up to large amounts of money in the long term, since "moments are the elements of profit." Marx, *Capital* vol. 1, 352.

Recalling again Abba Lerner's remark that an economic transaction
is a settled political problem, insurers and self-insurers that undercom-
pensated engaged in a kind of infrapolitics. They politicked at the edges
of economic transactions with employees by cutting corners and shifting
costs, while also seeking to avoid having their actions becoming overtly
politicized. Connor's report was an attempt at politicizing that
corner-cutting.[113]

The individualizing logic of insurance pushed some compensation
claims back into court as well. Recall Charles Weaver, injured in 1913
in his only eye, as discussed in Chapter 4. Travelers Insurance insured
Weaver's employer, the Maxwell Motor Company, and it was Travelers
that contested Weaver's compensation claim. Travelers also insured
Eugene Branconnier's employer, and employed Walter Badger and Louis
Doyle, the attorneys who contested Branconnier's compensation claim.[114]

Travelers was not unique in this behavior but, rather, exemplary of how
employers' liability insurers used the law in a zero-sum conflict over
whether injured people or insurance companies would get money. Lawyers
were the insurer's instrument in that conflict, and were well compensated
for playing that role. The attorney who represented Travelers in Weaver's
case was named Fred Vandeveer. He had a successful legal career that
funded owning a second home, and lived to be ninety years old.[115]

---

[113] The term "infrapolitics" comes from James C. Scott, *Domination and the Arts of
Resistance: Hidden Transcripts* (New Haven: Yale University Press, 1990). The term
refers to actions taken that are political but unobtrusive. Scott focuses on these kinds of
acts by subordinated people, but businesses too perform infrapolitics whenever they
violate the law. Alongside conflict over non-compensation there were ongoing processes
of depoliticizing employee injury, class relationships, and market dependency. Politiciza-
tion and depoliticization can be seen as occurring in different ways in keeping with
Durkheimian, Weberian, and Marxian understandings of class and society. See Wright,
Understanding Class, x–xi and 118–125, and Holdren, "Moral Economy as Structurally
Recurrent Interpellation: Reading Thompson Pessimistically." To borrow Wright's
metaphor of gameplay, sometimes politicizing a specific rule may be a way to depoliticize
the question of which game to play. Eugene Genovese made a similar point in different
terms. See Genovese, *Roll, Jordan, Roll*, 49.

[114] For some examples of similar cases where Travelers Insurance contested employees'
compensation claims to save money, see *In re Carter*, 221 Mass. 105; *In re Stacy*, 225
Mass. 174; and *Knight's Case*, 231 Mass. 142.

[115] Vandeveer served as the appellant's attorney in Weaver's case. Some of the documents
list the Maxwell Motor Company as the appellant and some listed Travelers Insurance
as a co-appellant. On Vandeveer's employment at Travelers, see *National Enameling &
Stamping Co. v. Fagan*, 115 Ill. App 590, 593 (4th Dist. 1904) and *The City of Detroit
Michigan, 1701–1922*, vol. 3 (Detroit: S. J. Clarke Publishing Company, 1922), 752.
The latter includes information about Vandeveer's life, including his second home.

Companies that paid lawyers like Vandeveer to win smaller compensation payments were, to borrow Pullman president David Crawford's phrase, making "enlightened expenditures" – spending a little to make or save a lot.[116] Over time, many such savings added up to a great deal of money kept in insurers' coffers. Depooling, the individualizing logic of insurance, was a response to market imperatives as organized within compensation laws and large corporations. In the face of these pressures, insurers used their lawyers to modulate the flow of wealth upward and the avalanche of costs downward. These lawyers became cost-management technicians carrying out the individualizing logic of insurance.[117]

CONCLUSION

Workmen's compensation laws defined injury risk and provided security in a financial sense. Compensation laws turned private employers into the guarantors of employee injury risk pools. Employers managed those pools according to their firms' financial interests rather than the security of society or the well-being of working-class people. In seeking to reduce their individual share of workmen's compensation risk, they acted in an individualizing fashion. Compensation laws took individual employers as a mechanism for social management. That mechanism was at odds with social security goals of some injury law reformers.[118] Attempts to provide

[116] D. A. Crawford to L. S. Hungerford, May 31, 1934, Employee and Labor Relations, Medicine and Sanitation, Administrative Subject Files, Pullman Corporation Records, Newberry Library, Chicago, IL.

[117] The phrase "cost-management technicians" is inspired by Ronald Gilson's discussion of lawyers as what he called transaction cost engineers. I discuss this further in the next chapter. Ronald J. Gilson, "Lawyers as Transaction Cost Engineers," in *The New Palgrave Dictionary of Economics and the Law* , ed. Peter Newman (New York: Stockton Press, 1998), 508–514.

[118] This is one reason why compensation laws should not be viewed as social insurance, though some historians have characterized compensation laws that way. See, for example, Moss, *Socializing Security*, 23, and Roy Lubove, *The Struggle for Social Security, 1900–1935* (Cambridge, MA: Harvard University Press, 1968), 45. This book follows economist Domenico Gagliardo in defining social insurance as involving state-provided insurance funds. Domenico Gagliardo, *American Social Insurance* (New York: Harper & Brothers, 1955), 19–20. The point is not that insurance must be state-run but that it must be open to all rather than bounded according to profit concerns. Only seven US states created compensation laws with state monopoly insurance funds. Ten other states created state funds that competed with private insurance; the remaining states required employers to privately secure their compensation risks. Compensation laws created "an employer mandate that a specific set of benefits be paid," as Fishback and Kantor put it, and mandated measures to secure payment of these benefits in a way that

security through the individualizing logic of insurance will always leave some people out. The individualizing logic of insurance requires sorting populations into members and non-members. Thus, while compensation laws created new risk pools into which some employees became enrolled, they also created excluded populations judged too risky to hire. Employers began to practice the commodification of working-class people in a new way that intensified the creation of a population marked as surplus to the economy's needs.

The incentives for businesses to discriminate in response to workmen's compensation laws were particularly intense for firms that self-insured, because they did not pool their compensation risks with other firms. These incentives were further intensified by the administrative and economic structures of large, fixed-capital-intensive manufacturers. That said, the differences between self-insurers and other companies were differences of degree, not of kind. Incentives to discriminate were built into all insurance arrangements under workmen's compensation.

The reformers discussed in earlier chapters believed that compensation laws would bring new security. These laws did bring some security to businesses, which could better calculate their likely employee injury costs, and so purchase insurance or budget funds for those costs, as in the case of so-called self-insurers. Working-class families gained some financial security, as they could count on losing only a portion of their income in the event of injury. Yet the benefits of these new forms of security were unevenly distributed, and brought about new sources of working-class insecurity. Compensation laws inflicted new insecurity in part because they treated employee injury as a problem to be insured by individual businesses. Businesses do not steer their actions primarily out of a sense of responsibility for the well-being of society or the working class as a whole. This fact is not a matter of the moral consciousness (or lack thereof) of individual business owners, but a matter of the imperatives imposed by market dependency. Businesses were mostly concerned with their own well-being within the market, not with either securing markets or the population writ large. That narrowness of concern was at least in part imposed by market imperatives.

retained a much larger role for market-based insurance institutions than for state insurance. Fishback and Kantor, *Prelude to the Welfare State*, 104, 148–171. Those programs were arguably social insurance, but by individualizing employers' costs they were still subject to discriminatory incentives.

The organization of compensation laws as insurance around individual workplaces fostered the creation of small risk pools, with some security provided to the people allowed into them. These laws also hardened the borders of those risk pools. Thus the proliferation of risk pools was also the proliferation of margins between them into which some people fell or, rather, were pushed. Employers came to act like insurers, guarding the borders of their risk communities, selecting some people for admission and others for exclusion in order to keep the community profitable. Insurance scholar Tom Baker calls this a "depooling effect," and argues that it is part of "the limits of insurance as an engine of social solidarity."[119] Because compensation laws created an overlap between belonging to risk communities and employment, this depooling effect pushed some people out of access to wages. They were in a sense made safe from the risks of injury within waged workplaces because they were not hired at all. That relative safety from employee injury came at the cost of poverty, and was a side effect of employers' real goal, the financial health of their companies. Employers prioritized the health of their businesses over the health of working-class people. That new priority would soon reorganize workplace-based medicine, as industrial physicians too became cost-management technicians.

[119] Baker, "Containing the Promise of Insurance," 259.

6

Discrimination Technicians and Human Weeding

In his report on the administration of workmen's compensation in New York, Jeremiah Connor highlighted the case of an injured worker who "had been examined by thirty-two physicians." The New York compensation law required employers to pay for the medical care of injured employees. The multiple examinations in this case, however, were not about medical care but rather about attempting to find ways to reduce the amount of compensation paid to the man. The law allowed employers to select the employees' physicians. That power over "the selection of attending physicians has worked to the disadvantage of the injured workman," Connor wrote, in part because "the physician who treats [the employee's] injuries and restores him to a working condition, later appears as a witness against him upon his application for compensation."[1] These physicians practiced medicine as surveillance of employees, for the financial benefit of businesses. Rather than providing care to the physical body of the individual injured person, these doctors provided care to the financial body of the corporation, and did so to the detriment of working-class people.

Connor lamented what he called the transformation of employee medical care "into a 'business' undertaking," wherein the physician's own business interest was less in line with the patient's well-being than it was with the employer's. This situation "destroyed the confidential relationship

---

[1] Jeremiah F. Conner, *Report of Investigation by Jeremiah F. Connor* (Albany: J. B. Lyon, 1919), 22–23. It is worth noting that the standard of health Connor wrote of was not one of flourishing or happiness, but ability to perform waged labor.

and the human interest as between the physician and patient."[2] Connor here decried the reshaping of medicine by the individualizing logic of insurance. The tyranny of the table reorganized medicine around a new inhuman business interest, inflicting on working-class people medical practices that could only euphemistically be called care. Compensation laws changed employers' economic environment. In response, they created new strategies to respond to that environment, and drew on medicine as a risk-avoidance tactic. This new use of medical technique changed the purposes of employer-provided medicine. It became, to borrow Edward Phelps's phrase, "conducted on a cold-blooded business basis."[3] The doctors who carried out this approach to medicine became financial tacticians, cost-management technicians.[4]

---

[2] Conner, *Report*, 23.

[3] Edward Bunnell Phelps, "Certain Grave Questions of Workmen's Compensation: Will It Lead to Discrimination against Married Men and Slightly Impaired Lives?," *The American Underwriter Magazine and Insurance Review* 42, no. 1 (July 1914): 1–10; 4.

[4] My understanding of physicians as cost-management technicians is inspired in part by Ronald Gilson's analysis of attorneys as managing transaction costs. See Ronald J. Gilson, "Lawyers as Transaction Cost Engineers," in *The New Palgrave Dictionary of Economics and the Law*, ed. Peter Newman (New York: Stockton Press, 1998), 508–514. A transaction cost is a cost built into using the market, such as the time or money required to gather information, and the fees paid to brokers and other intermediaries. These costs are legally structured in multiple ways. Gilson argued that lawyers are often a type of intermediary that market actors hire to help them pursue their objectives in the market. Lawyers and other intermediaries are part of the "organizational and transactional structure" through which market actors "economize" on transaction costs, by which he means seeking to reduce their costs (p. 508). Gilson's paradigm case of the lawyer as transaction cost engineer was the business lawyer designing legal instruments, but he suggests that lawyers engaging in litigation might be considered transaction cost engineers as well. The insurance company lawyers who litigated the cases discussed in Chapter 4 helped create new structures of incentives and new distributions of costs and risks. They were in a sense part of the process of engineering the market in labor power. I prefer to call these lawyers cost-management technicians, because they were engaged less in the conscious design of markets and more in a process of helping business reduce costs – economizing, as Gilson put it. The legal structure of the labor market emerged as an effect of those efforts at economizing. Cost-management technicians economize in a second sense as well, in that they help produce the world conceptually as a set of economic objects. As Chapter 5 discussed, part of what ideology does is (or is a name for how actors) produce understandings of the world as self-evident. Law formats the world, so to speak, as economic. Eli Cook uses the term "capitalization" to discuss what I have called formatting the world as economic. Cook uses the term "investmentality" to discuss the mental outlook and cultural/intellectual resources through which people become economic objects. Cook's work sheds light on the ways in which people have been priced over time, and helps denaturalize the social practice of pricing people. See Eli Cook, *The Pricing of Progress: Economic Indicators and the Capitalization of American Life* (Cambridge, MA: Harvard University Press, 2017). See also Margaret Jane Radin, *Contested Commodities: The Trouble with Trade in Sex,*

THE EXPANSION OF MEDICAL EXAMINATION
FOR FINANCIAL GAIN

For companies to minimize their exposure to potential liability for employee injury, they needed to be able to identify sources of liability. Many of the conditions that made an individual susceptible to a particularly expensive injury were not immediately apparent to the company officials who conducted hiring. Employees and applicants might not know they had such a condition, and even if they did, disclosing such a condition – and thus being less employable – was only in the employer's interest, not the employee's. Employers needed a reliable way to sift employees and applicants into acceptable and unacceptable risks. Medical examinations provided that device. Employers therefore expanded their programs of medical examinations in the aftermath of compensation laws.

The Ohio-based Youngstown Sheet and Tube Company started pre-employment medical examinations in response to a February 26, 1913, "amendment to the Workmen's Compensation Act, known as Section 22," which "permitted employers with sufficient financial responsibility to carry their own liability insurance." That is to say, the company expanded medical examinations directly in response to the self-insurance provisions of Ohio's compensation law. As their medical director would later put it, "it is hard for me to understand how any company can do

---

Children, Body Parts, and Other Things (Cambridge, MA: Harvard University Press, 2001). See as well the introduction to Marx's *Grundrisse* on the conceptual and social distribution of people to roles in production, which is also a distribution of people to the status as objects subjected to economic calculation. Karl Marx, *Grundrisse: Foundations of the Critique of Political Economy* (London: Allen Lane, 1973). Applying economic reasoning presupposes that prior formatting: for a person, place, thing, or experience to have a money price it must be comprehensible to value it in monetary terms. Lawyers as cost management technicians economized in this second sense insofar as they represented injuries and human beings as subject to dollar valuations and instrumental calculations. Lawyers were far from alone in this. Much of this book has been about arguing that policy reformers, compensation laws, and business officials did this in a variety of ways. So too did physicians, as this chapter argues. David M. Driesen and Shubha Ghosh, "The Functions of Transaction Costs: Rethinking Transaction Cost Minimization in a World of Friction," *Arizona Law Review* 47, no. 1 (2005): 61, cites scholars who explain compensation laws as driven by an effort to reduce transaction costs. That framework is itself morally thin or, to borrow Nancy Fraser's term, insufficiently bivalent. Nancy Fraser, "From Redistribution to Recognition? Dilemmas of Justice in a 'Postsocialist' Age," in Fraser, *Justice Interruptus: Critical Reflections on the "Postsocialist" Condition* (New York: Routledge, 1996), 19–22, 32. At worst, that morally thin conceptual framework treats injuries as solely a matter of efficiency rather than justice. At best, only distributive justice fits into that framework, which leaves out justice as recognition.

business without pre-employment examinations. If you are large enough to have your own liability insurance which the state permits you to have under this Section 22 which was adopted in 1913, you have an opportunity to save on your compensation."[5] The company acted out the individualizing logic of insurance as institutionalized in compensation laws. Medical examinations were the instrument that facilitated this action.

Youngstown Sheet and Tube was not unique in these actions. In 1914, the Ohio Industrial Commission studied the degree to which workers' employment prospects had changed due to Ohio's compensation law. The report included data on approximately forty companies employing a total of approximately 65,000 people. Of these, twenty-nine companies reported that physical examinations were required for job applicants.[6] Employers in other states had similar requirements. In his 1914 report, Iowa Industrial Commissioner Warren Garst quoted a letter from an Iowa manufacturer about physical examinations: "This company is having a physical examination made of every person now in its employ who is included in the Workmen's Compensation Act, for the purpose of ascertaining their present physical condition."[7] He said that after workmen's compensation laws, employers tended to "institut[e] a rigorous physical examination of [their] employes."[8] A year later, Welker Given, secretary of the Iowa Industrial Commission, observed that there was "a growing tendency to subject the workmen to a physical examination" conducted by physicians working for employers, with the result that "a good many men are thrown out of the benefits of the law."[9] In 1920

---

[5] P. H. Kennedy, "The Policy and Value of Pre-employment and Periodic Check-Up Physical Examinations," 31, in "Clinic on Health in Industry, under the Auspices of the Mahoning Valley Industrial Council with the Trumbull County Manufacturers' Association, the Ohio Manufacturers' Association, and the National Association of Manufacturers," Youngstown Country Club, Youngstown, Ohio, October 2, 1940, National Association of Manufacturers records, Series 7, Industrial Relations Dept. Records, Hagley Museum and Library, Wilmington, DE.

[6] *Bulletin of the Industrial Commission of Ohio* 2, no. 1 (January 1915): 8.

[7] Warren Garst, *First Biennial Report of the Iowa Industrial Commissioner to the Governor of the State of Iowa for the Period Ending June 30, 1914* (Des Moines: State of Iowa, 1914), 7. Rachel Marks details the spread of physical examinations to screen out disabled people as a response to workmen's compensation. Rachel Marks, "Effects of Early Workmen's Compensation Legislation on the Employment of the Handicapped, 1897–1915," *The Social Service Review* 25, no. 1 (1951), 60–78.

[8] *The Standard*, August 15, 1914, 175.

[9] *Correctionville News*, July 1, 1915. On the history of medical examinations in workplaces, see Angela Nugent, "Fit for Work: The Introduction of Physical Examinations in Industry," *Bulletin of the History of Medicine* 57 (1983): 578–595.

the National Industrial Conference Board surveyed companies about medical examination practices. Medical examinations had spread, and done so directly in response to compensation laws.[10] By 1925, forty-two US states had workmen's compensation legislation, and major US companies such as Pullman, the Crane Corporation, Western Electric, and International Harvester had enacted medical examinations for job applicants and employees, in order to screen out people judged physically defective. Workmen's compensation statutes changed the structure of employment discrimination, discussed in previous chapters in terms of an old and a new normal. That discrimination also became specifically medicalized in its practice, with industrial physicians on the front lines of the new exclusion.

INDUSTRIAL PHYSICIANS ORGANIZE

Employer demand for medicalized discrimination offered a growth opportunity for entrepreneurial industrial physicians, and came at a key moment in the development of industrial medicine as a field. In the early twentieth century, industrial physicians did not have very many professional peers. Alice Hamilton, an early leader in the field of occupational health and a social reform advocate, said that in the early days of her career, in the early twentieth century, with very few exceptions, "there were no medical men in the State of Illinois who specialized in the field of industrial medicine."[11] Even by 1919, after industrial medicine was developing as a field, there were only about a hundred physicians in

---

[10] F. L. Rector, "Physical Examination of Industrial Workers: Results of an Investigation by the Conference Board of Physicians in Industry," *The Journal of the American Medical Association* 75, no. 25 (December 1920): 1739–1741.

[11] Quoted in Jacqueline Karnell Corn, *Response to Occupational Health Hazards: A Historical Perspective* (New York: Van Nostrand Reinhold, 1992); see pp. 2–11 for a compressed but useful overview of concern with occupational health and safety in the medical field and in public policy prior from 1900 to 1935. The rest of her book focuses on occupational health from 1935 to 1990. See also Odin W. Anderson, *Health Services in the United States: A Growth Enterprise since 1875* (Ann Arbor: Health Administration Press, 1985), 1–112; Alan Derickson, *Workers Health, Workers Democracy: The Western Miners' Struggle, 1891–1925* (Ithaca: Cornell University Press, 1988); Jacqueline Corn, *Environment and Health in Nineteenth Century America: Two Case Studies* (New York: Peter Land, 1989); Jacqueline Corn, *Protecting the Health of Workers: The American Conference of Governmental Industrial Hygienists, 1938–1988* (Cincinnati: American Conference of Government Industrial Hygienists, 1989); David Rosner and Gerald Markowitz, eds., *Dying for Work: Workers' Safety and Health in Twentieth Century America* (Bloomington: Indiana University Press, 1987); and David Rosner and Gerald Markowitz, *Deadly Dust: Silicosis and the Politics of Occupational Disease in*

Illinois known to specialize in industrial medicine, the vast majority of them in Chicago. Some worked for multiple companies, "but the usual practice is for the industrial physician to take employment with only one large establishment and here he usually has the assistance of from one to three physicians." The field is relatively new and "by no means standardized" yet.[12]

Doctors who worked in industrial medicine often did not feel respected by other doctors. As Hamilton put it, "For a surgeon or physician to accept a position with a manufacturing company was to earn the contempt of his colleagues."[13] The disrespect of other doctors may have been in part because industrial physicians seemed to be siding with corporate officials that many other doctors saw as opponents of medical professionals. As sociologist Paul Starr has put it, at the end of the nineteenth century doctors felt threatened by competitors, including "company medical plans" and other "bureaucratically organized alternatives" to the prevailing institutional form of medical care, "independent solo practice." This "represented a threat not only to [physicians'] incomes, but also to their status and autonomy."[14] Industrial physicians may have appeared to other doctors as part of the problem. Starr argued that the medical profession developed greater economic power because doctors largely sold "services primarily to individual patients rather than organizations ... The medical profession ... insisted that salaried arrangements violated the integrity of the private doctor–patient relationship, and in the early decades of the twentieth century, doctors were able to use their growing market power to escape the threat of bureaucratic control and to preserve their own autonomy."[15] This was not the experience of industrial physicians, helping create the disconnect between them and the rest of the medical profession.

Twentieth-Century America (Princeton: Princeton University Press, 1994); David Rosner and Gerald Markowitz, "A Gift of God: The Public Health Controversy over Leaded Gasoline during the 1920s," *American Journal of Public Health* 7, no. 4 (April 1985): 344–352; Christopher Sellers, "The Public Health Service's Office of Industrial Hygiene and the Transformation of Industrial Medicine," *Bulletin of the History of Medicine* 65, no. 1 (Spring 1991): 42–73. See also Harry E. Mock, *Industrial Medicine and Surgery* (Philadelphia: W. B. Saunders and Company, 1919), 125–132, for an overviews of the field's early development.

[12] Health Insurance Commission of the State of Illinois, *Report of the Health Insurance Commission of the State of Illinois* (Springfield: Illinois State Journal Co., 1919), 74.

[13] Henry B. Selleck and Alfred H. Whittaker, *Occupational Health in America* (Detroit: Wayne State University Press, 1962), 59.

[14] Paul Starr, *The Social Transformation of American Medicine: The Rise of a Sovereign Profession and the Making of a Vast Industry* (New York: Basic Books, 1982), 22.

[15] Starr, *The Social Transformation of American Medicine*, 24.

Being enmeshed within corporate bureaucracy likely increased their desire to associate, for the sake of advocating for their interests and for professional camaraderie.

The need for association and a felt lack of status among other physicians explains the turn toward organization building among industrial physicians in the 1910s. In 1914 Harry Mock, the medical director at Sears, Roebuck and Company, convened a meeting to discuss forming a professional association. Attendees consisted of Chicago-area industrial physicians employed by companies including Peoples Gas Light and Coke, the Avery Company, the Crane Company, and International Harvester. The group constituted itself as an organizing committee that set about contacting doctors around the country, quickly garnering support from doctors at the Packard Motor Company, B. F. Goodrich, Bethlehem Steel, the New York Telephone Company, the Norton Company, and Ford.[16] In 1915, with the help of the Illinois Manufacturers Association, this group held a larger meeting to found an association, and incorporated itself officially. The Incorporating Committee of the fledgling American Association of Industrial Physicians and Surgeons (AAIPS) announced itself publicly at the first meetings of the National Safety Council's Health Service Section in October 1915. All industrial physicians were invited to attend the first annual meeting of the AAIPS, to be held in conjunction with the American Medical Association's first meeting, in June 1916 in Detroit.[17] No list remains of the attendees of the AAIPS's first conference or its founding members, but by 1917 the organization had 225 members, climbing to 275 in 1918 and 340 in 1919.[18] The rising numbers likely reflect the expansion of industrial medicine as a field.

As industrial physicians organized themselves, they articulated the importance of their field to employers, helping explain why their field helped meet employers' needs. That articulation tended to treat the working-class people physicians acted on in distinctly cold-blooded terms. In his 1919 book *Industrial Medicine and Surgery*, Harry Mock argued that "modern industrial concerns have employed experts to study their expensive, complicated machines, in order to preserve their mechanism and obtain their maximum efficiency," but these companies neglected the "human machine."[19] Another industrial physician, Robert Legge,

---

[16] Selleck and Whittaker, *Occupational Health in America*, 64.
[17] Selleck and Whittaker, *Occupational Health in America*, 68.
[18] Selleck and Whittaker, *Occupational Health in America*, 73–74, 83.
[19] Mock, *Industrial Medicine and Surgery*, 64.

spoke in terms of human machinery as well: "To secure the maximum efficiency from the human machine, the industrial surgeon, virtually the human engineer, acts as the agent for stabilizing labor, thereby facilitating production and helping the worker to do a better day's work, prolong the years of his activity and increase his compensation."[20] Physician C. E. Ford from the New York–based General Chemical Company similarly spoke to the economic importance of industrial medicine, arguing that "the productive labor of unhealthy workers is inferior to that of healthy workers."[21] What Legge did not say was that being judged as less productive also likely meant being consigned to worse health, due to the poverty that came from reduced employment prospects.

Physician J. H. Redfern too used the human machine metaphor, and underscored employers' financial interests in having that machine perform with maximum productivity. He argued that

wages paid to industrial workers in the average plant over a period of four years equals the cost of the plant. We go on painting, repairing, inspecting the building, but our "human machine" is neglected. If we go into our development program without health service, we are gambling our money for we may be spending considerable time and money trying to develop men to the high degree of proficiency to which we have aimed and suddenly find out that the individual has to leave us [for health reasons].[22]

Frank Purnell, president of the Youngstown Sheet and Tube Company, saw medical examinations as an important investment:

you go ahead and spend a million or a hundred thousand or two million dollars on a piece of equipment and you turn it over to three or four men to operate. You want to see that most men are in position to get the productive value out of that investment. You grease and oil and other things to see that the equipment is in working order and it is only fair to see that the men that operate the machine are in equal capacity.

No businessperson goes to market seeking to buy substandard material, Purnell implied, and that did not change when the material purchased happened to be a human being.[23]

[20] Robert Legge, "Industrial Medicine," *California State Journal of Medicine* 19, no. 2 (February 1921): 64. Quoted in C. E. Ford, "The Physician in Industry and His Relation to Community Problems," in *The Physician in Industry: A Symposium*, ed. National Industrial Conference Board (New York: National Industrial Conference Board, 1922), 12.

[21] Ford, "The Physician in Industry and His Relation to Community Problems," 13–14.

[22] Quoted in "Preliminary Survey of Physical Examinations for Employees in Industry," 5.

[23] "Clinic on Health in Industry," 4.

Industrial physician C. H. Watson of the American Telephone and Telegraph Company used this understanding to call for the extension of examinations beyond applicants, saying, "The plant engineer, after passing upon the integrity of newly acquired equipment, periodically carries out an inspection to determine its efficiency, its rate of depreciation, and its relationship to the other portions of the plant with which it must coordinate its functions. The same logic applies to the human plant equipment. Hence the physical examination of the employee in all its phases." In both applicant and employee examinations, the industrial physician's eye was to be on screening out individuals: "No person who constitutes either a menace to himself, a menace to others, or a menace to property, should be considered acceptable for employment. In plant terms, such an individual is a hazard just as is an unbalanced flywheel with a defective governor."[24] These similes figured workers as commodities that mattered to the degree that they were functional to businesses, and figured them as objects – "human plant equipment" – to be worked on by experts. Implicit in this vocabulary was the idea of discarding (or not purchasing at all) the people not considered worth working on. As William O'Neill Sherman, chief surgeon at the Carnegie-Illinois Steel Corporation, said:

[g]enerally speaking, industry commands the services of the best legal talent, engineers, chemists, accountants, metallurgists and other trained personnel. However, it has been somewhat reluctant to utilize the best [that] modern organized medicine has to offer. In the last analysis, the human element is the most important asset of industry. "Human engineering" can best be rendered by doctors who have an understanding of the problems confronting the employer, employee and public. They should be consulted more frequently and considered as a part of the plant organization.[25]

Physicians like Watson and Sherman emphasized that industrial medicine was fully compatible with treating human beings as commodities, and that the field offered companies important resources for doing so in an especially efficient and profitable manner.

"[I]t behooves industrial physicians to show in some concrete form what benefits [employers] may expect," wrote Harry Mock in his 1919 book on industrial medicine.[26] Mock named financial savings as a particularly important benefit of corporate use of industrial medicine, and

[24] C. H. Watson, "Physical Examinations: A Resume," in *The Physician in Industry*, 22–26; 22–23.
[25] "Clinic on Health in Industry," 26–27.
[26] Mock, *Industrial Medicine and Surgery*, 80.

"[o]ne of the greatest sources of saving to the employer is the physical selection of employees for work."[27] Specifically, this meant selection through the use of medical examinations administered by industrial physicians, justified specifically as a cost-saving measure for employers; the savings would arise from helping employers restrict their hiring. P. H. Kennedy, an industrial physician at Youngstown Sheet and Tube, similarly said that "physical examinations have a very definite role in the establishment of lower manufacturing costs."[28] Pullman's Thomas Crowder wrote that "[p]re-employment examinations are useful and have an economic value."[29]

Some industrial physicians appealed directly to the incentives created by compensation laws in order to underscore the value of industrial medicine due to identifying potentially risky employees and applicants. "The value of medical service in industry was emphasized," argued C. E. Ford, by compensation laws, because employers became required to pay for medical care for the injured.[30] Dr. Frank Rector similarly argued that compensation laws made medical examinations especially valuable. For Rector, examinations helped employers select among employees based on assessments of potential risk. "No method yet devised for estimating the compensation risk of a worker has surpassed the physical examination of applicants for employment, and the periodic re-examination of the employed force.... The careful physical examination of all workers and applicants for employment ... will do more than any other one thing to reduce the hazards of occupation and the amount of money spent in compensation."[31] Industrial physicians, like life insurance physicians, would help their employers create optimal risk pools, with member employees selected in order to reduce companies' liabilities.

REJECTIONS AND THE PUZZLING POWER OF MEDICINE

The human machine that industrial physicians optimized was not the individual worker but the collective workforce assembled by the employer.

---

[27] Mock, *Industrial Medicine and Surgery*, 86.   [28] "Clinic on Health in Industry," 18.

[29] Memo from T. S. Crowder to L. S. Hungerford., undated, Administrative Subject Files, Employee and Labor Relations, Medicine and Sanitation, Pullman Corporation Records, Newberry Library, Chicago, IL. In 1934, Pullman spent $24,538.02 ($478,000 inflation adjusted) on workplace injuries, about three percent of its 1934 wage bill. (US Bureau of Labor Statistics inflation calculator, http://data.bls.gov/cgi-bin/cpicalc.pl).

[30] Ford, "The Physician in Industry and His Relation to Community Problems," 9.

[31] Frank L. Rector, "Relation of the Physician in Industry to Workmen's Compensation Laws," in *The Physician in Industry*, 60.

Individual employees were cogs within that machine, job applicants were prospective cogs; physicians inspected those human components for defects, ensuring that defective cogs were discarded or were not purchased in the first place. This was not a theoretical matter. Physicians discussed the numbers of people they rejected.

Medical examinations in response to compensation laws were frequent and widespread in American businesses. The Ohio Industrial Commission found that twenty-nine of the forty companies approached for its 1914 survey practiced medicalized gatekeeping. The twenty-six of these companies that kept records examined 23,118 applicants and rejected 1,040 "owing to physical inefficiency," a rejection rate of about 4 percent.[32] The report noted that the actual rejection rates would be higher but unrecorded because "physical examinations are usually only given to those who have prospects of securing employment. Applicants who are maimed, or in poor physical condition or undesirable for the work, are usually rejected by the employment officer without referring such applicants to the medical offices. In such cases, of course, no record appears in connection with physical examinations."[33]

The National Industrial Conference Board reported on a similar survey in 1920. Thirty-four companies responded. Those firms employed 410,106 people, for an average of more than 12,000 employees per firm. Of the respondents, twenty-four listed the number of persons examined in the previous year. "[I]n plants employing a total of 209,777 males, there were 178,367 physical examinations of applicants for employment and in plants employing 19,632 females, there were 29,074 examinations." This means these twenty-four companies examined more than 8,000 applicants per year per company.[34] The National Industrial Conference Board found that "[i]n plants where records have been kept, an average of from

---

[32] *Bulletin of the Industrial Commission of Ohio* 2, no. 1 (January 1915): 12. For a discussion of the history of the idea of efficiency see Jennifer Alexander, *The Mantra of Efficiency: From Waterwheel to Social Control* (Baltimore: Johns Hopkins University Press, 2008). The term "physical inefficiency" as with the term "unfit" conjures eugenic overtones to the twenty-first-century mind. The term likely was intended that way.

[33] *Bulletin of the Industrial Commission of Ohio*, 12. Among "the principal defects" that the examinations screened for were "heart disease, hernia, venereal diseases, contagious diseases, flat foot, deformity, amputations or other evidence of serious injuries, pyorrhea, and chronic stomach and kidney disorders" (p. 12).

[34] F. L. Rector, "Physical Examination of Industrial Workers: Results of an Investigation by the Conference Board of Physicians in Industry," *The Journal of the American Medical Association* 75, no. 25 (December 1920): 1739–1741.

three to five percent of all applicants examined have been refused employment because of physical defects."[35] The study found that "the average percentage of rejected applicants for employment in the 56 plants investigated by the National Industrial Conference Board was only 4.6."[36] "As a rule from 8 to 10 percent of applicants will be found to be under par and need careful placement, whereas about 2 – 5 percent have to be rejected."[37] Of course, the numbers of people actually excluded from employment would have been even higher, not only due to employer decisions but also because as people became aware of medical examinations, some would not even apply.

THE PUZZLE OF STANDARDIZED WEEDING AT PULLMAN

The Pullman company provides an example of the practices of medical examinations within a single corporation. Pullman also served as an exemplar in its day, one that medical directors at companies around the country looked to. Thomas Crowder, Pullman's first medical director, was actively involved in the process of creating the AAIPS and served in multiple officer roles. He corresponded with medical directors at many companies who sought information about Pullman's practices. The professionalization and organization of industrial physicians helped those physicians help their employers. Through their conferences and correspondence, AAIPS members were able to enjoy collegial association and to efficiently and effectively develop best practices for medicalized employment discrimination.

Pullman's upper management understood there to be external pressures on the company to discriminate, and instructed mid-level managers to figure out how the company could respond. Once the company determined that employment discrimination was a financially wise course of action, management ordered their subordinates to figure out how to best conduct that exclusion. Industrial physicians became tasked with removing human weeds from company risk pools.

---

[35] National Industrial Conference Board, *Health Service in Industry: Research Report Number 34, January, 1921* (New York: National Industrial Conference Board, 1921), 40.

[36] Rector, "Physical Examination of Industrial Workers," 1741.

[37] "Preliminary Survey of Physical Examinations for Employees in Industry – 1927, Compiled by the Library Division, October 1927, Henry L. Doherty & Co.," 7, National Industrial Conference Board records, Series 5, Wages to Workmen's Compensation, Hagley Museum and Library, Wilmington, DE.

To exclude impaired people, employers had to first define what counted as an impairment. That definition came at first from law: impairments were any characteristics that would lead to additional compensation after injury. What law defined as compensable was a moving target, which employers perceived as a threat of rising liability and hence increasing cost. Employers sought to manage two kinds of financial risks under compensation laws: conditions that were currently compensable and conditions with any likelihood of becoming compensable in the future. Employers thus excluded not only people who they saw as an immediate compensation risk under the current law but also people who they thought the law might turn into a compensation risk in the future. Employers thus tended to collapse the distinction between impairment and potential impairment.

The threat of future legal changes further expanding injury liability shaped companies' use of medical examinations. Employers worried about who was currently a risk to hire, but also about who might become a bad risk in the future. Any physical condition might become such a risk, even if it currently was not. For example, during internal discussions within Pullman about medical examinations, Pullman's Safety Director Harry Guilbert raised concerns about employee syphilis as a potential cost to Pullman, after the company discovered at least three cases of employees who suffered workplace injuries that were complicated by syphilis in 1923. In general, Pullman officials tended to react to individual instances like this as evidence of a potentially large and previously undetected threat; because they anticipated continuing expansion of injury liability, officials tended to err on the side of greater exclusivity in hiring in response. The growing practice of employment discrimination in turn further expanded the appeal and use of medical examinations at Pullman. For example, Guilbert's concern about syphilis arose because of a welder who claimed to be going blind due to his work. Guilbert noted that "the Ohio [Industrial] commission has ruled that compensation for the loss of vision shall be based upon the actual physical impairment suffered by the claimant before correction and not after correction by the use of glasses." A new ruling meant a new risk had been created. Guilbert added that the company had recently had a case where "a man lost the entire sight of one eye for which we will have to pay him, although judging by the glasses he was wearing at the time of the accident, he only had about 10% vision in the eye that was destroyed, but, of course, we had no record of this previous to the injury."[38] Had the company had medical records on this man, they could have argued that they were liable for less loss of sight.

When a company worked out definitions of conditions for exclusion, it completed one step in the process of puzzling out how to most profitably discriminate. A new conceptual problem then appeared, that of how to identify individuals who fell under that definition. Often these conditions were not immediately visible to hiring personnel, as illustrated by Pullman management's uncertainty as to whether or not the company actually employed one-eyed people. Indeed, individual persons themselves might not know that their bodies counted as impaired. At the 1917 conference of the International Association of Industrial Accident Boards and Commissions, an organization of workmen's compensation administrators, Dudley Holman, the IAIABC's president, suggested that people with one sighted eye may not always know they had sight in only one eye. "How many of us know exactly what our vision is, and how many men do you suppose are working in industry today who have never had an accident to their eyes, so far as they know, and who are yet blind in one eye?" Holman asked conference attendees to imagine a worker who had "worked along during all his life under the assumption that he had two good eyes" only to find in an accident that the remaining eye was in fact not fully sighted. Identifying these kinds of impairments required medical expertise.

To figure out how to best exclude, Pullman's medical director Thomas Crowder began with a diagnostic examination of the company, asking what Pullman was already doing. He began corresponding with the physicians who served as the immediate point of contact between the company and its employees and applicants. Initially he simply asked why doctors marked certain candidates for rejection.[39] The examining physicians cited various reasons for rejecting applicants. A doctor employed by Pullman in St. Louis said that he rejected applicants "for epilepsy if we can find out the individual is subject to it. They are also turned down if they are missing fingers or parts of fingers. They are also rejected for

---

[38] Guilbert to Crawford, December 27, 1923, Employee and Labor Relations Medicine and Sanitation, Administrative Subject Files, 1905–1968; Labor Relations 1942–1964; Medical Examinations, Truck Drivers, and Chauffeurs, 1956–1961, Pullman Corporation Records. See also Crowder to E. F. Carry, November 14, 1923, re: "Preemployment Physical Examination of Employees."

[39] T. R. Crowder, "Instruction for Examination of Yard Help," undated, Employee and Labor Relations, Medicine and Sanitation, Administrative Subject Files, Pullman Corporation Records, Newberry Library, Chicago, IL.

marked deformities of the arms or legs."[40] A Pullman doctor from Atlanta said that "hypertension, heart disease, hernia, and defective vision are disqualifying defects for all types of applicants."[41] Another Pullman doctor wrote, "We have no very definite list of defects for which we reject. We try to pass judgement on a man's ability to do the work for which he is being employed," adding that "accepting and rejecting men in this work is largely a matter of personal opinion, and we probably reject some men who might be safely employed. I am sure we at times accept men for employment whom we afterwards wish we had rejected."[42]

The initial variation at Pullman fit with what the Ohio Industrial Commission found in its 1914 study of physical examinations. The report concluded that, in general, physical examinations "were not conducted along exact lines of scientific investigation, but instead, each type of examination was arranged to point out the defects it seemed important to disclose in relation to the particular requirements of the establishment or the ideas of those in charge."[43] Over time, however, examinations would become more systematic, though still subordinated to "the ideas of those in charge" in business. This was the pattern in general, and at Pullman. Crowder began systematizing rejections at Pullman, by requiring that all facilities send reports each month including the number of applicants examined, passed, and rejected, and by formulating standard policies on which applicants to reject.

The changes he introduced were in part a matter of raising the bar or, rather, further closing the gate. Any one doctor's individual reason to exclude became an instruction for all doctors to exclude for that same reason. In general, the more that businesses used industrial medicine to identify people not to hire, the more this practice became systematized. Some doctors specified lists of particular conditions that were unacceptable in employees. Soon, however, industrial physicians began to create categories that rated applicants on a scale. In order to sort people into

---

[40] W. H. Spoirman to Thomas Crowder, June 20, 1934, Employee and Labor Relations, Medicine and Sanitation, Administrative Subject Files, Pullman Corporation Records, Newberry Library, Chicago, IL.

[41] Dr. Daniel Elkin to Crowder, June 19, 1934. Employee and Labor Relations, Medicine and Sanitation, Administrative Subject Files, Pullman Corporation Records, Newberry Library, Chicago, IL.

[42] Dr. R. J. De Motte to Thomas Crowder, June 26, 1934, Employee and Labor Relations, Medicine and Sanitation, Administrative Subject Files, Pullman Corporation Records, Newberry Library, Chicago, IL.

[43] *Bulletin of the Industrial Commission of Ohio* 2, no. 1 (January 1915): 8.

categories, the company had to have standard examination procedures so that doctors knew what to look for.[44] To put it another way, sorting applicants and employees' bodies into categories based on degrees of acceptability required epistemological construction as well as construction of knowledge-generating techniques. The knowledge produced by physical examinations was not only descriptive but constitutive. That is, while companies made decisions about who to exclude because of pre-existing corporeal conditions (such as having one eye or one hand, or epilepsy), decisions about what to look for and who to exclude helped create the categories that made people unacceptable to hire.

Pullman began using an A through E scale. Examining physicians were to record "all physical defects and diseases found" and group applicants as follows:

A – Men of good physique without defects or diseases.

B – Men with defects or diseases of slight importance, not handicapped for work. (Such as carious teeth, large tonsils, small varicocele, moderately defective vision, etc.)

C – Men with defects or diseases constituting slight handicaps, or temporary handicaps amenable to corrections. (Such as symptomless heart diseases, large varicocele, hernia, bad pyorrhea, acute diseases, etc.)

D – Men with defects or diseases constituting serious or permanent handicaps, but able to work. (Such as heart disease, nephritis, chronic infections, very bad hernias, etc.)

E – Men with defects or diseases constituting serious or permanent handicaps which make them unfit for work.[45]

Crowder also noted that conducting these examinations had required Pullman to hire many more medical personnel. By 1926, the company employed sixty-one medical examiners, who examined 2,791 applicants that year. (They accepted 2506 and rejected 285, a 10 percent rejection rate.)[46] These applicants made up over one-quarter of the people that Pullman doctors saw each year.

---

[44] Physicians actively created a new state of affairs, changing the social world they sought to know by virtue of their knowledge. For a philosophical reflection on this condition with regard to knowledge about society, see Ian Hacking, *Historical Ontology* (Cambridge, MA: Harvard University Press, 2002).

[45] Crowder to all medical examiners, May 29, 1923, Employee and Labor Relations Medicine and Sanitation, Administrative Subject Files, 1905–1968, Pullman Corporation Records.

[46] Crowder to Sterling B. Taylor, March 25, 1926, Employee and Labor Relations Medicine and Sanitation, Administrative Subject Files, 1905–1968, Pullman Corporation Records.

Medical examinations also required companies to develop their information management and knowledge production techniques: medical examinations needed to be standardized, and needed to produce data that could be passed upward within the corporate chain of command. For example, at Pullman Thomas Crowder had to correspond with Pullman physicians about their examination practices, calculate statistical data based on the results of this correspondence, and formulate and communicate new policies in response to the results of these data. For someone in Crowder's position, industrial medicine was largely removed both from individuals' bodies and from caring for individuals' health. Medical examinations were for employers a technique for financial savings, a tactic they waged on employees and applicants as part of the company's battle for profits.

Once Crowder puzzled out the best practices for medicalized employment discrimination, medical examination became an easily deployable tool. That tool in turn made it possible for the company to take new steps to stay ahead of the shifting line of liability in the law. The ongoing presence of dangers in the workplace, the threat of changes in the legal distribution of liability, the political economy of risk-averse firms, and the growing efficacy of techniques for medicalized discrimination all combined to create pressure for exclusion to be ratcheted up, not dialed down.

The standards Crowder propagated do not seem to have limited the causes for rejection anywhere in the company. Rather, if doctors at one facility rejected people for some cause, Crowder made that into a cause for rejection at all facilities. An internal document, "Instructions for Examination of Yard Help," included under causes for rejection "blindness in one eye" – the job required 20/40 vision in one eye and 20/60 in the other at worst; "marked defective hearing"; heart disease; suspicion of tuberculosis; hernia; "major crippling deformities"; and pregnancy, among other causes.[47] Pullman cast a broad net in terms of viewing people as medically unfit to hire. Anyone who would suffer a more expensive injury in the event of an accident was likely to be considered a poor hiring decision.

By the late 1920s, Pullman was routinely turning away applicants in large numbers. Thomas Crowder wrote to another Pullman official noting

[47] Untitled, undated document in the files of Thomas Crowder, Employee and Labor Relations Medicine and Sanitation, Administrative Subject Files, 1905–1968; Pullman Corporation Records. The item's placement in Crowder's file suggests it was probably from 1930 or 1931.

TABLE 6.1 *Examinee classifications at Pullman, 1926*

Classification[a]	Number of people	Percentage of total
A	2,601	24.1
B	4,810	44.5
C	2,878	26.6
D	487	4.5
E	30	.3

[a] See text for explanation of classification categories.

that due to the results of physical examinations, "[r]ejections at [Pullman's manufacturing facility in] St. Louis were 21.5% last year [in 1929], 17.7% in 1928, and 15.5% in 1927.... In Chicago last year 10% of yard applicants were rejected on the medical findings."[48] Pullman officials did not comment on the changing rate of rejections. Perhaps people with disabilities applied more often for work at Pullman. Perhaps Pullman officials preferred higher rates of rejection, as a way to assure greater "fitness" among employees. These figures were higher but basically in keeping with what Crowder saw happening around the country. As he put it, "some of the leading industrial physicians in the country [have] informed me that rejections [at their companies] average from one to fifteen percent."[49]

Crowder recorded that in 1926 Pullman examined 10,806 people, about 25 percent of them applicants and the rest of them employees. Table 6.1 lists how the company classified these examinees in its categories.

Only people in category A were considered impairment free. Thus over 75 percent of examinees were considered to have some physical impairment. For these 10,806 examinees, physicians found 16,135 "defects," an average of about 1.5 per person.[50] This fit with Crowder's observations in another company memo that "thorough and competent examinations ... show physical defects in a large proportion of men."[51]

[48] Thomas Crowder, May 27, 1930, Administrative Subject Files, Employee and Labor Relations, Medicine and Sanitation, Pullman Corporation Records, Newberry Library, Chicago, IL.

[49] Thomas Crowder, May 27, 1930, Administrative Subject Files, Employee and Labor Relations, Medicine and Sanitation, Pullman Corporation Records.

[50] Crowder to Sterling B. Taylor, March 25, 1926, Employee and Labor Relations Medicine and Sanitation, Administrative Subject Files, 1905–1968, Pullman Corporation Records.

[51] Crowder to Keeley, September 14, 1922, Employee and Labor Relations Medicine and Sanitation, Administrative Subject Files, 1905–1968, Pullman Corporation Records.

By 1930, Pullman had a program of physical examinations in almost all of the company's facilities. Policy changes at Pullman were informed by discussions among industrial physicians as specialists networked across firms and drew on their experiences at their companies. Crowder and his colleagues extrapolated from experience in response to unclear or fuzzy probabilities: How likely would someone be to get hurt? Which people would be more hurt than usual by injury? Which injuries were likely to be most expensive, given past practice? In doing so, Crowder and company sought to get ahead of the changing legal curve with regard to liability.

In particular, physicians discussed the reasons for rejections, and how to systematize these rejections. C. E. Ford listed rejection reasons, including:

Organic disease – including uncompensated heart disease, disease of the circulatory system, stomach, liver, kidneys, etc. Loss of or defective vision. Deafness or disease of the ears likely to lead thereto. Disease of the nervous system. Hernia, unless operated upon or unless the company is released from legal responsibility. Communicable disease. Amputations. Defective mentality.[52]

Similarly, the Youngstown Sheet and Tube Company did not hire people with poor vision, high blood pressure, heart disease, "syphilitic disease of heart, blood vessels, and nervous system," hernia, bone disease, impaired joint function due to disease, being overweight or underweight, "marked curvature of the spine," or any other "conditions that would detract noticeable [*sic*] from applicant's ability or efficiency, or would be a source of danger to himself or fellow employees."[53]

Ford said that medical examinations should sort applicants into one of four categories:

1. Individuals physically and mentally fit for any job
2. Individuals physically fit for any employment but below par in development or by reason of minor defect, who by treatment may be placed in Class 1
3. Individuals fit for limited employment when certified to by plant physician
4. Individuals unfit for any employment.[54]

[52] Ford, "The Physician in Industry and His Relation to Community Problems," 10.
[53] "Clinic on Health in Industry," 18.
[54] Ford, "The Physician in Industry and His Relation to Community Problems," 10.

R. S. Quinby, another industrial physician, proposed a similar four-group classification system, listing employees as "fit for any work in the plant," "fit for any job but having slight physical defects," "fit only for certain work when specifically approved by physician," and "unfit for work in the plant."[55]

THE CONSTRICTION OF MEDICAL EXAMINATION
FOR FINANCIAL GAIN

As employers responded to the tyranny of the table, more and more companies began to require that people submit to inspection – being touched by a stranger, being looked over in a cursory fashion rather than actually seen in any human way – as a condition for employment. The inspection was conducted by a medical professional, but over time the elements of the practice that could appreciably be called "medical care" declined. That is to say, form followed function. P. H. Kennedy said that medical examinations could be "conducted with mass production methods and at very little cost."[56] These "mass production methods" included two basic elements: making the examinations faster and standardizing the process, neither of which offered any medical or health-improving benefit to the individuals examined. Many people in leading roles in industrial medicine agreed with Kennedy. Helena Williams wrote:

There is a distinction between the physical examination which is conducted in many industries as a basis for the selection of labor and the periodic physical examination which is made as a basis for health promotion.... [T]he examination which is used for the selection of labor is a relatively simple examination. The examination which is required as a basis of advice and counsel to an individual generally has to be very painstaking examination, and involves not only the physical examination itself but a considerable amount of time in discussing the case with the individual.[57]

That is to say, medical examination as a form of care directed toward the examinee differed from medical examination as a form of gatekeeping directed toward the composition of employer risk pools. Medical examinations conducted in order to screen out applicants and employees who might pose liability risks to an employer could be conducted much faster than examinations for the examinees' benefit. "It is the experience of

---

[55] Quoted in "Preliminary Survey of Physical Examinations for Employees in Industry," 7.
[56] "Clinic on Health in Industry," 18.
[57] Quoted in "Preliminary Survey of Physical Examinations for Employees in Industry," 1.

industry that from 5 to 15 minutes is usually occupied in each examination. This, of course, is insufficient to give a thorough examination but for a pre-employment examination this would be satisfactory."[58] As the National Industrial Conference Board put it,

[s]peed is often essential in industrial examinations in order to avoid delay in the employment department and undue waiting in the medical department.... The usual physical examination in industry is neither exhaustive nor conclusive.... [T]he consensus of opinion seems to favor the limiting of the physical examination to determine the worker's fitness for employment in a particular type of work and to discovering defects which are likely to impair his general usefulness.[59]

This examination took between five and ten minutes.[60] Other doctors argued for even faster examinations. Industrial physician Irving Clark declared, "The usual time allotted to the physical examination is on the average five to six minutes."[61] The New England Conference of Industrial Physicians said that "[o]rdinarily such an examination can be made in 5 minutes."[62] Youngstown Sheet and Tube's Dr. Kennedy described an examination procedure that was faster still. "Such an examination does not require more than three minutes time if the doctor has a clerk present to take his dictation as he proceeds with the examination."[63] Given that clerks' hourly pay was likely cheaper than that of physicians, this additional investment in staff time could result in a savings by reducing the physicians' time per examination. Kennedy detailed the methods involved in this three-minute examination "conducted with mass production methods" as follows:

the applicants enter booths arranged on one side of the waiting room where they remove every item of clothing. In the nude [they leave] the opposite side of the booth one at a time to enter the examination room ... arranged so that the doctor has an opportunity to see them enter and leave the room. In this way the examiner's eye can at a glance detect the essential abnormalities of the arms, legs, back, and inguinal regions. The applicant steps on a scale to be weighed and measured, and then must make a half-turn while standing on the scales before his blood pressure is taken and a stethoscopic examination of the heart made.[64]

---

[58] National Industrial Conference Board, *Medical Care of Industrial Workers*, 30.
[59] National Industrial Conference Board, *Medical Care of Industrial Workers*, 27.
[60] National Industrial Conference Board, *Medical Care of Industrial Workers*, 22.
[61] W. Irving Clark, *Health Service in Industry* (New York: Macmillan, 1922), 74.
[62] Quoted in "Preliminary Survey of Physical Examinations for Employees in Industry," 20.
[63] "Clinic on Health in Industry," 18.
[64] "Clinic on Health in Industry," 18. This method made the most of physicians' time by using a particular arrangement of space, a particular architecture, and investment in materials. In a sense, medical screening programs involved a version of the political

Kennedy noted that the examinations did not involve taking any medical history, admitting that they did not have any medical value for the individuals examined. For Kennedy there was no real alternative because of the link between medical examination and employment. "When a man is getting a job and you start asking him all about his past medical history, you have as much chance of getting him to tell the truth as a complete stranger would if he asked you to sign a blank check."[65] Some industrial physicians criticized the rising speed of medical examinations conducted using "mass production methods," decrying that "too often" company doctors carried out "superficial inspection" with the only goal being "rejection of the evidently unfit." This inspection "consists of a hasty survey for obvious defects and apparent sickness."[66]

C. H. Watson wrote that "the physical examination of the applicant is entirely inadequate from the standpoint of proper medical health supervision." He added that

particular effort should be made, in the formulation of a standard physical examination plan, to bring out the fact that we are searching for a few cardinal points on which to pass judgment as to employment of an individual. In other words, it should be very definitely understood by the medical man entering industry that he is not carrying out a hospital, a dispensary, or even a private office examination of a patient.... Once this method is in operation, it will be found that the average time consumed will not be prohibitive from the stand-point of costs. The maximum length of time for the physical examination of an applicant should not be more than fifteen minutes, and, in many instances, not over six or eight.[67]

economy of speed that Christopher Tomlins and others have identified as operating in machinery-intensive industry. Christopher Tomlins, *Law, Labor and Ideology in the Early American Republic* (Cambridge: Cambridge University Press, 1993), 322–326; Alfred Chandler, *The Visible Hand: The Managerial Revolution in American Business* (Cambridge, MA: Belknap Press of Harvard University Press, 1977), 281–283. This economy of speed, however, is not specifically defined technologically but politically and financially. The goal of spending money on the physical space of the examination site, like investments in machinery, was to allow the work to be conducted more quickly in order to ultimately save money by getting the most out of physicians' labor. That goal was written into the materials, and those materials reinforced that goal.

[65] "Clinic on Health in Industry," 18.

[66] G. M. Kober, and E. R. Hayhurst, *Industrial Health* (Philadelphia: P. Blakiston's Son and Company, 1924), 129. The discussions of medical examinations surveyed here were not only descriptive of the range of practices in industrial medicine but were prescriptive as well. These works formed part of the process through which industrial physicians decided how to practice industrial medicine, collectively as they built their field in its early days, and individually as new physicians came into the field. These works formed a part of the ideological process of subjection and qualification of new industrial physicians. Goran Therborn, *The Ideology of Power and the Power of Ideology* (London: Verso, 1980), 17–20, 46–48.

[67] Watson, "Physical Examinations: A Resume," 22–23.

As Irving Clark put it, "[s]peed in examination is essential." Achieving speed required "concentrat[ing] on the points of industrial rather than medical importance ... what may be called industrial physical defects."[68]

In addition to becoming faster, medical examinations became more standardized over time, as illustrated by the spread of medical forms. In his introduction to the National Industrial Conference Board 1922 symposium, "The Physician in Industry," industrial physician John Moorhead of the Conference Board of Physicians in Industry described standardization of medical examinations via forms as one of the principle tasks of industrial physicians' professional organizations.[69] Toward this end, several leaders in industrial medicine published works collecting medical forms developed at specific companies and proposing new ones. These collections of forms offered individual practitioners and their corporate employers a resource for standardizing the practices of medical examinations. They helped companies carry out the epistemological or categorical construction needed in order to run their medical programs.

Medical forms also helped firms govern the lowest-level practitioners who actually conducted medical examinations. Forms were tools with which individual examining physicians did their work on the bodies of applicants and employees. They were tools that both reflected and shaped the tools' wielders.[70] Forms helped managerial personnel to supervise medical examiners and to structure the medical examination around managerial priorities. Forms also standardized the interactions between medical personnel and the human objects they acted on: medical examiners could follow the procedures listed on the examination forms, looking at the person's body, and looking away from their humanity, in the routinized manner prescribed in the form. Overall, medical examinations were used by industrial physicians in service of employers' financial goals, specifically, risk management. Care for an individual person's health and well-being was at best a secondary priority in these processes. These examinations helped inflict distributive injustice on people excluded from employment, and denied recognition

---

[68] Clark, *Health Service in Industry*, 74.   [69] *The Physician in Industry*, 2.

[70] This point is a kind of miniaturized analogy to the criticism of the instrumentalist conception of law and the state. On this, see Tomlins, *Law, Labor and Ideology in the Early American Republic*, 304; Nicos Poulantzas, "Preliminaries to the Study of Hegemony in the State" and "Towards a Democratic Socialism," in *The Poulantzas Reader: Marxism, Law and the State*, ed. James Martin (London: Verso, 2008), 74–119 and 361–364; Michael Heinrich, *Introduction to the Three Volumes of Karl Marx's Capital*, trans. Alexander Locascio (New York: Monthly Review Press, 2012), 199–218.

to all the examinees, whether hired or not. Furthermore, those examined were treated to physical contact carried out via "mass production methods," touched and looked at as an object through processes that prioritized speed and employer financial concerns.

HUMAN CAPITAL INVESTMENT

In some respects, what I have detailed here within industrial medicine was a decline. The field's center of gravity shifted to exclusion as medical examinations in workplaces were routinized around companies' efforts to avoid liability. In the field's early days, industrial medicine was not focused on liability reduction but instead admitted a wider range of practices. Yet industrial medicine always had a relatively narrow scope in terms of how the field conceptualized its purposes. Space considerations here prohibit a comprehensive overview of industrial medicine prior to compensation laws. A few examples can help illustrate the simultaneous breadth and narrowness of industrial medicine prior to compensation laws. I present this compressed history in order to make clear that my discussion of industrial medicine after compensation laws does not express an uncritical and nostalgic perspective on earlier industrial medicine.

In 1906, physicians, social workers, and other concerned individuals formed the Chicago Tuberculosis Institute. In 1912 the Institute published a pamphlet titled "A Plan of Examination of Employees for Tuberculosis." The Plan argued that for physicians in industry and companies employing them, "[t]he watchwords should be: education, detection, control."[71] The

---

[71] *A Plan of Examination of Employees for Tuberculosis* (Chicago: Committee on Factories of the Chicago Tuberculosis Institute, 1912), 13. Like Progressive Era public health efforts more broadly, factory-focused anti-tuberculosis efforts expressed what historian Daniel Burnstein calls this era's "comprehensive social vision," a vision within which ideas of health played a key role. This social vision manifested in efforts to identify and root out whatever was considered unclean or potentially infectious. Daniel Eli Burnstein, *Next to Godliness: Confronting Dirt and Despair in Progressive Era New York City* (Urbana: University of Illinois Press, 2006), 3. Spreading belief in the scientific theory that bacteria caused illnesses like tuberculosis, cholera, and typhoid fed and changed this emphasis on health. Physicians sought to place themselves in important roles within the world imagined by this social vision and claimed special expertise in identification of people who carried infectious diseases (Burnstein, *Next to Godliness*, p. 14). Paul Starr argues that physicians saw public health as a potential incursion on their territory. Physicians sought to deal with this incursion by positioning themselves as meeting public health needs, arguing that their expertise was especially important in controlling the spread of disease. Starr, *The Social Transformation of American Medicine*, 183–194.

pamphlet praised Sears, Roebuck and Company for having "for some time given special attention to tuberculosis in their examination of employes."[72] As a result of the Institute's education work, its proposals for the expansion of medical detection and control were adopted at multiple other businesses. International Harvester, Montgomery Ward, the Chicago Telephone Company, and Swift & Company all followed the example of Sears. Anti-tuberculosis efforts were one source of the growth of the field of industrial medicine.[73]

These efforts were arguably the most laudable insofar as they placed the most emphasis on improving working-class health. Even so, the primary claims made in favor of medical examinations for tuberculosis did not mainly prioritize working-class well-being as a good so much as they took working-class health as a useful secondary objective en route to another, more important goal.

The "Plan of Examination of Employees for Tuberculosis," for example, declared, "The hand of the engineer is on the throttle of the manufacturing machinery; the hand of the physician should be on the health of the working force; a higher standard of health means greater efficiency."[74] In this imagery working people appear as a factor of production, like machinery, and appeared as an object on which a controlling, supervisory hand must rest. The engineer with his hand on the throttle of machinery partially determined the pace at which a machine would wear out. The physician, with his hand on the throttle of the workforce, helped determine the same for employees.

As part of this claim, Starr argues that physicians helped shift the emphasis in public health "from the environment to the individual," which he sees as exemplified by the growth of medical examinations (p. 192).

[72] *A Plan of Examination of Employees for Tuberculosis*, 8.

[73] Both Harry Mock and Irving Clark considered anti-tuberculosis work as key to the formation of the field of industrial medicine. See Mock, *Industrial Medicine and Surgery*, 128, and W. Irving Clark, Jr., "Tuberculosis and Heart Disease among Industrial Workers," in *The Physician in Industry*, 42–47.

[74] *A Plan of Examination of Employees for Tuberculosis*, 13. This quote recalls Marx's observation that "experience shows to the intelligent observer how rapidly and firmly capitalist production has seized the vital forces of the people at their very roots." Karl Marx, *Capital: A Critique of Political Economy*, vol. 1 (London: Penguin, 1990), 380. Marx's overriding concern in this chapter was the rapidity with which workers were used up in production, with terrible effects on their lives. Marx had much less to say about other ways in which capitalism might grip "the vital forces of the people," probably because he wrote before many significant developments in industrial medicine and public health occurred.

The growth of medical examinations at Pullman illustrates the instrumental purposes that defined industrial medicine early on, and shows a drift away from serving employee health. When Pullman first hired Thomas Crowder as its medical director in 1905, the company ordered him to address public fears that ventilation in Pullman's signature sleeping cars might pose a threat to passengers' health. The company feared that harms to passengers could be a source of financial liability as well as a source of harm to the company's reputation. Crowder spoke at numerous conferences and wrote articles and books on the issue of sleeping car ventilation. Under his watch Pullman introduced new fans and forms of ventilation and temperature control in sleeper cars, and changed the bedding in those cars, adding additional cover layers on sleeping berths in the attempt to minimize contact between successive passengers.[75] The heart of Crowder's work, however, was to argue that there was no serious problem of sleeping car ventilation. Crowder's conclusion after studying the matter was that passengers sometimes felt ill aboard sleeping cars because they had become overheated. If a passenger began to feel ill in a sleeping car, they probably just needed to open a window. This is a fairly innocuous episode. The structure of this episode – Crowder being handed a technically defined problem with great freedom to operate but within narrowly defined parameters – would recur several times at Pullman, sometimes in less innocuous ways, as part of changes in the field of industrial medicine and the role the discipline played in American business.

After sleeping car ventilation, Pullman would soon face another problem of ventilation and cost: occupational health effects of lead paint exposure for Pullman employees. Pullman came to care about lead exposure due to a new law passed in Illinois. This law itself was conceptualized largely in instrumental terms. In 1911 the Illinois Occupational Health Commission published a report that detailed the danger of lead paint exposure. That report appealed to economic reasoning to stress the importance of working-class health, stating that poor employee health caused "the interruption of the use of costly machinery and other capital." In general, the report declared, workers "in health are a source of wealth to the nation." The report thus expressed an instrumental approach to working-class health similar to that of anti-tuberculosis efforts.

---

[75] John H. White, *The American Railroad Passenger Car*, vol. 2 (Baltimore: Johns Hopkins University Press, 1978), 406. See also Thomas R. Crowder, "A Study of the Ventilation of Sleeping Cars," *Journal of the American Public Health Association* 1, no. 12 (December 1911): 920–992.

Social reform advocate and physician Alice Hamilton led the Occupational Disease Commission's investigation into the health effects of lead. Her portion of the report noted that painting and sanding the ceilings of railways cars such as Pullman's signature luxury cars posed a particularly serious danger to workers due to exposure to lead paint dust. For her research, Dr. Hamilton interviewed employees suffering the effects of lead poisoning. In her autobiography she wrote about how these stories distressed and moved her:

> as I would pass through Pullman on the train in the course of my journeyings, I would curse it in my soul, picturing what was going on there and realizing how powerless I was to do anything about it. But suddenly I found to my relief that there was a chance to bring about a change. I had poured out my story to Miss [Jane] Addams and she made me repeat it to Mrs. Joseph T. Bowen, one of the first and staunchest friends of Hull-House, and a member of that all-too-small class of wealthy people who feel a direct responsibility toward the sources of their wealth.[76]

Hamilton wrote that "the facts were brought to Mrs. Bowen's attention and that made her decide to take up the whole question of accidents and industrial disease among the employes of this company of which she is a stockholder." Louise de Koven Bowen was a wealthy reformer and settlement house activist who held many shares of Pullman stock.[77] Bowen used her influence at Pullman to get Hamilton and another investigator access to the company in order to document in greater detail the problems of industrial disease and workplace injury at the company. Bowen sent the report to Pullman's president and demanded a meeting. After Bowen threatened to take the matter public, Pullman officials met with her. The company first decided to confirm the findings of Hamilton's report by ordering "a thorough physical examination made of all the men employed in work which exposed them to industrial diseases." These examinations confirmed the Hamilton report's findings, and company officials began to take steps to improve conditions at Pullman.[78]

---

[76] Alice Hamilton, *Exploring the Dangerous Trades: The Autobiography of Alice Hamilton* (Boston: Northeastern University Press, 1985), 158.

[77] For more on Bowen and some of her other reform activities, see Elizabeth J. Clapp, *Mothers of All Children: Women Reformers and the Rise of Juvenile Courts in Progressive Era America* (University Park: Pennsylvania State University Press, 1998), 185–190.

[78] Alice Hamilton, "What One Stockholder Did," *The Survey*, June 1, 1912, 387–389; Louise de Koven Bowen, *Growing Up with a City* (New York: Macmillan 1926), 166–167. Bowen's experiences at Pullman encouraged her to attempt to intervene over work hours and wages at International Harvester, another company in which she was a shareholder, and at U.S. Steel (pp. 167–170).

In March 1911, Illinois passed a new law on occupational disease, in direct response to the work of the Occupational Disease Commission. As the Commission's report had suggested, the new law mandated that companies conduct the sorts of medical examinations of employees that Pullman had just begun to conduct. Employers were required to carry out medical examinations of employees at any company where workers came "into direct contact with the poisonous agencies or injurious processes referred to" in the report, and examining physicians were to report any positive findings to the Illinois State Board of Health.[79] These medical examinations were to be conducted "by a competent licensed physician for the purpose of ascertaining if there exists in any employee any industrial or occupational disease or illness."[80] The Illinois legislature agreed with this, writing these suggestions into law. Largely due to Bowen's efforts, Pullman was well-placed to comply with the Illinois law, and was the first company to do so. Pullman introduced medical examinations for employees exposed to lead as well as washing-up stations and other practices designed to mitigate lead exposure. Pullman was praised for these efforts, which likely did improve employee health.[81] It is worth underscoring, however, that employee health was an instrumental good for Pullman, something it took action on due to legislative requirement and fear of negative publicity.

In its response to sleeping car ventilation and to lead paint exposure, Pullman officials used company physicians and the physical health of persons as tools in service to the health of the corporation. With sleeping car ventilation, the company responded to the possibilities of negative responses from the market. With the problem of employees' exposure to lead paint, Pullman officials acted in part because the law made them do so, and in part because of the threat of negative publicity. The issue of lead

---

[79] "Workers Health Measure Passes," *Chicago Daily Tribune* March 29, 1911, 11. The Illinois Commission report was influential on other states' occupational safety laws and led directly to a federal commission on the matter. As Pullman's manufacturing plants were centered in Illinois, these other laws had less effect than the Illinois law, but other manufacturers would have also had to begin physical examinations as a result of similar laws around the country. In an earlier article, "Disease and the Workers" the *Chicago Daily Tribune* wrote that "[h]umanity and social economy both demand this expenditure." *Chicago Daily Tribune*, January 13, 1911, 10.

[80] *Report of Commission on Occupational Diseases*, 158.

[81] George Moses Price, *The Modern Factory: Safety, Sanitation and Welfare* (New York: John Wiley & Sons, 1914), 322, 324–325. See also Hamilton, "What One Stockholder Did," 389.

exposure in particular facilitated growth in Pullman's medical department and spurred the development of industrial medicine as a corporate risk management practice.[82] The issue of lead paint exposure also marks an important development in the emergence of employees' bodies as a key concern in the company's management of financial uncertainty and of medical examinations as a technique for this management.

Industrial medicine at Pullman would soon be expanded even further, as the company encountered another problem for which industrial medicine seemed to be the answer: a perceived threat to public health posed by employees who handled food. This problem too was the result of legal requirements, and here too medical examinations were key practical and conceptual tools for detection and control. As Pullman responded to this issue, the company further increased its focus on managing employees as a source of risk, thereby increasing the importance of medical examinations as an ongoing practice to monitor operations. In its train car service, Pullman employed people who handled food. Numerous cities and states passed laws in the early 1910s requiring medical examinations of employees who handled food, out of fear of food transmitting illness to consumers. As a company operating across the United States, Pullman fell under multiple jurisdictions, and the company needed to conform to the laws in every state in which it operated food service. And, thus, food handler laws too caused an expansion of medical examination at Pullman.

In its approach to food handling, Pullman's goal was to promote health, but not that of its employees. Rather, employees were conceptualized as a source of risk. This was a kind of biopolitics aimed at protecting the nation – or at least the population of Pullman customers – by knowing about but not seeking to improve the health of Pullman's employees. In 1913 Pullman employed approximately 700 food handlers. The company began by requiring applicants for food handling positions to submit to what Crowder called "a cursory examination which is reasonably

---

[82] David Rosner and Gerald Markowitz's *Dying for Work* remains an excellent work on lead paint exposure and much more in the history of occupational safety and health. That history is important for several reasons, including the ways it foregrounds the human effects of business decisions. Those decisions are systematically produced and are predictable in a capitalist society. For more on lead poisoning, see Christian Warren, *Brush with Death: A Social History of Lead Poisoning* (London: Johns Hopkins University Press, 2000). Warren discusses Pullman briefly (p. 52), noting that immigrant workers did some of the most dangerous work at Pullman, with their employer and their co-workers rarely informing them of the risks.

effective in weeding out those having infectious diseases."[83] Here as with the later use of medical examinations to reduce compensation liability, industrial medicine both individualized and aggregated. Medical examinations helped produce a population of food handlers deemed to be safe, and did so by setting up a boundary around that population. Where those excluded from work went was not Pullman's concern.[84] The health of the larger public and the health of Pullman employees were here treated as a zero-sum game, with Pullman emphasizing both public health and employee exclusion because it was profitable to do so.

Having briefly surveyed some moments in the development of industrial medicine prior to compensation laws, it is now possible to more clearly state the kind of decline in industrial medicine that came with the tyranny of the table. In an echo of the narrowing of the legal meaning of injury that I have called moral thinning, industrial medicine too became narrower. There was a prior moment when industrial medicine's purposes were broader, admitting of a wider range of medical practices that served working-class health and well-being – sometimes. More specifically, industrial medicine served working-class health instrumentally, when it was profitable. The centrality of profit was part of the field from its inception, as was the objectification and use of working-class people.

The story of industrial medicine before and after compensation laws is one of both change and continuity. Arguably in its early days industrial medicine sometimes distributed access to medical care. Even when it did so, however, often the goal was not one of distributive justice and the field did not tend to treat working-class health as a good in itself. Rather, the distribution of medical care was incidental to other priorities held to be more important than working-class health. Industrial medicine provided

---

[83] Given the brevity of the exam, Crowder added, "[i]t is still possible, however, that those in the early stages of tuberculosis might get by." "Physical Examination of Porters, Suggestion of District Superintendent Rittenhouse Regarding," July 16, 1913, Employee and Labor Relations Medicine and Sanitation, Administrative Subject Files, 1905–1968, Pullman Corporation Records, Newberry Library, Chicago, IL.

[84] Pullman's management of risks to customers could take a racist cast. A Pullman official named E. F. Carry wrote in 1922 that "it is desirable for us to develop the status of our colored help, particularly the porters, as regards venereal diseases." Carry anticipated legal change requiring the company to examine car service personnel: "Unquestionably laws will shortly be passed requiring the examination of porters, in addition to those who handle food. I believe that our porters are above the average, but being colored, it is taken for granted that they are in the class that runs 50% to 60% venereal." E. F. Carry to Hungerford, September 7, 1922, Employee and Labor Relations Medicine and Sanitation, Administrative Subject Files, 1905–1968, Pullman Corporation Records, Newberry Library, Chicago, IL.

medical care in a recognition-free manner, acting on people as objects. I argued above that after compensation laws industrial medicine came to focus on medical technique involving neither distribution of medical care nor recognition, summarized in what multiple commentators called "weeding out." By analogy, when industrial medicine did distribute access to medical care, it was in effect treating working-class people as crops. Better a crop than a weed, if one has only those two options, but better still a human being. That was only minimally an option within industrial medicine even in the field's best moments. Having spent its early years alternatively rooting out human weeds and tending human crops as law and profit variably dictated, the field was equipped to act when compensation laws changed what counted as profitable. Companies quickly repurposed the profit-centered, recognitionless practice of medicine to focus even more narrowly on exclusion for the sake of liability avoidance.

QUIET MEN'S BURDENS

After criticizing industrial medicine as I have, I want to stress that the industrial physicians who carried out human weeding were neither monsters nor villains, at least not in the cartoonish sense. Frank Pedley, for example, a Quebec-based industrial physician, seems to have regretted what the field became and what it did. In 1930 Pedley made a speech at the annual meeting of the International Association of Industrial Accident Boards and Commissions. In his talk, "Workmen's Compensation Act in Relation to Handicapped Individuals," Pedley argued that as a result of Quebec's workmen's compensation law "[m]any employers are unwilling to engage men with various handicaps, particularly men who have lost an arm, or a leg, or the sight of one eye, because if the opposite member should be lost the liability is very materially increased."[85] He suggested that "[s]uch men [as] are usually classed by medical examiners as substandard risks ... frequently fail to secure employment in consequence. Yet is it to be assumed that all these individuals are to be deprived of the opportunity to earn a livelihood?" Pedley sardonically remarked, "Starvation is not a satisfactory treatment for the handicapped."[86]

---

[85] United States Bureau of Labor Statistics, *Bulletin of the Bureau of Labor Statistics* 536 (1931): 249–250.
[86] United States Bureau of Labor Statistics, *Bulletin of the Bureau of Labor Statistics* 536 (1931): 251.

Thomas Crowder was present during Pedley's speech, and was the first person to respond in discussion. Crowder said, "A job is the thing the handicapped workman needs most. Without it the extra compensation he might receive for injury is entirely nonoperative. The remedy for this condition is not a medical one, but a remedy is what is needed."[87] As Crowder once wondered in an internal memo wherein he recommended greater medicalized discrimination, "[t]he question which immediately occurs to me is, who hires those rejected?"[88] Crowder knew full well what he had helped Pullman do. He knew from personal experience.

Crowder did not set out to be an industrial physician. He had intended to follow the family profession and become a doctor like his brother, father, and grandfather. A profile of Crowder published in 1935 declared that he "wanted to be an internist" in keeping with the family tradition. Crowder attended the highly regarded Rush Medical College, graduating in 1897. While at Rush, Crowder would work in a laboratory and department run by Ludvig Hektoen, a physician known for his scientific advances. This was a boon to the young Crowder, as in this period the medical profession was increasingly concerned with being considered scientific.[89] After graduating from medical school in 1897, Crowder interned for a year and a half at Cook County Hospital in Chicago. In this period hospital experience came to be viewed as central to the training and qualification of physicians.[90] Crowder's work at Cook County Hospital helped make him a well-qualified physician. His next positions, from 1901 to 1905, as a fellow in the study of pathology at Rush and as a medical instructor at Rush, were both high-status positions for an early career.[91] In 1902–1903, while a fellow at Rush, Crowder studied in Vienna, Austria.[92] In going to Vienna, Crowder further advanced his career, because the rising generation of American doctors looked to Austria and Germany as centers of medical expertise grounded in science.[93] On returning to the United States, with his teaching and fellow position at

[87] United States Bureau of Labor Statistics, *Bulletin of the Bureau of Labor Statistics* 536 (1931): 252.

[88] T. R. Crowder, "Medical Examinations – Shops," undated, Employee and Labor Relations, Medicine and Sanitation, Administrative Subject Files, Pullman Corporation Records.

[89] Martin Fischer, *Martin B. Wherry: Bacteriologist* (Springfield: Thomas, 1938), 35.

[90] Charles Rosenberg, *The Care of Strangers: The Rise of America's Hospital System* (New York: Basic Books, 1987), 184.

[91] DePauw University, *Alumnal Record* (Greencastle: Depauw University, 1915), 204.

[92] Selleck and Whittaker, *Occupational Health in America*, 134.

[93] Rosenberg, *The Care of Strangers*, 174.

Rush and his recent European education, Crowder was well placed to pursue a promising career in his desired field of internal medicine.

That goal would be cut short due to hearing loss. As the 1935 profile put it, Crowder "did not go very willingly" out of internal medicine and into industrial medicine. He "love[d] his work, and he did not want to leave it." I have not been able to identify the source of Crowder's deafness, but the 1935 profile states clearly that he left internal medicine due to "an infirmity – a disability of hearing, which made even auscultation difficult."[94] Auscultation meant listening to a patient's body and was a central technique required to practice internal medicine. One colleague said that Crowder "was seriously handicapped by deafness."[95] Another colleague, J. S. Felton, said that Crowder was quiet in social interaction, "possibly because of some deafness-related shyness and withdrawal." His hearing impairment meant that "oral communication was difficult [for Crowder], but he did express himself well in writing." Felton said that Crowder's hearing impairment was the reason that he stopped practicing internal medicine and began to work at Pullman, adding that "[f]ew ever discussed Dr. Crowder's loss of hearing with him."[96] Whether congenital or acquired, it seems clear that Crowder did not like to discuss his impairment and that he was able to succeed as an industrial physician despite this impairment. The discipline of internal medicine did not allow Crowder employment as a result of his impaired hearing. This barrier to his chosen field is what compelled him to change professional tracks, leading to his career in the new field of industrial medicine. In that field, at his employer's instructions, ironically, he helped construct barriers to many other disabled people's employment.

Again, industrial physicians like Crowder were not monsters. The 1935 profile described Crowder in its title as "One of those Quiet Men who Carry a Heavy Burden and Do It Well."[97] His burdens were multiple, including hearing loss and the employment barriers he suffered.

---

[94] "Thomas Reid Crowder, M.D., Honorary Life Member, Conference of State & Provincial Health Authorities of North America, 'One of Those Quiet Men Who Carry a Heavy Burden and Do It Well,'" *Industrial Medicine*, 4, no. 9 (September 1935). In a story he wrote for his children in 1926, in which he described some events in his own childhood, Crowder related hearing a dog bark and gave no indication of childhood hearing impairment. Thomas Crowder, "To Alice and Doodie and Tommy," May 6, 1926, Cornelia Meigs Papers, Rauner Special Collections Library, Dartmouth College.

[95] Selleck and Whittaker, *Occupational Health in America*, 193.

[96] J. S. Felton, "Thomas R. Crowder, M.D. Retrospection in Environmental Health," *Journal of Occupational Medicine* 8, no. 7 (July 1966): 377–382, 378–379.

[97] "Thomas Reid Crowder, M.D., Honorary Life Member."

The profile depicted Crowder as well-loved by colleagues. One colleague stressed that even after Crowder lost his hearing, still "he could always hear the voice of a patient in distress."[98] That sensitivity to suffering is not apparent in any of the policies he wrote. It is apparent in his parenting. To entertain his children, he told stories about his own childhood dog, Jack. In 1925 his wife, Grace Meigs Crowder, passed away. He wrote movingly to his children about their deceased mother, and he told them about his emotional responses to the loss of Jack the dog in attempt to help his children cope with their own grief. He took pains as well to keep his children in contact with their mother's family, especially their aunt. He sometimes facilitated that contact via taking his children to his office. As one of his daughters wrote in a letter to one of her aunts, "I am writing this letter in Papa's office. I like to typewrite."[99] That same typewriter may be the one at which he typed his story about the Jack the dog. That office typewriter facilitated a portion of the deep humanity Crowder displayed as a parent. And it was at that office typewriter that Crowder crafted policies that harmed so many working-class people. Walter Benjamin's angel of history, drifting across the Illinois skies from Cherry to Chicago, would have looked down and seen that Thomas Crowder was not a monster, and thus found his actions and their institutional context

---

[98] Selleck and Whittaker, *Occupational Health in America*, 193.

[99] Alice Crowder to Cornelia Meigs, 1929, Papers of Cornelia Meigs, Dartmouth College Library, New Hampshire. My hope here is to evoke Crowder's complex personhood, to use sociologist Avery Gordon's phrase. Avery F. Gordon, *Ghostly Matters: Haunting and the Sociological Imagination*, 2nd ed. (Minneapolis: University of Minnesota Press, 2008), 4–5. As Gordon has put it, "even those who haunt our dominant institutions and their systems of value are haunted too by things they sometimes have names for and sometimes do not" (p. 5). Perhaps Crowder's actions haunted him; perhaps he managed to exorcise the guilt and memory of what he did. In terms of his actions and their effects on others, it does not matter. At the same time, that his actions and the actions of many others like him were the acts of complex human beings, not cartoon villains, matters a great deal for understanding these events. It was not the individual character of these people that explains their actions, but their institutional contexts and the labors of domination and exclusion they were compelled to perform. That Crowder retained some of his humanity is certainly not good enough, but perhaps there is some hopeful kernel to be found there, that systems of domination may fully subordinate but do not necessarily fully extinguish the human spark of the people who staff them. It would be naïve to expect the spark of humanity within the middle management of the world to do anything whatsoever to alter the course of our society, but that this spark remains may be some evidence that humanity can persist and, with the vehicle of mass movements, might become more than a spark. Then again, perhaps this is just another cost of dehumanizing institutions, that in harming their victims they also harm the people they compel to carry out the labors of dehumanization.

all the more horrifying. The machinery of injustice does not need monsters to operate.

CONCLUSION

Employers crafted strategies of exclusion in response to the changed incentives under compensation laws, and they ordered industrial physicians to solve the technical problems required to execute those strategies. Industrial physicians came in practice to emphasize one of the Chicago Tuberculosis Institute's watchwords above all: detection. Specifically, they sought to detect people who were potential sources of greater liability to the physicians' employers. The doctors became discrimination technicians standing as gatekeepers around employers' risk pools. They surveilled employees and applicants using "mass production techniques," practicing medical technique but not medical care. To borrow Jeremiah Connor's words, within industrial medicine "the human interest as between the physician and patient" was lost. The physicians were, of course, still human beings, and it simply must be the case that some of them had an impulse to feel guilty about their role in inflicting exclusion on disabled people. If they did feel guilty, their guilt does not seem to have shaped their actions. Crowder certainly was aware of the effects of the policies he helped craft. Perhaps he and other industrial physicians found abstractions to help rationalize or to stop thinking altogether about their actions. Abstractions like "impairment," C.E. Ford's grades 3 and 4, Crowder's grades D and E, tabular presentation of numbers and the streamlined representational schema available within medical forms may have served as filters to help people who sought to avert their eyes from the humanity of the people whose exclusion they organized. If these empathy-inhibiting abstractions worked, then they served as both a comfort for industrial physicians and a reduction of their own humanity. Perhaps these abstractions failed, so that industrial physicians simply did their jobs and felt bad about it, privately: men who carried heavy burdens quietly, their guilt just another of the many human costs that rolled downward while profits flowed upward.

Conclusion

Resistance and Aftermath

This book begins to come to an end. The storm does not. In the contemporary United States, approximately 5,000 people die as employees each year.[1] This means someone in the United States dies from a workplace-related injury approximately every two hours. Go see a film. By the time it ends, someone has died in a workplace accident. Compared with the early twentieth century, 5,000 deaths per year may seem like relatively few. Still, 5,000 is higher than the number of victims of the terrorist attacks of September 11, 2001, and higher than the US military personnel killed in Iraq from 2003 to 2013.[2]

---

[1] United States Bureau of Labor Statistics, "Census of Fatal Occupational Injuries News Release," December 18, 2018,www.bls.gov/news.release/cfoi.htm, accessed June 15, 2019. There have been approximately 90,000 fatal employee accidents in the United State in the twenty-first century. This figure is calculated from the Bureau of Labor Statistics December 18, 2018, news release and its "1992–2002 Census of Fatal Occupational Injuries," www.bls.gov/iif/oshwc/cfoi/cftbo186.pdf, accessed June 15, 2019. See also AFL-CIO, *Death on the Job: The Toll of Neglect. A National and State-by-State Profile of Worker Safety and Health in the United States*, www.aflcio.org/content/download/174867/4158803/1647_DOTJ2016.pdf, accessed January 6, 2017. Non-fatal injuries remain frequent as well. In recent years, almost 900,000 people per year in the United States have reported workplace injuries serious enough to require time off from work. United States Bureau of Labor Statistics, "Employer-Reported Workplace Injuries and Illnesses (Annual) News Release," November 8, 2018, www.bls.gov/news.release/osh.htm, accessed June 15, 2019. Injuries are widely underreported as well, especially among the most vulnerable of employees. See Annette Bernhardt et al., *Broken Laws, Unprotected Workers: Violations of Employment and Labor Laws in America's Cities* (New York: National Employment Law Project, 2009).

[2] For the number of US military personnel killed, see "Faces of the Fallen," *The Washington Post*, http://apps.washingtonpost.com/national/fallen/, accessed April 3, 2014. This count does not include Iraqi casualties, about which see Iraq Body Count, www.iraqbodycount.org,

There is something uncomfortable in those juxtapositions. There should be. Lives and deaths are singular, incomparable, non-fungible. To treat them otherwise is to trespass on recognition, on our shared humanity. The often-lethal violence of employment is another such trespass. This book can be thought of as a historical investigation into the machine-like regularity with which these trespasses on our humanity happen in our society. Again and again, predictably, people at work lose hands, eyes, faces, lives, loved ones. They endure suffering and loss that overflows measurement. Then they enter into legal processes that hand them small sums of money. Nothing personal, just business.

When do the losses from injury end? Do they ever? When I was eighteen a few hundred pounds of lumber fell on me at work. When did that moment end? Has it yet? I would not say I was traumatized by this injury. At the time, I wasn't even particularly angry. It was unpleasant and my hand healed and I went on with my life. This episode was in a sense over in just a few weeks, after the bone healed. Much more often I have had memories of my younger brothers' workplace injuries (the ones I've heard of, anyway). I felt much more frightened about their injuries and remained upset about their injuries much longer than I did about my own. Now and again ever since I have remembered those instances and felt afraid about what still could happen to my brothers at their jobs. My experiences of injury are far smaller and less severe than what Marguerite and Florence Murray or Samuel and Salina Howard must have experienced. If I felt afraid, they must have felt sheer terror.

Employee injuries are, to borrow from sociologist Avery Gordon, ghostly matters.[3] They haunt the living. As William Faulkner wrote, "the past is never dead. It's not even past." How many people at any given moment have been living with past-yet-present experiences of injury, the people whose bodies were injured and the people whose loved

accessed April 5, 2014. Similarly the count of employment-related fatalities in the United States does not count all the employment-related fatalities directly related to the US economy, such as injuries at facilities owned by US companies but operated in other countries. Overall, the International Labour Organization estimates that there are two million employment-derived fatalities annually in the global economy. International Labour Organization, *Safety in Numbers: Pointers for a Global Safety Culture at Work* (Geneva: International Labour Organization, 2003), 1. This means 5,000 such fatalities each day. International Labour Organization, "Work-Related Fatalities Reach 2 Million Annually," www.ilo.org/global/about-the-ilo/media-centre/press-releases/WCMS_007789/lang--en/index.htm, accessed April 14, 2014.

3 Avery F. Gordon, *Ghostly Matters: Haunting and the Sociological Imagination*, 2nd ed. (Minneapolis: University of Minnesota Press, 2008).

ones were injured? Perhaps there is no forgetting and no end to injury on the part of injured people and their loved ones. Meanwhile within the law there is no remembering.

The tyranny of the table brought both new poverty and denial of recognition. At least some people saw it coming, in a quick glance over the shoulder of the angel of history. In a 1901 report on Britain's workmen's compensation law, a researcher named A. Maurice Low pointed out that the law had begun to cause employment discrimination against older and physically impaired employees. Low's report was published by the US Department of Labor. This means that at least some of the people who helped bring about compensation laws knew the consequences. Perhaps, like Thomas Crowder, they too were burdened by this knowledge, and bore that burden quietly, privately. Low rationalized: the new exclusion was, he wrote, "an unfortunate but perhaps unavoidable corollary to the effort made to improve general conditions," since "bring[ing] about 'the greatest good for the greatest number' ... entails some suffering on the minority."[4] From the 1910s through the 1930s, the greater good resulting from injury law reform brought new suffering to a minority in the United States. Employers converted people with disabilities from a "statistical minority into a political minority," in the words of sociologist Claire Liachowitz.[5] Employers added more people to the social position of "disabled person" and changed the forms of oppression that went along with that social position. If there was a greatest good accomplished here, it was one antithetical to the good of a great many individuals forced to live among the wreckage of the storm of history.

Reformers like Crystal Eastman and William Hard called for biopolitical policies to care for the working class, for reasons of justice. Other reformers like Charles Henderson called for biopolitical policies for less laudable reasons of economic stability and xenophobic eugenic concerns. All of these reformers shared concern for a large aggregate of the national population or the population of the working class in the United States. Businesses, on the other hand, practiced a much more limited biopolitics, caring only for a much more localized population: their own workforce. Disabled people were pushed out of those smaller biopolitical

---

[4] A. Maurice Low, "The British Workmen's Compensation Act and Its Operation," *Bulletin of the Department of Labor* 6, no. 32 (January 1901): 103–132; 118.

[5] Claire H. Liachowitz, *Disability as a Social Construct: Legislative Roots* (Philadelphia: University of Pennsylvania Press, 1988), 46; see also 45–61 for discussion of compensation laws.

communities, and thus rendered a population surplus to businesses' requirements and not granted biopolitical care.[6] The people who were allowed entry to employment were offered less care than before as well, as industrial medicine made care for human crops less of a priority than the removal of human weeds.[7]

---

[6] Surplus populations at least in the early twentieth century were subject to the underside of biopolitics – alongside the management of the life of some populations, other populations were marked as being left to die. Foucault summarized this as a power "to make live and to let die." Michel Foucault, *"Society Must Be Defended"*: *Lectures at the Collège de France, 1975–1976* (New York: Picador, 2003), 241.

[7] Throughout these processes, employee injury law and markets acted ideologically, depicting working-class human beings as more object than subject, and specifically as economic objects. Robert Knox has argued that "one of law's key roles is to integrate the working class into capitalism." Knox examines unions as forms of political subjects both conceptualized and partially constituted by law. He argues that the specifics of this integration change over time, yet the legal positions available to the working class "ultimately all remained within the coordinates of capitalist social relations." Robert Knox, "Law, Neoliberalism and the Constitution of Political Subjectivity: The Case of Organised Labour," in *Neoliberal Legality: Understanding the Role of Law in the Neoliberal Project*, ed. Honor Brabazon (New York: Routledge, 2017), 92–118; 95. Employee injury law similarly carried out the social integration of working-class people, organizing their distribution and consumption, and similarly remained entirely within the limited range of possibility present within capitalism. In this case, however, for both the reformers who called for compensation laws and within those laws themselves, that integration was not so much as political subjects than as depoliticized economic objects – labor power for the instrumental use of employers and the national economy. This was less subjectivity than it was subjection. I suspect that part of the difference between labor law and employment law lies in the former offering a range of collective political subjectivities and the latter a range of positions that are either individualized rather than collective or conceptualized as economic rather than political. Knox argues that a similar conceptual substitution of political with economic has occurred as neoliberalism has taken hold in British law. He thus characterizes neoliberalism not as a retraction of state action or as deregulatory but rather as actively intervening in society to impose individualism. Christopher Tomlins has narrated a similar pattern that occurred in the early nineteenth-century United States, as early unions presented themselves – and, arguably, work itself – as both civic and collective in nature, while courts tended to conceptualize them as economic and to see collectivity as illegitimate interference in the market. See Christopher Tomlins, *Law, Labor and Ideology in the Early American Republic*, (Cambridge: Cambridge University Press, 1993). In addition, Knox suggests that where political subjectivity continues to exist under neoliberalism, it exists as an attenuated politics, in that the economy is hived off as apolitical, which is to say, the split between economic and political is rendered outside the domain of politics. This implies a limited capacity for law to contribute to overcoming that split. If anything, I would argue, law is both artifact and agent of that split. My thoughts here are influenced by Chris O'Kane's writing. O'Kane reformulates Marx's critique of political economy and Adorno's social theory in terms of one another. See Chris O'Kane, "On the Development of the Critique of Political Economy as a Critical Social Theory of Economic Objectivity," *Historical Materialism* 26, no. 1 (2018): 175–193, and Chris O'Kane, "'Society Maintains Itself Despite All the Catastrophes That May Eventuate':

All of this can be thought of as a story of three kinds of machines: a financial machinery of employment that left many people in poverty and subjected them to employers' power of private government, physical machinery that continued to break bones and rend flesh, and a new machinery of exclusion and abstraction built by compensation laws. Crowder and company quietly swallowed and rationalized their guilt over their role in these various machines. Other people did not go so quietly.

Some workers and unions pushed back. A 1914 Iowa labor assembly urged political action against the new pressures on workers introduced by compensation laws. They called on the government to "protect our more unfortunate brothers to retain their employment."[8] Delegates at an American Federation of Labor convention that same year similarly called for changes to the law.[9] At that convention the AFL's Executive Council reported that "the attention of workers should be called to a condition dangerous to their welfare which has developed out of social insurance and welfare provisions – the requirement of physical examination of workers as a condition requisite for employment or for continuation of employment."[10] One convention delegate, P. J. Conlon from the Alexandria, Virginia, Trades Council, put forward a resolution criticizing physical examinations. Conlon's resolution decried "[t]he tendency of employers of labor to force upon their employes a physical examination, under the pretext that it is a necessary requirement to comply with the compensation laws." Conlon's resolution called for the AFL to formulate a response to the issue of physical examinations, a response that would "become the universal policy of all affiliated unions in this matter."[11]

Critical Theory, Negative Totality, and Crisis," *Constellations* 25, no. 2 (June 2018): 287–301. My thoughts have also been influenced by the writing of Rob Hunter on the blog *Legal Form*, work in a similar theoretical vein to that of O'Kane but more directly applied to law. See https://legalform.blog, accessed June 7, 2019. See also the essays by O'Kane and Hunter in the forthcoming *Elgar Research Handbook on Law and Marxism*.

[8] Ottumwa Trades and Labor Assembly to Governor Clarke, December 31, 1914, Multiple Governors Correspondence, State Historical Society of Iowa, Des Moines, Iowa.

[9] *Insurance Monitor*, January 1914, 602. See the *Weekly Underwriter*, November 21, 1914, 592.

[10] American Federation of Labor, *Report of the Proceedings of the Thirty Fourth Annual Connection of the American Federation of Labor Held at Philadelphia, Pennsylvania, November 9 to 21* (Washington, DC: Law Reporter Printing, 1914), 67.

[11] American Federation of Labor, *Report of the Proceedings of the Thirty Fourth Annual Connection*, 417. These statements form part of unions' processes of self-governance. Unions are institutions of governance, governing themselves, their members, other unions, and waged workplaces. As such, the interaction between law, employers, and

Instead of Conlon's resolution, the AFL Convention passed a resolution from Frank Dujay, the president of a local federation of electrical workers in New York, stating that the AFL should demand a change in the law to make pre-employment physical examinations illegal.[12] In this resolution, the AFL-affiliated unions proposed to deal with the problem of physical examination by lobbying state government to amend compensation laws.

Dujay worked at the General Electric plant in Schenectady, New York. Earlier in 1914 GE had implemented physical examinations in response to compensation laws. Dujay called for the New York State Industrial Commission to intervene to stop these examinations, but the Commission declared itself powerless. Members of the AFL argued to the New York compensation commission that "the privilege of employers being self-insurers" should be removed from the compensation statute. Robert E. Dowling, chair of the New York Commission, responded by arguing that "the law should not be amended, but in such cases as the Federation of Labor suggested, there should be a complaint lodged with the Commission. If after an investigation such discrimination was found, he should not be allowed to act as a self-Insurer under the provisions of the law."[13] In part, Dowling was arguing about which part of state government ought to act in order to respond to this problem: the legislature or the Commission. Discrimination by self-insurers was not, Dowling suggested, an issue for the legislature to take up. Rather, the issue could be taken up administratively by the Commission overseeing workmen's compensation. Having gotten no satisfaction from the Commission, Dujay took up the GE workers' objections through the AFL and called for legislation. The events at the GE plant in Schenectady were what led New York Industrial Commissioner John Mitchell to criticize employers' use of physical examinations. Even though the commission could not

---

unions was the interaction between multiple centers of governing authority. These different authorities could and did conflict, as they imagined and sought to create different relationships among the ensemble of institutions governing American economic life. Like states, businesses, and other institutions of governance, unions "puzzle before they power." Hugh Heclo, *Modern Social Politics in Britain and Sweden: From Relief to Income Maintenance* (New Haven: Yale University Press, 1974), 305, and Margot Canaday, *The Straight State: Sexuality and Citizenship in Twentieth-Century America* (Princeton: Princeton University Press, 2009), 3.

[12] American Federation of Labor, *Report of the Proceedings of the Thirty Fourth Annual Connection*, 257.
[13] *The Spectator*, December 24, 1914, 356.

force GE to change its behavior, Mitchell could add his voice to the chorus of objections. This fact may have also influenced the AFL's call for legislative change, since clearly the agency administering the compensation law could not resolve the matter.

Ultimately, the 1914 AFL convention passed a resolution calling for elimination of employers' liability insurance companies from the compensation system and the establishment of state insurance companies with funds administered by the state compensation commissions.[14] In 1916 John P. White, president of the United Mine Workers of America, issued a similar call for the state to organize workmen's compensation insurance. In a speech at a conference on social insurance in Washington, DC, White said that physical examinations were so serious a matter that, if they were to happen at all, they

should be undertaken only on the assurance that the public welfare demands it and that the results are worth the sacrifice of that personal sanctity which our institutions have thrown about the individual. This, in my judgment, is another way of saying that the state, not the employer, should undertake such examination, assuming always that public policy demands compulsory examination at all.... If physical examination of all persons is demanded on the broad grounds of social welfare, then let it be administered by the state.[15]

The call for state insurance and state-run physical examinations amounted to a demand to remove the construction and distribution of risk pools from private insurance markets or self-insuring employers.

Union officials objected to insurance serving as what legal scholars Tom Baker and Jonathan Simon have called "delegated state power." Baker and Simon write that the state often chooses to forgo creating its "own criteria for access to vital economic freedoms like operating an automobile or a business (which would be politically controversial and even, perhaps, unconstitutional)." Instead, "the state mandates that a person wishing to engage in any such activity first obtain some form of insurance." This hands over decisions about who can engage in those "vital economic freedoms" to insurers. "Motivated by controlling losses they have contracted to pay, the companies set up their own norms of

---

[14] American Federation of Labor, *Report of the Proceedings of the Thirty Fourth Annual Connection*, 96.

[15] John P. White, "Compulsory Physical Examination," *The Shoe Workers' Journal* 17, no. 12 (December 1916): 3–4. White here depicted the state as the representative of society and the guardian of social welfare, occupying a conceptual framework similar to social liberalism.

conduct, which they enforce." Insurance is thus "one of the greatest
sources of regulatory authority over private life."[16] With regard to injury
law and physical examinations, the AFL opposed the reorganization of
employers' governing power in the form of actuarial gatekeeping. In
calling for state insurance rather than market insurance, the AFL hoped
to delink employment and insurance and thus alleviate incentives toward
employment discrimination.

In these events, workers and unions proposed state action to solve the
problems created by employers' responses to workmen's compensation.
In addition to lobbying and calling for legislative change, unions opposed
the extension of physical examination and employment discrimination
through strikes or threats of strikes. At the 1914 AFL convention Frank
Dujay called on AFL affiliates to "refus[e] to permit their membership to
stand for any kind of physical examination" tied to compensation laws.
This was an attempt to get unions to govern their members in such a way
that would shape employers' behavior. Dujay's proposal is another
reminder that unions were groups of people governing themselves, in the
sense of shaping each other. Union conventions and communications were
not a process of simply relaying pre-existing information but were part of a
constitutive process of building and maintaining collective opinion within
unions. The 1914 convention did not pass Dujay's resolution. Such a
policy would have amounted to a requirement for union members to strike
whenever an employer practiced physical examinations, at least examinations of union members. Even without Dujay's idea becoming AFL policy,
such strikes did occur. GE workers had threatened to strike, and another
delegate at the 1914 convention noted that there had been strikes over
physical examinations in New York in two different union locals.[17]

In 1916, United Mine Workers president John White articulated a
claim about freedom and dignity in opposition to "[c]ompulsory physical
examination." These examinations were "an interference with the personal life of the individual." White quoted another union official, Andrew
Furuseth, saying that industry would "scrap the whole human race if they
keep on" and continued that "we are in great danger of losing entirely the
human equation in industry, and with it the freedom of the individual."[18]

---

[16] Tom Baker and Jonathan Simon, "Embracing Risk," in *Embracing Risk: The Changing Culture of Insurance and Responsibility*, ed. Baker and Simon (Chicago: University of Chicago Press, 2002), 13. The same could (and should) be said of employment.

[17] American Federation of Labor, *Report of the Proceedings of the Thirty Fourth Annual Connection*, 824.

[18] White, "Compulsory Physical Examination," 3–4.

The UMW also evoked a duty for employers to care for employees: "The compensation law does not give to the operators the right to require men to pass a physical examination before securing employment. Furthermore, examinations would work a great injury and injustice to thousands of men employed in the mines of Illinois." The union declared in no uncertain terms that "the coal companies must employ the physically unfit as well as the physically fit, and that for us to take this position is working no injustice to any particular coal company, for the reason that every coal company will be required to do identically the same thing."[19] The union continued, "We hold that it is the duty of the industry to take care of its physical wrecks, as well as the physically fit, and that from a standpoint of humanity and justice it devolves upon those who have charge of the industry to see that this is done." District 12's president, Frank Farrington, informed members of this decision in an official circular titled plainly "Oppose Physical Examinations of Workers." The circular added that "we shall oppose with all the strength of our organization any attempt on the part of the coal operators to establish a practice which means that men who cannot pass a physical examination are to be discarded and scrapped as industrial wrecks."[20]

In 1917 the executive board of United Mine Workers District 12 in Illinois decided to "serve notice" to mining companies that the union disapproved of companies "requiring applicants for employment to pass a physical examination as a result of Illinois' workmen's compensation law. The Miners' Union will not tolerate the establishment of this practice in Illinois," the union wrote to the companies, "even though we may be put to the undesired necessity of ordering a strike to prevent it being done." Employers had introduced physical examinations to control one kind of uncertainty, uncertainty of costs as introduced by workmen's compensation laws. The UMW replied to mine owners by threatening another kind of uncertainty, disruption of business by strikes.[21]

Again in 1917, the same year as the United Mine Workers conflict with the Illinois mine owners, miners affiliated with the Industrial Workers of

[19] The union here displayed an attitude Ruth O'Brien noted in the early twentieth-century labor movement, that unions could create improvements for workers "without violating the individual rights of either workers or employers." Ruth O'Brien, *Workers' Paradox: The Republican Origins of New Deal Labor Policy, 1886–1935* (Chapel Hill: University of North Carolina Press, 1998), 8.

[20] F. Farrington, "Oppose Physical Examination of Workers," *United Mine Workers Journal* 28, no. 16 (August 16, 1917): 7.

[21] Farrington, "Oppose Physical Examination of Workers," 7.

the World struck in Bisbee, Arizona.[22] While the IWW and United Mine Workers were not on particularly friendly terms, the *United Mine Workers Journal* ran an article by Harold Callender portraying the strikers and their demands sympathetically. First on the list of demands was "abolition of the physical examination required now by the companies."[23]

The 1917 miners' strikes were not the last time unions took up the issue of physical examinations. Strikers listed the end to physical examinations in their demands in the 1919 steel strike in Pennsylvania, which led to the Great Steel Strike that shut down much of the steel industry.[24] In 1921 an IWW publication ran an article arguing that railroads had introduced both age limits and physical examination in response to railway workers' strikes as early as 1894. In 1922 the International Association of Machinists issued a nine-point platform of its political and social aims, which included "abolishing personal record and physical examination requirements."[25] In 1927 in Colorado

[22] For more on the history of the Bisbee strike, see Melvyn Dubofsky, *We Shall Be All: A History of the Industrial Workers of the World* (Chicago: Quadrangle Books, 1969), 10–11, 220–224.

[23] Harold Callender, "Copper Is King: Facts about the Bisbee Deportation," *United Mine Workers Journal* 28, no. 18 (August 30, 1917): 9. For another contemporary account of events in Bisbee, see "The Arizona Copper Strike," *The Outlook*, July 25, 1917, 466–468. During the Bisbee strike, a group of business and political officials put out a pamphlet supporting the Phelps Dodge Company. The pamphlet defended physical examinations and listed reasons for rejection that will be familiar to readers by now: "In order to protect the safety of employees as well as to guard the employers from undue loss through the operation of the Compensation Act and the Employers' Liability Law, all applicants for employment are required to pass a physical examination. No one afflicted with any contagious disease such as syphilis, tuberculosis, or chronic ulcers will be accepted. In addition, defective eyesight, or the loss of an eye, rupture, kidney disease, or heart disease, are causes for rejection. Men over 45 years of age are advised to correspond with mining companies before coming to the district." "Mining Conditions in Bisbee Arizona," in University of Arizona Library Special Collections, The Bisbee Deportation: A University of Arizona Web Exhibit, www.library.arizona.edu/exhibits/bisbee/docs/mincon.html, accessed March 1, 1914.

[24] Jacob Margolis, "The Present Crisis in the Steel Industry," *Socialist Review* 8, no. 1 (December 1919): 31. The strikers' demands were recognition of the union, collective bargaining, an eight-hour workday, an increase in pay, the abolition of physical examinations, and the introduction of a check-off system of dues collection. For another contemporary account that also mentions the end to physical examinations as a demand in this strike, see "Steel Strike Declared in Industry," *Locomotive Firemen and Enginemen's Magazine* 67, no. 6 (September 15, 1919): 10–12. For an overview of the steel strike, see David Brody, *Steelworkers in America: The Nonunion Era* (Cambridge, MA: Harvard University Press, 1960), 231–262.

[25] International Association of Machinists, "Declaration of Principles," *Machinists Monthly Journal* 34, no. 1 (January 1922): 5.

IWW–affiliated miners struck again, listing the end of physical examinations among their demands.[26]

A strike statement by the IWW miners appealed to the experience of physical examination, through what was probably intended as a pointed joke: "We do not propose to be stripped before going to work and then be stripped again when we get our paycheck. One of the strippings must be abolished now. We will tend to the other later."[27] The comparison may have been humorous to some readers, or it may have made them angry, or both. Miners were forced to partially or fully disrobe and to be handled by a doctor, one who was probably moving quickly and in dehumanizing fashion according to what Youngstown Sheet and Tube's company physician P. H. Kennedy had called "mass production methods."[28] Clearly, the IWW the miners found this objectionable.

All of these efforts failed. Employers did as they did. The machineries ground on. Whatever agency workers exercised collectively, it was not enough in this context to turn the storm of "progress." It remains to be seen if and when workers will in later contexts be able to do so. Yet within these failed efforts were cogent criticisms of the course of events. In the state-focused appeals of the AFL we can find support for a government that takes working-class well-being as a genuine priority. Within the UMW's strike threats we can find support for workers and unions as having their own governing authority over their workplaces and their lives. We can also find notions of human dignity.

I discuss this opposition to employers' use of medical examinations because it demonstrates that some people understood the consequences of what I have called the tyranny of the table, and understood it as a matter of injustice. Indeed, there were multiples kinds of claims about justice and injustice made within the labor movement. Some of those claims had been articulable under the tyranny of the trial, and many

---

[26] Jonathan Rees, "X, XX, and X-3: Spy Reports from the Colorado Fuel & Iron Company Archives," *Colorado Heritage* (Winter 2004): 28–41; 29–30.

[27] T. A. Rickard, "Labor Agitators, Mr. Roosevelt, and Others," *Mining and Scientific Press*, August 18, 1917, 242.

[28] P. H. Kennedy, "The Policy and Value of Pre-employment and Periodic Check-Up Physical Examinations," 18, "Clinic on Health in Industry, under the Auspices of the Mahoning Valley Industrial Council with the Trumbull County Manufacturers' Association, the Ohio Manufacturers' Association, and the National Association of Manufacturers," Youngstown Country Club, Youngstown, Ohio, October 2, 1940, National Association of Manufacturers records, Series 7, Industrial Relations Dept. Records, Hagley Museum and Library, Wilmington, DE.

others had not been. The IWW's objection to waged labor itself, for example, could not be turned into any legally recognizable claim in a courtroom. With the tyranny of the table, the law's already limited capacity to express justice claims became even more narrow. Compensation laws further depoliticized injury, employment, and the (de)valuation of human beings in dollar amounts. These laws placed markets, prices, and the ongoing pricing of persons even further from moral and political consideration.

The stakes were high for those people pushed out of employment. "Starvation," said industrial physician Frank Pedley in 1931, "is not a satisfactory treatment for the handicapped." Pullman's Thomas Crowder agreed with Pedley, saying: "A job is the thing the handicapped workman needs most."[29] Both conveniently overlooked their own roles in writing and implementing the plans that placed jobs out of reach of many people. Some of the people subjected to employment discrimination no doubt managed to find incomes somehow. While few people may have actually starved due to employment discrimination in response to compensation laws, what is certain is that those excluded from employment were exposed to harm as a result of their exclusion.[30]

Those pushed out of employment by employers' responses to liability law saw their lives worsened, and their responses to this worsening were largely private and individualized, with few public or collective resources made available to them. The people who got hired or remained employed would, to paraphrase Foucault, be "made to live" in various ways, as individuals and as a population. The people without work would be left to die, or not; the institutions governing injury were relatively indifferent to their fates.

In 1935, in response to the poverty and unemployment widespread in the Great Depression, the US Congress passed the Social Security Act, which created new ways for people to get access to money. The law

---

[29] United States Bureau of Labor Statistics, *Bulletin of the Bureau of Labor Statistics* 536 (1931), 251.

[30] It is not clear to me what should count as just a "few" when it comes to starvation. In 1931, there were twenty reported deaths from starvation in New York. Raymond Richards, *Closing the Door to Destitution: The Shaping of the Social Security Acts of the United States and New Zealand* (University Park: Pennsylvania University Press, 1994), 76. That year *Popular Science* magazine claimed "only a small number of people actually have died in this country from starvation," adding, "but millions are on short rations and may continue to do so for some time." "Grain Rots and Men Starve," *Popular Science* 119, no. 5 (November 1931): 70.

attenuated but maintained the link between employment and income, in that Social Security insurance payments derived in part from labor market performance – higher paid workers would receive higher Social Security payments – and in that Social Security applied only to some populations. People with disabilities were not included in the Social Security Act when it was passed and they remained excluded until 1956.[31] Thus many of the people pushed out of work by employers in response to compensation laws were initially ineligible for Social Security. They remained a population surplus to economic requirements, the possessors of labor power that many employers refused to buy.

To sum up the metaphorical balance sheet, workmen's compensation was straightforwardly fairer than the court-based system: it left fewer people with their injuries uncompensated, and so for many people it mitigated some of the poverty resulting from injury. The court-based system left too many people's injuries uncompensated. Any number of uncompensated injuries is too many. That compensation laws compensated more injuries should be considered an improvement in terms of fairness regarding distribution of wealth and social costs. At the same time, compensation laws were poorer in meaning. They narrowed the legal valuation of persons, injuries, and experiences. This restriction, which I have called the moral thinning of injury, impoverished the law's conception of injury and of humanity. It is surely more just that an injured employee receives compensation than not. It is also surely more just that human beings and human losses be conceptualized and valued within our legal system as more than simply economic units. If our options are constrained to two unfair and inhumane systems of law, then workmen's compensation is the better option. But surely if history is to have any meaningful place in how we think about our society, one of its roles

---

[31] Richard Verville, *War, Politics, and Philanthropy: The History of Rehabilitation Medicine* (Lanham: University Press of America, 2009), 143–144. See also Deborah A. Stone, *The Disabled State* (Philadelphia: Temple University Press, 1984), 68–71. Historian Alan Dawley has argued that the Roosevelt administration brought about something "truly new" in 1935, managing via the Social Security Act and similar legislation to reconcile "capitalism and social reform." Alan Dawley, *Struggles for Justice: Social Responsibility and the Liberal State* (Cambridge, MA: Harvard University Press, 1991), 378. Similarly, Roy Lubove called the Social Security Act of 1935 "a revolution in American social welfare." Roy Lubove, *The Struggle for Social Security, 1900–1935*, 2nd ed. (Pittsburgh: University of Pittsburgh Press, 1986), 179. The exclusion of people with disabilities does not support these enthusiastic assessments.

should be to trouble our willingness to merely settle for the better of two unfair and inhumane options.[32]

As E. P. Thompson once put it, "[t]he injury which advanced industrial capitalism did, and which the market society did, was to define human relations as being primarily economic."[33] This was part of capitalism's pervasive "tendency to reduce all human relationships to economic definitions."[34] That reduction, at least when applied to human beings, is a denial of recognition. This is what compensation laws did. Compensation laws were, to use another phrase of Thompson's, "a product of a political economy which diminished human reciprocities to the wages-nexus."[35] Compensation laws also helped actively produce that diminishment of humanity. As political theorist Nicos Poulantzas has put it, "the body is not simply a biological entity, but a political institution."[36] Compensation laws changed the institution of the working-class body, formatting it not as a political institution (let alone as a human being) but as a market institution. These laws depoliticized employment, employee injury, and employment discrimination. Compensation laws were in one sense a government intrusion in the market, policy regulating the economy. They

---

[32] Leon Fink's suggestion that we rename the Progressive Era "the Long Gilded Age" is a salutary one that encourages us not to settle, or at least to be more aware and less complacent when we do so. Leon Fink, *The Long Gilded Age: American Capitalism and the Lessons of a New World Order* (Philadelphia: University of Pennsylvania Press, 2014). For other work that similarly argues that there is little that is meaningfully progressive about the Progressive Era, see Shelton Stromquist, *Reinventing "The People": The Progressive Movement, the Class Problem, and the Origins of Modern Liberalism* (Urbana: University of Illinois Press, 2006), and David Huyssen, *Progressive Inequality: Rich and Poor in New York, 1890–1920* (Cambridge, MA: Harvard University Press, 2014).

[33] Michael Merrill, "An Interview with E. P. Thompson," *Radical History Review*, no. 12 (Fall 1976): 4–25.

[34] E. P. Thompson, "The Peculiarities of the English," *Socialist Register* 2 (1965): 311–362, 356.

[35] E. P. Thompson, "The Moral Economy of the English Crowed in the Eighteenth Century," in E. P. Thompson, *Customs in Common: Studies in Traditional Popular Culture* (London: Merlin Press, 1991), 185–258; 258. Thompson's phrase was not intended as about employee injury law; it was about how historians misunderstood bread riots. The phrase is apt, however, for thinking about compensation laws, no doubt because Thompson meant the point as a combination of historiographic criticism and social criticism. Thompson objected to what he considered an economistic intellectual framework that conceded too much to the culture of capitalism. Margaret Radin calls that kind of framework "universal commodification." Margaret Jane Radin, *Contested Commodities: The Trouble with Trade in Sex, Children, Body Parts, and Other Things* (Cambridge, MA: Harvard University Press, 2001), 1–15.

[36] Nicos Poulantzas, *State, Power, Socialism* (London: New Left Books, 1978), 29.

were in another sense law shoring up the market, preserving the economy, further reducing the legal space for any ways of valuing human beings other than in the monetary values set by employers. This is to say, compensation extended the reach of the market, making the United States into even more of a market society. It is repugnant that within that society life and limb were, in Edward Glackin's words, "too cheap." Equally repugnant is the social compulsion to price lives and limbs at all.

Coda

Narrative, Machinery, Law

Over the years as I have discussed my work with friends, colleagues, and students, I have often been asked what improvements might be made to the law to remedy or at least mitigate the uglier parts of the story my book tells. Any such improvements should seek to promote both justice as recognition and justice as distribution. In terms of justice as recognition, the law could require victim impact panels in the event of every injury, requiring the presence of every company official in the chain of command connected to the injury in question: from the shift supervisor to the plant manager to the company's CEO and board of directors. These panels would make them bear some inconvenience, and more importantly make them sit and hear the human truths of injury. Those impact panels could be televised as well. This public airing would allow more room in the law for treating the injured and their experiences with the gravity and dignity they deserve, more room for attending to human suffering and singularity.

This matters because injuries create losses that are non-fungible. These losses fit poorly if at all into a notion of financial compensation. While of course it is better that those who suffer receive money than that they do not, at some fundamental level their losses are noncompensable.[1] Physician, reformer, and social investigator Alice Hamilton highlighted the

---

[1] Barbara Welke discusses the non-fungible human costs of accidents in Barbra Young Welke, "The Cowboy Suit Tragedy: Spreading Risk, Owning Hazard in the Modern American Consumer Economy," *Journal of American History* 1, no. 1 (June 2014): 97–121, and Barbara Young Welke, "Owning Hazard: A Tragedy," *UC Irvine Law Review* 1, no. 3 (September 2011): 693–771.

noncompensability of injuries in her memoir reflecting on her involvement in occupational health in the early twentieth century: "There is
something strange in speaking of 'accident and sickness compensation.'
What could 'compensate' anyone for an amputated leg or a paralyzed leg,
or even an attack of lead colic, to say nothing of the loss of a husband or
son?"[2] Journalist and reform advocate William Hard expressed a similar
sentiment in 1910:

For the agony of the crushed arm, for the torment of the scorched body ... and for
the whole hideous host of things like them, following upon the half million
accidents that happen to American workmen every year, there can be no compensation. Nor can there be compensation for what follows the telling of the tale by
some fellow-workman at the door of his stricken comrade's home.... We cannot
translate into dollars and cents the infinite torture, physical and mental, of
America's 500,000 annual industrial accidents.[3]

We cannot translate, because recognition cannot be expressed in a dollar
amount. When it comes to injury and loss, justice as recognition requires
stories.[4]

---

[2] Alice Hamilton, *Exploring the Dangerous Trades: The Autobiography of Alice Hamilton*
(Boston: Northeastern University Press, 1985), 114.
[3] William Hard, *Injured in the Course of Duty* (New York: Ridgway Company, 1910), 38.
[4] Thomas Crowder's life offers a case in point. He told stories to grieve for the loss of his
wife, Grace Meigs Crowder, to help his children grieve for their mother, and to facilitate a
relationship between the children and their aunts. In his essay "A Place for Stories,"
historian William Cronon argues that stories are central to the writing of history and to
human social life. Storytelling is the "necessary core" of history writing. William Cronon,
"A Place for Stories: Nature, History, and Narrative," *Journal of American History* 78,
no. 4 (March 1992): 1347–1376, 1349. Narrative, Cronon argues, "is fundamental to the
way we humans organize our experience" (p. 1368). The moral philosopher Alasdair
MacIntyre would agree, arguing that human life is fundamentally narrative in character,
which is to say that a non-narrative description of human life or lives leaves out everything
important about people. To put it another way, for MacIntyre, human life is comprehensible as such only through narrative. A non-narrative life would not be recognizable as
human life. See Alasdair MacIntyre, *After Virtue: A Study in Moral Theory* (Notre Dame:
University of Notre Dame Press, 1981), 204–225. See also Richard Rorty, *Truth and
Progress: Philosophical Papers*, vol. 3 (Cambridge: Cambridge University Press, 1998),
172. Rorty writes that "novels rather than moral treatises are the most useful vehicles of
moral education" (p. 12). For Cronon stories are also key to moral reflection: "narratives
remain our chief moral compass in the world." Cronon, "A Place for Stories," 1375. This
means as well that for Cronon history is always a moral discipline, a discipline where
morality is inextricably bound up with what historians do. History has a "moral center,"
one inextricable from the role of narrative in the discipline. Cronon, "A Place for Stories,"
1370. This is not to say that all historians share the same moral outlook – indeed,
historians disagree greatly about the moral content of the field; arguably, that disagreement is part of what constitutes the field. The point, rather, is that history is always in part
a moral enterprise of some sort.

While there were a great many limits to what I have referred to as the tyranny of the trial, that system of employee injury law permitted stories about injury, stories woven with values beyond the pecuniary, stories that made claims about injury as a possible moral and political wrong. That system did not go far enough in what it allowed to be subject to dispute, but the loss of what it did allow should trouble us. In the court-based system of employee injury law, people could say things like *after my injuries I feel I am not myself, I fear for my future, I worry that no one will ever love me or marry me, and this feels like a blow to my dignity.* They could say, *I can't hug my children anymore.* They could say, *my hands were part of me. I used to play piano.* They could say, in effect, *my self-concept has been damaged, this harm not only has reduced my earning ability but also has hurt me as a human being, it has hurt me by changing the ways I used to live my life and to regard myself and so give meaning to myself: it has hurt my understanding of myself as a self.* They could say as well, *I suffered. My fingers were caught between the steam rollers, the bones crushed, the skin burnt off, the muscle cooked. I smelled my own flesh cooking. I was trapped there for fifteen minutes.* All of these facets of employee injury were real in people's lives. They remain so. Employee injury law could be reformed to permit them more of a legal life and hence more social visibility.

Compensation laws could be reformed to create greater distributive justice as well. Employee injury law could provide lifetime pensions to the injured, at a living wage. That living wage could be set at some genuinely generous payment level, such as the salary of the highest paid employee of an enterprise. In addition, the government could provide a universal basic income set at a living wage, a job guarantee, and universal healthcare; all of these steps would reduce the pressures on employees to obey employers' orders at the risk of their own safety. The government could also offer full protection from employer retaliation for employees who report injuries, including retaliation in the form of deportation of undocumented immigrants (this could be done by granting immunity to any immigration proceedings for people reporting workplace injuries; this could also be done by ending deportation).

These changes may seem utopian, in part because they require fundamental changes to power relations in our society. For example, a victim impact panel for employee injury would require employees to have protection from firing and retaliation, which would mean carving out exceptions to at-will employment – or, better, ending it altogether. I am, frankly, pessimistic that any of these changes would be implemented, at least without massive social upheaval. Part of my point in suggesting these changes has been to note that the problems in employee injury law are to an important extent not solvable within the narrow scope of employee injury law, because employee injury law is further down the assembly line within the machinery of society. The real changes we need are further up the line, and in the design of the social machinery.

I want to also note the limits of storytelling as justice: Samuel Howard wrote his story of suffering in the Cherry Mine disaster, while he watched his younger brother die and then died himself. Greater recognition of losses like that of Howard and his family would be an improvement, but far better would be to hold those responsible accountable; better still would be to create an economy that does not kill. That change too would require significant redesign of the machinery of society.

MACHINERY

As I have written this book I have repeatedly returned to a passage from Frank Norris's 1902 short story "A Deal in Wheat." Norris described people living through "a crisis that at any moment might culminate in tragedy." Financial ruin led one of these people to a bleak epiphany: "Dimly he began to see the significance of things. Caught once in the cogs and wheels of a great and terrible engine, he had seen – none better – its workings."[5] It is not necessarily true that those ground under history's wheels better understand the machinery of history. I have experienced something like the economic insecurity Norris described, having repeatedly been caught in the great and terrible engines of various labor markets, pulled between the cogs of landlords and the wheels of employers. I have personal and familial experience with employee injury. I experienced harm as well in writing this book. To borrow the title of a Jeanette Winterson novel, this is a book written on the body; perhaps all books are. I wrote the book in part as a requirement of my job, and, like most jobs, this one has marked my body and my life – early signs of carpal tunnel from too much typing, back pain from prolonged sitting, and so on. These experiences did not provide me with insight. For the most part, I felt more than thought about these experiences, and in getting on with my life I swallowed most of those feelings, trying to put those experiences behind me. It was only when I was quite far into this book that

---

[5] Frank Norris, *A Deal in Wheat and Other Stories of the New and Old West* (New York: Doubleday Page, 1903), 25.

I "dimly ... began to see the significance" of occupational safety and health issues in my own life.

We live in "a great and terrible engine" that has, over and over again, predictably, caught and ground human lives in its "cogs and wheels." The catching and grinding of human beings in our society has taken many forms, including employment discrimination and literal harm to people's bodies. The terrible engine has changed over time. Some cogs wore out and were replaced; some new parts were added. Injury law reform reorganized but did not repurpose this machinery. The catching and grinding continued – innovated but not interrupted.[6] Further, the machinery of our society and the effects of that machinery are hidden by a curtain. Taking a long look behind that curtain helps us see that revising employee injury law can achieve only limited justice.

Another literary passage I returned to while writing this book is from John Steinbeck's *Grapes of Wrath*. This passage illustrates the understanding of agency and structure that informs this book. A farmer facing eviction after foreclosure confronted the tractor driver knocking down foreclosed houses. When the farmer threatened to shoot him, the tractor driver responded by invoking the threat of hanging. If the farmer used his weapon, other men with weapons – namely, the police – would come, and the weapon of the hangman's noose would eventually be used against the

---

[6] As Christopher Tomlins writes, in history there are many "repetitive regularities." Christopher Tomlins, "After Critical Legal History: Scope, Scale, Structure," *Annual Review of Law and Social Science* 8, no. 1 (December 2012): 31–68; 36. These regularities mean, among other things, that contingency has limited use as a conceptual tool for historical explanation. It is possible that multiple events contingently take the same shape, but why they take the same rather than a different shape is at least some of the time better explained by resort to a concept of social structure, rather than contingency. Moishe Postone makes a similar point about the limits of the concepts of both agency and contingency for historical explanation. Patterns of social practice like those Tomlins calls repetitive regularities "cannot convincingly be explained in local and contingent terms. They strongly suggest the existence of general structural constraints on political, social, and economic decisions, as well as dynamic forces not fully subject to political control." Moishe Postone, "The Current Crisis and the Anachronism of Value: A Marxian Reading," *Continental Thought & Theory* 1, no. 4 (October 2017): 38–54, 41. For a history of how US academics came to turn away from examining structure in ways akin to what Postone discusses, see Daniel T. Rodgers, *Age of Fracture* (Cambridge, MA: Belknap Press, 2010). I have sought to examine employee injuries as one such regularity, and to take that regularity as symbol for the social structures that produce those injuries and their (mis) handling by law. I have been inspired as well by Marcus Rediker's work on slave ships, which took those ships both as sites of terrible brutality without which the system of slavery could not exist and as symbols of slavery as a whole. See Marcus Rediker, *The Slave Ship: A Human History* (New York: Viking, 2007).

farmer. The gun and the noose were only two of the three weapons in the scene. The third was the tractor, though the law would not call the tractor driver's actions violence.

The tractor driver tried to absolve himself to the farmer: "It's not me. There's nothing I can do. I'll lose my job if I don't do it." Tractor drivers are fungible, any one will do. So are the police that the tractor driver invoked. They, like the driver, also need paychecks. Seeking an individual agent to blame, the farmer asked, "Who gave you orders? I'll go after him. He's the one to kill." "You're wrong," replied the driver. "He got his orders from the bank." Fungibility scales upward. A bank can get a new president. The driver continued, "Maybe there's nobody to shoot. Maybe the thing isn't men at all."[7] The problems facing Steinbeck's farmer were not simply a matter of unsympathetic individuals. The problem was bigger and more diffuse.

If a bank or a finance company owned the land, the owner man said, The Bank – or the Company – needs – wants – insists – must have – as though the Bank or the Company were a monster, with thought and feeling, which had ensnared them.... We're sorry. It's not us. It's the monster. The bank isn't like a man.... The bank is something else than men. It happens that every man in a bank hates what the bank does, and yet the bank does it. The bank is something more than men, I tell you. It's the monster. Men made it, but they can't control it.[8]

As depicted here, the American economy and society had a kind of independent and impersonal movement in which numerous people took part, while experiencing their participation as compelled by collective social practices with no single directing center. Their actions were the result of institutional and structural pressures rather than individual character or agency. In capitalism people live out roles in a kind of social machinery. Some push on others who push on others who push on others, cogs and wheels in a great and terrible engine.

To change the metaphor from machinery to drama, the actors in the story my book tells were playing parts in a script, a social drama they didn't write. Marx refers at one point to individuals as character-masks.

---

[7] John Steinbeck, *The Grapes of Wrath* (New York: Penguin, 2006), 38. For a similar situation involving a railroad conductor compelled to enforce Jim Crow laws, see Barbara Young Welke, *Recasting American Liberty: Gender, Race, Law, and the Railroad Revolution, 1865–1920* (New York: Cambridge University Press, 2001), 369–370. For a theoretical discussion of agency and its limits for historical scholarship, see Walter Johnson, "On Agency," *Journal of Social History* 37, no. 1 (Autumn 2003): 113–124.

[8] Steinbeck, *The Grapes of Wrath*, 36.

The idea is that while an individual who plays Hamlet may put his or her idiosyncratic spin on that part, the part is the part. Whatever variations the actor introduces, an actor playing Hamlet is still playing the part of Hamlet. Similarly, a social actor playing out the social role of employer is playing the role of an employer despite any individual flourishes they bring to the part. They didn't write the macro-level script. Capitalism writes the script, market dependency directs the play.[9] Living this way could shape the subjectivity – the moral character – of the people involved. With enough repetition, the part an actor plays can begin to shape the person of the actor. To quote Steinbeck again:

Some of the owner men were kind because they hated what they had to do, and some of them were angry because they hated to be cruel, and some of them were cold because they had long ago found that one could not be an owner unless one were cold. And all of them were caught in something larger than themselves. Some of them hated the mathematics that drove them, and some were afraid, and some worshipped the mathematics because it provided a refuge from thought and from feeling.[10]

While some people had more reach than others, everyone's scope of conscious action and immediate influence was limited, and everyone

---

[9] I am here describing capitalism as a social totality, an entity wherein the individual people who compose it are subjected to that entity. The famous television trope of the so-called Mexican Standoff – wherein three or more people face off pointing guns at each other – and a traffic jam on the highway both partially illustrate the concept of social totality. These are situations that in a sense consist of individuals, yet those individuals act in relationship to each other in ways that shape each other's behavior such that no individual can, through individual action alone, exit the situation. For a useful overview of the concept of totality, see Lars Heitmann, "Society as 'Totality': On the Negative-Dialectical Presentation of Capitalist Socialization," in *The Sage Handbook of Frankfurt School Critical Theory*, vol. 2, ed. Beverley Best, Werner Bonefeld, and Chris O'Kane (London: Sage Publications, 2018), 589–606. I discuss the relationship between law and capitalism, and the importance of the concept of totality to understanding that relationship, in Nate Holdren, "Some Hasty Musings on Matters Legal and Economic," *Legal Form*, https://legalform.blog/2018/11/18/some-hasty-musings-on-matters-legal-and-economic-nate-holdren/, accessed November 18, 2018.

[10] This passage can be read as depicting the effects of morally thin vocabularies on people in low-level positions of institutional power. The study of such people can be considered what historian Steven Zdatny has called "history from the middle up." Steven Zdatny, *The Politics of Survival: Artisans in Twentieth-Century France* (Oxford: Oxford University Press, 1990), ix. As the spatial term "middle" indicates, these actors exist between the operations of top-down and bottom-up operations of power. Karen Ho's *Liquidated* is an example of how this kind of study can illuminate economic life. Study of these actors demonstrates that economic life "is infused with the organizational strategies" of the social actors who simultaneously make and "are subject to the market." Karen Ho, *Liquidated: An Ethnography of Wall Street* (Durham: Duke University Press, 2009), 6.

had to find ways to live with their role. Thomas Crowder was one of the many tractor drivers in the processes this book has described, answering to various owner men compelled by market imperatives. As long as market imperatives remain the driving force, the animating logic to the patterns in our society, violent injustice of one kind or another will follow, whether the weapon used is a tractor or a gun or a typewriter.

LAW

Let us follow "the owner of money and the owner of labour-power" out of the "noisy sphere" of the market, wrote Karl Marx at a key juncture in *Capital*, and proceed to "the hidden abode of production on whose threshold there hangs the notice 'No admittance except on business.'" On leaving the labor market, "the money-owner now strides out in front as a capitalist; the possessor of labour-power follows as his worker." The employee "is timid and holds back, like someone who has brought his own hide to market and now has nothing else to expect but – a tanning." This book has scrutinized the point of contact between production and market, the place where Marx's capitalist hung the sign "No admittance except on business."[11] This notice expressed the governing power of employers in multiple ways. Legal change transformed the ways employers commodified people and created newly impersonal and market-based ways of talking about "tanning," the injuries endured by many wage earners. As a result, Marx's notice and the governing power behind it changed as well. What did not change, however, was what Marx called "the general law of capitalist accumulation." In capitalism, the accumulation of wealth is "at the same time accumulation of misery."[12] The subordination of society to capitalism's simultaneous accumulation of wealth and misery has been carried out by law.

[11] Marx, *Capital*, vol. 1, 280.
[12] Misery of various kinds is woven in to capitalism, making the accumulation of wealth and the accumulation of misery as inextricable from each other as two sides of a coin. Marx, *Capital*, vol. 1, 799–800. See also Chris O'Kane, "On the Development of the Critique of Political Economy as a Critical Social Theory of Economic Objectivity," *Historical Materialism* 26, no. 1 (2018): 175–193; Chris O'Kane, "'Society Maintains Itself Despite All the Catastrophes That May Eventuate': Critical Theory, Negative Totality, and Crisis," *Constellations* 25, no. 2 (June 2018): 287–301.

The violence and injustice this book has described have been law's violence, law's injustice.[13] All of the building blocks of the social processes described in this story have been legally constituted, from the money to the authority to the persons. In Christopher Tomlins's words, law is key to "the allocation of directive authority over the deployment of labor power in the employment relationship."[14] Law constitutes both the authority of some people to render others objects of instrumental use and the range of socially allowed and disallowed forms of that use. The conditions under which buyers and sellers encounter one another in markets are created, maintained, and remade by law. This includes the buyers and sellers of labor power. Furthermore, law sets the terms according to which capitalists can use labor power after its purchase. And law approves and naturalizes the expectations that people are objects of use.

Compensation laws, then, were not primarily a matter of reigning in the market, subordinating the economy to society and so reducing injustice. They stabilized the market, organizing and redistributing injustice. Compensation laws protected society from the market, but that protection drew on market ways of thinking and valuing – the abstractions of commodification – and extended those abstractions, shrinking the legal space for other ways of valuing working-class people. In the end, compensation laws regularized the commodification of those people. That is,

---

[13] For a meditation on law and violence, see Robert Cover, "Violence and the Word," *Yale Law Journal* 95, no. 8 (July 1986): 1601–1629. I agree with Cover that law "depends upon the social practice of violence for its efficacy" (p. 1613). In effect, Cover's point is that much of the time law is violence, and so understanding law requires understanding the centrality of violence to law, and the violence law perpetrates. Part of my point in this book has been to suggest a similarly close relationship between capitalism and violence, and between capitalism and legality. I disagree, however, with Cover's assertion that "law is the attempt to build future worlds" (p. 1602, note 2). For a counterpoint in the form of a poem, see Bertolt Brecht, "Song of the Courts," in *The Collected Poems of Bertolt Brecht*, ed. and trans. Tom Kuhn and David Constantine (New York: Liveright, 2018), 401. At least within capitalism, law is the attempt to maintain this world and prevent alternative futures. I discuss these matters in Holdren, "Some Hasty Musings on Matters Legal and Economic." I hold out more hope than Cover seemed to, at least as expressed in "Violence and the Word," that a human society without violence is possible. See also the discussion of violence and of Cover in Ian Haney López, *White by Law: The Legal Construction of Race*, revised ed. (New York: New York University Press, 2006), 85.

[14] Christopher Tomlins, "Subordination, Authority, Law: Subjects in Labor History," *International Labor and Working-Class History*, no. 47 (Spring 1995): 56–90, 68. See also Christopher Tomlins, "The State, the Unions, and the Critical Synthesis in Labor Law History: A 25-Year Retrospect," *Labor History* 54, no. 2 (2013): 208–221.

compensation laws commodified working-class people to protect society from the corrosive effects that market practices could have on markets themselves. Hence, rather than the double movement of market harming society and society reacting against the market, compensation laws were a double movement of market-dependent society becoming unstable then stabilizing itself. They were the self-protection, through law, of market society.

As I have written this book, the present, and even more so the future, has been worrisome. Quite simply, I fear for my children and the grandchildren I hope to have. Peter Frase has recently sketched out some futures worth fearing, some of them catastrophically dystopian, apocalyptic futures full of crashes and home to terrible human drama at a large scale.[15] Quietly dystopian futures stand as another threat: quiet because of an enforced silence, anomic alienated futures empty of meaning and possessed of inhuman indifference. Each of these futures is in a sense already the present for some people in the world. Historical time and human society are woven from multiple strands. Benjamin's angel has seen so many braided threads of human inhumanity. This has been our history, it is our present. It could stop being our future.

Law can at best mitigate the harms to individual persons, and often law serves to regulate – to standardize, render predictable and stable – and to legitimize the production, distribution, and consumption of new human raw material. One human cog breaks, another is led to fill their place, and many are waiting within the reserve army of labor. And so while there are clearly some better and worse versions of capitalism possible, we should not lower our aspirations to merely a better capitalism. We must bide our time, to be sure, and in doing so we will be tempted both to settle and to forget that we are settling. The horizons of our imagination can shrink so that we become like the proverbial frog in the well who thinks the sky is no bigger than the well's mouth. We need to be aware of that pressure on our imaginations, much of that pressure coming from the law, so we can maintain our aspiration to go beyond settling for those needs and rights that are merely basic. More bread, better compensation for injury, but, at least in the long term, roses too – and a society that does not harm and kill and does not measure human worth through inhumane mechanisms. Then perhaps

---

[15] Peter Frase, *Four Futures* (London: Verso, 2016).

the storm might end, Benjamin's angel could rest, stop fearing the future and begin to truly mourn the dead. In the words of Steinbeck's farmer: "We all got to figure. There's some way to stop this. It's not like lightning or earthquakes. We've got a bad thing made by men, and by God that's something we can change."[16]

---

[16] Steinbeck, *Grapes of Wrath*, 38.

Index

AAIPS, 224, 229. *See* American Association of Industrial Physicians and Surgeons
ability/disability, 46
actuarial self-awareness, 108
Addams, Jane, 244
Aetna, as under-compensating company, 213
age discrimination, 182–183
aggregation
  of injuries, 62, 81
  in injury law, 66
agricultural work, exclusion in compensation law, 177
Alexander, E. D., 195
Allen, Newton, 54
Allen, Ora, 55
Althusser, Louis, 211
ambulance chasers, 69
American Association of Industrial Physicians and Surgeons (AAIPS), 224, 229
American Association for Labor Legislation, 56
American Economics Association, 56
American Federation of Labor
  appeals of, 263
  compensation laws supported by, 111
  court-based injury law as preference, 105
  on discrimination against married men, 181
  on discrimination by self-insurers, 198
  opposition to medical exams, 257
  support for state monopoly insurance, 260

American Mining Congress, on compensation legislation, 123
American Red Cross
  Cherry mine relief as template, 125
  injury outlook on, 88
American Steel and Wire Company, lawsuits against, 95
Anderson, Elizabeth, 7
anti-tuberculosis efforts, 242
Asher, Robert, 103
assumption of risk rule, 20
Atherton, Charles, 132
attorneys. *See* lawyers
at-will employment, 203

Badger, Walter, 214
Bagehot, Walter
  Economic Studies, 91
Bailiff, Mrs. Thomas, 131
Baker, Ella, 9, 12
Baker, Tom, 201, 204, 206, 217, 259
Barker, A. P., 43
battle fatalities, comparison with, 77
Beck, Ulrich, 204
Belick, Estella, 29
Bellamy, Paul
  on actuarial self-awareness, 108
  on compensation laws, 95
  on lawsuit outcomes, 79, 95
benefit-sharing dependents, 202
Benjamin, Walter, 2, 17, 118, 132, 277
Berman, David, 67
Between the World and Me (Coates), 3

Bickle, Ernest, 126
biopolitics, 16
  capitalist needs reflected in, 87
  Foucault on, 65
  recognition vs., 74, 78
  reformers' views on, 255
  state's well-being and, 85
Bisbee strike (1917), 262
Blaine, John, 69
Blake, William, 133
Blom, Nettie
  indignity suffered by, 35
  injury of, 1
  lawsuit of, 4, 8, 25
Blumenthal, Susanna, 36
body parts, dollar value of, 5
body retrieval/funerals, 126
boundary struggles, 9
Bouvier, John, 40
Bowen, Mrs. Joseph T., 244
Bowen, Louise de Koven, 244
Boyd, James Harrington
  on employer negligence, 79
  on "human conservation", 87
  on industrial hazard exposure, 64
  on injury/fatality statistics, 76
  on uncompensated injuries, 80
Boydston, Jeanne
  Home and Work, 92
Branconnier, Eugene
  compensation granted to, 152
  distributive justice for, 156
  Travelers response to, 214
Brand, James, 60
Bureau of Labor Statistics
  on employee fatalities in 2001, 132
  on goggles at Pullman, 163
Burhop, W. H., 195
Burke, Thomas, 122
Burnstein, Daniel, 241
business-protection perspective, 84, 93
Buswell, Henry, 37

California Supreme Court, Liptak decision,
  162
Callahan, F. R., 164
Callender, Harold, 262
Capital: A Critique of Political Economy
  (Marx), 275
capitalism, 7, 275
  at-will employment in, 203

on class conflict, 7
  compensation as minimal impact on, 175
  on human relationships as economic, 266
  human roles in, 274
  self-interest in, 200
capitalists
  risk avoidance by, 101
  trade associations of, 109
*Care and Education of Crippled Children in
  the United States* (Reeves), 139
Carlin, Kathryn
  award for injuries, 4, 28
  lawsuit of, 8
Carry, E. F., 162–163, 247
Central Railroad, 31
Central Railroad v. Richards, 32
Cherry Mine fire, 119
  administrative matter vs. murder?, 132
  diary of deceased miner(s), 127–128
  family members of, 119
  names of deceased, 129
  surviving miners, 128
Cherry Relief Commission
  control over women/families, 125
  relief provided by, 120, 124
Chicago Daily News, on ironworker
  accidents, 63, 78
Chicago packinghouse workers, 25
Chicago Tuberculosis Institute
  "A Plan of Examination of Employees for
    Tuberculosis", 241–242
  watchwords for, 252
Chicago, Milwaukee and St. Paul Railroad,
  127, 133
Chicago, Rock Island and Pacific Railroad,
  26
children, wage-earning employment at age
  fourteen, 126
Church, R. W., 121
civic obligation, 76
Clark, Irving
  on formation of industrial medicine, 242
  on medical exam speed, 238
Clark, John Bates, 102
class conflict, 105
class relationships, 7
Coates, Ta-Nehisi, 3
Cole, Thomas R., 182
collective thought, 55
collectivity, 65
commensurability, 114

commodification, 16, 33–34
  artificial/genuine, 50
  as core of employee injury law, 20
  facets of, 114
  incomplete, 149
  of people, 92
  Radin on, 36
  risk as factor in, 205
  universal, 173
  in workmen's compensation, 113
commodities, Marx on, 6
Commons, John R.
  as academic, 56
  on safety incentives, 189
compensable injury risk, 230
compensation laws. *See* workmen's
    compensation
compensation policy formation, 68
Conference Board of Physicians in Industry,
    240
Conlon, P. J., 257
Connor, Jeremiah, 213, 218, 252
consciousness, 9
contingency, 12, 272
contracts
  implicit in employment, 23
  insurance in, 66
  as outcome of protracted struggle, 37
contributory negligence rule, 20
Conyngton, Mary, 179
Cook, Eli, 219
Cooley, Thomas, 37
corporate restructuring/merging
  employee injury/fatality exposure from,
    102
  as risk avoidance, 100, 108
court-based system, 36, 78
Cover, Robert, 276
Crane Company, medical screening as
    competitive requirement, 206–207
Crawford, David, 165, 215
Cronon, William, 269
Crowder, Grace Meigs, 251, 269
Crowder, Thomas
  awareness of actions, 249, 251, 257
  background of, 251–252
  on economics of medical exams, 227
  on job needs of handicapped workers,
    249, 264
  market imperatives as driver for, 275
  rejection criteria of, 232

roles in AAIPS, 229
  on sleeping car ventilation, 243
  storytelling of, 269
  survey of Pullman physicians, 231

Dawley, Alan, 110, 265
Dawson, Miles
  business-protection perspective of, 93
  on economics of injury, 85
  as legal counsel to striking garment
    workers, 69, 86
  on liability insurance costs, 96
  on waste in court-based injury law, 69, 95
"Deal in Wheat" (Norris), 271
DeArmand, J. A., 42, 44
death benefits, 181
"Death Calendar in Industry for Allegheny
    County", 61
defects/impairments. *See also* disability/
    disabilities
  defects screened for, 228, 231, 236
  definition of, 176, 210, 230
  exclusion criteria, 231
Department of Labor, 107
depression of 1893, corporate restructuring/
    merging as response to, 100
diary, of Samuel Howard, 127–128
disability/disabilities, 138. *See also* disabled
    workers; impairment, definition of
  contemporary view of, 138
  gender differences in connotations, 46
  as social and political condition, 47
  as socially constructed marginalization, 47
  ubiquity in Progressive Era, 138–139
disabled workers
  discrimination
    financially incentivized, 173
    moral reservations about, 170
    at Pullman Corporation, 159–166
    wage, 152, 155
  employment prospects for, 138–140, 168
  equality of, 158
  marginalization/exclusion of, 149–151
  segregation of, 150
  Social Security exclusion of, 265
  starvation of, 264
  as surplus population, 256
  waiving rights to compensation, 170, 172
discrimination. *See also under* insurance
  against disabled workers. *See under*
    disabled workers

discrimination. (cont.)
  against married men, 179, 182
  age, 182–183
  family size as factor in, 181, 188
  legitimating, 209
  wage. *See* wage discrimination
disfigurement, masculine/feminine, 49
distributive injustice, 34
domestic work, exclusion in compensation
    law, 177–178
Dowling, Robert E., 258
Downey, E. H.
  on compensable injuries, 25
  History of Labor Legislation in Iowa, 76
  on no-fault accidents, 79
  on uncompensated injuries, 80
Doyle, Louis, 214
Duffy, T. J., 198
Dujay, Frank, 199, 258, 260

Earling, Albert J., 120
Eastman, Crystal
  biopolitical policies advocated by, 255
  on compensable injuries, 25
  condescension of, 58
  on cost of workplace injuries, 72
  "Death Calendar in Industry for
      Allegheny County", 61
  on justice as recognition, 74
  on no-fault accidents, 79
  on statistics, 67
  "Temper of the Workers under Trial", 53
  on uncompensated injuries, 80
  work of, 57–60
  Work-Accidents and the Law, 53, 60
  working-class treatment by, 115
Economic Studies (Bagehot), 91
economic/moral facets, 19
economy, non-lethal, 271
Eisner, Marc, 101
Electrical Alliance (union), 199
Elliott, Sarah Barnwell, 121
Ely, Richard, 91
Empire Companies, 170
employees
  coercion of, 7
  as commodities, 226
  as financial risk, 180
  instrumentalization of, 12
  protection from retaliation, 270
  role of, 10

employer–employee cooperation, 103
employers
  accountability requirements for, 271
  as gatekeepers of risk pools, 175, 215
  lawsuit outcomes, 95
  legal defenses of, 20, 25, 81, 98
  liability insurance costs, 96
employing class, working class vs., 106
employment, 51
  at-will, 203
  commodification. *See* commodification
  as contractual, 37
  damages from
    non-pecuniary, 26, 39
    pecuniary, 25
  distributive injustice, 34–36
  legal assumptions about, 19–24
  moral logic, 36
  as political, 209
  as voluntary, 21–22
  regulating, 110
employment law, 107
English Compensation Act, 124
equality, 156
equivalency, in human losses, 50
Estis, Matt, 42
eugenics, 88
European compensation laws, 125
Evans, William D., 144
experience rating, 203

Fair Labor Standards Act, 107
Fall, Charles, 24
  on contracts, 23
  on employer responsibility, 37
families
  dislocation of, 73
  dissolution of, 70
  injury impact on, 72
  as source of future workers, 91
Farrington, F., 261
Farwell, Nicholas, 20, 23
*Farwell v. Boston and Worcester R.R.
    Corp*, 20
fathers, damages for loss of a virtuous
    daughter, 49
Faulkner, William, 254
fault negligence, 79
fees vs. fines, 38
fellow servant rule, 19, 37
Felton, J. S., 250

financial liability, one-eyed employees as, 160
Fishback, Price, 96–97, 215
fixed-capital-intensive firms, 100
food handlers, 246
Ford, C. E., 225, 227, 236, 252
Ford, Henry, 167
Ford Motor Company, exceptional
    treatment of disabled workers, 167
Fors, Clarence, 171
Foucault, Michel
    on biopolitics, 16, 32, 65
    on surplus populations, 256
    on veridiction, 27
Frankel, Lee, 70
Frase, Peter, 277
Fraser, Nancy
    on boundary struggles, 9
    on class, 12
    on justice as redistribution/recognition,
        11
    on social reproduction crisis, 90
French, Nathaniel, 89
Friedman, Lawrence, 93
full redress, 39
fungibility, 114
Furuseth, Andrew, 260
future speculation, in compensation
    determination, 29

Gagliardo, Domenico, 215
Garland-Thompson, Rosemary, 150
Garst, Warren, 124
    on age/disabilities discrimination, 183
    discrimination as concern, 212
    on impaired risks, 176
    insurance company responses to, 187
    on non-discriminatory compensation
        laws, 201
    on pre-employment medical
        examinations, 221
    on self-insurance, 186
    on waiving the right to workmen's
        compensation, 172
Garwin, John, 146, 156
Geertz, Clifford, 33
gender differences
    in compensation income, 28
    in court testimony, 43
    in pay scales, 178
    in power relationships, 49
    in risk taking, 36

General Contractors Association, 205, 209
General Electric
    discrimination at, 168
    employee terminations, 199
    medical exams by, 258
Genovese, Eugene, 212
Georgia Circuit Court, 40
Georgia Supreme Court ruling, 31
German compensation laws, 67, 104
Gettysburg battle fatalities, comparison
    with, 77
Gillette, George, 69, 86
Gilson, Ronald, 215
Given, Welker, 221
Glaberman, Martin, 9
Glackin, Edward J.
    business-protection perspective of, 93, 98
    on court-based injury law, 84
    on financial effects of injury, 74
    on ironworker accidents, 78
    on liability insurance costs, 96
    "Life and Limb Too Cheap", 112, 267
Gompers, Samuel, 111
Goodhart v. Pennsylvania R.R. Co., 41
Gordon, Avery, 17, 251, 254
Grapes of Wrath (Steinbeck), 272
Gray, Fred, 87, 118
Great Steel Strike, 262
Guglielmi, Maria, 125
Guilbert, Harry
    on one-eyed employees, 160, 162–163,
        230
    on syphilis, 230

Hamilton, Alice
    on industrial medicine doctors, 222
    on lead paint exposure, 244
    on non-fungible losses, 268
Hard, William
    biopolitical policies advocated by, 255
    estimates of, 74–78
    Injured in the Course of Duty, 53
    on justice as recognition, 74
    on litigation-based injury law, 81
    no-fault accident estimates, 79
    on non-fungible losses, 269
    on uncompensated injuries, 80
    work of, 57–60
    working class treatment by, 115
Harrar, James, 210
Haywood, William D., 105

hazard pay, 23
hegemony, 212
Henderson, Charles
  biopolitical policies advocated by, 255
  as compensation law proponent, 99
  on court-based injury compensation, 80
  on segregating injured "degenerates", 88
  as social investigator, 56
  on work hazards, 77
Hine, Lewis, 60
History of Labor Legislation in Iowa
    (Downey), 76
Hobbs, R. A. Mansfield, on self-insurance,
    195–196, 200
Holman, Dudley, 231
Home and Work (Boydston), 92
Hookstadt, Carl, 198
  on accident prevention as self-insurance
    benefit, 200
  on discrimination against disabled
    workers, 168
  on fear of retaliation, 198
  on goggles at Pullman, 163
Horan, Caley, 204
Horner, William H., 193
Howard, Alfred, 119
Howard, Salina, 119, 126
Howard, Samuel
  in Cherry mine fire, 119
  diary of, 127–128, 271
  Robinson's relationship with, 126
Huber, I. K., 169
Hull House, 244
human worth in dollar amounts, 36
Hungerford, L. S., 160
husbands, damages for loss of wife's
    "consortium", 49
Huyssen, David, 57

Idaho governor's murder, 105
ideology, 83, 200, 211, 239, 256
Illinois Bureau of Labor Statistics, 119, 123
Illinois Employers' Liability Commission,
    72–73
Illinois Manufacturers Association, 110
Illinois Occupational Health Commission,
    on lead paint exposure, 243
Illinois occupational health legislation, 245
Illinois Steel Company, 54, 75, 77
Illinois Supreme Court, eye loss decision,
    162

impaired risks, 176
impairment, 176, 230. *See* defects/
    impairments
industrial medicine, 218, 252. *See also*
    industrial physicians; pre-
    employment medical examinations
  before compensation laws, 241–248
  formation of, 242
Industrial Medicine and Surgery (Mock),
    224
industrial physicians
  as cost-management technicians,
    222–227
  as non-monsters, 251–252
industrial violence, 1
Industrial Workers of the World
  on Cherry mine deaths as wanton
    slaughter, 132
  Haywood as leader in, 105
  opposition to medical exams, 262
  on working class and employing class,
    106
inegalitarian wages, 113
inflation adjustments, 181
infrapolitics, 214
Ingalls, Wallace, 71
Injured in the Course of Duty (Hard), 53
injured workers. *See also* work-related
    injuries
  advocates for, 53
  biopolitics, 64–68
  documentation of, 55
  injury frequency, 64, 75
  pain and suffering for increased awards,
    97
  physical appearance of injuries, 42, 46
  singularity/individuality of, 58, 61
    definition of, 58
    as distancing from, 63
  weekly payments to, 111
injuries, compounded, 137
  court decisions
    on partial disability, 140–149
    on total disability, 152–158
  disabilities discrimination, 149–152
  employment of disabled workers,
    138–140
  Pullman risk avoidance, 158–166
  risk-averse employers, 167
injuries, ubiquity in Progressive Era,
    138–139

injury law, 4
  court-based system of, 15
    distributive injustice of, 78
    injuries and loss depicted in, 59
    shortcomings of, 78, 93
    social meaning of, 38
    strife/militancy created by, 103
    as wasteful, 68–74
    workmen's compensation vs., 265
  growth of, 57
  insurance in, 66
  lawsuit frequency, 95
  mutual moral obligations in, 37
  state reforms, 98
  uncertainties in, 95
  unemployment risk as factor in, 157
instrumental-reform perspective, 84, 87, 93
insurance, 175–177, 217
  behavior changes from, 204
  cherry picking by, 191
  as cold-blooded business, 207–208
  as communities of privilege, 204
  cost management with lawyers, 215
  discrimination
    marital status/age as basis for, 179
    reasons for, 185–191
  legitimating inequality, 209–211
  low settlements from, 69
  pooled risks in, 201
  as risk-control measure, 71, 102
  as risk-pooling, 66, 110, 176
  selection practiced by, 201
  self-insurance. *See* self-insurance
  as state monopoly. *See* state monopoly
    insurance
  as transfer of wealth, 205
  types of, 185
  underpayment of claims, 213
  as a worldview, 66, 108, 177
insurance company statistics, in
    compensation payments, 31, 34
Insurance Federation of Iowa, 187–188
International Association of Industrial
    Accident Boards and Commission,
    231, 248
International Association of Machinists, 262
International Harvester, 101, 103, 121, 244
investmentality, 219
involuntary retirement, 183
Iowa Employers' Liability Commission, 89,
    191

Iowa Industrial Commission, 221
Iowa Supreme Court
  on assumption of unimpaired workers,
    141
  Jennings decision, 156
  partial disability ruling of, 146
ironworker accidents, 60, 63, 77
IWW. *See* Industrial Workers of the World

Jackson, Justice, 31–32
Jaeggi, Rahel, 9, 90
Jennings, I. B., 146, 156
Jennings v. Mason City Sewer Pipe Co., 147
Jevons, William, 91
Jones, Marian Moser, 88
Joyce, Howard, 39
Joyce, Joseph, 39
judicial morality plays, 52
Jungle, The (Sinclair), 25
justice as recognition, 35, 74, 76

Kantor, Shawn, 96–97, 215
Karsten, Peter, 97
Kennedy, P. H., on medical exams
  as lowering costs, 227
  with mass production methods,
    237, 263
  speed of, 238
Kopitar, Gisalle, 163
Kudlick, Catherine, 149
Kurana, Rakesh, 200

Labatt, Charles, 20–21
labor history, Thompsonian, 117
labor law, employment law vs., 107
labor pricing, as compensation determinant,
    112
labor relations, 103
laissez-faire school of sociologists, 21
lawsuits. *See* injury law
lawyers
  as cost-management technicians, 215
  in injury cases, 69
lead paint exposure, 243, 245
Lears, Jackson, 67
legal history, 11
Legge, Robert, 224
legitimation via insurance, 209, 211
Lente, Antonio, 157
Lerner, Abba, 209, 214
Levy, Jonathan, 20, 23, 36, 176

liability, shifting line of, 234
liability, at Pullman
    employee termination, 163, 165
    one-eyed employees as, 159–160
    for sleeping car ventilation, 243, 245
    workers with illnesses as, 165
liability insurance
    compensation laws as preferable to, 102
    cost of, 96, 123
Liachowitz, Claire, 255
Liberatore, Matteo
    on living wage, 91
    Principles of Political Economy, 90
life insurance statistics, in compensation
    payments, 31, 34
"Life and Limb Too Cheap" (Glackin), 112,
    267
Lipincott, Henry, 205
Liptak, John, 162
living wage, 91
Livingston, James, 101
London, Jack, 26
Longmore, Paul, 149
Lopez, Ian Haney, 173
Lord and Taylor, 210
Los Angeles Times, on age discrimination,
    184
Low, Maurice
    on age/disabilities discrimination, 183
    on employer selection, 184
Lubove, Roy, 265
Lucci, Frank, 157
Ludwig, Martha, 45
Lusk, F. T., 31
Lynch, Charles, 1

MacIntyre, Alasdair, 269
mangle injuries (laundry facilities)
    Nettie Blom, 1
    Kathryn Carlin, 4, 28
    Marguerite Murray, 26, 28–29
    in Richardson's fiction, 28, 139
maritime rules of risk management, 20, 176
market imperatives, 101
    restructuring/merging as response to, 101
    uncertainties from, 101
    workmen's compensation as intervention
    in, 8–9
market price of injuries, 27
marketless losses, 39
Marks, Rachel, 221

marriageability, impact on, 49
Marshall, Alfred, 91
Marx, Karl
    Capital: A Critique of Political Economy,
    275
    on class, 7
    on commodification, 33
    on commodities, 6
    on individuals as character-masks, 273
    on surplus population, 26
    on workers used up in production, 242
Mason, Fred, 181
Massachusetts Industrial Board, on age/
    disability discrimination, 183–184
Massachusetts Industrial Commission, total
    disability decision, 153
Maxwell Motor Company, 142–144, 214
McInerny, Mary, 42, 47
McKeown, Robert, 200
McKinley, William, murder of, 106
medical examinations, 220. *See also* pre-
    employment medical examinations
    of food handlers, 247
    industry use of, 228
    information management systems for,
    234
    mass production methods for, 237–241,
    263
    at Pullman Corporation, 229–237
    speed of, 238
    standardization of, 239–240
    union pushback, 257
Meiksins-Wood, Ellen, 12
mental suffering, 43
Mercer, Hugh, 71, 94
merger wave, 100–101, 108
Michigan compensation, 141
Michigan Supreme Court, partial disability
    ruling of, 145
military deaths, comparison with, 77
mining accidents, fatalities from, 1. *See also*
    Cherry mine fire
Minnesota Employees' Compensation
    Commission, 68
Minnesota Supreme Court
    decisions in favor of employees, 95
    Garwin decision, 156
    partial disability ruling of, 146
Missouri Division of Mine Inspections,
    compensation law supported by, 124
Mitchell, John, 197, 209, 258

Mock, Harry
  on cost savings from medical exams, 226
  Industrial Medicine and Surgery, 224
  role in AAIPS, 224
monetary equivalence, 114
Moorhead, John, 240
moral/economic facets, 19
moral imagination, 7
moral logic, 36
moral thinning
  with compensation laws, 247
  with eye injuries valued in dollars, 164
  of injury law, 16, 173, 265
  loss of recognition as, 116
  under tyranny of the table, 116
  in workmen's compensation, 116
moral worth of the injured, 58
mortality tables, 32
Murphy, Jerry, 160
Murray, Florence
  on dollar value of care, 30
  injury description by, 42
  on mental suffering, 43
  on pain and suffering, 41
  testimony of, 30, 47
Murray, Marguerite
  award for injuries
    amount of, 26, 35, 94
    calculation of, 28–29
    court instructions on, 43
    injuries of, 41
mutual insurance programs, 186

National Association of Manufacturers (NAM), 110
National Civic Federation, 110
National Conference on Workmen's Compensation for Industrial Accidents, 75
National Industrial Conference Board
  on applicant rejection rates, 228
  on medical examination speed, 238
  medical examination survey by, 222
National Labor Relations Board, 107
National Metal Trades Association, 110
National Safety Council, on cost of industrial accidents, 164
Nease, W. A., 169
Nease v. Hughes Stone, 169
Neill, Charles, 69

New England Conference of Industrial Physicians, on medical examination speed, 238
New York Court of Appeals, total disability decision, 155, 158
New York Employers' Liability Commission, 56
New York Self-Insurers' Association, 192, 195
New York State Federation of Labor, on discrimination against married men, 181
New York State Industrial Commission, 258
New York Workmen's Compensation Commission
  on discrimination, 181
  as powerless on discrimination, 199
  on private insurers, 187
  on self-insurance, 197
Nielsen, Kim, 150
no-fault accidents, 79
non-pecuniary damages, 38, 49
normate, 150, 152
Norris, Frank
  "A Deal in Wheat", 271

objectification, 114
occupational health legislation, 245
Ohio Employers Liability Commission, 64, 77
Ohio Industrial Commission, 198
  defects screened for, 228
  on pre-employment medical examinations, 221, 232
  on rejection rates, 228
Oklahoma Supreme Court, Nease decision, 169
one-eyed applicants/employees, Pullman policy on, 159–166
Open Court, on Cherry mine settlement, 121, 125
Osgood, William, 28
owning hazard, 50

pain and suffering, 40, 97
Panzieri, Raniero, 101
Parks, Joseph, 74
Paxson, Justice, 32
pecuniary/non-pecuniary damages. See *under* employment
Pedley, Frank, 172, 248, 264

Pennsylvania self-insurers, 193
Pennsylvania Supreme Court
Goodhart decision, 41
Lente decision, 157
Steinbrunner decision, 31
Perkins, George, 101, 103
Phelps, Edward Bunnell
on employment discrimination, 176–177,
202
on insurance as cold-blooded business,
207
on medicine as cold-blooded business, 219
physical appearance of injuries, 42, 46
Pietruska, Jamie, 66, 100
Pinch, J. W., 45
Plan of Examination of Employees for
Tuberculosis (Chicago Tuberculosis
Institute), 241–242
Polanyi, Karl, 50, 99
police/judiciary, as defending employers, 106
political economy, 90
political radicalism, 103
Postone, Moishe, 272
Poulantzas, Nicos, 266
poverty, as generated by capitalism, 26
pre-employment medical examinations,
220–222, 227–229, 239. *See also*
medical examinations
at Pullman, 229–237
mass production methods for, 237–241
standardization of, 240
pre-injury wages
as compensation determinant, 4, 29,
112–113, 141, 155, 179
gender differences in, 28
gender/racial differences in, 179
price vs. recompense, 40
Priestley v. Fowler, 22
Principles of Political Economy
(Liberatore), 90
private economy, 91
private government, 7, 207, 257
probability, predictability and, 66
prostitution, 72–73
public wealth, 91
Pullman Corporation. *See also* liability, at
Pullman
occupational health steps at, 245
risk avoidance (discrimination) at, 158
risk management
lead paint exposure, 245

as racist, 247
sleeping car ventilation, 243, 245
screening at, 235
Purnell, Frank, 225

Quinby, R. S., 237

racialized compensation exclusion, 178
racialized pay scales, 178–179
Radin, Margaret, on commodification, 36,
114, 149, 173
railroad employees, eye loss risk, 163
Ransom, Roger L., 182
recognition
decline of, 60–64
eclipsed by tyranny of the table, 15
instrumental-reform perspective vs., 87
limitations of, 55
of losses, 271
recompense vs. price, 40
Rector, Frank, 227
Redfern, J. H., 225
Rediker, Marcus, 12
Reeves, Edith
"Care and Education of Crippled
Children in the United States,"
139
retaliation, 3
Richardson, Dorothy, 139
risk
avoidance of, 101–102
boundaries around, 204
company cherry picking, 191
definition of, 176
experience rating in, 203
minimum standard of, 202
risk management
corporate mergers as, 108
insurance as, 71
maritime rules of, 20, 176
at Pullman
as racist, 247
lead paint exposure, 245
Rittenhouse, J. A., 158, 160, 166–167
Robinson, Mamie, 126
Roosevelt, Theodore, 110
Rorty, Richard, 269
Rose, Sarah, 150–151, 170
Rubinow, Isaac, 64, 196
Russell Sage Foundation, 53, 56
Ryan, Harwood E., 196–197

safety improvements
 goggles as, 160, 162, 164
 insurance as incentive for, 189, 200
Sampson, Henry, 146
Sandel, Michael, 38
Sartre, Jean-Paul, 9
Sayer, Henry D., on self-insurance, 193,
 195, 200
Schmidt, James
 on industrial violence, 1
 on legal proceedings as judicial morality
 plays, 52, 117
Schmitt, Carl, 106
Schwab, Jacob
 distributive justice for, 156
 New York Court of Appeals decision for,
 153
Schweik, Susan, 150
Scott, James C., 214
Scott, Thomas, 162
Sears, Roebuck and Company, anti-
 tuberculosis efforts of, 242
security, in the face of uncertainty,
 64–68
Sedgwick, Theodore, 27, 46
self-evident facts, 211
self-insurance, 191–201
 compensation adoption dates and, 194
 cost savings from, 195
 de-pooling effect of, 201, 216
 requirements for, 186
 as risk-averse, 201
 self-insuring companies, 191
 states with, 190, 193–194
Shaw, Lemuel, 20, 23, 36
Sherman, William O'Neill, 226
Simon, Jonathan, 259
Sinclair, Upton
 Jungle, The, 25
slavery, Coates on, 3
sleeping car ventilation, 243, 245
Smallwood, Stephanie, 33
social context, 8
Social Creed of the Churches (Ward), 124
social disrespect, financial considerations,
 180
social imagination, 7, 19
social insurance, 216
social reform-oriented magazines, 56
social reproduction crisis, 90
Social Security, 264

social totality, 274
social viewpoint, 71
socialism, risk avoidance as step toward,
 102
Socialist Party, on Cherry Mine deaths as
 murder, 132
social-justice reform perspective, 84, 87, 93
St. Paul Coal Company, 119, 123
Starr, Paul, 223, 241
state legislation, 111
state monopoly insurance
 Garst on, 187
 opposition to, 189–190
 states with, 190, 215
 union support for, 259
state's well-being, 93
state-employer retaliatory violence, 105
statistical reasoning, 32
statistics
 as dehumanizing injuries, 61
 in determining compensation payments,
 31, 34
 in injury law, 67
 on fatalities in 2001, 132
 for work-related injuries, 77, 164, 253
 steel strike in Pennsylvania (1919), 262
steelworker accidents, 54, 57
Steinbeck, John
 Grapes of Wrath, 272
Steinbrunner, Mrs., 31
Steinbrunner v. Railway Co., 32
Steinfeld, Robert, 10, 22
Stone, Deborah, 204, 209
storytelling, as justice, 270
strikes
 business support of Phelps Dodge
 Company, 262
 of Iron Molders' Union, 105
 in Pennsylvania, 262
 over physical examinations, 260, 262
subsumption, 208
surplus population
 disabled as, 208, 256
 excluded workers as, 216
 Foucault on, 256
 Marx on, 26
 older workers as, 183
Sutch, Richard, 182
Sutherland, J. G., 38–39, 46
syphilis, workplace injuries complicated by,
 230

tables of value, of body parts, 5
"Temper of the Workers under Trial",
	53
Therborn, Goran, 83
*Thomas D. Scott v. Killisnoo Packing
	Company of Alaska*, 162
Thompson, E. P., 12, 24, 58, 266
Tomlins, Christopher, 61, 173, 272, 276
Travelers Insurance Company
	on discrimination, 188–189
	on exclusionary hiring, 198
	on self-insurance, 191, 196
	on state monopoly insurance, 190
	as under-compensating company, 213
Tripp, Joseph, 103
tuberculosis awareness, 241
tyranny of the table, 5. *See also*
	discrimination; medical
	examinations; pre-employment
	medical examinations
	beginnings of, 82
	body parts and monetary equivalence,
		114
	context of, 10
	disabled workers worth under, 158
	industrial medicine use under, 237, 247
	injury values standardized by, 115
	injustices under, 136–137, 175
	moral thinning under, 116
	recognition eclipsed by, 15
	shift to, 111, 135
tyranny of the trial, 6
	courtroom stories under, 270
	disabled workers worth under,
		148, 172
	injustice from, 25, 51
	shift from, 111, 135
	termination of, 52, 82
	uncompensated injuries from, 94
	use concurrent with compensation laws,
		173

Umansky, Lauri, 149
uncompensated injuries, 265
	Bellamy on, 79
	estimates of, 25
	fatalities, 80
	reformers' findings, 79
	Ward on, 124
underpayment of claims, 213
underwriting as boundary setting, 209

unions
	on discrimination against married men, 181
	as illegitimate market interference, 256
	on one-eyed applicants/employees, 167
	opposition from, 105, 257
	on private insurers, 186
	state repressive power against, 106
United Mine Workers of America
	monument, 131
	opposition to medical exams, 259, 261
	strike threats, 263
US Circuit Court of Appeals, San Francisco,
	eye loss decision, 162
US Industrial Commission, on employers'
	legal defenses, 81
U.S. Steel, 101, 103, 244

value, according to income, as social rank
	continuation, 29
Vandeveer, Fred, 214
venereal disease, as exclusion criterion, 230,
	247
veridiction, 27, 50, 67
*Vicksburg and Meridian Railroad Company
	v. Putnam*, 40
victim impact panels, public airing of, 268
violence, 105
voluntary accident relief plans, 104
Voorhies, George, 40

wage discrimination
	by age, 182
	disabled workers, 152, 155
	by race/gender, 28, 178
	as reflected in Social Security, 265
wage premium for hazards, 23
war comparisons, 77
Ward, Harry Frederick
	Social Creed of the Churches, 124
Watson, Archibald, 43
Watson, C. H., on medical exams, 226, 239
wealth accumulation, 275
Weaver, Charles
	claim contested by Travelers, 214
	compensation received by, 141–142, 145,
		147
	court-based injury law impact on, 137
	employment of, 138
	injuries, compounded, 137
	legal proceedings of, 142–146
	Lente decision implications, 157

Weber, Max, 207
Weeks, Edward, 38
Welch, Kimberly, 116
Welfare Federation of Cleveland, 140, 167
Welke, Barbara, 32, 50, 151
White, John P., 259–260
Whitney, Albert W., 187, 189
Wilcox, Fred, 170
Williams, Helena, 237
Williams, John, 120, 125
Williams, Raymond, 212
Winterson, Jeanette, 271
Wisconsin Industrial Commission, 171, 195, 200
Wisconsin River Paper and Pulp Company, 171
Witt, John, 32
women's work
  economic importance of, 48, 92
  exclusion in compensation law, 177–178
  as source of future workers, 91, 182
Wood, Gregory, 183
Work-Accidents and the Law (Eastman), 53, 60
working class, 7. *See also* working-class families
  collective action of, 109
  commodification of, 34, 115
  cost of workplace injuries for, 72
  as economic objects, 256
  emotions/depth of feeling, 58
  employing class vs., 106
  funerals as meaningful to, 127
  health improvements for, 242
  healthcare as incidental, 247
  industrial violence experienced by, 51
  instrumentalization of, 10
  nonpecuniary values of, 126
  as objects "fit for use", 89
  protection from economic consequences, 74
  as valuable to the economy, 86
  as valuable raw material, 89
working-class families
  as source of future workers, 92, 182
  size of, 181, 188
  value of, 89
workmen's compensation
  abled character of US law, 151, 276
  death benefits, 181

Department of Labor oversight, 107
  differences by state, 189
  evolution of, 84
  employer risk exposure, 93
  impact on children/future labor, 89
  Pullman's concern about, 161
  state legislation for/role in, 111–115, 122
  state's well-being factored in, 85–89, 93
  US vs. other countries, 123
  exclusions in, 177
  features of
    assumption of unimpaired workers, 140
    as conflict avoidance, 103
    deritualization, 117
    as meeting capitalists' needs, 106
    as predictable expense, 98
    value of injury as payment determination, 111
  as gendered terminology, 9
  impaired and "poor" risk exclusion, 205
  injuries, compounded. *See* injuries, compounded
  insurance costs as motivation for, 97
  moral thinning in, 116, 265
  non-fungible losses from, 268
  pre-injury wages as determinant. *See* pre-injury wages
  safety incentivized by, 164
  shortcomings of, 16, 264–267
  states with, 194
  union pushback, 105
Workmen's Compensation Service Bureau, 187
work-related injuries, 253–257. *See also* defects/impairments; injured workers; injuries; injury law
  awards for
    amount of, 4, 26, 141–142
    calculation of, 28–29, 141, 155
    in Michigan, 141
    proposed improvements for, 270
    social meaning of, 38
    two-tier system for, 148
  compensable, 25
  economics of, 86
  estimates of, 1–2
  eugenics of, 88
  fatalities, 1–2, 253–254
  Holdren's experience with, 4–6, 54, 254, 271
  insuring and budgeting for, 99

work-related injuries (cont.)
  living wage impact of, 92
  market price of, 27
  parsed by multiple events, 141, 144
  pecuniary/non-pecuniary damages. *See
    under* employment
  physical appearance of, 42, 46
  poverty from, 81

  statistical data for, 253
  uncompensated. *See* uncompensated
    injuries
  under-reporting of, 3, 5, 54
Wright, Edwin, 75

Youngstown Sheet and Tube Company,
  220, 236

Made in the USA
Monee, IL
20 January 2023

25754298R00184